AF496541

ARABIC ART

Prisse d'Avennes

ARABIC ART

After Monuments in Cairo

Foreword
Clara Schmidt

200 plates

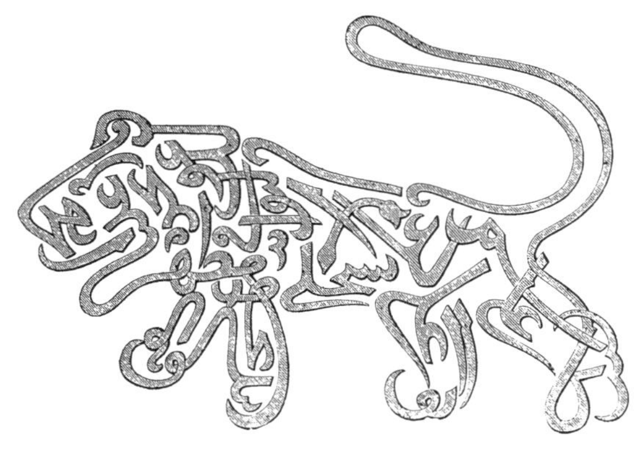

L'Aventurine

We would like to thank the Bibliothèque Forney in Paris
for allowing us to reproduce the plates from their copy of
L'Art arabe d'après les monuments du Kaire.

Translation : Juanita Steichen

ISBN 2-914199-16-3

PRISSE D'AVENNES
IN SEARCH OF TRUTH

Achille Constant Théodore Emile Prisse d'Avennes had already entered the last stages of his life when *L'Art arabe d'après les monuments du Kaire*[1] was published in 1877. This impassioned, impetuous and uncompromising man had spent more than seventeen years in Egypt. His publications as well as his voluminous notes, documents, drawings and watercolors bear witness to the diversity of his interests and the scope of his vision.

A pure product of the 19th century, Prisse was born in 1807 in Avesnes-sur-Helpe in the north of France, received training to be an architect and engineer. These studies would serve him well sharpening his vision and aiding him in the execution of his drawings recognized for their meticulous preciseness.

In 1826, the quest of a lost Arcadia led him to Greece where he participated in the War of Independance against the Ottoman Empire. Orphan at age 7, modelled by Byronic romanticism, Prisse viewed this first voyage to the Orient as synonymous with adventure and the point of departure of his life journey. At the same time throughout Europe, this voyage was being transformed into a veritable educational system for youth and took on the trappings of an established institution.

France and England were the first nations to realize that their future ruling classes would gain from being confronted with the reality of other civilizations. The equivalent in France of the *Grand Tour* undertaken by English aristocrats, a voyage around the Mediterranean was intended for the French elite, be they from literary, artistic or scientific backgrounds. Over time, the voyage to the Orient acquired validity rivalling with the traditional voyage to Rome, a venerable tradition completely given over to the study of ruins. This time, however, other values were in the balance. The study of ruins still exerted its attraction and the nostalgia of a Golden Age still motivated the "Tour" of certain men of letters but from that time forward, it was vital to go ahead and spread civilization to the ancient lands.

Indeed, Volney's travel commentaries[2] dating from the late 18th century were used to corroborate a new vision of the Orient. Conflicting with England's political policies, Napoleon Bonaparte championed the theory that a country such as Egypt could regain its past glory if it were enlightened by a nation such as France. To this end, the country must be studied and then modernized. It is significant that the Campaign of Egypt was carried out not only by an army but also scientists armed with all sorts of measuring and research equipment for physics, astronomy, chemistry and surgery. These were to permit the exact observation of the world that was to be discovered.[3] New notions emerged from this enormous project, among them the concept of truth in history. It would become a guiding principle in the later work of Prisse d'Avennes and would prevail in his observation and narrative methods.

In 1827 Prisse d'Avennes followed Governor Ibrahim Pasha to Egypt and remained there until 1844. During this first period in Egypt, he was in turn civil engineer and hydrographer for Mehemet Ali and later teacher at the fortified domain of Dumiyat. He learned Arabic and became to comprehend Islamic culture, noting numerous observations and executing drawings concerning architecture and local customs. He frequented the Saint-Simonians whom he received in Alexandria in 1833. Although he never actually joined their ranks, he nonetheless shared their values and ideals of creating bonds among the peoples and opening the pursuit of happiness to all.

From 1836 until his departure for France in 1844, Prisse d'Avennes devoted himself to the study of Egyptology. He concentrated his attention on a certain number of buildings in Luxor and Karnak, producing many drawings and watercolors; he learned to decode hieroglyphics. His activities brought him in rivalry with the foremost egyptologists of his times, notably Lepsius, while others like Champollion-Figeac admired his work.

Upon his return to Paris, Prisse d'Avennes'one concern was to return to Egypt in order to complete his studies and have them published. He set off once again in 1858 like Maxime Du Camp who he knew from Paris; both would be sent the same year on an two-year official mission sponsored by the Ministry of Public Education.

1. *L'Art arabe d'après les monuments du Kaire*, Veuve Morel, Paris, 1877.
2. Volney. *Le Voyage en Syrie et en Égypte*, Paris, 1787.
3. The findings of this expedition were recorded in the celebrated publication, *Description de l'Égypte ou Recueil des observations et des recherches qui ont été faites en Égypte pendant l'expédition de l'armée Française*, Imprimerie Impériale, Paris, 1809-1822. 9 volumes of text and 12 volumes of plates.

Realizing how little time he had and probably eager to substantiate the reality of his views, he hired a photographer, A. Jarrot. The daguerreotype was brand new; it appeared to be rapid, precise and seemed to possess documentary qualities superior to those of drawings. A total objectivity was conferred to the camera obscura which was even recommended for use by artists: "Having thus submitted their works to the test of truth, painters and sculptors will definitely abandon the excessive exaggeration and the false interpretations of Antiquity, because they will realize they are contradicted by fact and rejected by the public. Thus artists expert in perspective will no longer compose according views of monuments and renowned sites to their own tastes and will no longer render the noble Alhambra with the proportions of the Coloseum".[4] Photography was perfectly adapted for use on archeaological expeditions; moreover, the inventors especially recommended it for Egyptology.

A certain number of plates of *Arabic Art* were reproduced from daguerreotypes. Photography permitted Prisse d'Avennes to satisfy a pressing desire for realistic reconstitution and to give readers views truly "after nature".

Since the 1830's, the taste for the Orient and exoticism was constantly growing in literary as well as in artistic circles. At the first Great Exhibition in London in 1851, a generalized crisis was apparent in the decorative arts. Artists seemed only capable of creating mediocre works consisting of vulgar pastiches of past styles. A reform of the esthetics within "industrial arts" appeared indispensable. Owen Jones would take on the role of the theoretician; he codified his views on style and decorative composition in the famous propositions of *The Grammar of Ornament.*[5] From 1837, important publications in this context began to appear, veritable encyclopedias of ornament with colored illustrations realized in chromolithography.

The Orient became a vital source of inspiration for a world avid for novel forms – the fabrics, for example, presented by the India Company at the Great Exhibition of 1851 caused a sensation. Jones had previously published *Plans, Elevations, Sections and Details of the Alhambra*[6] with chromolithographic illustrations. In much the same manner as *Arabic Art* which Prisse d'Avennes would publish some thirty years later, Jones'work also revealed the beauty of Islamic art. The intentions of the two authors, however, were diametrically opposed. Through his analytical method of the study of ornamental art Jones was seeking industrial applications. Prisse d'Avennes had a more idealistic vision. While the plates in Jones'work remain descriptive without any relief and present elements out of context reflecting a purely functional esthetics, Prisse d'Avennes'works presents a dichotomy which he explained in the following terms: "In saving these treasures largely unknown to most scholars and artists from oblivion, we have allowed the public to contemplate and appreciate in their true aspects one of the most remarkable periods of the history of art long left unexplored, while at the same time providing modern decorative arts, and architecture as well, with materials which allow them to renounce banality and pedestrian inventiveness which have so justly upset those lofty souls professing the cult of the beautiful." A picturesque, romantic vision is confronted with a descriptive, scientific one, more closely related to an ethnological study than a desire to nurture Western eclecticism.

In his later years, Prisse d'Avennes published two major works: *L'Art arabe d'après les monuments du Kaire* in 1877, and *Histoire de l'art égyptien depuis les temps les plus reculés jusqu'à la domination romaine,* two years later in 1879.

Although *Arabic Art* by Prisse d'Avennes was originally presented as an anthology of ornamentation, it was also one of the first publications of "modern" archeaology.[7] His desire was to attest to the splendors of Arabic art as the expression of a highly evolved civilization on the brink of extinction so that it might help westerners comprehend their own history. Like Viollet-le-Duc in France, Prisse led an impassioned fight for the protection of historical monuments, for the restoration and maintenance of these affirmations of "one of the most amazing civilizations which history has recorded".

A reference in the field, the book offers a wide vision of Arab art in the areas of architecture, decoration and the applied arts. The picturesque Cairo as it was experienced by European travellers of the 1860's comes to life through the descriptions and images of this inveterate adventurer. An irresistable *mélange* of romanticism and historicity, this encyclopedia with its incredible graphic scope bears witness to the diversity and value of Islamic Art as seen through the rigorous and scientific eye of a 19th century Westerner.

Clara SCHMIDT

4. The inaugural address of the Fine Arts Academy of Venice, 1852. P. Selvatico Estense, "L'Arte insegnata nelle Accademie secondo le norme scientifiche", quoted in Italo Zannier, *Le Grand Tour*, Venice, 1997, p. 23.

5. Owen Jones, *The Grammar of Ornament,* Quaritch, London, 1865. French and English editions were both published the same year.

6. Owen Jones and Jules Goury. *Plans, Elevations, Sections and Details of the Alhambra,* 1836-1845.

7. Prior to his work, few travellers had shown interest in contemporary oriental architecture. Pascal Coste, an architect from Marseilles, published a rare study on the subject: *Architecture arabe et monuments du Kaire,* 1837-1839.

ANALYSIS OF THE PLATES

We have adopted a methodical classification by groups and subgroups in chronological order as the basis of analysis of the two hundred plates of our atlas.

These groups are fifteen in number, as follows:

1. Architecture: General Views and Details
2. Architecture: Ornamentation and Decoration
3. Coverings and Tilings
4. Ceilings
5. Panelling: Overall and Details
6. Doors
7. Porcelain Tiles and Imitations
8. Woodwork: Moucharabyeh and wooden grilles, Overall and Details
9. Interiors
10. Stained Glass and Glasswork
11. Textiles and Carpets
12. Arms and Armour
13. Civil and Religious Furniture: Copper Plate and Damascening
14. Manuscripts: Bindings and Applications of Paper Cutouts
15. Korans

This new method of classification will allow us to take in at a glance artistic procedures and their successive developments.

Our original intention had been to write a special descriptive notice for each plate, but we were soon obliged to acknowledge that this would lead to useless repetition. Most of the interesting descriptions, as may be easily seen, have been inserted in Chapters 8, 9, 10 and 11 where they are perfectly illustrated by our plates. Our decision to make use of an entirely different sort of analysis is thereby clearly understandable.

Plates I to XLIII
ARCHITECTURE
General Views and Details

This group, the most important of all, assembles forty-three plates which offer an approximately complete representation of all component parts of architecture, both in regard to exteriors and interiors, and to details having a special relation with the art of construction itself. It will thus be possible, through the particularities that they reveal, to definitively compare the processes of the Arab people with those of other nations, and to determine the place occupied by the Arabic style in comparison to other styles.

We have already expressed our personal ideas on the different methods adopted by the Arabs in preceding chapters[1]; we will content ourselves here with completing these with some general insights. We must still observe that, in the analysis of the plates in this group, we have abstained from discussing the ornamentation and decoration put forth by these specimens of the art of construction, to only address the specific object of our study on general architecture, reflected in our selection of plates. We will deal with these other aspects during the analysis of the plates in the second group.

But, all the while inviting the reader to refer to the small plates in the text as far as the plans are concerned, and to the special developments contained in the preceding chapters, we feel it important however to draw particular attention to the claim disclosed, therein, to wit that Arabic mosques were not constructed, as was believed for a long time, according to a uniform, predetermined plan, and that the plans of the temples of Mecca and of Medina never served as prototypes.

Let it not be forgotten that we have also pointed out the successive modifications and restorations of many mosques since the Turkish conquest, which have altered them; but that, as a general rule, the architect or the person in charge of directing work neglected, nearly always, to precede the execution of the work with a special plan, and that when such a plan did exist, it was almost never followed.

We will also take care to remind the reader of important points discussed in the general description of mosques, that in regard to the the sacred enclosure, a predetermined plan for all religious edifices appears to be easily recognisable, and that mosques containing tombs were the only ones to feature domes and cupolas.

Views and Details.—The plates forming this subgroup, and to which we have taken care to refer the reader in the chapters and paragraphs devoted to the art of construction, show us with what great understanding of the particular needs of Oriental civilisation, from Ahmad ibn Tulun until the Turkish conquest, were all component parts of the shell raised. We were unable, unfortunately to give, as the starting point of this nearly complete series, the marvellous façade that the luxury-loving founder of al-Qatayab had built in the 9th century of our era (3rd century of the Hegira), nor specimens from civil architecture, because the magnificent palaces are today only ruins; however, an in-depth study of Plates I and II still gives an idea of the splendid Ahmad ibn Tulun Mosque, the prototype of Islamic Art, today converted into a refuge for beggars and damaged, as we have already said, in the process of adapting it to its new purpose.

1. See Prisse d'Avennes, *L'Art arabe d'après les ornements du Kaire*, Volume of texts, same publisher.

The view of the interior of the maqsurah (Pl. I), taken near the pulpit, or minbar, gives a clear view of those long galleries where an entire population of believers come at the hour of prayer to hear, in the calm shade, the voice of the imam who guides them.

Plate IV has allowed us to borrow from the 10th century (4th of the Hegira) a very important specimen of the main courtyard of a mosque. All praises pale, we believe, following the contemplation of a vision such as this. Let us observe again that we say nothing, for the moment, of the profusion of ornamentations covering and surmounting every part of the masonry.

Plate VI represents, under the name of Bab al-Azab, bestowed by the Janissaries in modern times, the principal gate of the citadel; in times gone by, it was called Bab al-Silsileh, the *Gate of the Chain.* Despite the removal of the armorial bearings from above the entrance opening, its present condition gives an idea of the state in which it was left by Sultan Baybars, whose coat of arms on the other side may still be seen. This gate led to the Diwan and to the palace, residence of the prince.

Plate VII, the gate of the Palace of Baybars, is intended to give an exact idea of princely dwellings, during these times of sedition and uprisings which threatened destruction at any moment. This palace also figures in the plates of the great work about the Expedition of Egypt, but the caricatures portrayed before the door fail to render the costumes of the Mamelukes during this brilliant period.

We have succeeded in assembling various precious documents on Arabic Art of the 14th century, reproduced in Plates IX, X, XI, XII, XIII, XIV, XV, XVI, XVII and XVIII. Among these, a single disparate item is to be noted in the gate of the Sultan Hussein Mosque (Pl. XI), built, it is believed, by a Christian architect inspired by the most remarkable Islamic monuments of India. It is thus, in Egypt, a monument apart.

We draw attention as well to the door of the house in Shirawi Street (Pl. XII); tradition has it that it was part of the house of the qâdy of one of the four orthodox sects of Islamism. It is the only one of this type still encountered today in Cairo, but the mosaics of the spandrels appear to us to have been renovated at diverse periods.

As for the Sepulchral Mosque of Sultan Barquq (Pl. XVII), it is one of the most vast and splendid mosques of the Necropolis of Cairo. Beneath one of the cupolas are buried both the Princess Sakhrah and the son of Barquq; according to Mr Mehren, the Russian Orientalist, the son of Barquq was responsible for numerous additions which would be, in consequence, posterior to the main structure.

The 15th century (Pl. XII to XXV) in the Qaytbay Mosque, and the 16th century in the sepulchral monument of al-Ghuri (Pl. XXVI) furnish us with the last original tentatives of Arabic art *per se.* After the conquest, the influence of Byzantine architecture, appropriated by the Turks, made itself felt, and monuments were reduced to more or less careful copies of this architecture.

The sides of the interior of the tomb of Qansu al-Ghuri are covered in alternating panels of red and black marble, gilded and with intaglio engraving. Each slab bears different designs formed of Kufic letters and others, displaying pious phrases, simulating lamps, flower-pots and other varied designs. The 16th century also offers what is known as the tomb of Sultan Tarabay (Pl. XXVII), although it is atributed to a former governor of Thebaid. This tomb is located to the north of the citadel.

The tomb attributed to Mahmud Janum (Pl. XXVIII) is already topped with the crescent moon; Janum was one of the nephews of Sultan Qaytbay, and it is to him that is owed a beautiful mosque whose openwork windows are of remarkable beauty.

Amongst the few interesting constructions of its time, the 17th century gives us the opportunity to represent the interior façade of an Iwan (Pl. XXXI). The exterior door of the harem of a house belonging to the emir shows us, in its Maq'ad or Iwan, a room fulfilling the same function as the Mandarah; a small special staircase above a stable led to it.

Plates XXXIV, XXXV, XXXVI, XXXVII, XXXVIII and XXXIX allow us to recognise that the 18th century was slightly more fertile and varied in its different representations; it is the fall of the Mameluke sultans, themselves but waning members of the splendour of the Fatimid Califate, which caused the spring of original inspiration of Arabic Art, once so surprising and hardy, to dry up, perhaps forever.

We have reproduced a sepulchral monument of the 18th century including a Sibil, (Pl. XXXIV), quite well-preserved and enclosing all the parts considered by the Arabs as indispensable for it to be complete, that is to say, a school, and a water cistern or drinking trough. This edifice is crowned with a pyramidal dome and set in a small courtyard where the family of the deceased may withdraw from indiscreet eyes and be alone in its pain. The façade, moreover, shows a small room where travellers may rest and pray: next to it is a cistern whose latticework window allows the drawing of water, always avidly sought after in this arid plain. We were unable to decipher the inscription embedded above the grille, and which doubtless evokes the name of the pious deceased. This selection is intended to provide an example of those edifices sometimes reunited in the Arabic world around a sepulchral monument known as Waqfs, or pious foundations; entire caravans lodge and water here, while at the same time meeting with a Qibla for the direction of prayer.

Plate XXXV offers us a curious specimen of baldaquin tombs, very numerous around the tomb of the Imam Chafey; the Mamelukes bought these ready-made, and the practice continues today near cemeteries, be it by Turks or Italians.

Plate XXXVI represents a Sibil or fountain from the 18th century. This monument initially included a cistern which provided water to the public fountain and to a school located above.

Plate XXXVIII represents Hammam al-Talat, the only door worthy of reproduction among all the baths still in Cairo. Hammam al-Talat, which means the *Bath of Tuesday*, is situated at the entrance of the Jewish Quarter. This truly original stone chain, patiently chiselled out of a section of limestone, seems to hang from the top of the frieze as if waiting for the lamp, attached to a small bracket awkwardly applied to the latticework of the window, to be suspended from it.

Although from a more modern century, the house represented in Plate XXXIX, known as the House of the Page, or Young Master, Bait al-Shalabi, is almost a copy of Bait al-Amir.

Plans, Overalls and Details.—In Plates V, VIII, XVII, XXX and XXXIII, we have given the plans and elevations of five mosques, each from a different century; moreover, five other plans figure in the small plates in the text.[1] Those of the atlas belong to the 12th, 14th, 16th and 17th centuries; the first is that of the Great Mosque. They will undoubtedly confirm the exactness of our appreciations regarding this capital question of architecture, especially after the diffusion of the substantiated error which claimed that the reputedly sacred plans of the temples of Mecca and of Medina had served since immemorial time as the obligatory model for the construction of all mosques; we cannot insist enough on this point, whatever little interest this may appear to hold for European nations. Until the Turkish dominion, the widest diversity reigned in the construction plans of religious edifices. The five plates which represent such very remarkable specimens of mosques are irrefutable proof of this.

This is why we have felt it necessary to dwell at length upon the motive behind the reproduction of Plate XXX, representing the mosque of Sinanieh. This mosque is one of the first under Turkish dominance; it was constructed, near Dumiyat, under the care of Sinan-Pasha whose name it bears. Its plan features a vast rotunda, covered with a dome of large dimensions, like the Church of Sta. Sophia in Constantinople. The four corners are filled by niches, and a balcony runs around the cupola at the base of the vault, forming the *Tekassir* for the use of women. Although this monument is not in Cairo, its plate has been given to show the transformations in mosque building plans during the period of Ottoman dominion. We have also deemed it necessary to restore the arcades to their original ogival form, previously tranformed into cissoidal arcades in the extensive works by the Expedition of Egypt.

Details.—We have wanted to give the fewest possible plates of details, for the veritable interest of this work lies in the reproduction of our chosen motifs, especially in regard to ornamentation and the surprising transformations the Arabic genius could bring about within it. After the five plates of details proposed (Pl. III, V, VIII, XXII and XXXIII), Plates XIV and XV are of true interest. It was impossible to have executed the ensemble from which they were taken, for it has since disappeared. These two plates represent the most important part of the minaret of the Muhammad ibn Qala'un Mosque; placed end to end, they provide a nearly complete reproduction of this handsome minaret, which resembles those in Andalusia worked in plaster as is this one. Taken together, it may be said that in reality the whole is represented.

Plate XXII shows a part of the minaret of the Mosque of Qaytbay, reproduced on a remarkable scale which clearly indicates the great care we have taken to provide only the finest models.

The fragment of the Ahmad ibn Tulun Mosque in Plate III serves to demonstrate that it is only at a very late date, and only under the Turkish yoke, that it became habitual to adorn the axis of minarets with a Crescent; previously, a stone container took its place.

Finally, the two fragments which compose Plate XXIII are large-scale reproductions of one of the most splendid fountains of the 15th century, the Sibil of Qaytbay; the difficulty in executing the details fails to fully render its beauty.

Parallels.—We had at first intended to provide numerous plates which would have allowed the comparison of all component parts of the Arabic style, within the different countries having borne the yoke of Islamism; but we have had to restrain ourselves for fear of overstepping the limits which seemed imposed upon us by our title. We have confined ourselves to comparing amongst themselves the so-varied specimens of columns, minarets and domes.

Columns and Pillars. (Pl. XLIII)—The columns of Moresque edifices constantly offer indigenous capitals full of grace and elegance; these are rarely encountered in Egypt, where architects have almost always employed the capitals and columns of the Late Empire, which they assembled as best they could.

So it is with great difficulty that we have been able to put together the attractive specimens of Arabic Art from different periods represented in this plate:

1. See Prisse d'Avennes, *L'Art arabe d'après les monuments du Kaire,* volume of texts, same publisher.

No. 1.—Column from the large windows of Sidi Hussein al-Sadaka, one of the handsomest, richest and most ancient specimens of columns: nothing analogous is to be found any longer in Cairo (10th century).

No. 2.—Pillar of the mihrab in the tomb of Yusuf al-Maz. This pillar is 2.5 metres in height, the base and the capital each 0.25 metres around. This octagonal pillar is of white marble, covered in gilded arabesques. The chevrons of the shaft are gilded on an azure background and the intervals, red on the capitals and bases; the sides parallel to the structure are blue, and the diagonals red. The whole, in rather poor taste, moreover, was selected solely to show coloured motifs rather rare today.

No. 3.—Pillar of the mihrab of the Mosque of Qaytbay (cf No. 15).

No. 4.—Pillar of the niche of the gate of Gama Sultan Hussein.

No. 5.—Mosque at the entrance of Darb al-Barabras; column manufactured in Carrare.

No. 6 and 7.—Capital and base of columns of the mihrab of Gama Saleh Ayoub, across from the Moristan. Circle of pewter below the capital. Capital 0.41 metres in height; shaft 1.9 metres.

No. 8 and 9.—Capitals of columns engaged in the pier of the arcades of the Ahmad Ibn Tulun Mosque. The details of these capitals vary slightly from one end to the other of this vast and beautiful mosque (10th century).

No. 10.—Capital of the small pillar of the minbar of the Mosque of Daoud-Pasha (15th century).

No. 11.—Another capital of the same type.

No. 12.—Capital of a column in white marble, behind the Mosque of al-Moyed.

No. 13.—Capital of the column or pillar of the mihrab of the Mosque of Sultan Barquq.

No. 14.—Capital of a pillar of the mihrab near the Mosque of Qaytbay.

No. 15.—Detail of the pillar of the mihrab of the Mosque of Qaytbay. The shaft is covered in arabesques of a rather pure style yielding a charming diagram.

Domes and Minarets.—Minarets and domes were the parts of mosques which offered the most variety. Unfortunately, few minarets and domes of the Golden Age remain; however after careful searching, we have been able to compose Plates XXIV, XXV and XXIX which offer assuredly precious subjects for study.

The elegant cupola which forms the principal motif in Plate XXIV was still seen, several years ago, toward that part of the cemetery of Karafeh designated by the name of Turab al-Imam. Upon our last journey to Egypt, we were unable to find it again. In 1843, it was already damaged, and it is probable that it disappeared beneath Arab pick axes. A fairly frequent defect in the construction of walls, where stones are used in facing without being bound to the fill of rubble, has brought about the ruin of this edifice; but the ravages of man have contributed more to its destruction than the ravages of time. This view was lithographed by Mr Girault de Praogey, after his daguerreotypes.

The minaret on the left (No. 2) which in days of yore was part of a sepulchral monument in ruins today, can be seen in in the large avenue of Turab al-Imam.

The minaret on the right (No. 3) belongs to a a small mosque located south-west of the city, between Bab Tulun and the interior Qaytbay Mosque: it is called, we believe, mosque of al-Qalmi. Today, the two minarets still remain, but the charming cupola forming the middle of the plate no longer exists; however, there are still photographs which allow us to confirm the exactitude of this plate.

The dome and minarets of the Mosque of Kair-Bekieh were built under the orders of one of the Mamelukes who betrayed the last sultan of Egypt, al-Ghuri, at the battle delivering Cairo to the Ottomans. Although covered in honour by Selim, he was not any happier; held in contempt by all, he died scorned and in shame. The monument he caused to be built may be seen as the last breath of Islamic Art.

The comparison of two such opposed periods of Arabic Art as drawn on Plate XXV between the 15th and the 17th century make it obvious to us that the brain that conceived this marvellous jewel, the Mosque of al-Bordayny, heard protests and perhaps even violent reactions against this decadence and decrepitude known under the name of Turkish Art.

The motifs composing Plates XL, XLI and XLII which offer such a numerous and remarkable diversity of domes, were taken from various tombs in the cemetery of Karafeh, to the south and the north of Cairo.

Plate I

MOSQUE OF AHMAD IBN TULUN

Interior of the Maqsurah (9th century)

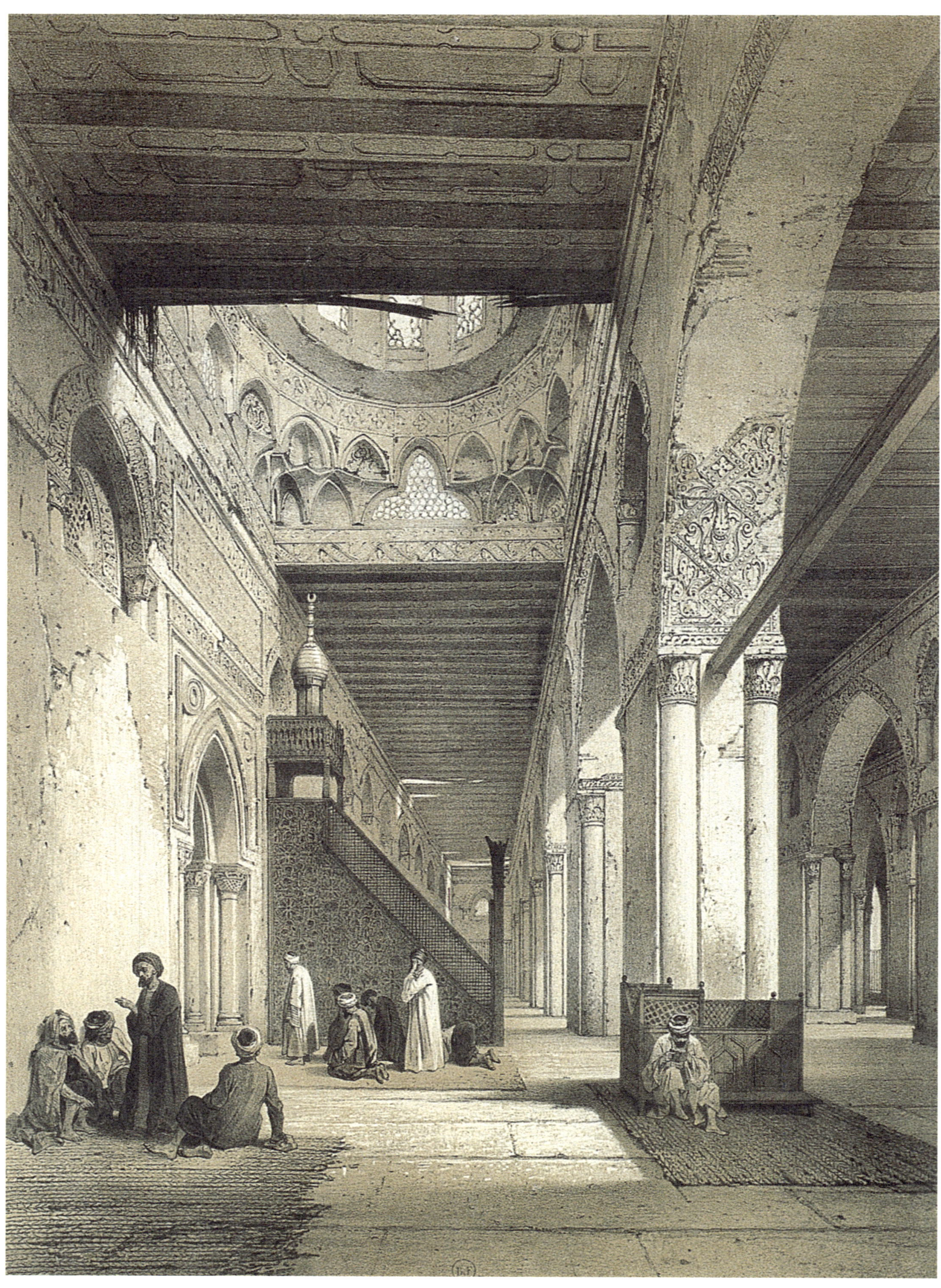

MOSQUE OF AHMAD IBN TULUN

Plate II

Arcade and Interior Windows (9th century)

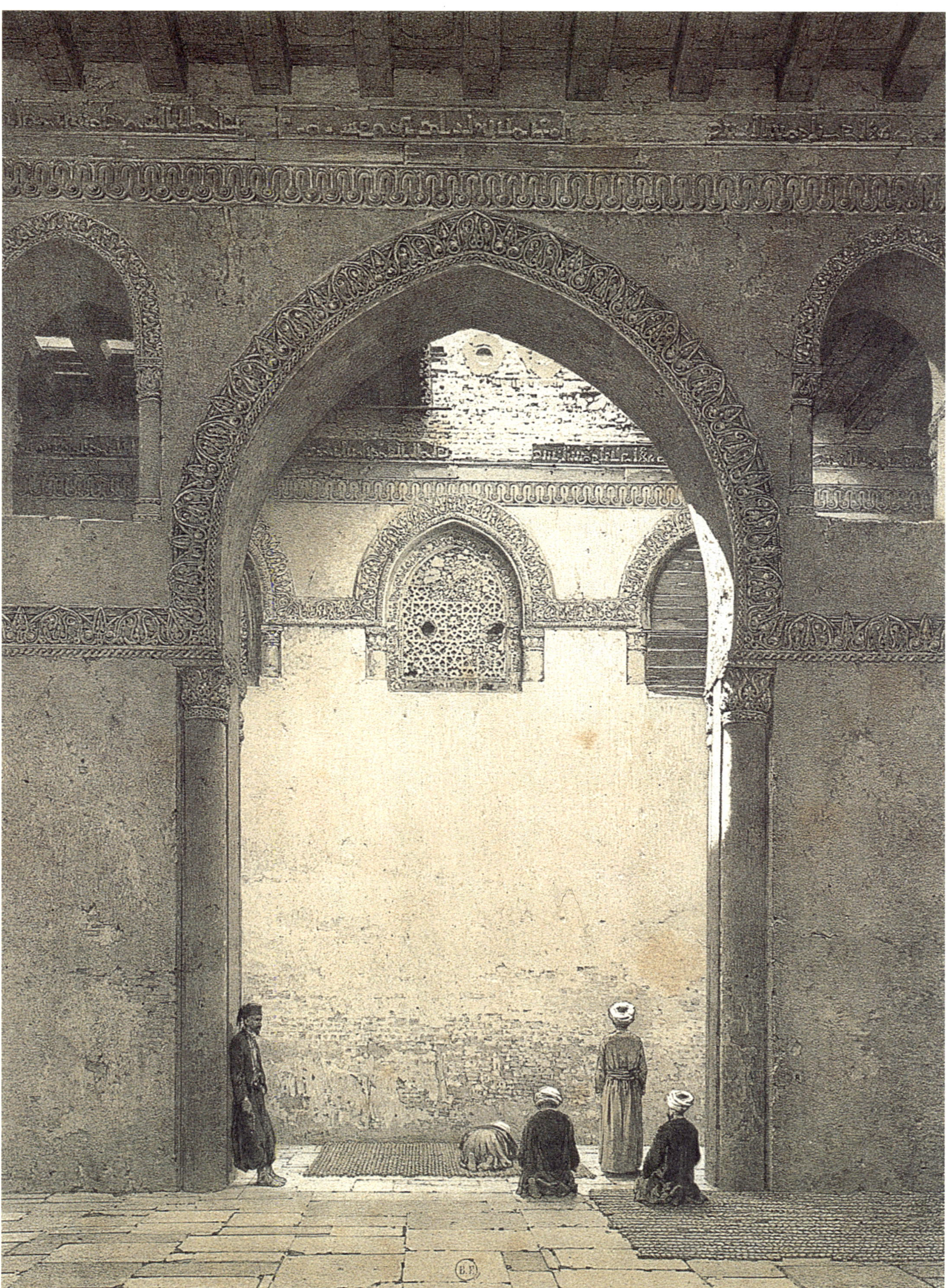

MOSQUE OF AHMAD IBN TULUN

Details

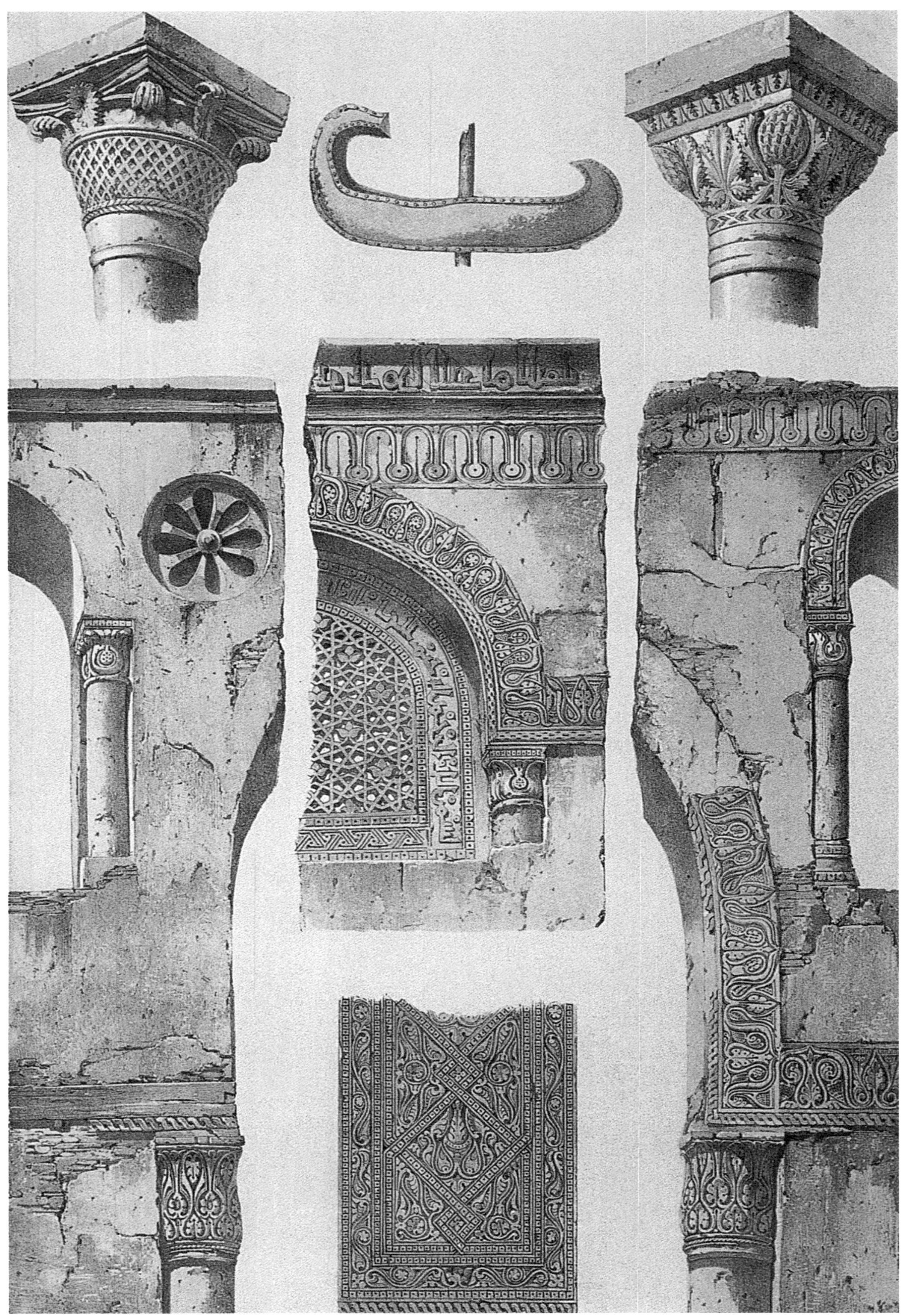

MOSQUE OF AL-AZHAR
View of the Main Courtyard (9th to 18th centuries)

Plate IV

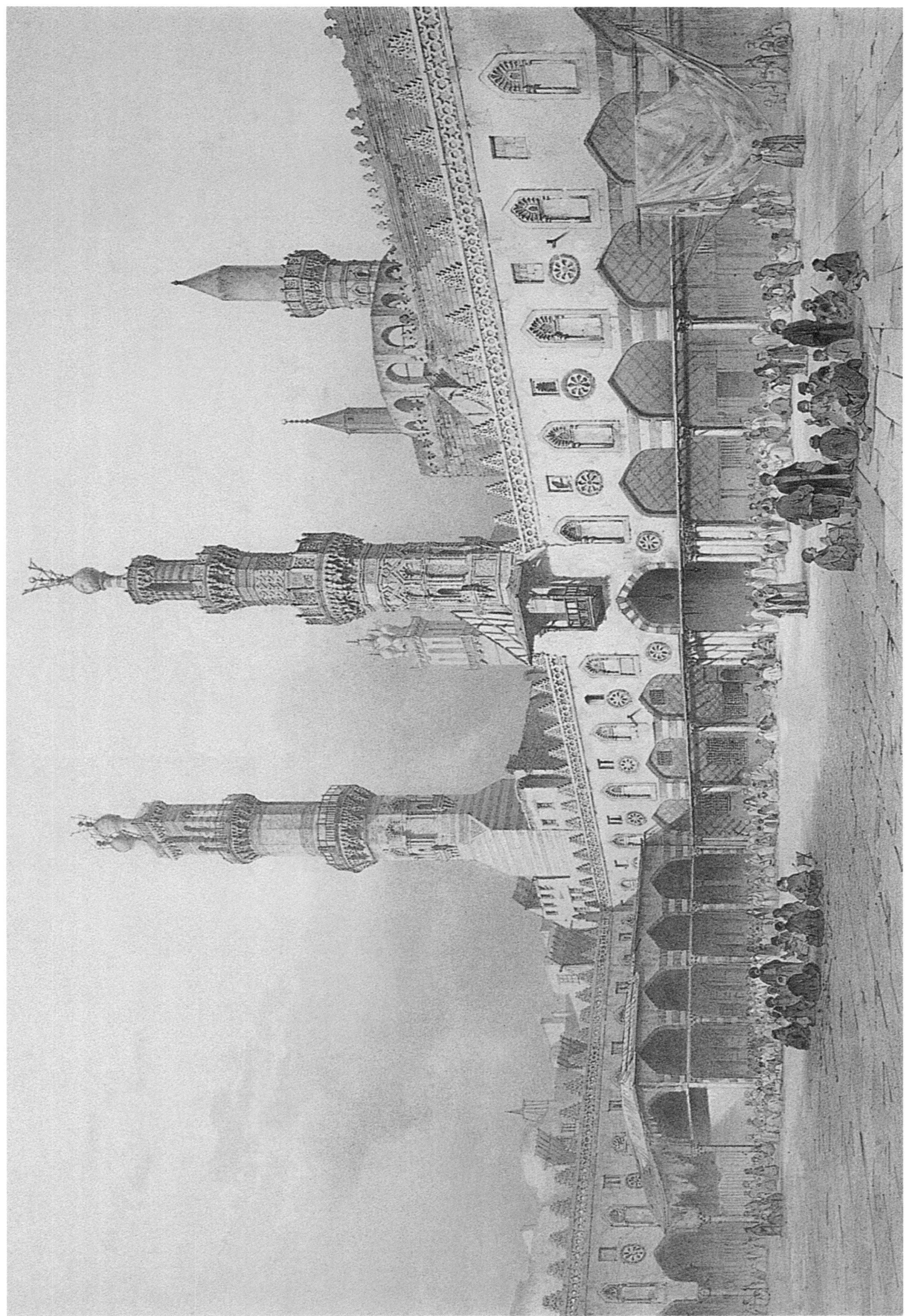

Plate V

MOSQUE OF TELAY ABU RIZK

Plan, Section, Elevation and Details (12th century)

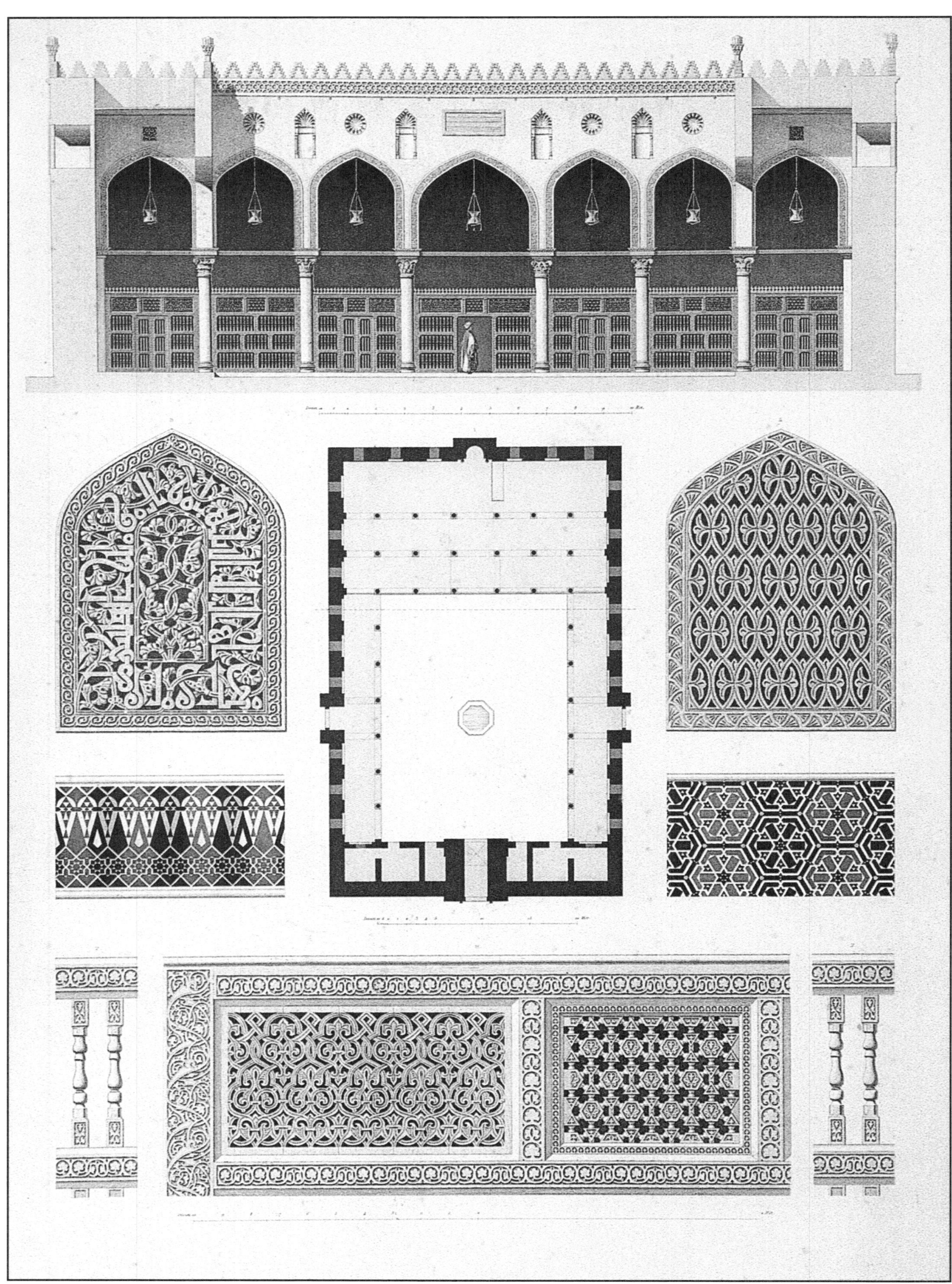

MAIN GATE OF THE CITADEL

Plate VI

Bab al-Azab (13th century)

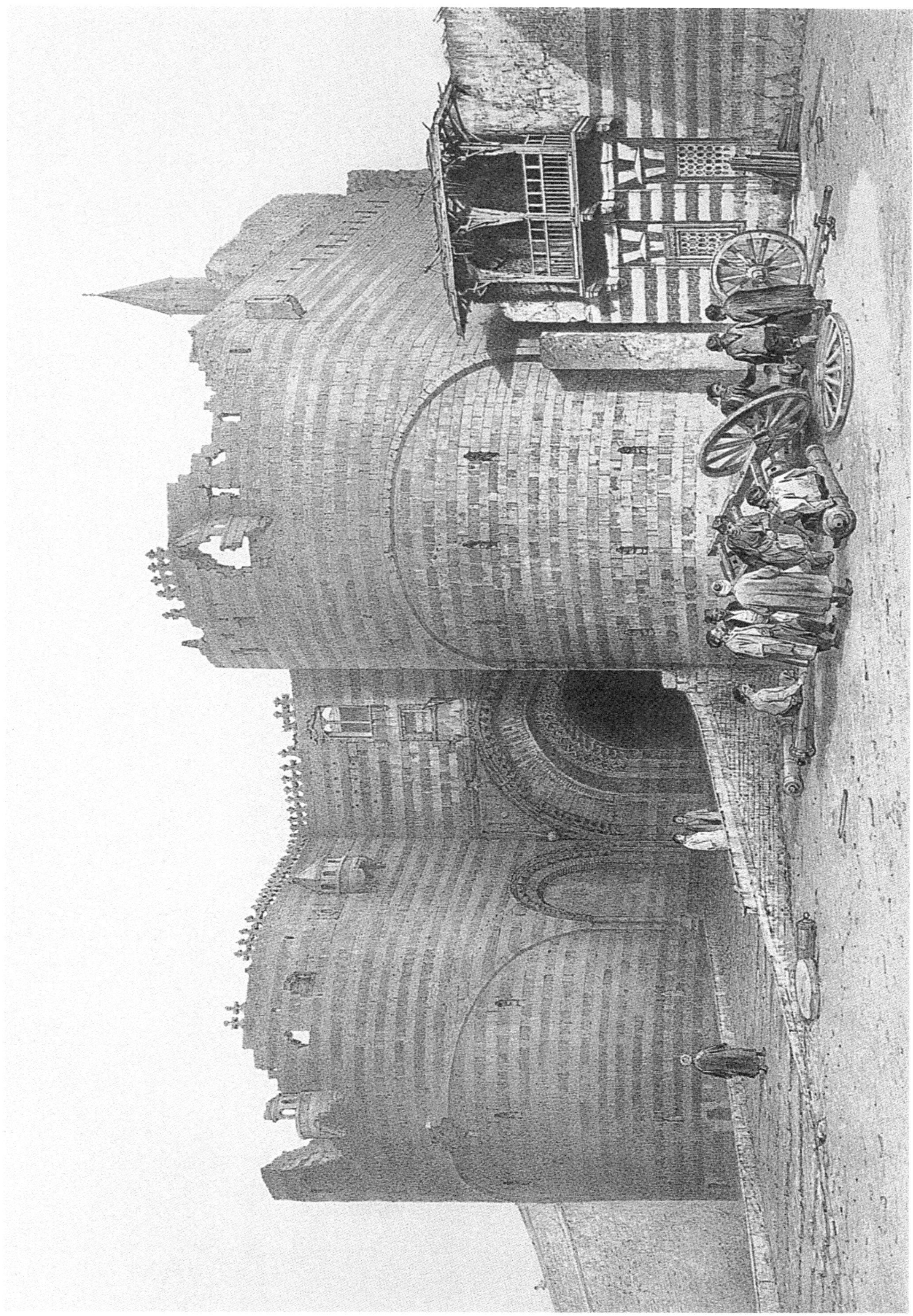

Plate VII

GATE, PALACE OF SULTAN BAYBARS
(13th century)

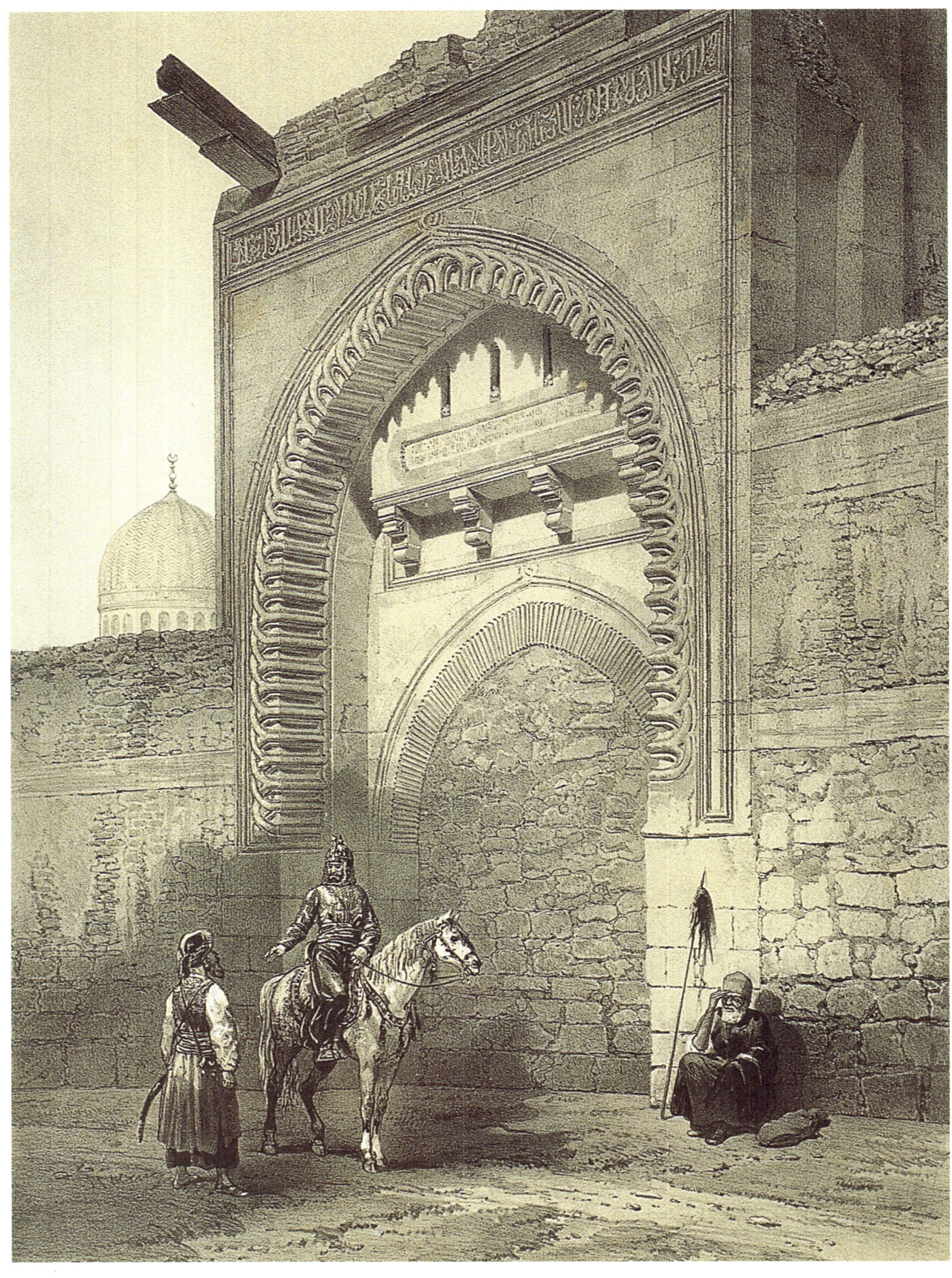

MOSQUE OF AL-DAHER (EXTRA MUROS)

Plan, Section, Elevation and Details (13th century)

Plate VIII

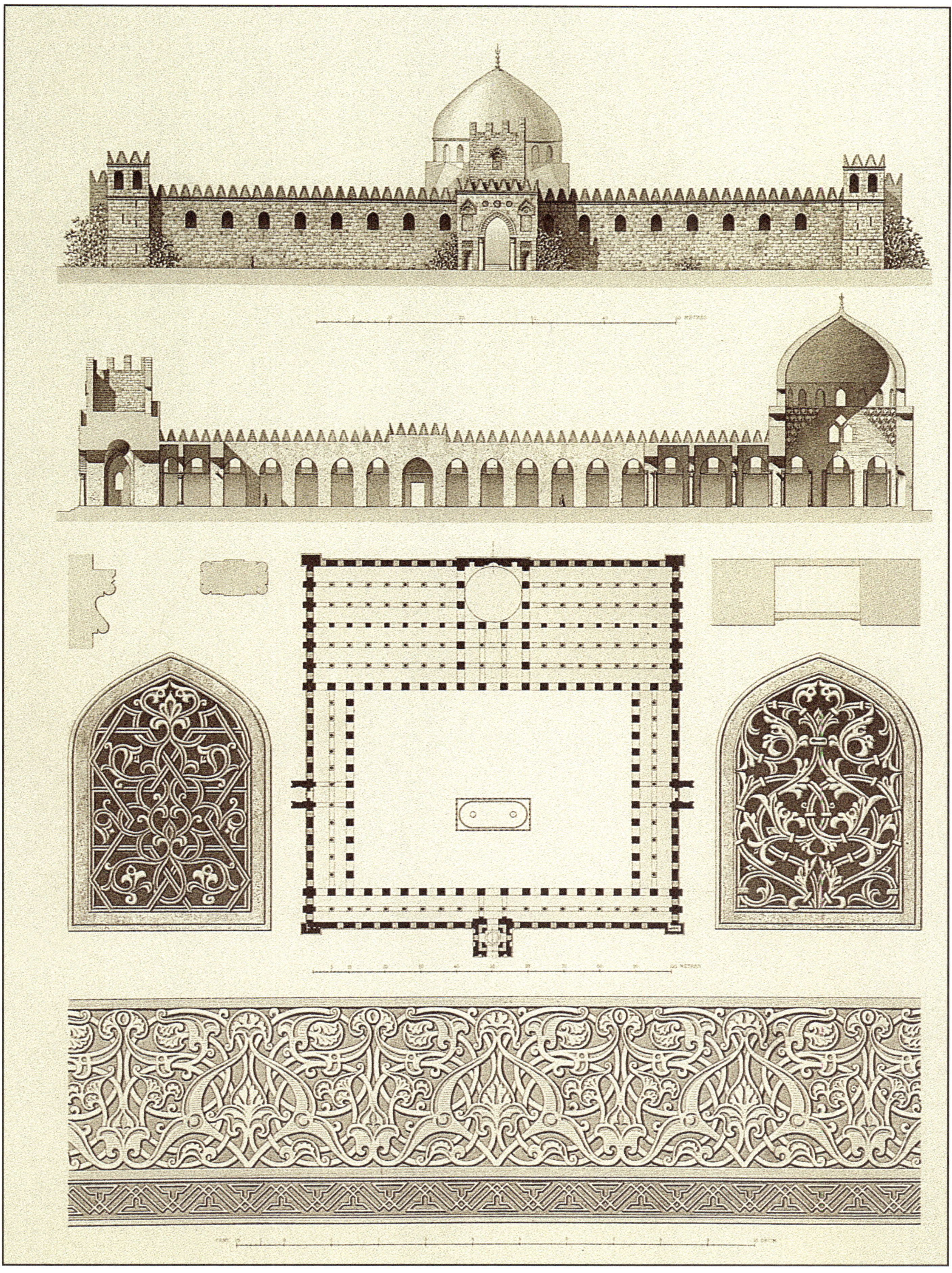

TEKIEH SHEIKH HUSSEIN SADAKA

Large Window in the Dome (XIVᵉ century)

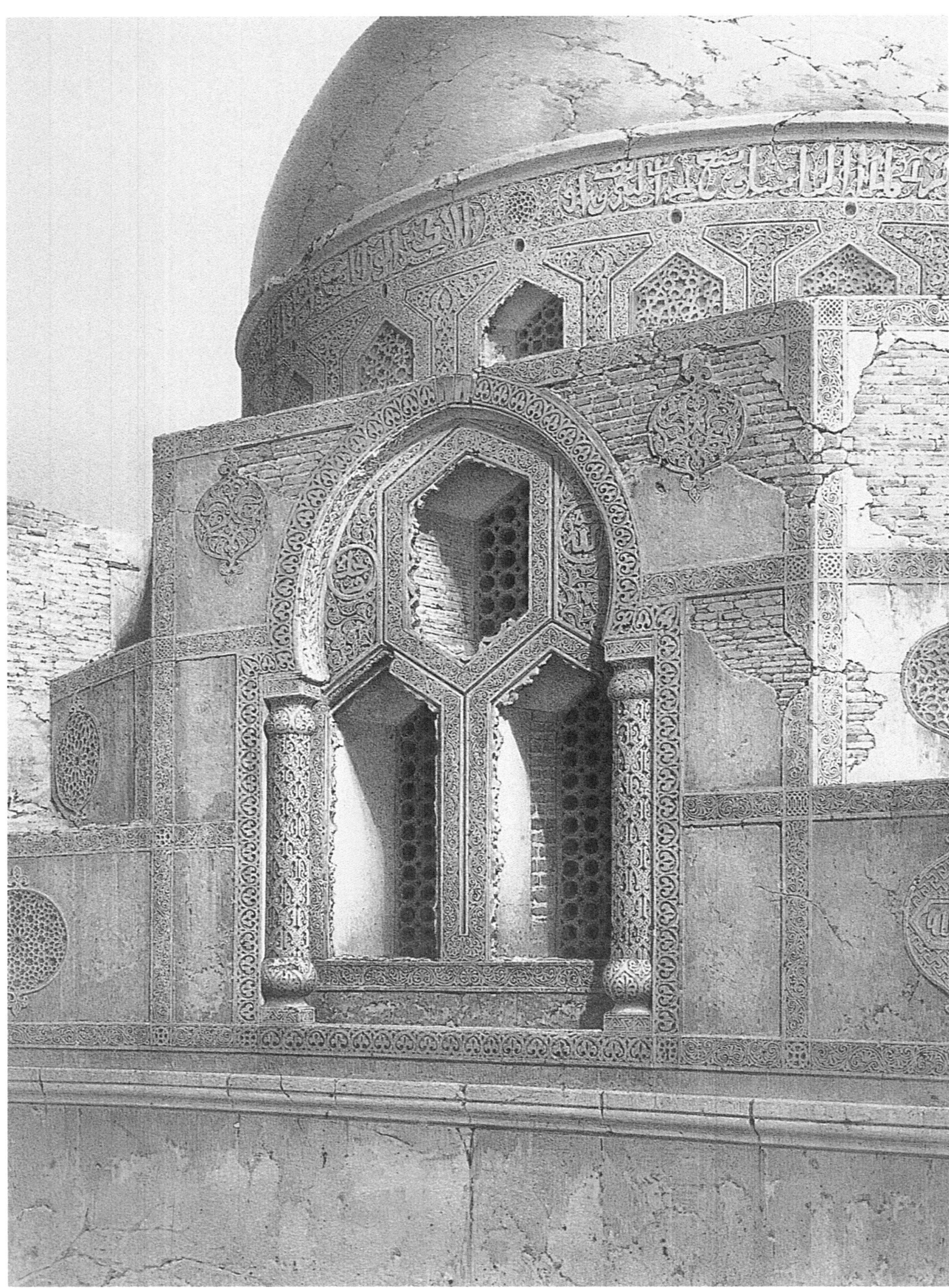

MOSQUE OF BAYBARSIEH

Minaret (14th century)

Plate X

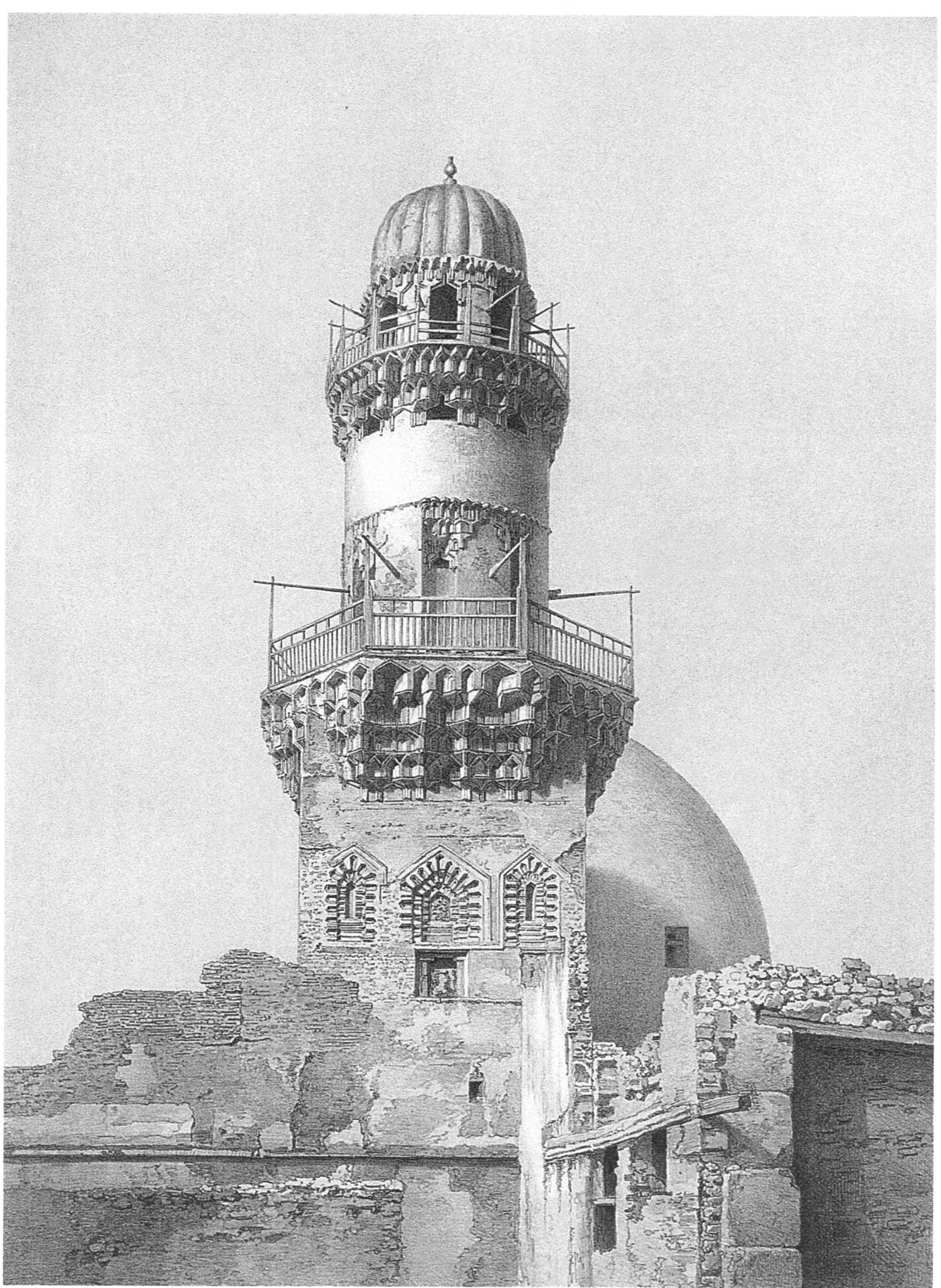

Plate XI

MOSQUE OF SULTAN HUSSEIN

Large Door (14th century)

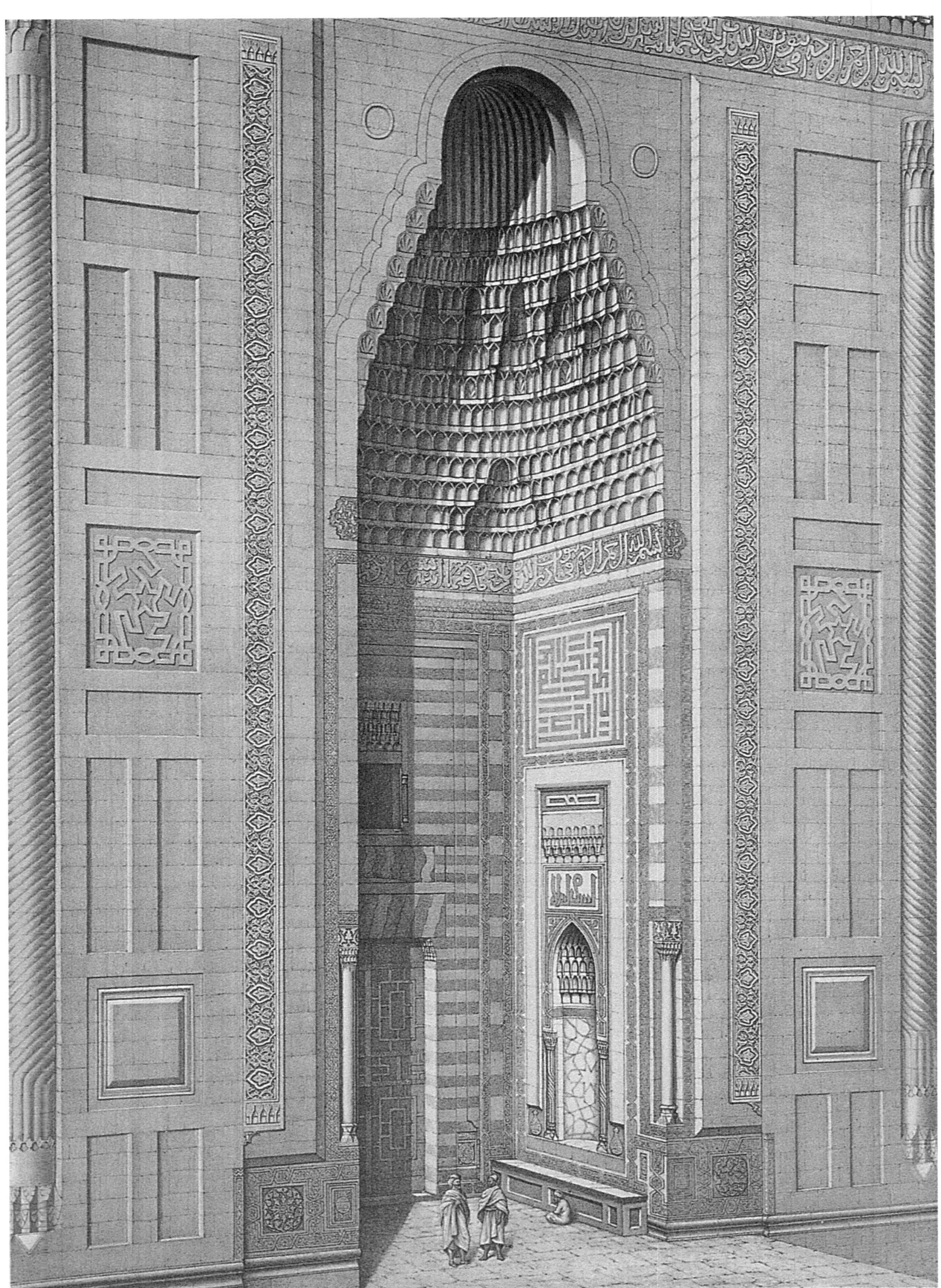

DOOR OF A HOUSE, SHIRAWI STREET, CAIRO (14th century)

Plate XII

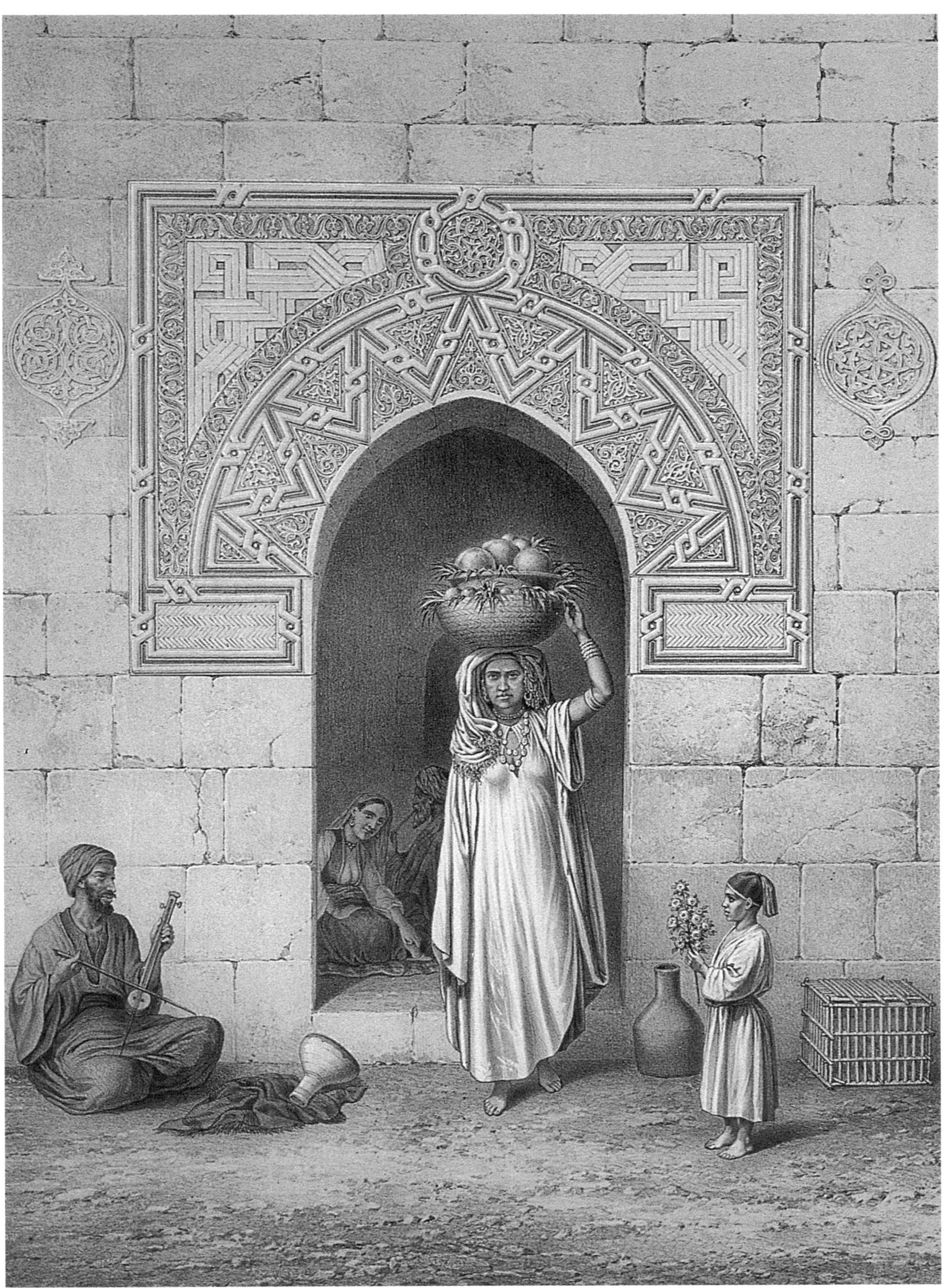

Plate XIII

MOSQUE OF MUHAMMAD IBN QALA'UN

View of the Mihrab (14th century)

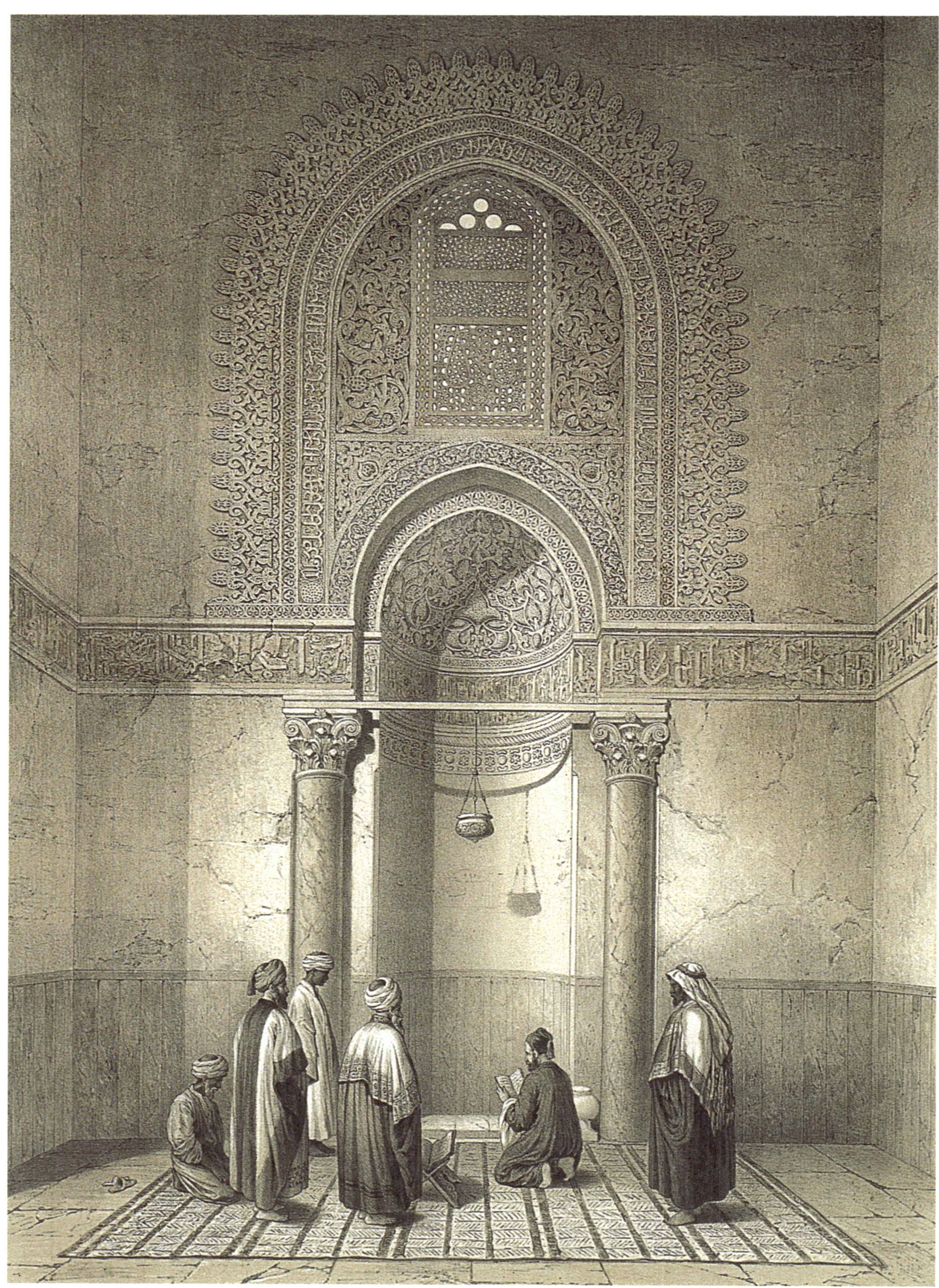

MOSQUE OF MUHAMMAD IBN QALA'UN

Plate XIV

Details of the Minaret (14th century)

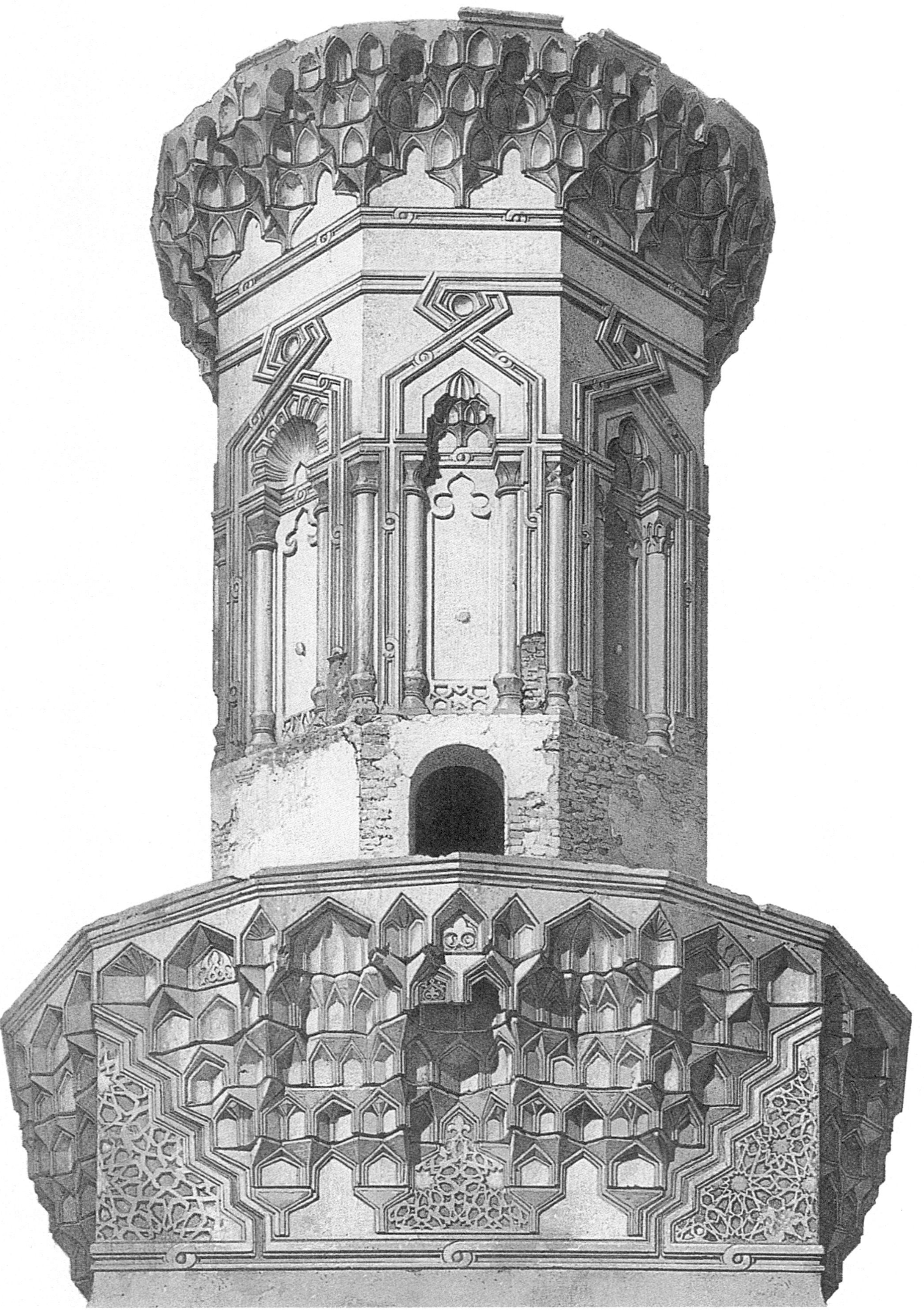

Plate XV

MOSQUE OF MUHAMMAD IBN QALA'UN

Details of the Minaret (14th century)

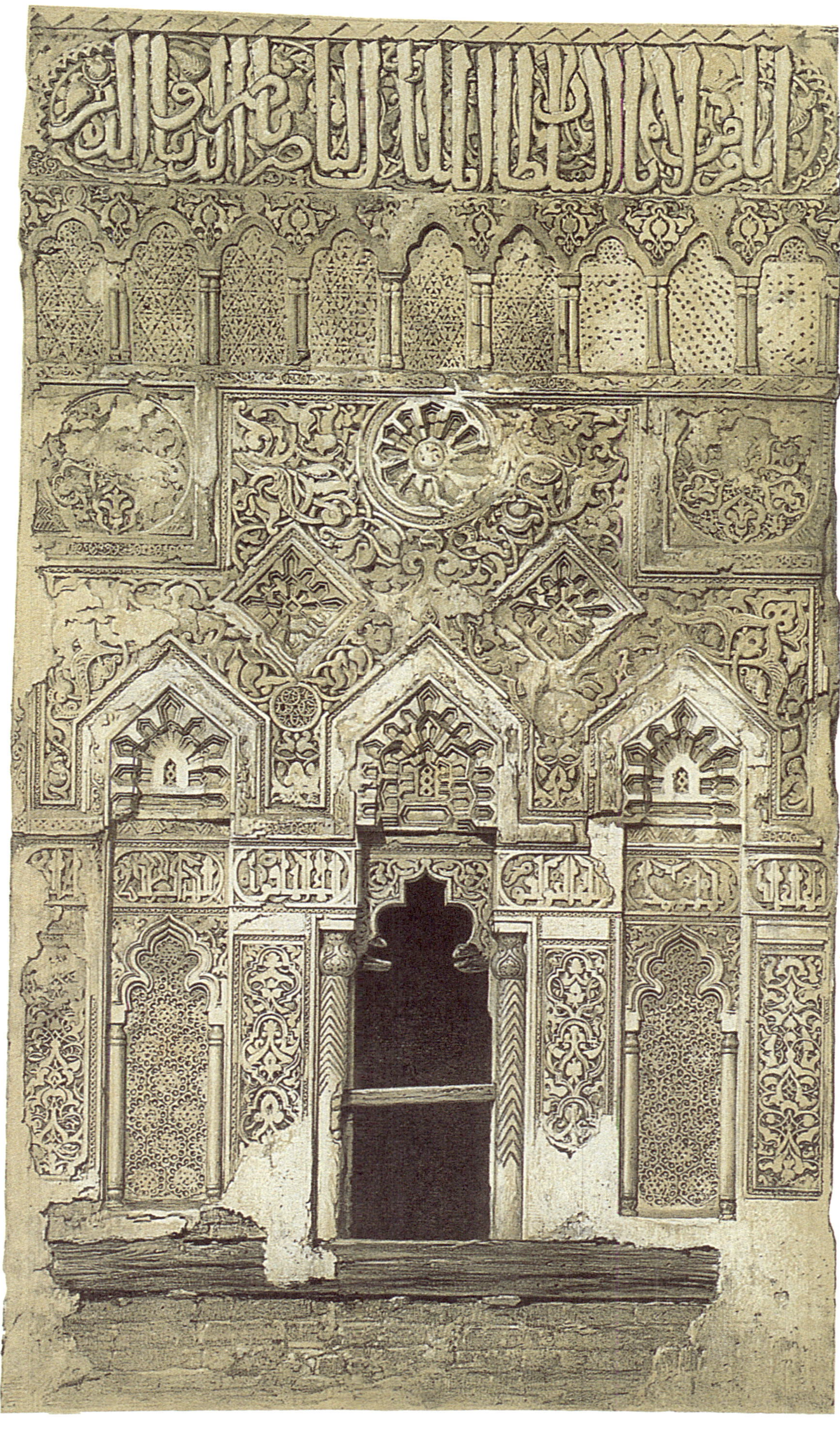

TOMB OF SULTAN QALA'UN
(14th century)

Plate XVI

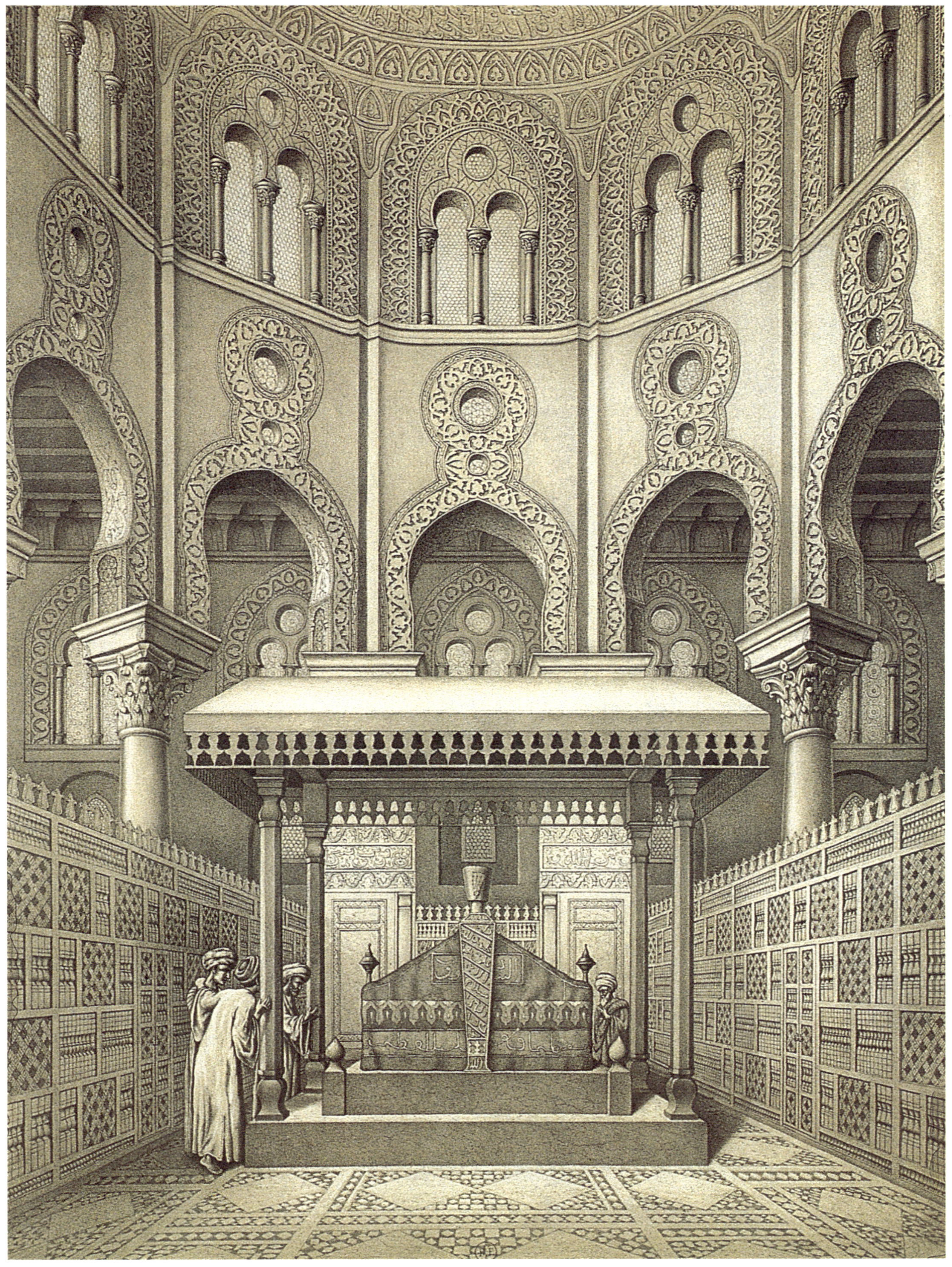

Plate XVII

SEPULCHRAL MOSQUE OF SULTAN BARQUQ

Present State, Plan and Section (14th century)

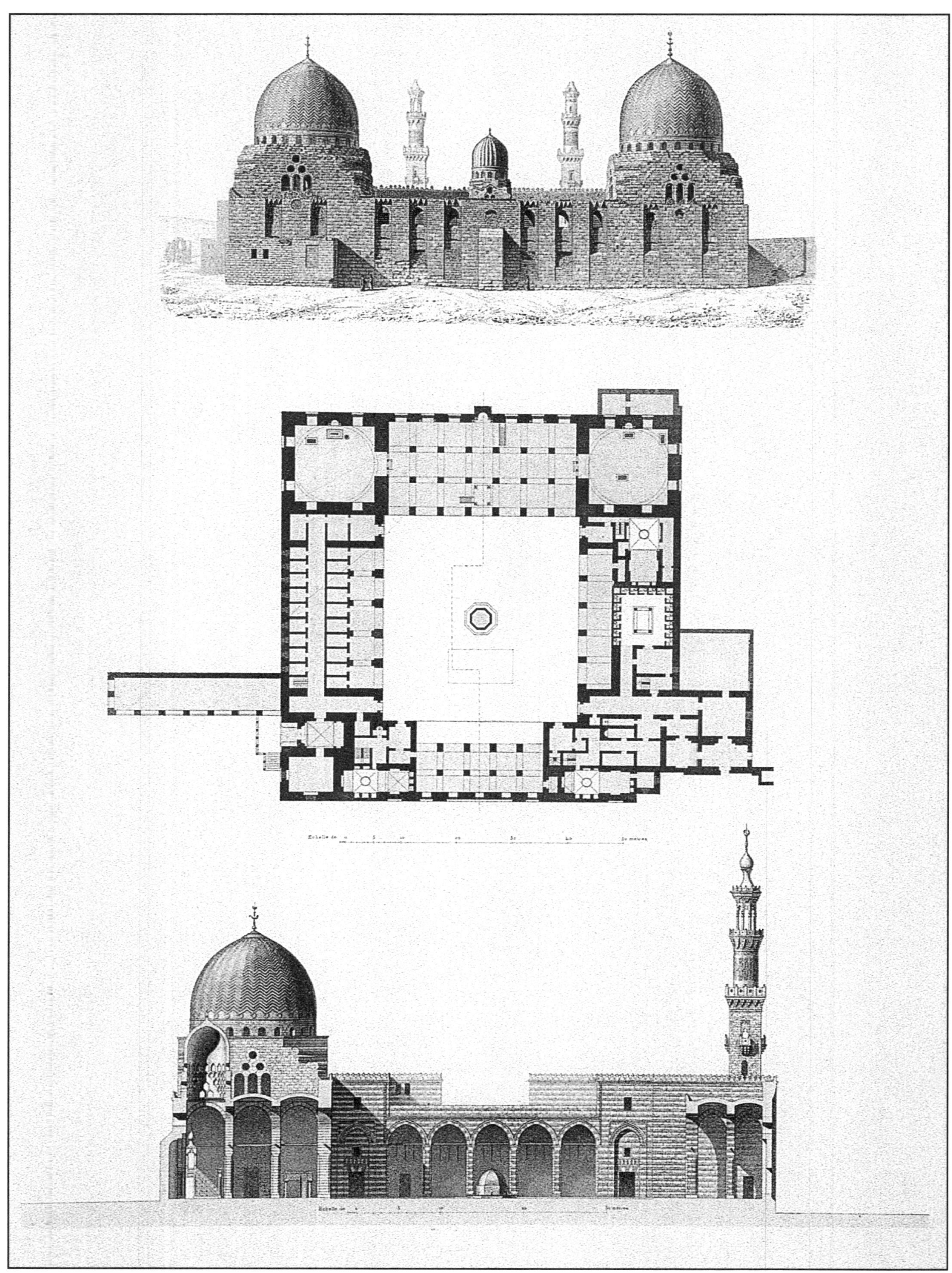

SEPULCHRAL MOSQUE OF SULTAN BARQUQ **Plate XVIII**

Door of the Tomb (14th century)

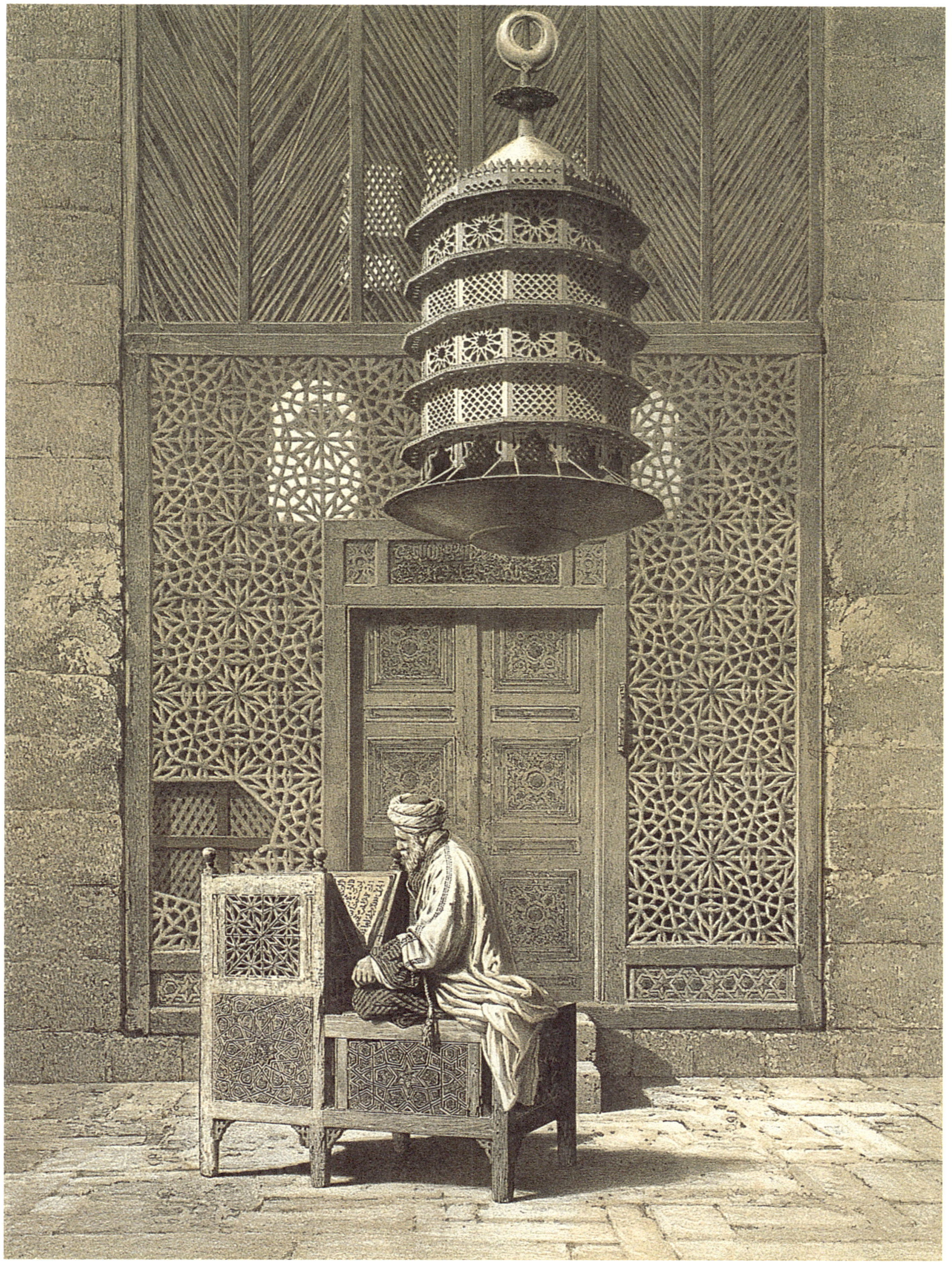

Plate XIX

MAUSOLEUM OF QAYTBAY
(15th century)

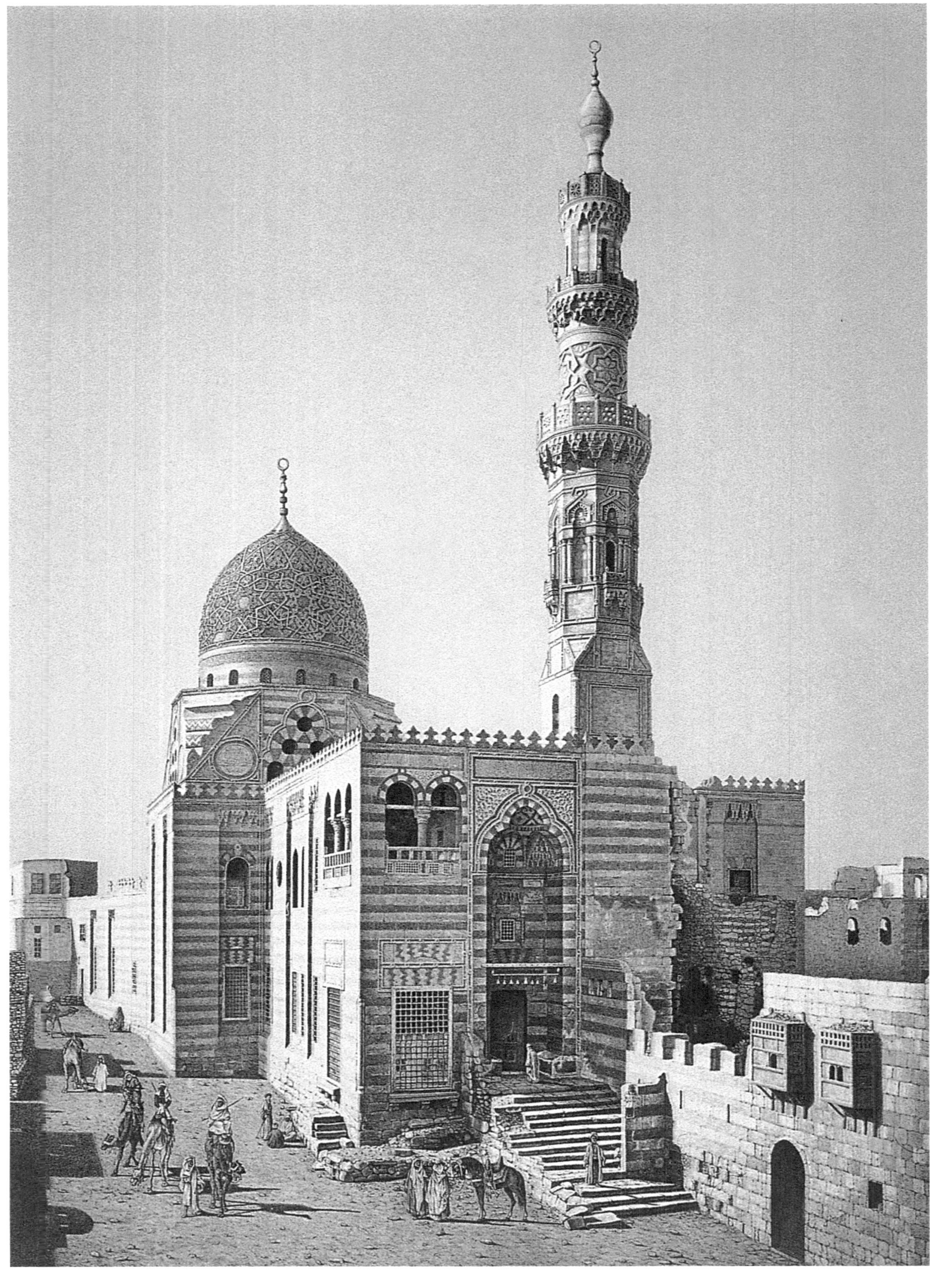

MAUSOLEUM OF QAYTBAY (INTRA MUROS)
One of the Sides (15th century)

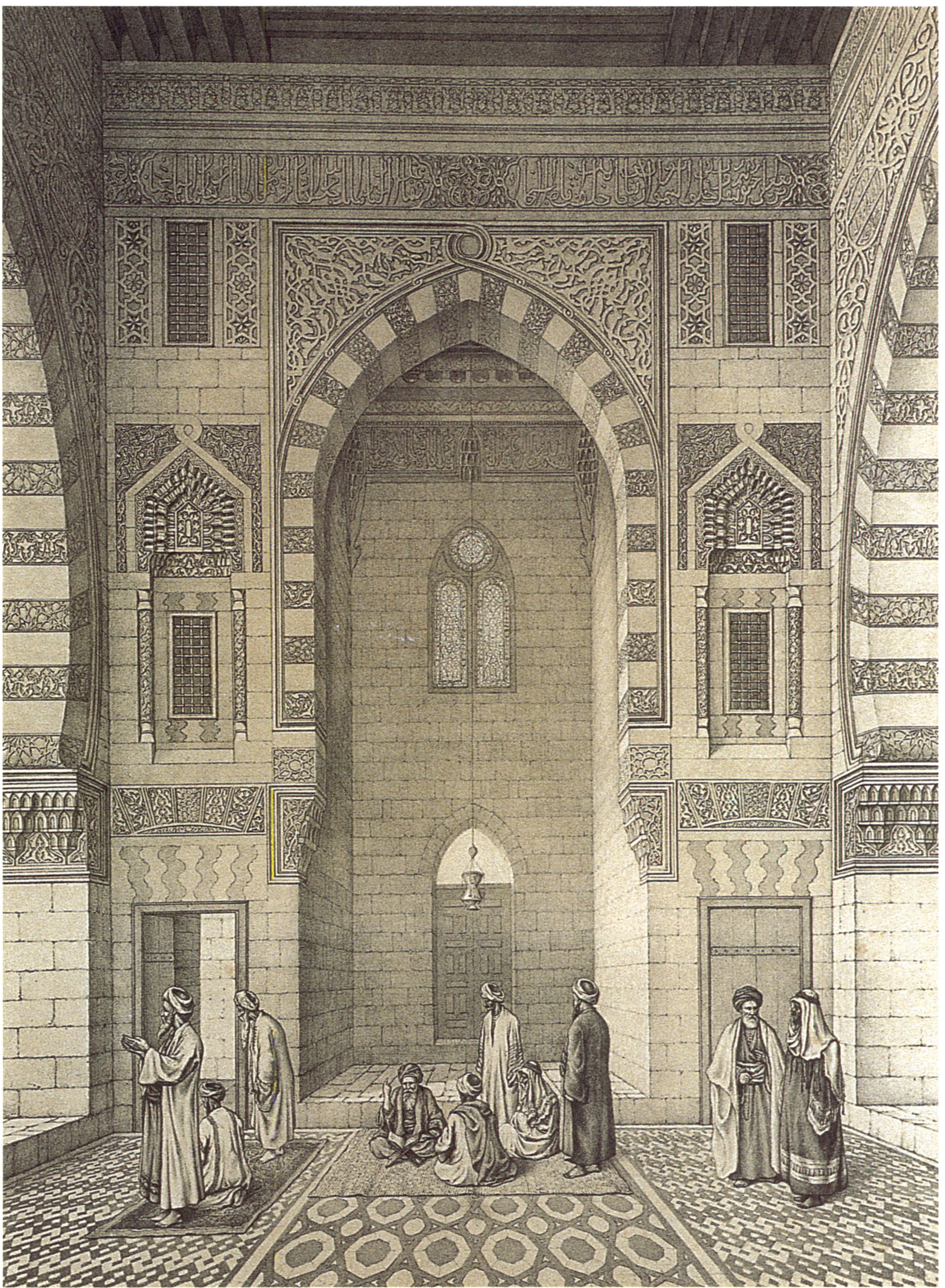

Plate XXI SEPULCHRAL MOSQUE OF QAYTBAY (INTRA MUROS)

Side with the Mihrab (15th century)

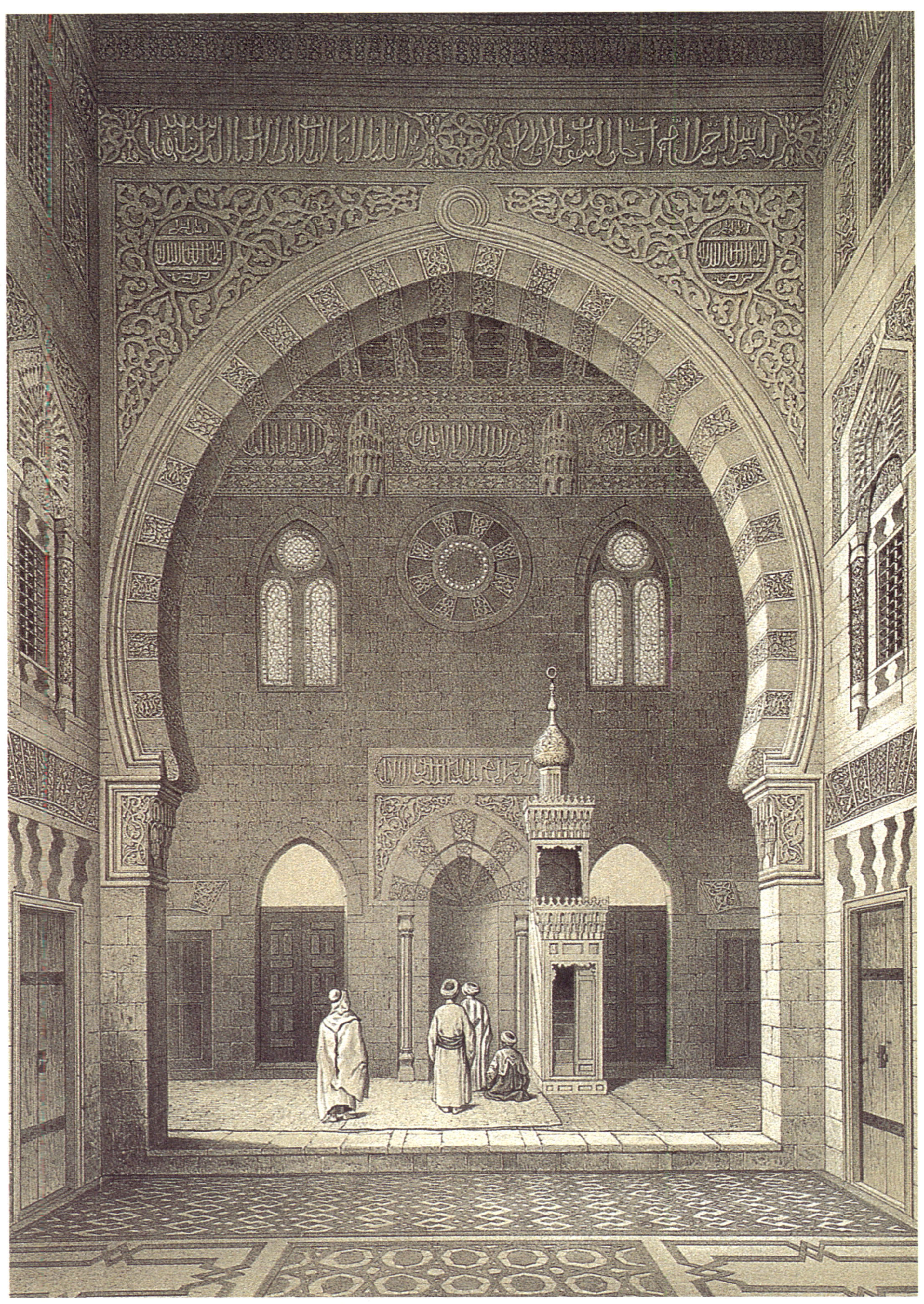

SEPULCHRAL MOSQUE OF QAYTBAY

Minaret and Details (15th century)

Plate XXII

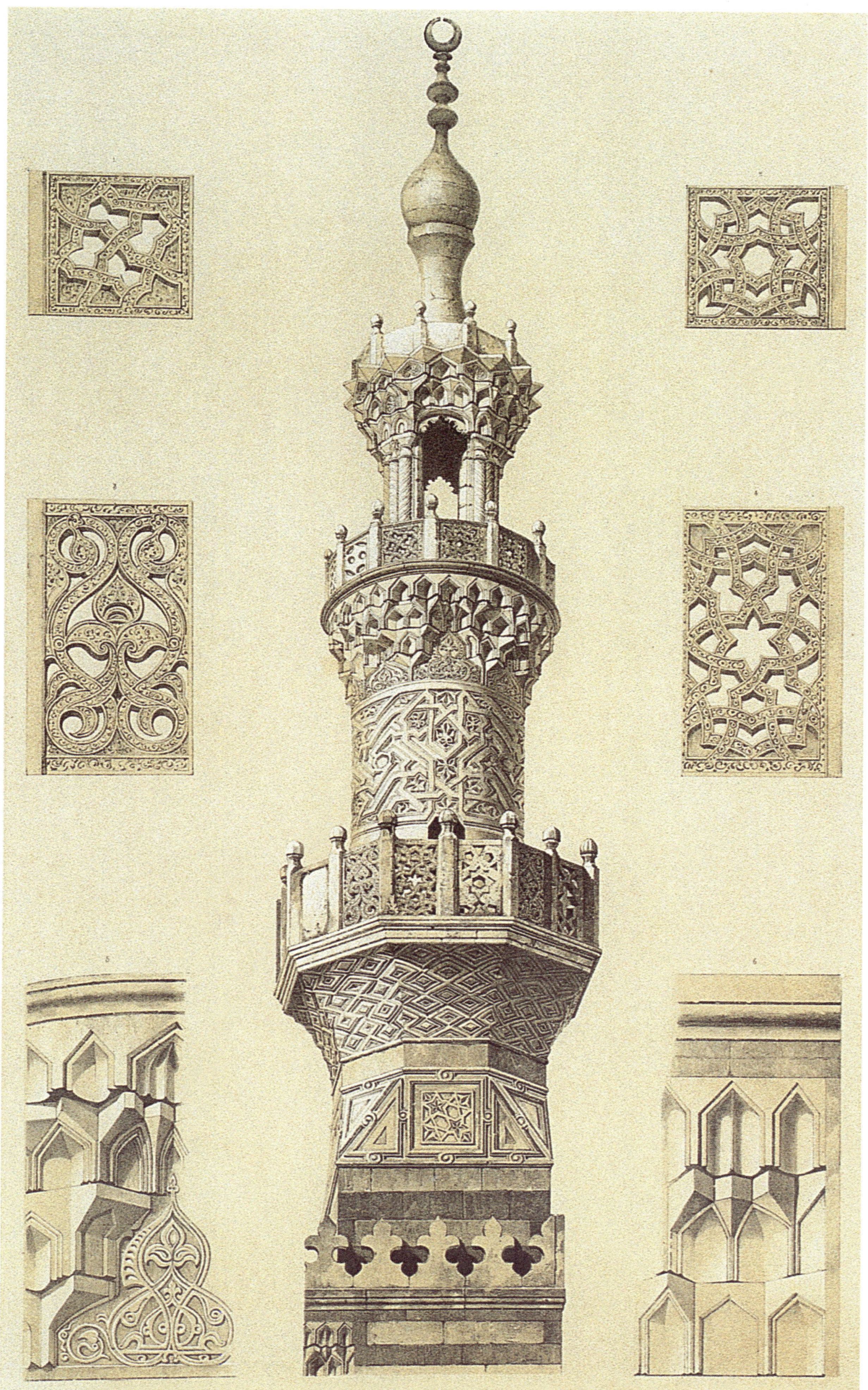

Plate XXIII

SIBIL OF QAYTBAY, NEAR ROUMELYEH

Parts of the Façade (15th century)

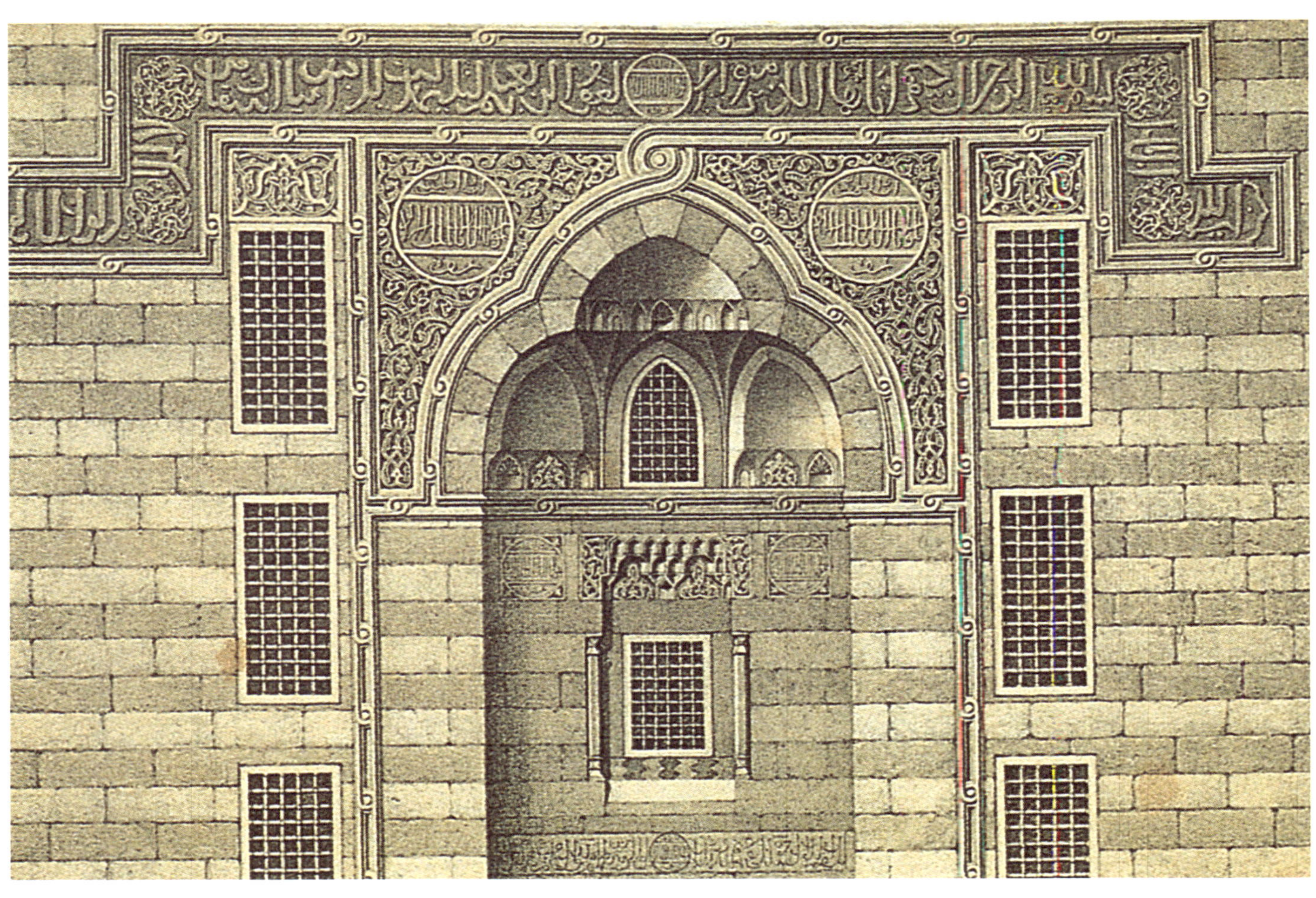

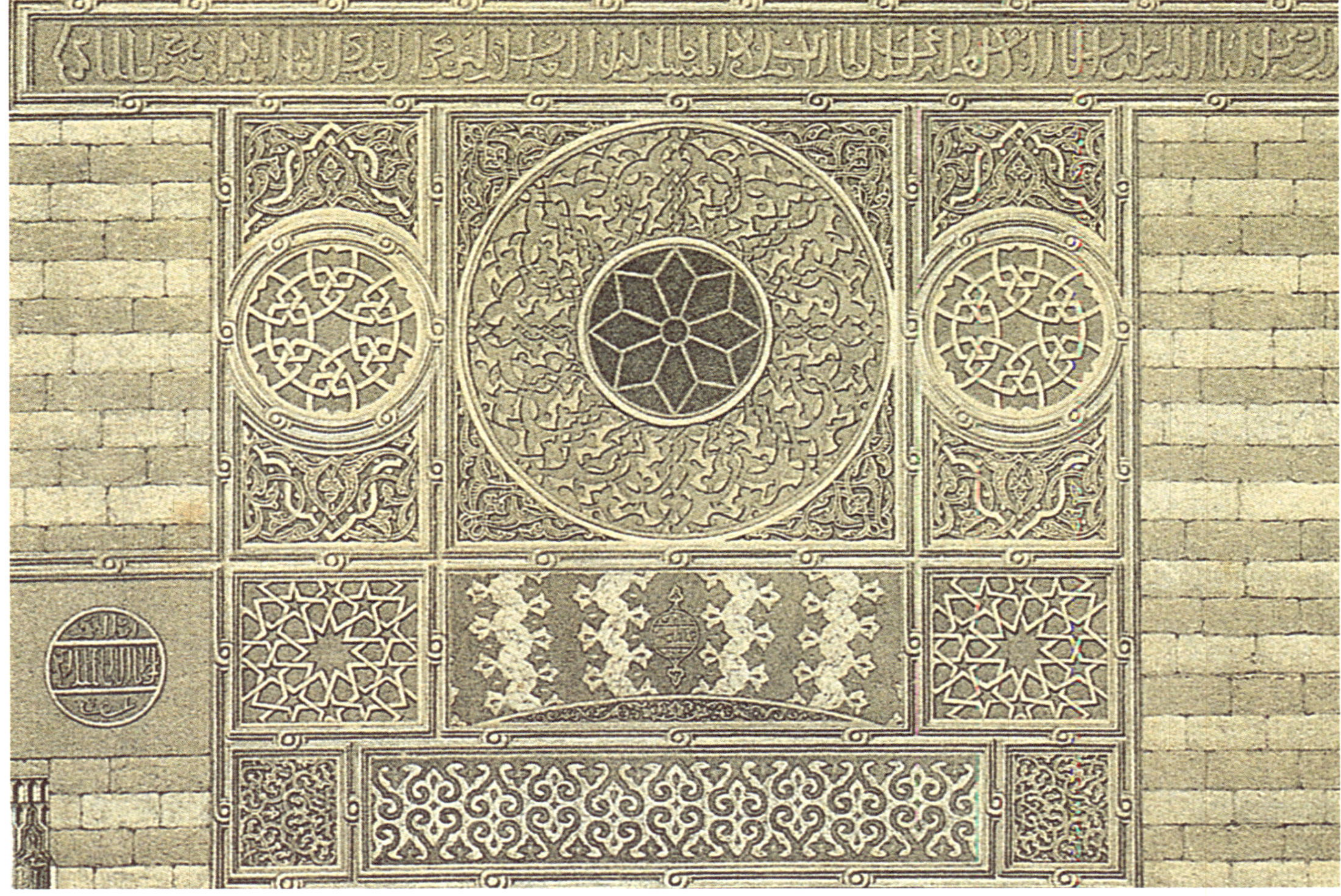

TOMB AND MINARETS

Plate XXIV

Tourab al-Imam. Mosque of al-Qalmi (15th and 16th centuries)

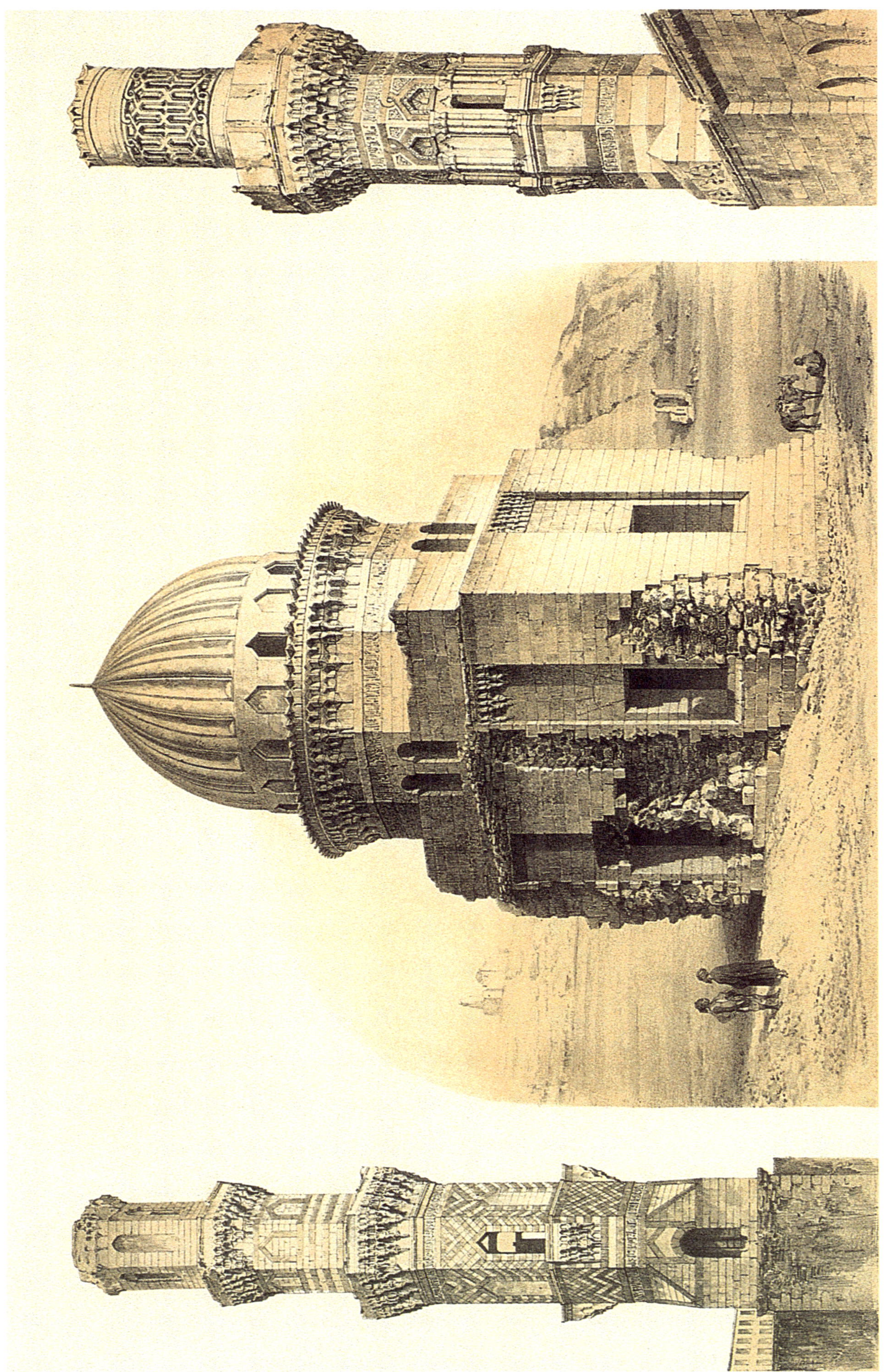

Plate XXV

MINARETS

Mosque of Nasrieh. Mosque of al-Bordayni (15th and 17th centuries)

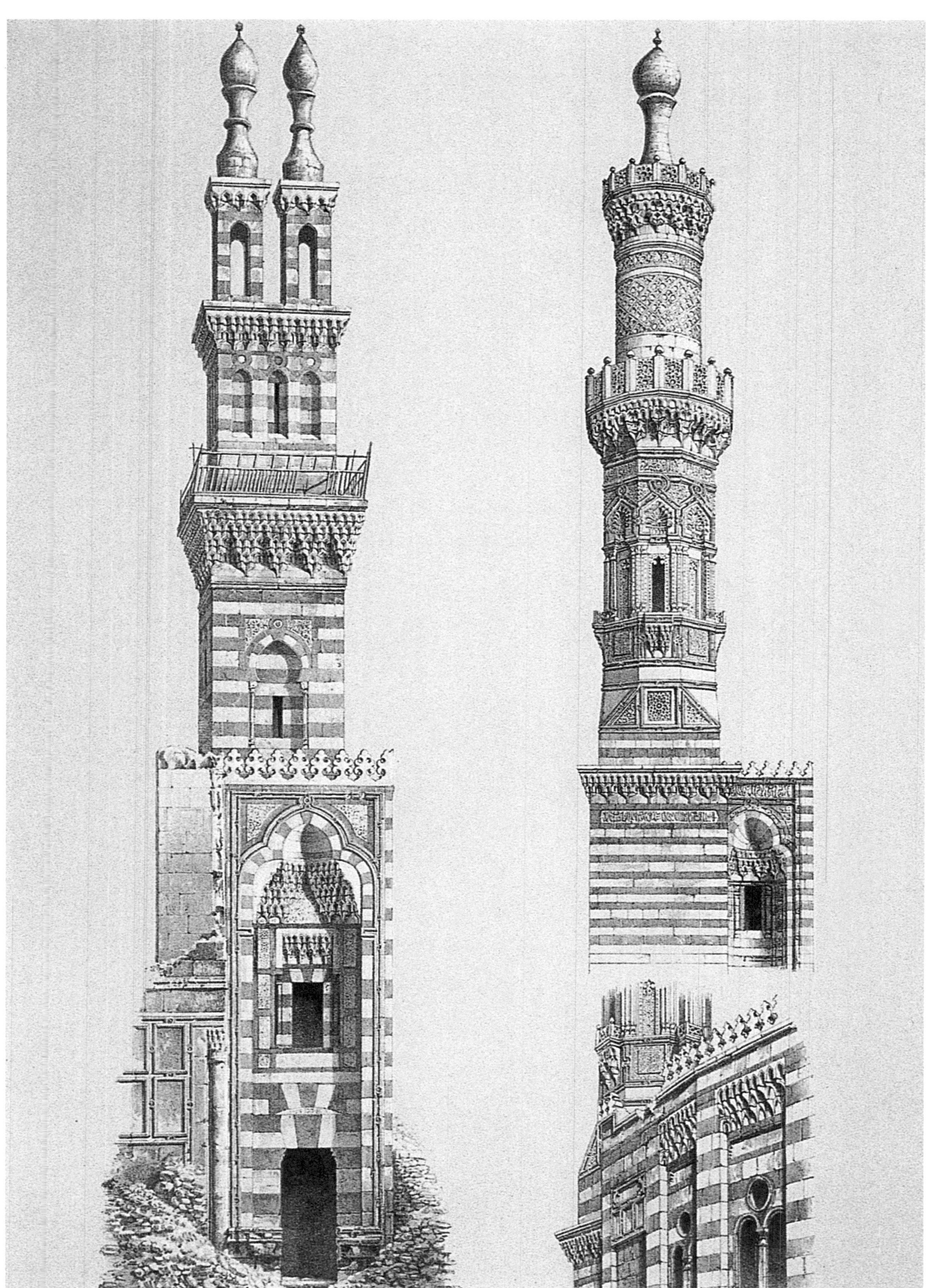

MOSQUE AND TOMB OF AL-GHURI
(16th century)

Plate XXVI

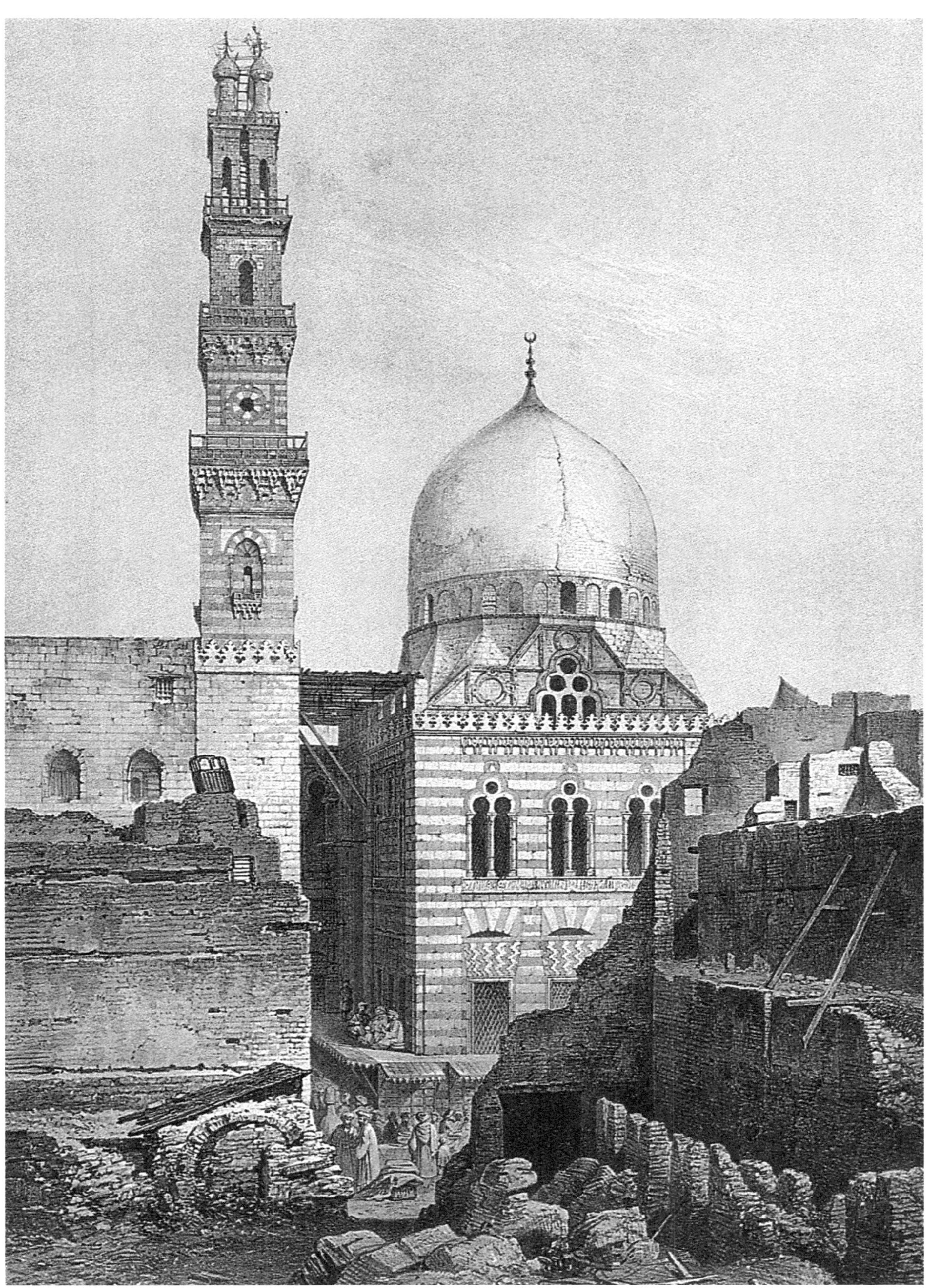

Plate XXVII

TOMB OF SULTAN TARABAY
(16th century)

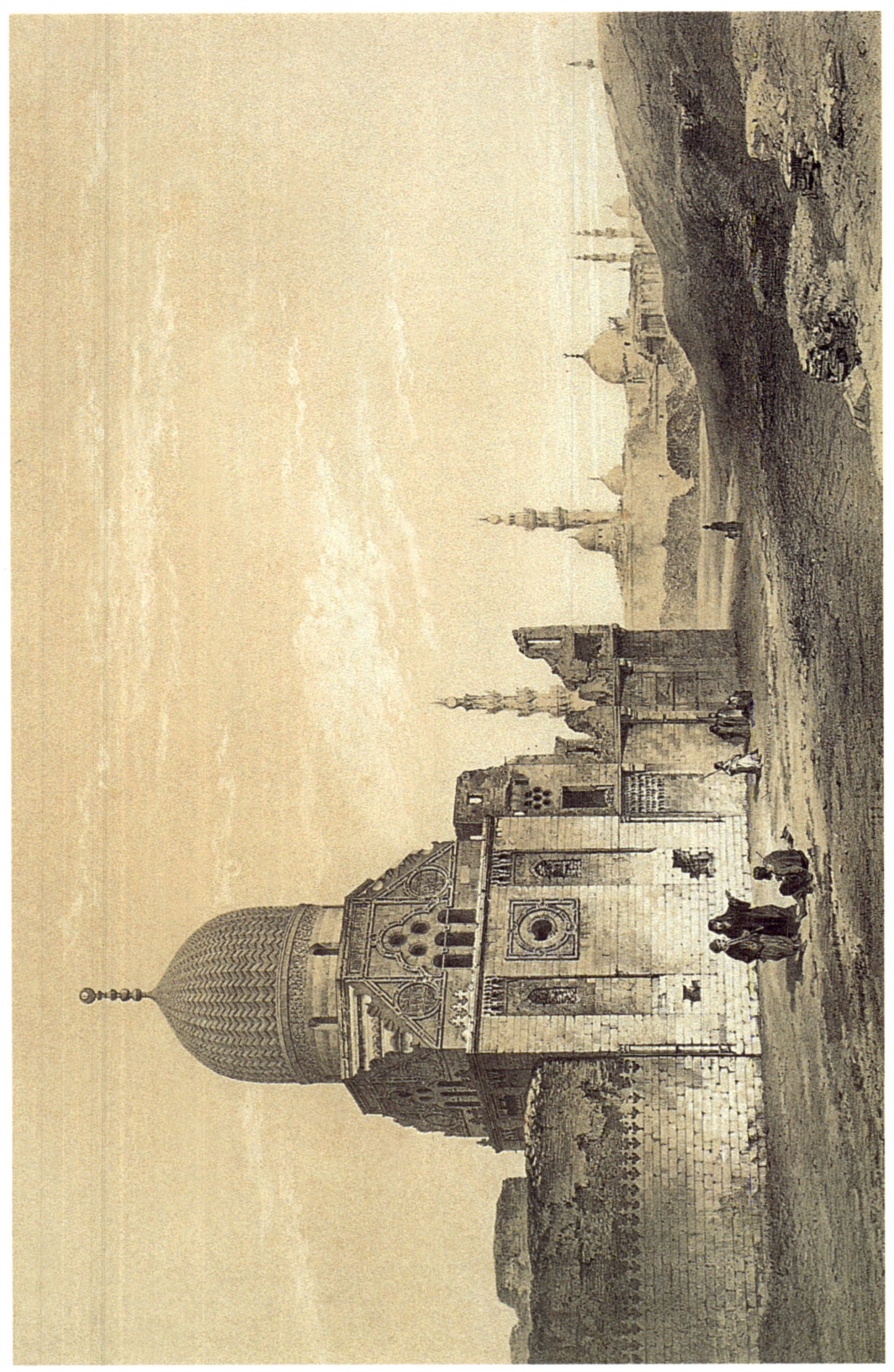

TOMB ATTRIBUTED TO MAHMUD JANUM

(16th century)

Plate XXVIII

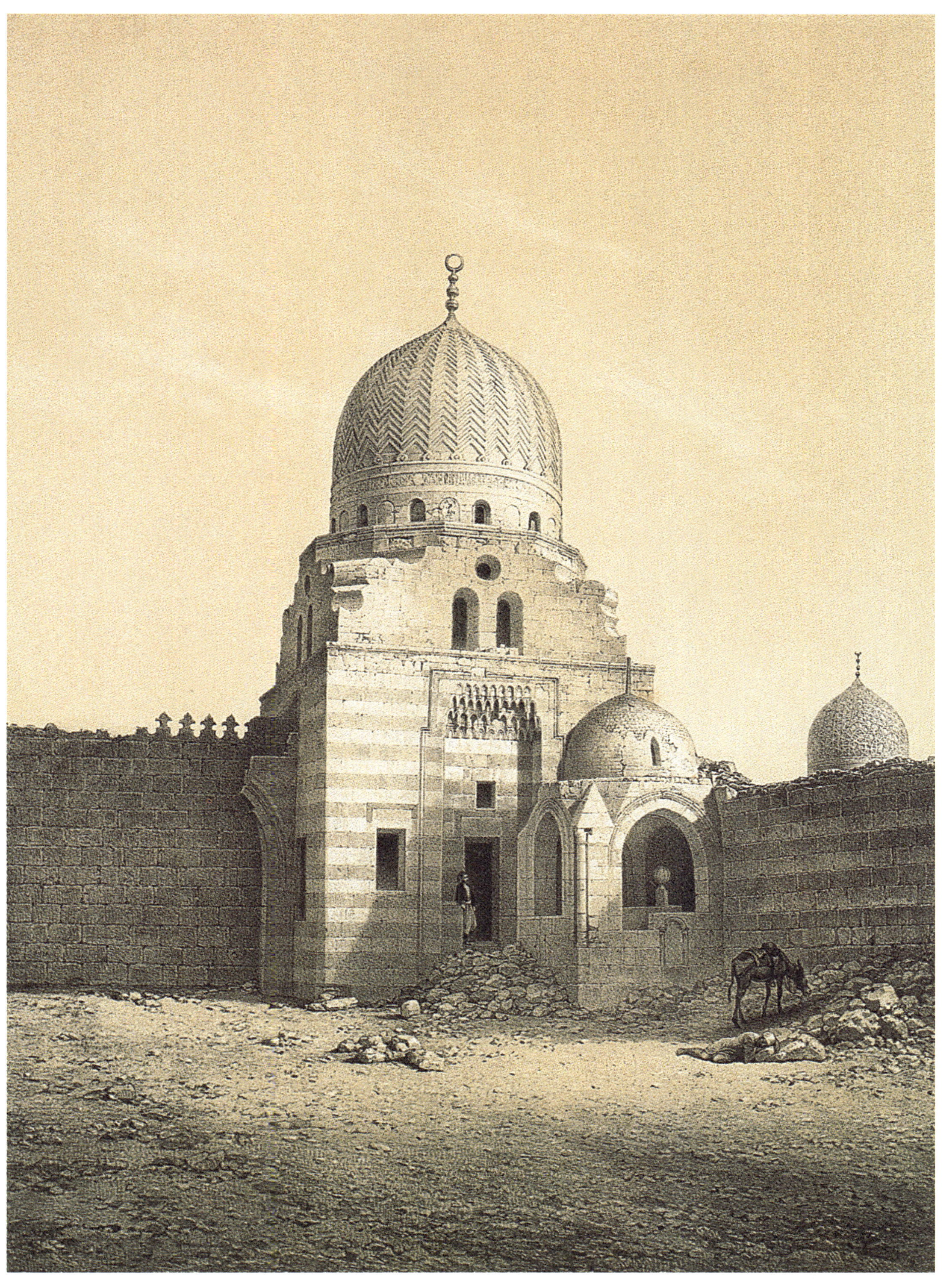

Plate XXIX

MOSQUE OF KHAIR-BEKIEH

Dome and Minaret (16th century)

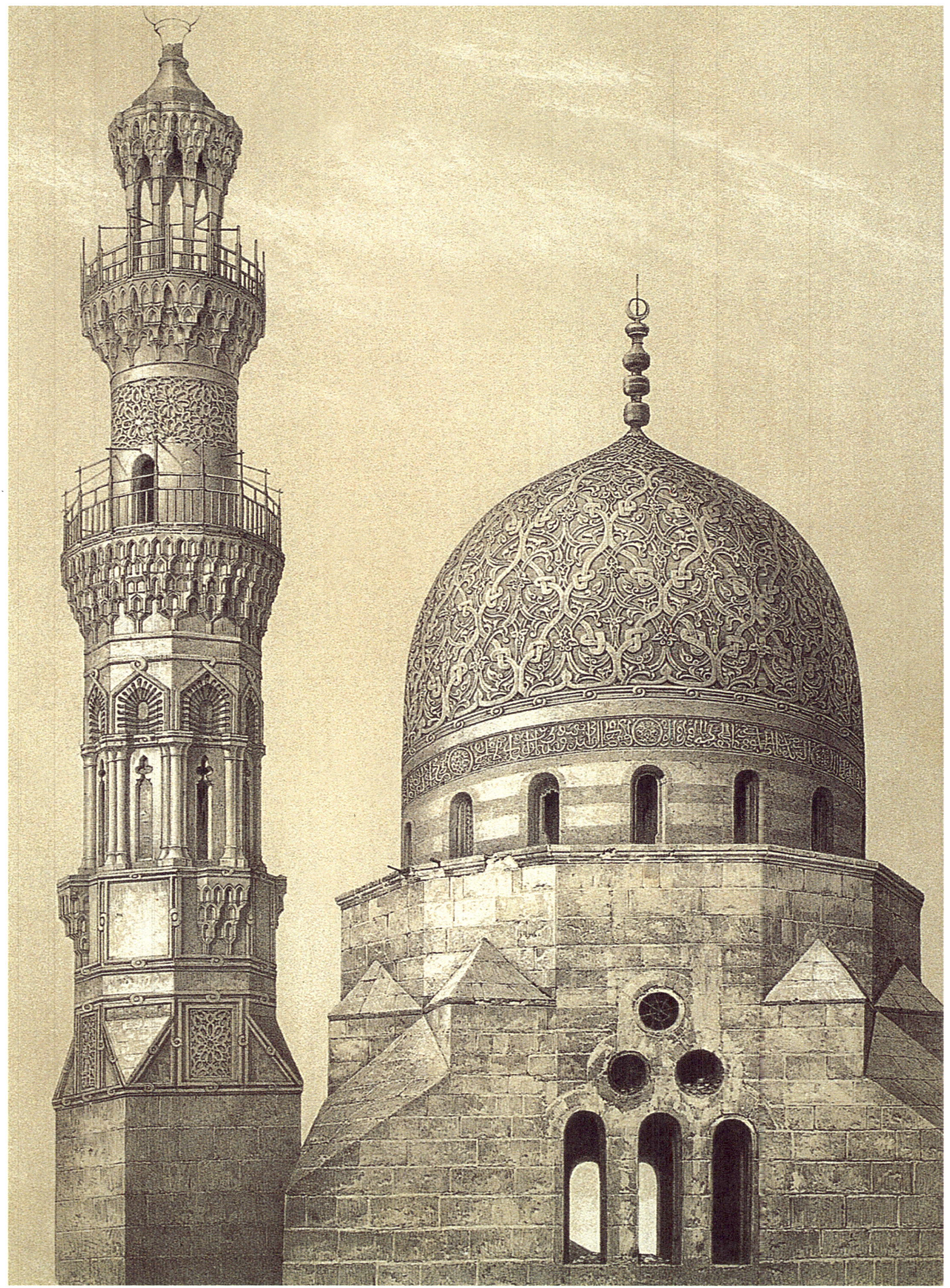

MOSQUE OF SINANIEH
(16th century)

Plate XXX

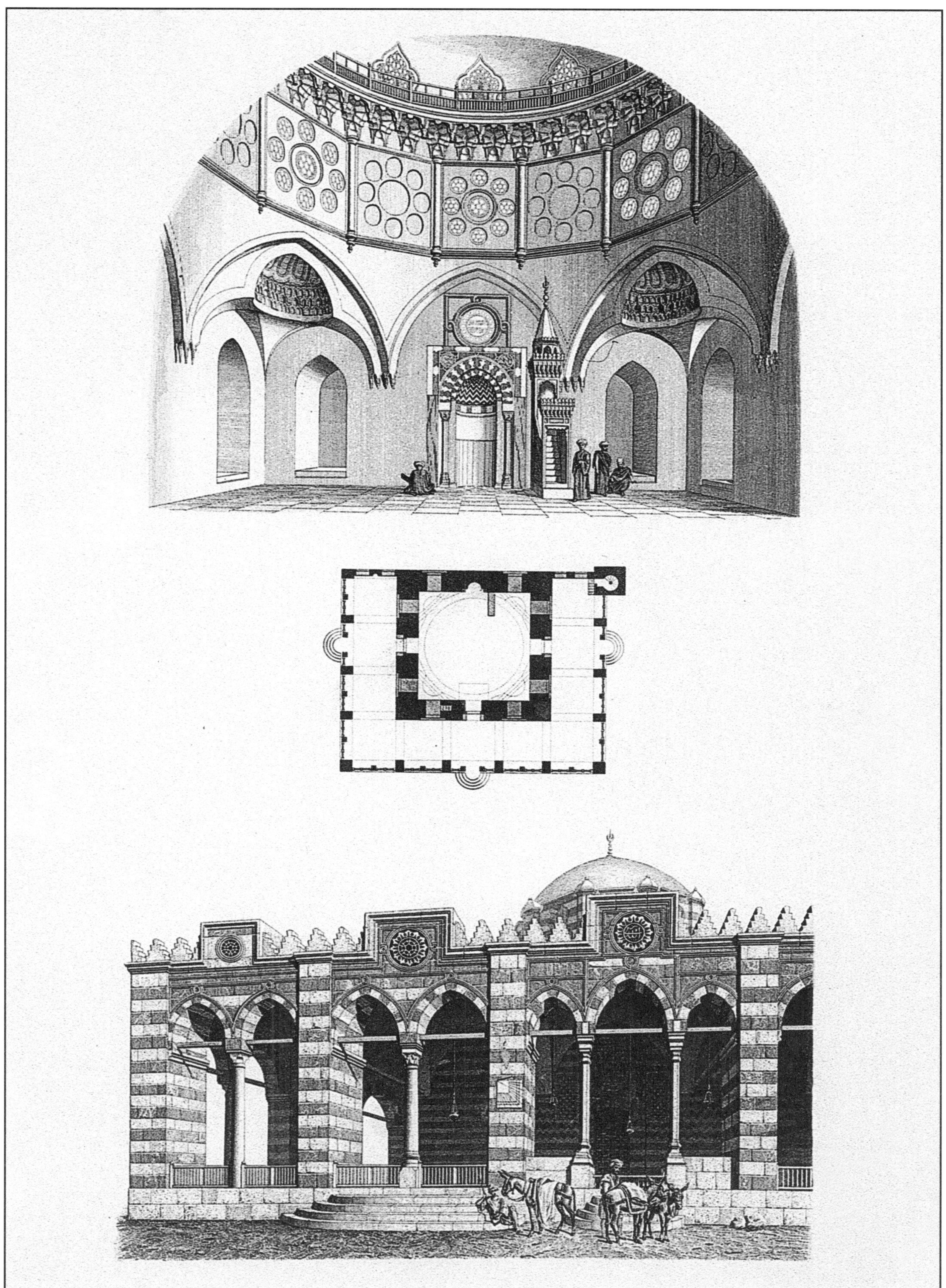

Plate XXXI

HOUSE KNOWN AS BAIT AL-AMIR

Façade of the Maq'ad or Iwan on the Courtyard (17th century)

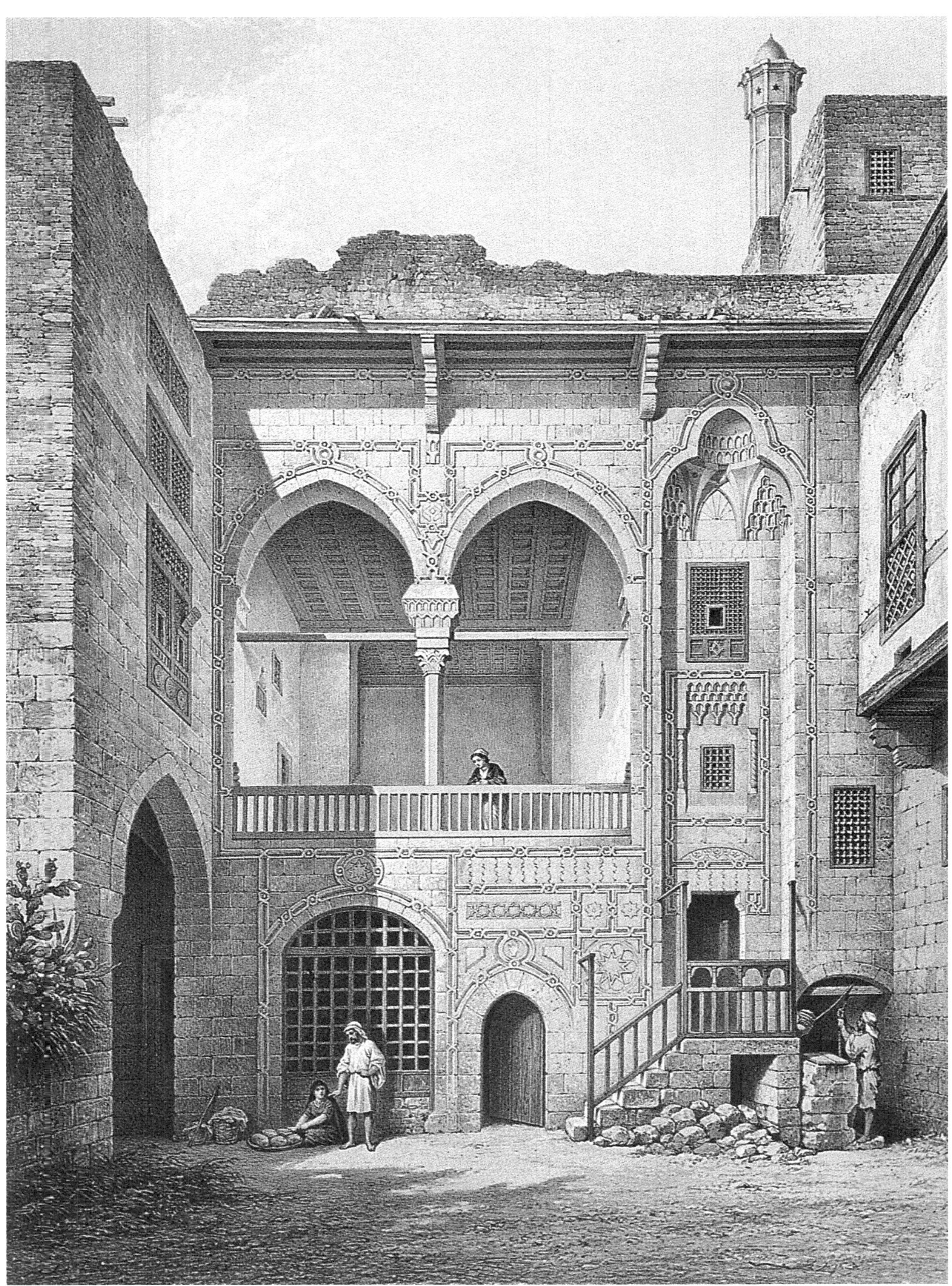

BAIT AL-AMIR **Plate XXXII**

Outer Door of the Harem (17th century)

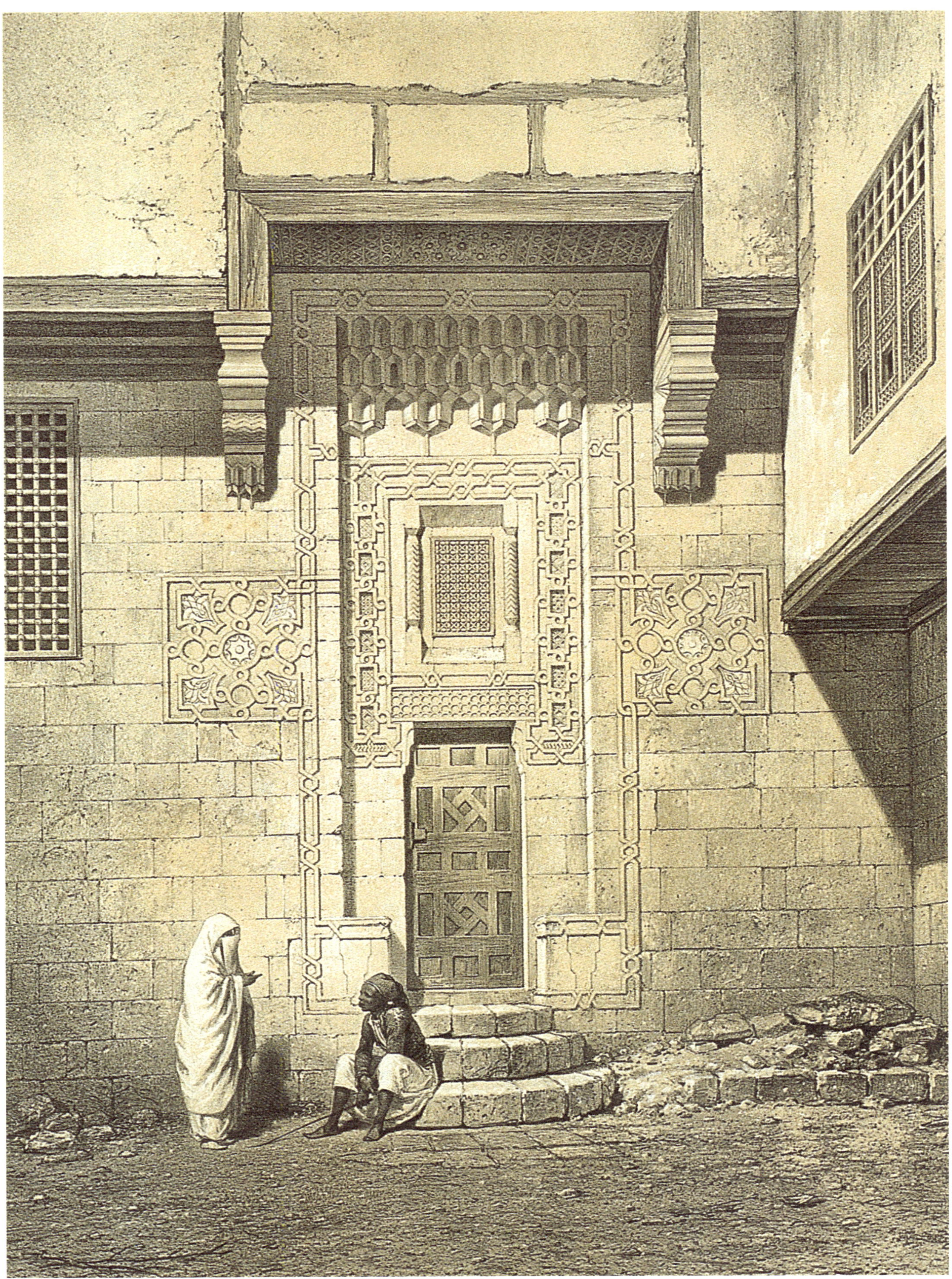

Plate XXXIII

MOSQUE OF AL-BORDAYNI

Plan, Elevations and Details (17th century)

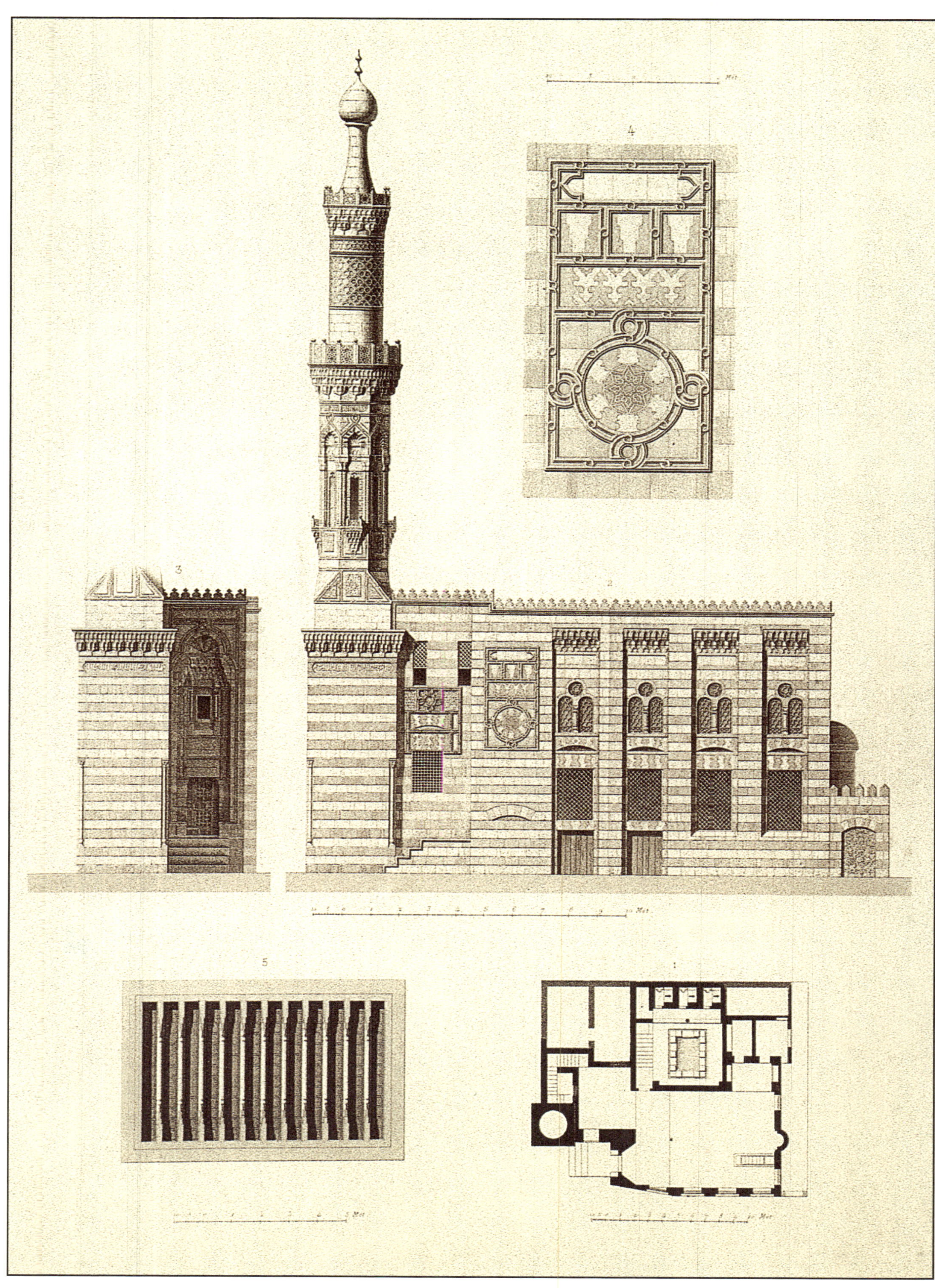

MAUSOLEUM NEAR KIMAN AL-GIUSHI
(18th century)

Plate XXXIV

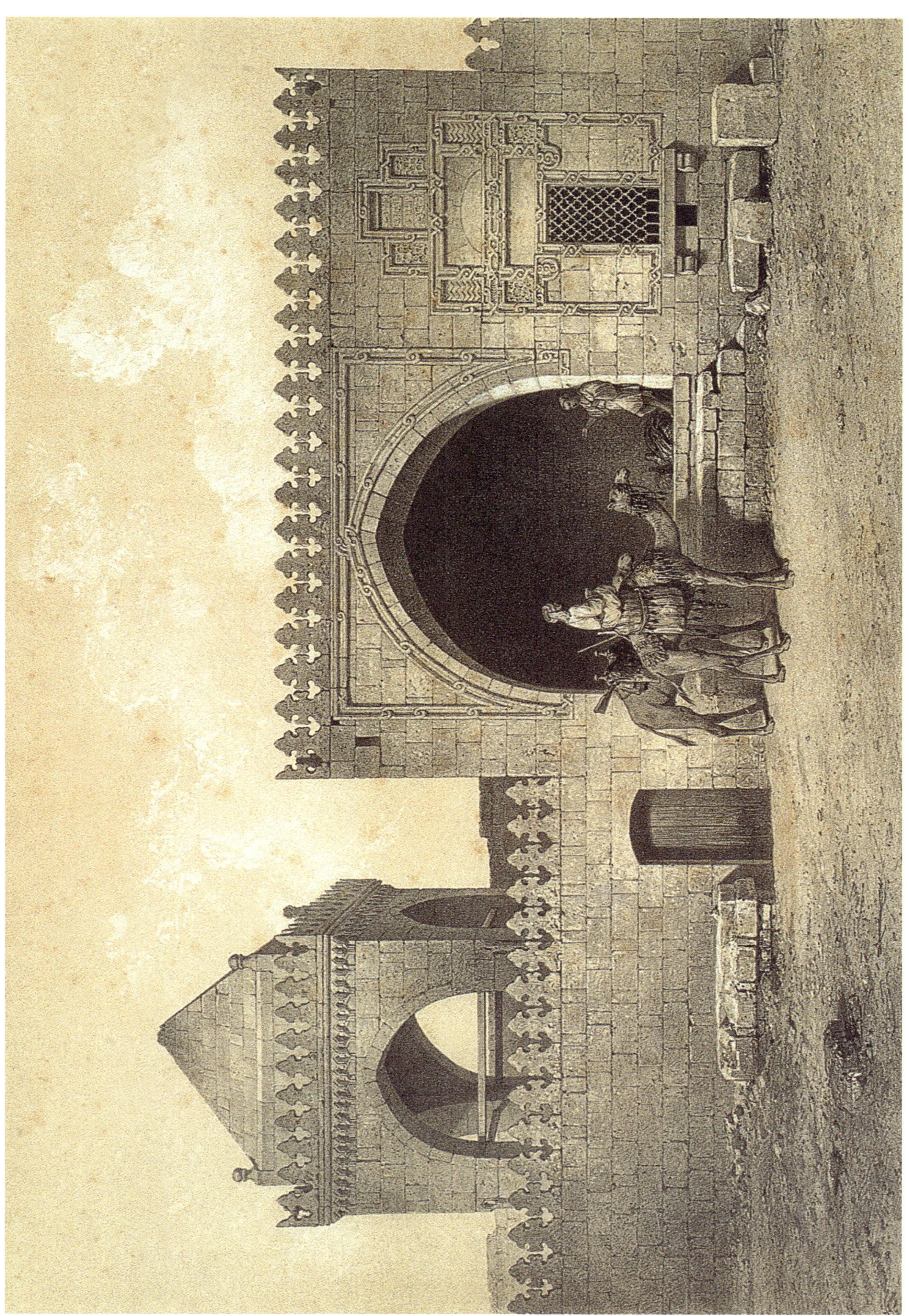

Plate XXXV

TOMB OF AN AMIR

In the Cemetery of Karafeh (18th century)

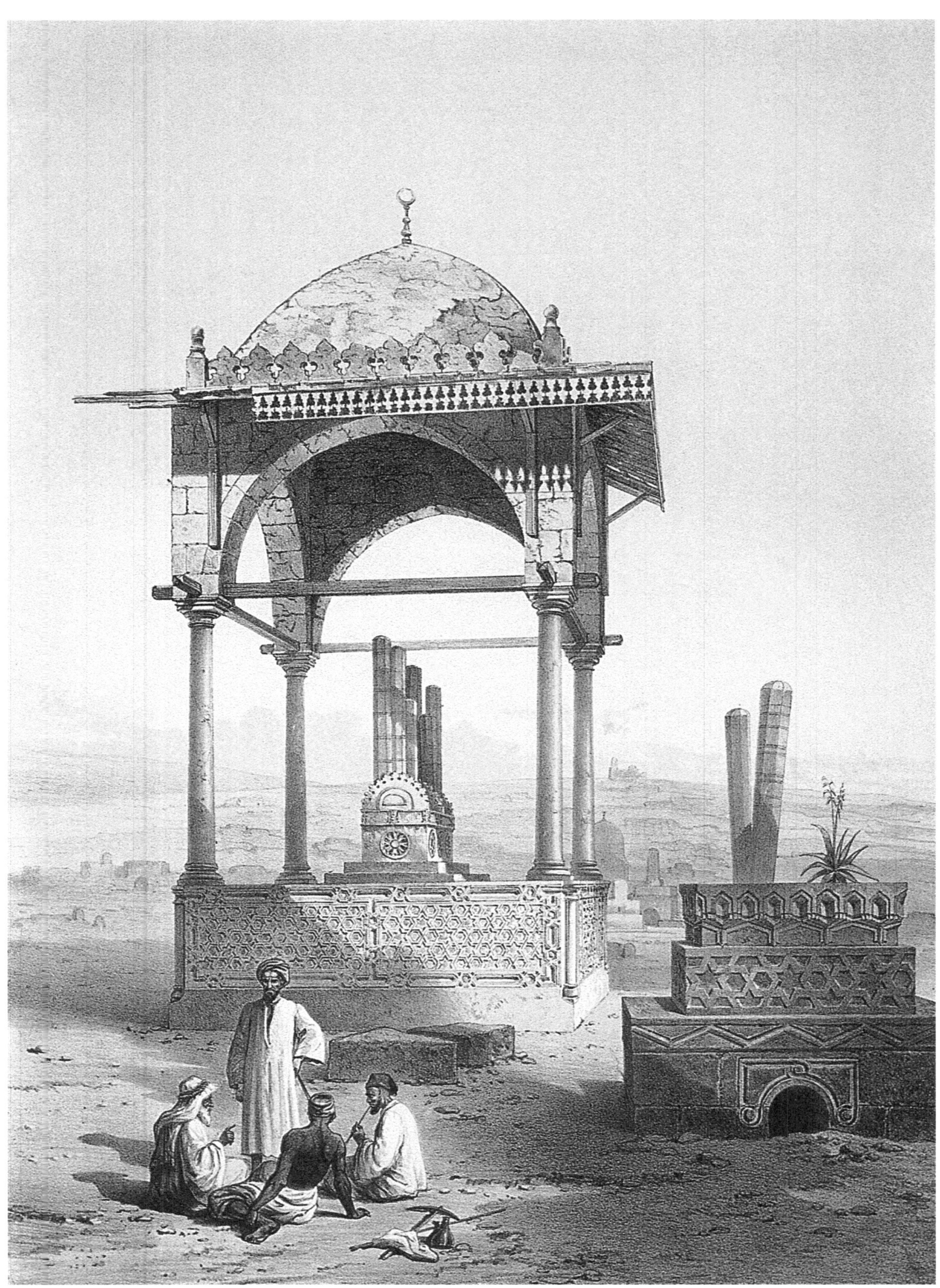

SIBIL OF AHMAD HUSSEIN MARGUSH (18th century)

Plate XXXVI

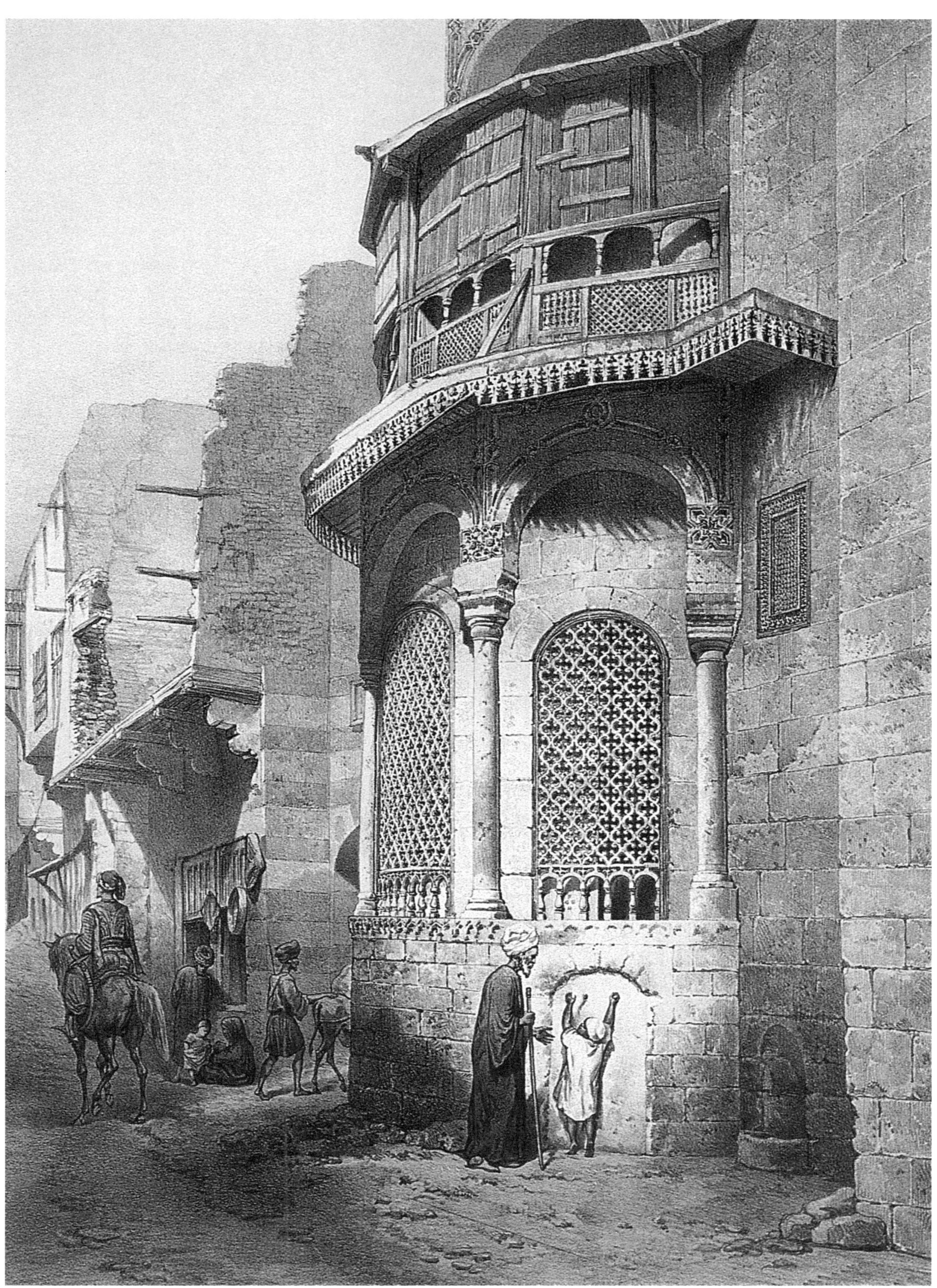

Plate XXXVII

ZAWYET OF ABD AL-RAHMAN YAHIA
(18th century)

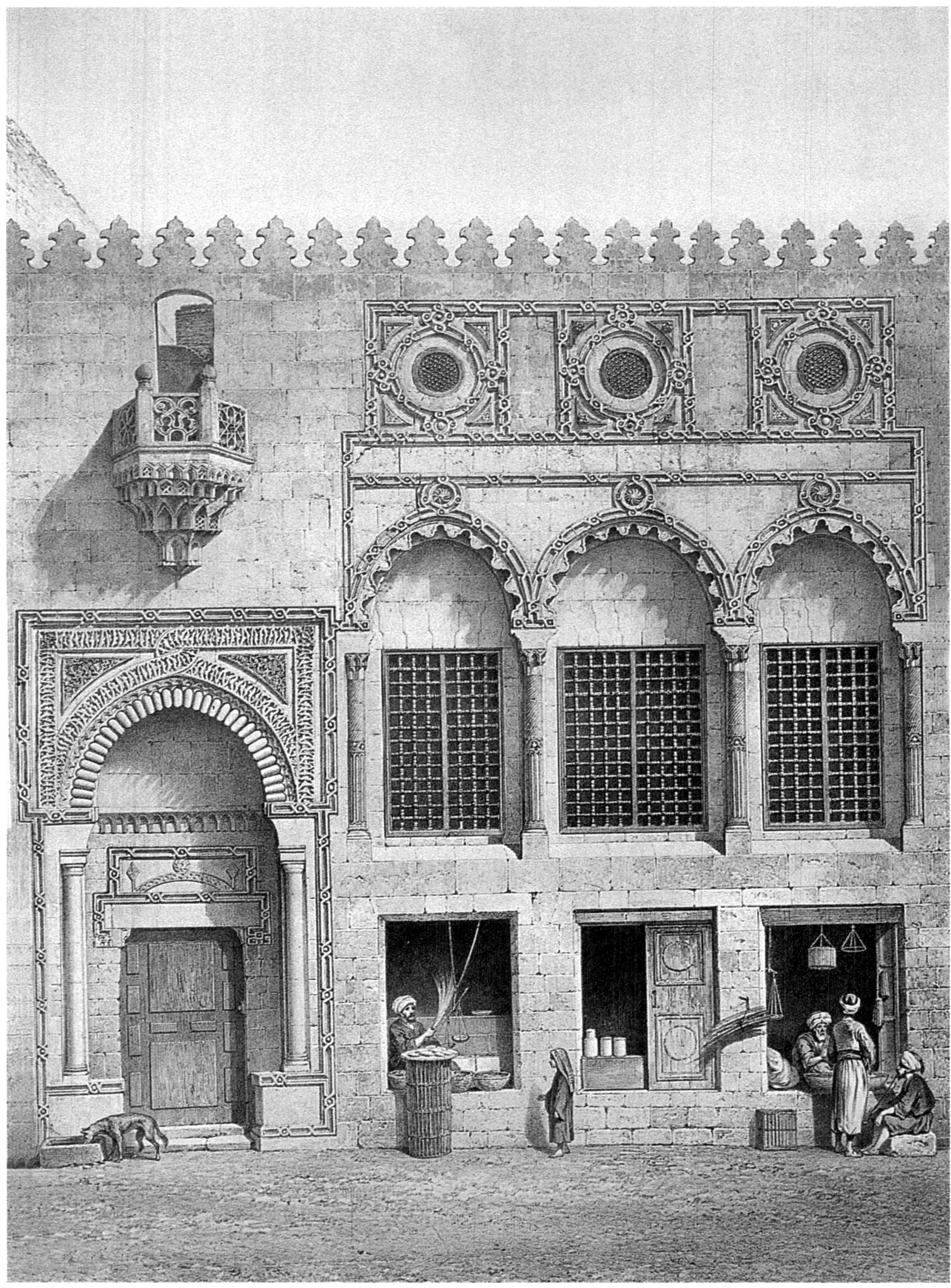

DOOR OF THE BATH OF HAMMAM AL-TALAT

(18th century)

Plate XXXVIII

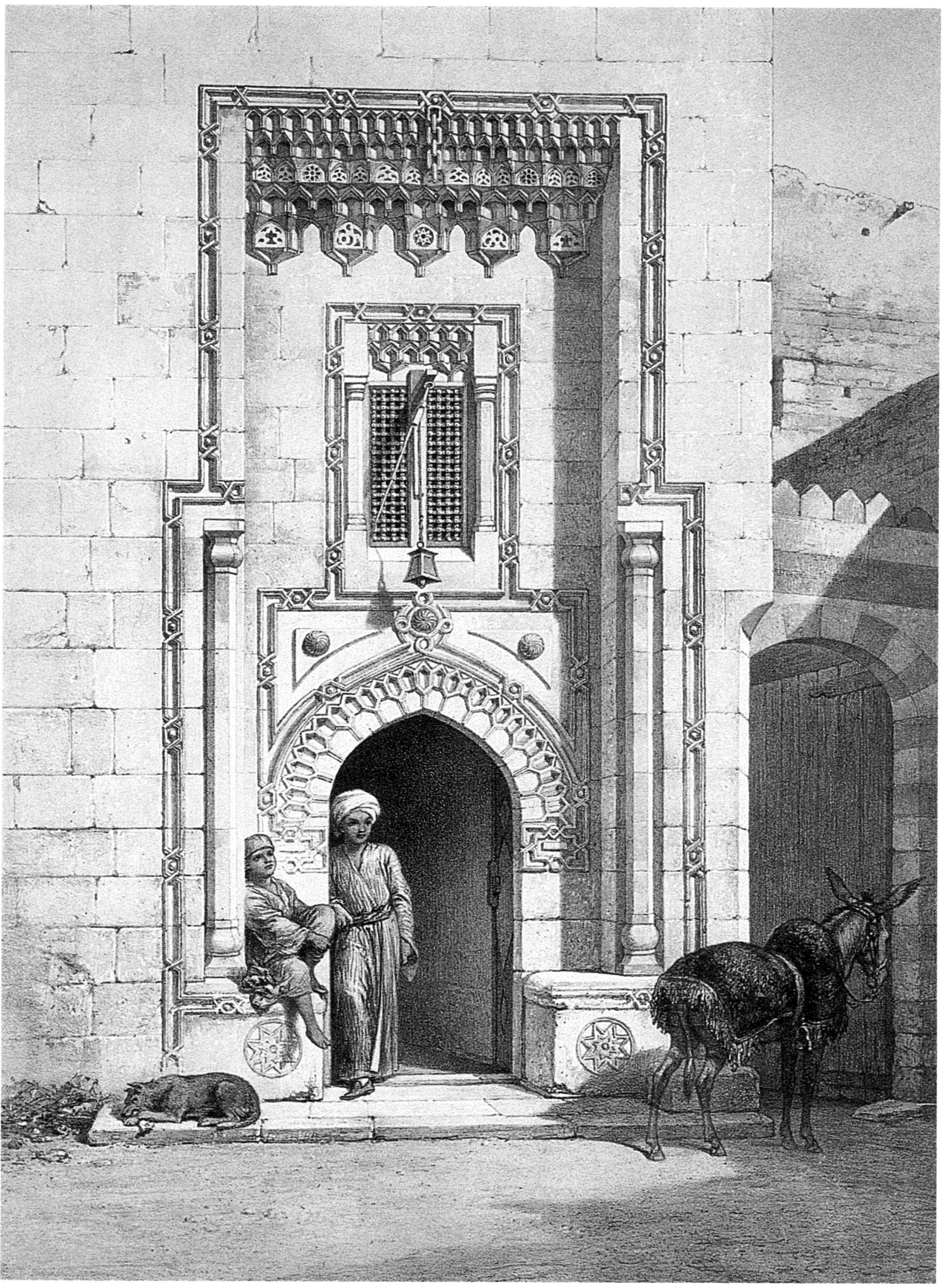

Plate XXXIX

HOUSE KNOWN AS BAIT AL-SHALABI

Interior Façade on the Courtyard (18th century)

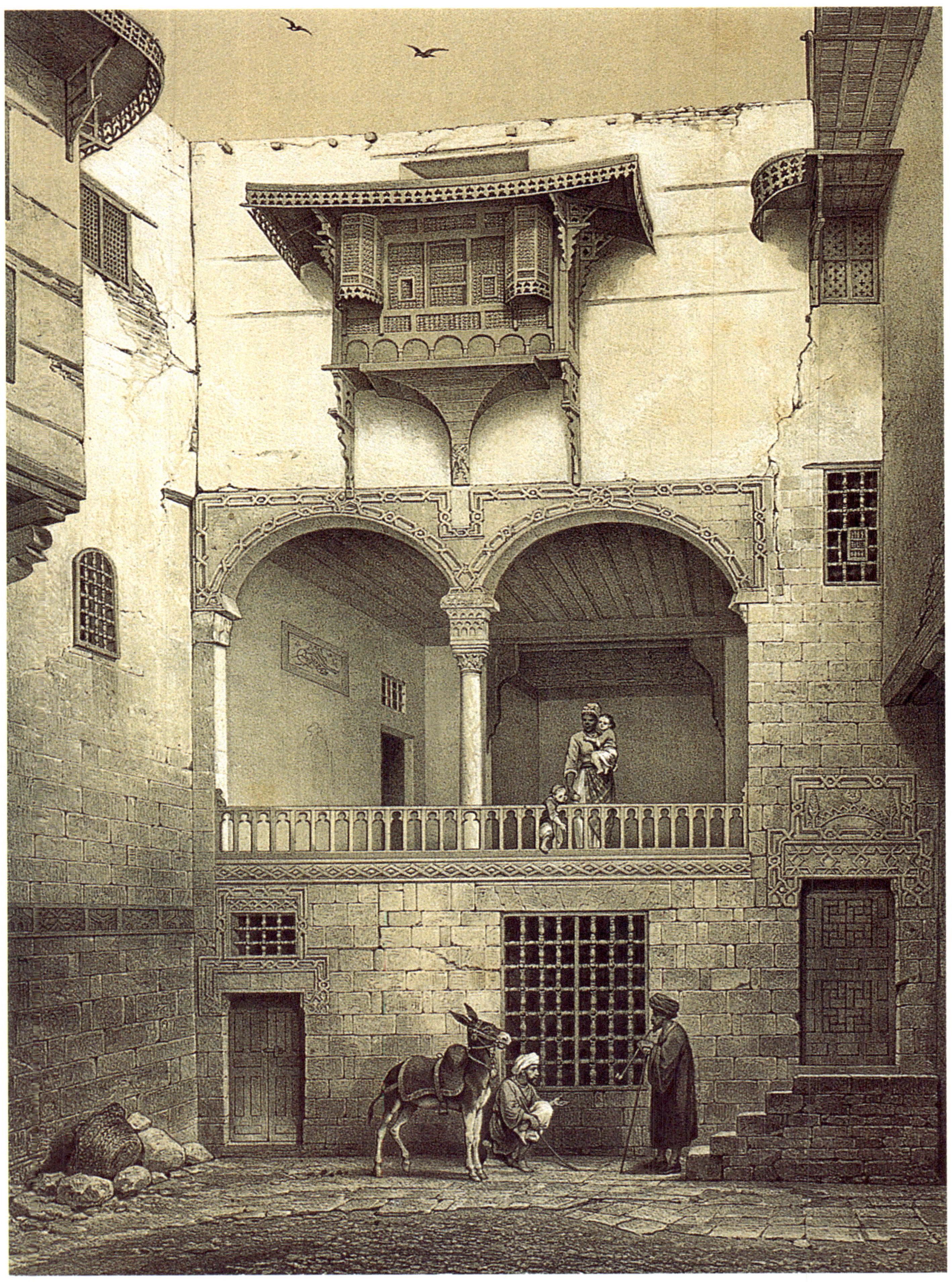

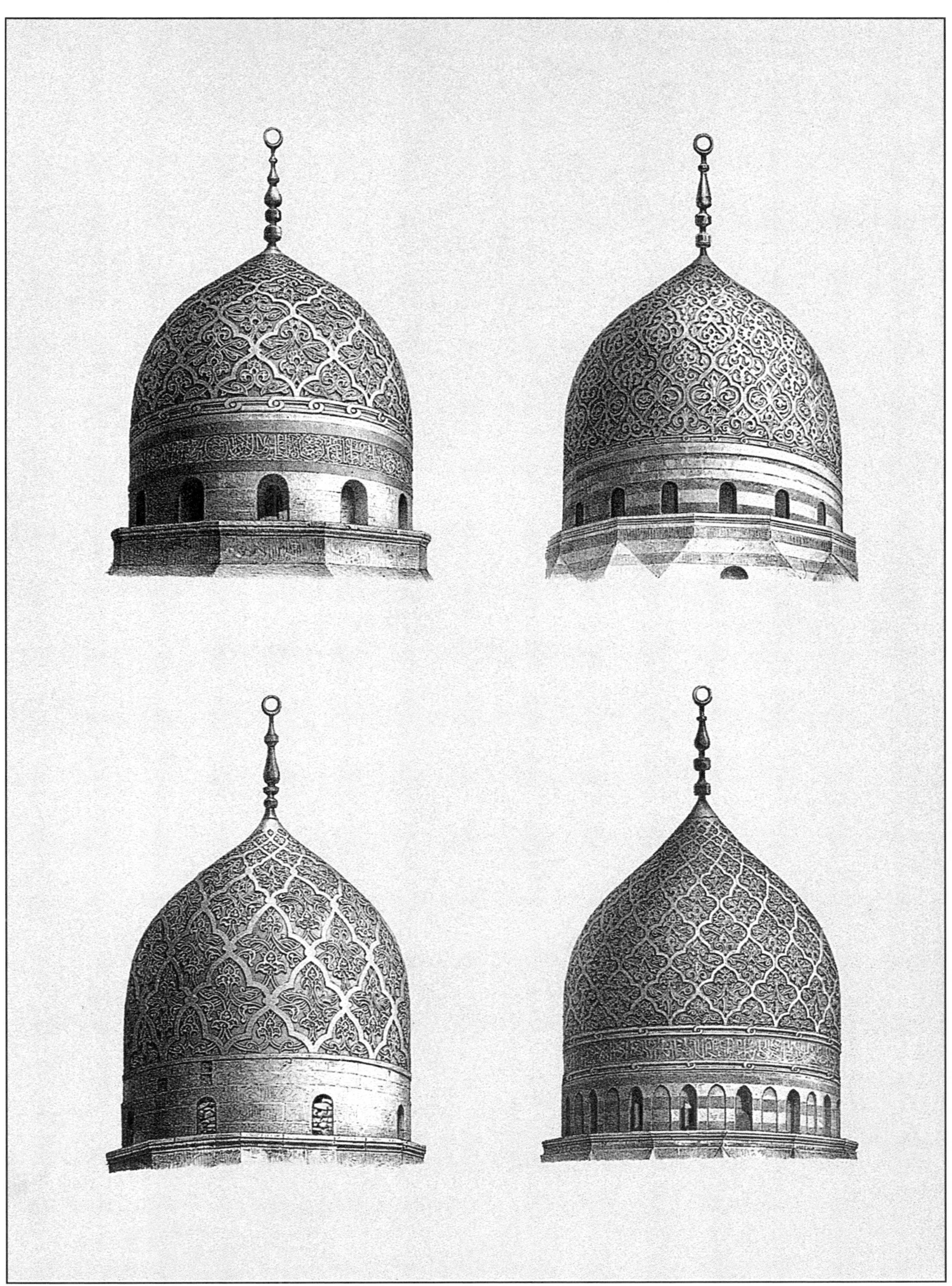

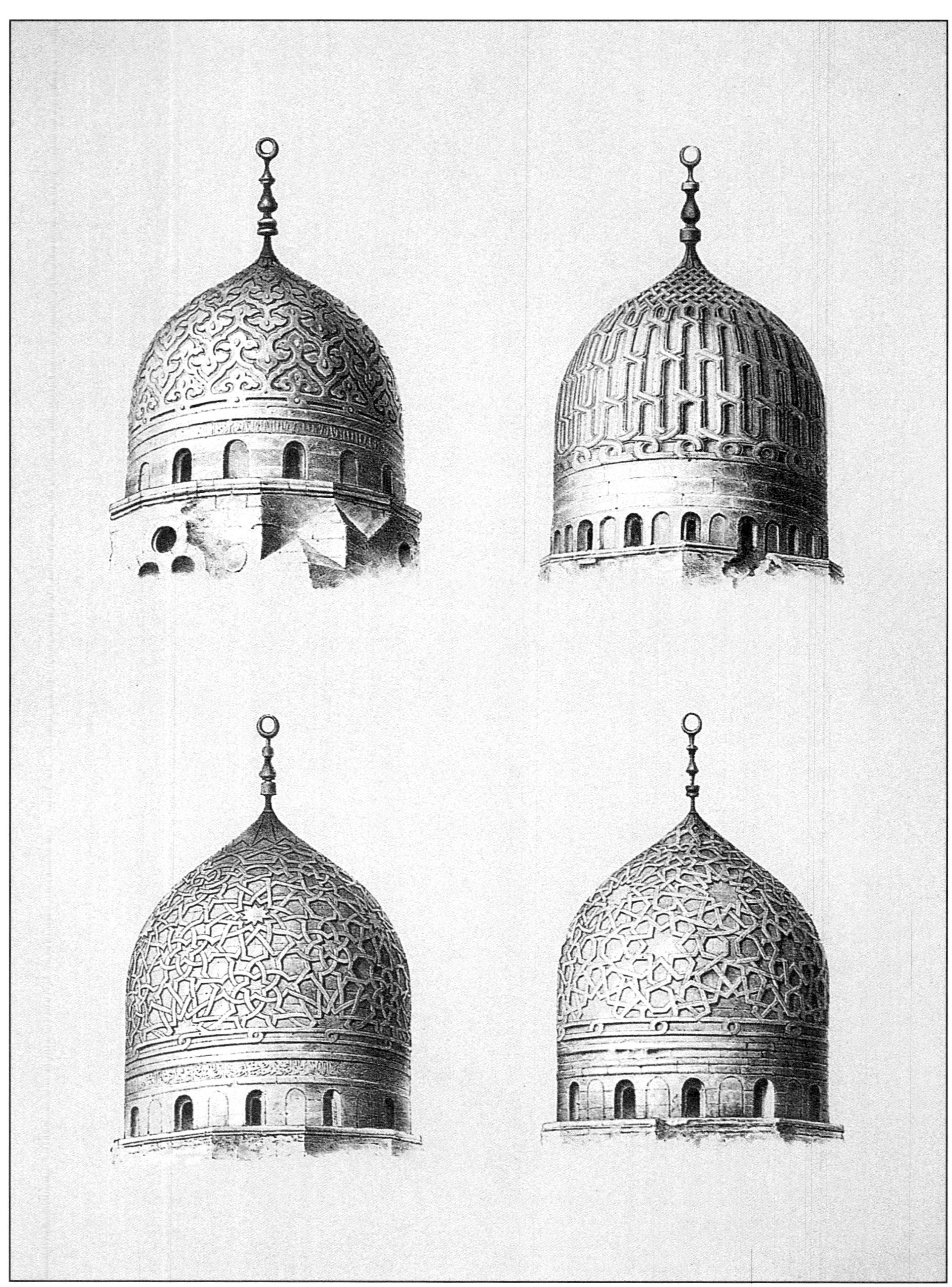

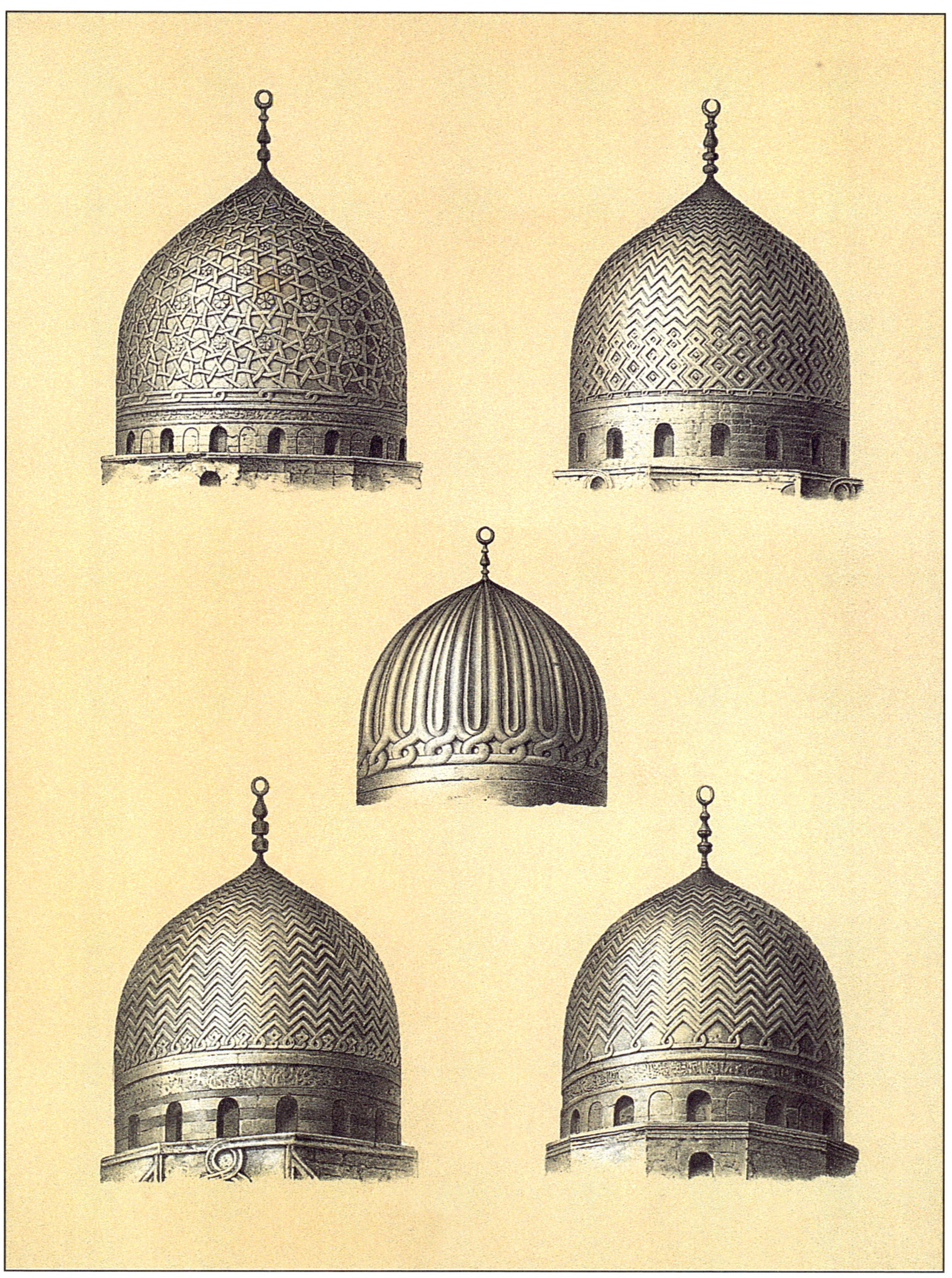

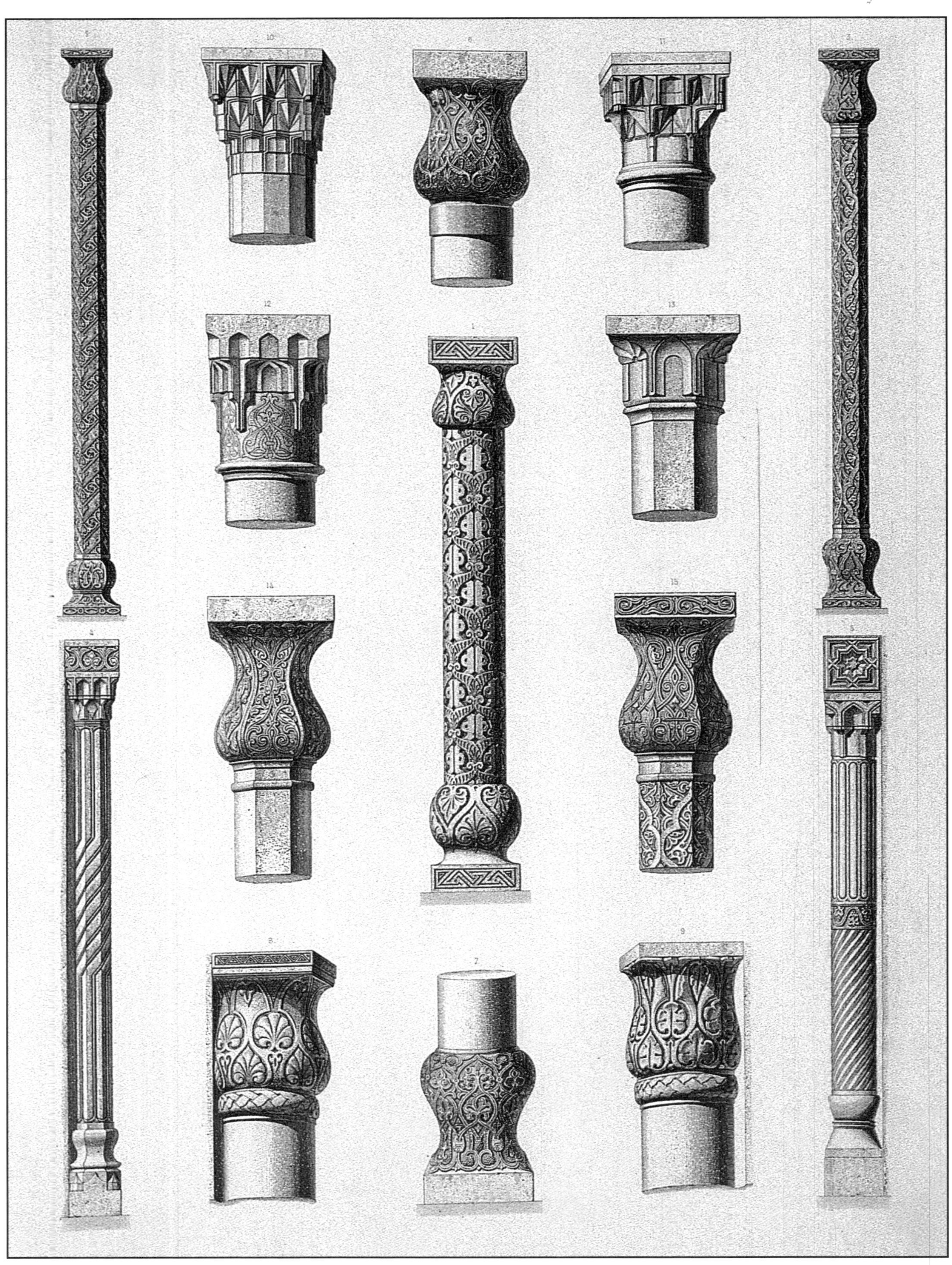

Plates XLIV to XLVII
ARCHITECTURE
Ornamentation and Decoration

We have analysed the forty-three plates of the atlas comprised within the first group, but only concerning architecture *per se* and construction; we would therefore like to remind the reader that a large part of our reflections on decoration and ornamentation in architecture will apply as much to the plates of the first group as to the four plates which constitute the second.

It may perhaps be said that the Arabic abhorrence of nudity led to a desire to perceive the whims of imagination in visible form. Everything about, from buildings to furniture, from weapons to clothing, became so many bare objects to be dressed by fancy.

At first glance, the application of Arabic ornamental practices to buildings presents a particular cachet; but, although obliged to follow the precepts of the Koran and only touch upon that not concerning man himself, they nevertheless covered and surmounted stone and framework with the most marvellous ornamental conceptions; such as is seen in the plate representing part of the al-Azhar Mosque. Certain misconceptions must be abandoned, for although the Mohammedans in their haste borrowed ideas and materials from all around, they were in no way ignorant; on the contrary, there have been amongst them an incredible number of eminent men, renowned for their knowledge, particularly Arabs and Persians.

"The purest decorative science, rightly says our regretted friend, Adalbert de Neaumont, the most exquisite taste, have embroidered, cut out, braided, levelled, and carved these interlacings, flowers and animals, whose infinite yet always geometrical complications set the mind in search of the law which creates such marvellous arabesques."

Prodigious efforts of imagination were required in order to vary the repetitious monotony of the characters of the alphabet; Arabic artists succeeded in rendering it monumental by adding, in the form of interlacing, these whimsical ornaments that were then coloured to add again to the decoration.

In all these Arabic edifices, ornaments are nearly always placed with much taste and discernment, the higher ones being always the largest and the least confused. However, there is a notable difference, as we have already said, between arabesques carved in stone and those carved in plaster.

Let us draw attention, in this respect, to the use of stone railings, a type of gate or openwork that is no longer seen today in Islamic buildings. These were in stone only, cut and carved in different patterns. Generally nine centimetres thick, they show a variety in the unity of the decoration most pleasing to the eye, so much the whole appears symmetrical at first glance.

Mosque of Ahmad ibn Tulun (Pl. XLIV).—We have given the details of the ornamentation seen in Plate XLIV in order to indicate precisely the known point of departure for this type of work. They demonstrate that in the 9th century (3rd century of the Hegira), Arabic religious buildings were already the object of minutious ornamentation research; we regret not having numbered them so as to make them better-known. Sculpted in plaster without the use of conventional models, they are scattered throughout the vast Ahmad ibn Tulun Mosque. These are indeed specimens of Arabic Art in a completely original form. Nothing in the 9th century resembled this ornamentation; the feeling is even that of a *sui generis* work, resembled by few others from this period on.

These ornaments, very simple, moreover, principally decorated intrados, jambs and windows in varied ways. Interior decoration, at this period, differed completely from exterior decoration. From without, mosques presented only smooth walls, doors were bare of any ornamentation and stalactites were not yet visible.

Tekieh Sheikh Hussein Sadaka (Pl. XLV).—Plate XLV shows the principal part of the exterior decoration of the dome, frieze, piers and windows of Tekieh Sheikh Hussein Sadaka.

The *chemsieh* or windows are all different and present some interest. The general rule, especially at this period, required that those of the dome be in the form of rectilinear interlacings, and those on the other side, in the form of more or less symmetrical arabesques. Here then, all is varied: piers, windows and frieze, yet all is in perfect harmony. The dome must have, we believe, been covered in arabesques, to judge by the several fragments which have resisted the ravages of time and man.

The escutcheons used as fillers break the monotony here and there upon the smooth walls.

Mosque of Qaysun (Pl. XLVI).—The windows of the Qaysun Mosque are in very poor condition, as is the entire edifice; situated at a great height, they are of highly varied decoration. However, the decoration repeats itself in a sufficiently large number of motifs, allowing us to complete each of the damaged parts through comparison with latticework of the same type from another grille. All the windows have a cissoidal arch with plaster columnettes presenting identical bases and capitals. These windows are thought to be the work of a foreign architect. The flowerbeds decorating the perimeter of the rectangular plaster surrounds bring to mind the charming point-lace in the tomb of al-Gaouly and a few other edifices from the same period.

Bait al-Amir. Crowning of the Bath Door (Pl. XLVII).—This masterpiece of ornamentation, which stands out from all we have seen, adorned the top of the the bath door in the residence of an amir, situated across from the door of Shirawi, street Bein al-Qasrein. This pampiniform panel, despite its great age, still shows vestiges of two different illuminations or colourings which are very difficult to date. In one, probably the more ancient of the two, the vine leaves which come out from a central vase, adorned with arabesques, seem to have been gilded as in the splendid mihrab erected by Caliph Walid in the ancient Mosque of Damascus. The narrowest border is yellow while the largest and most protuberant one runs about this splendid panel and forms a tore which the artist forgot to shadow and colour in red to set it off from the whole.

In another place, the colouring is perhaps more recent; the leaves are pale green, the vine branches dark green and the grapes blue, the whole less harmonious than the other, for that which is modern is gaudy. Escutcheons decorate the walls.

MOSQUE OF AHMAD IBN TULUN

Ornamental Details (9th century)

Plate XLIV

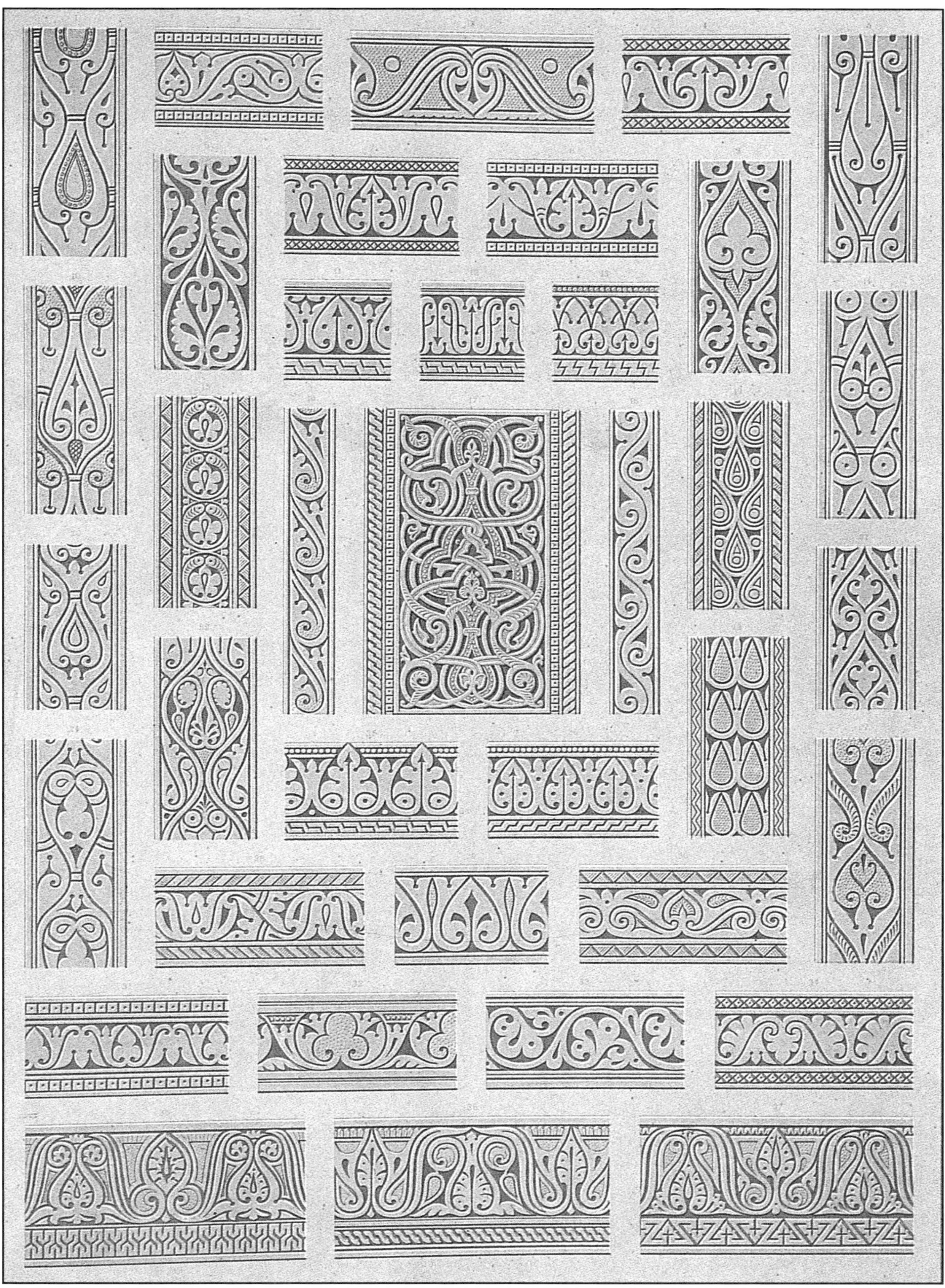

Plate XLV

TEKIEH SHEIKH HUSSEIN SADAKA

Fragments of Decoration of the Dome (14th century)

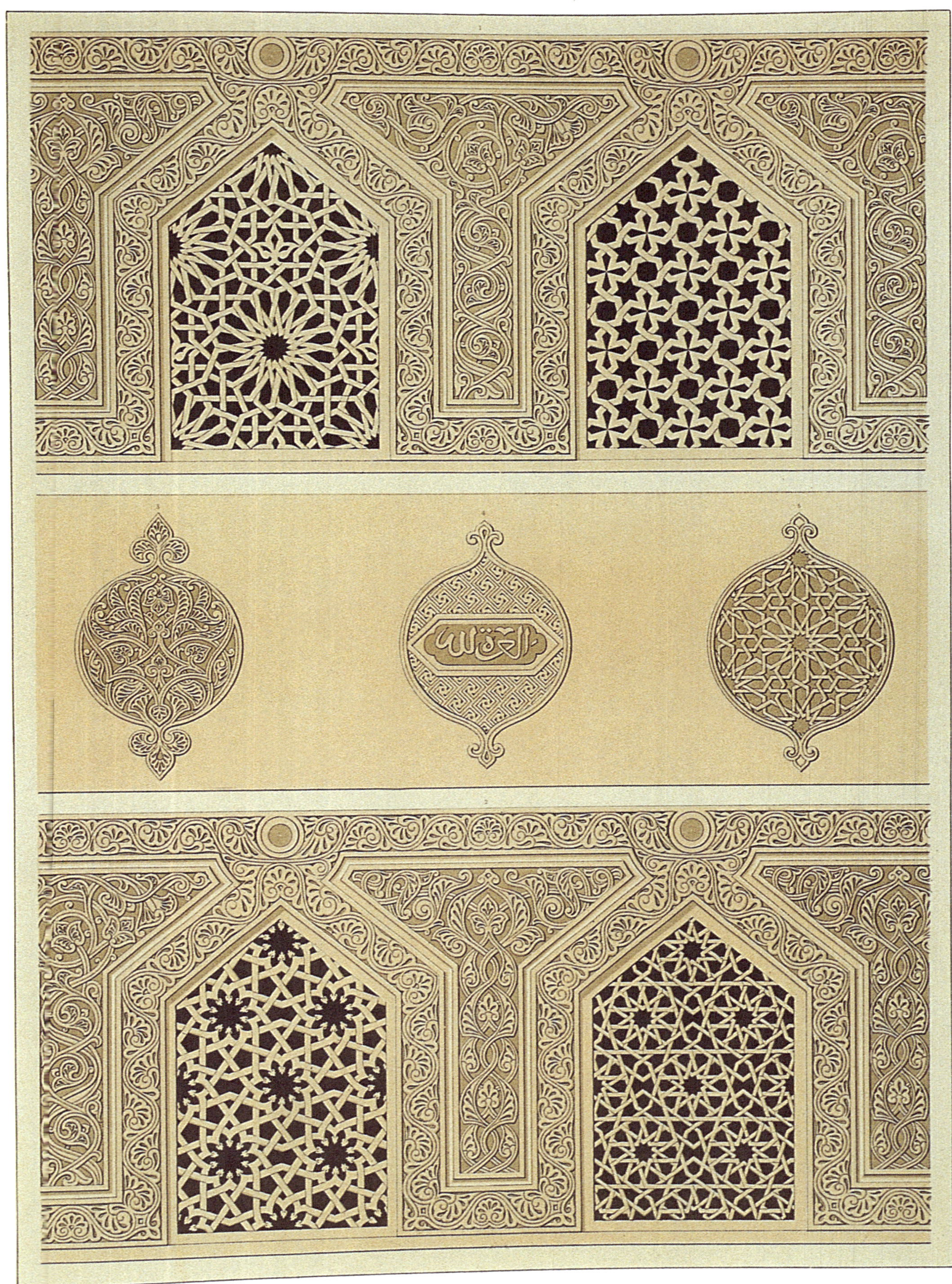

MOSQUE OF QAYSUN

Decoration on Interior Windows (14th century)

Plate XLVI

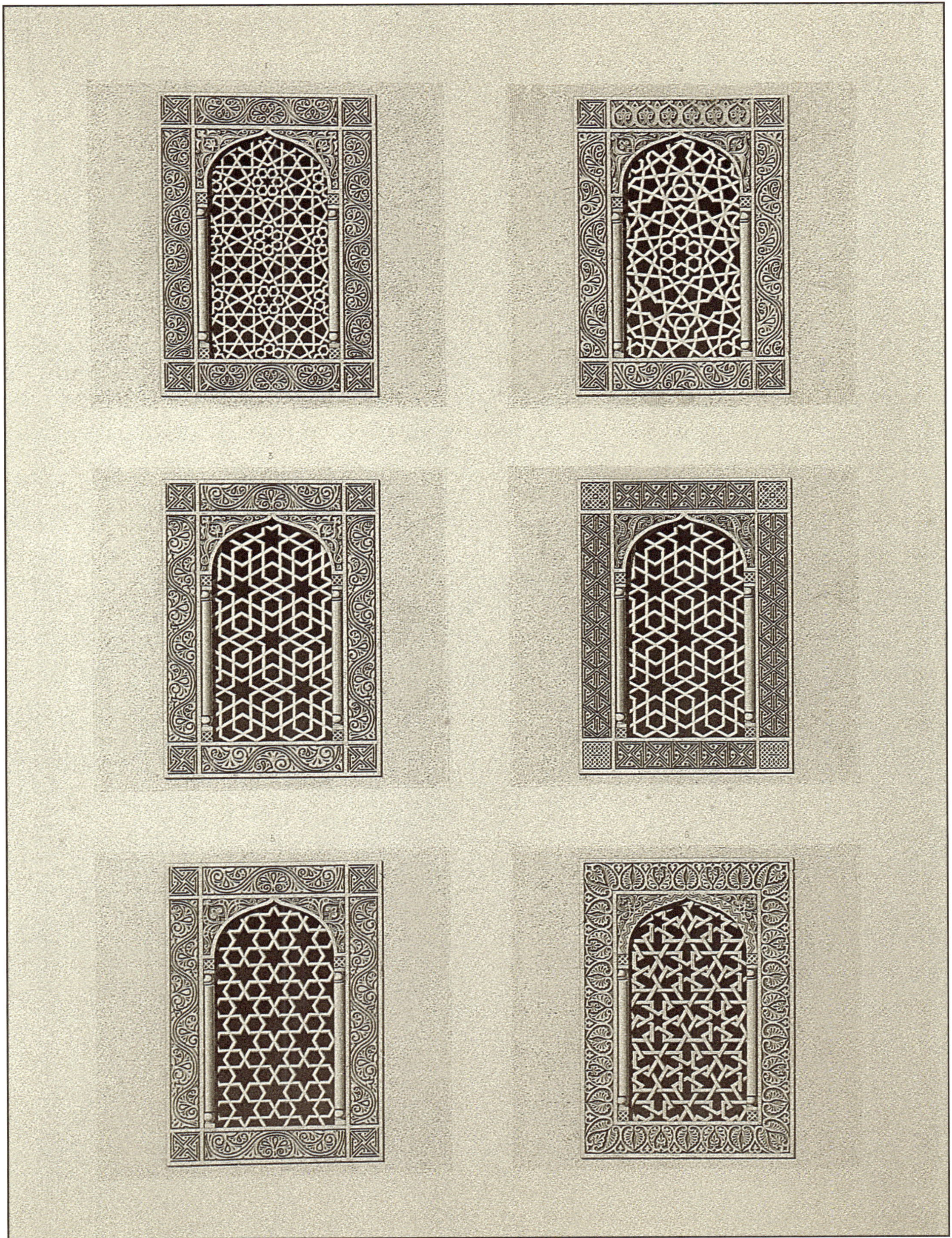

Plate XLVII

BEIT AL-AMIR

Crowning on the Bath Door (17th century)

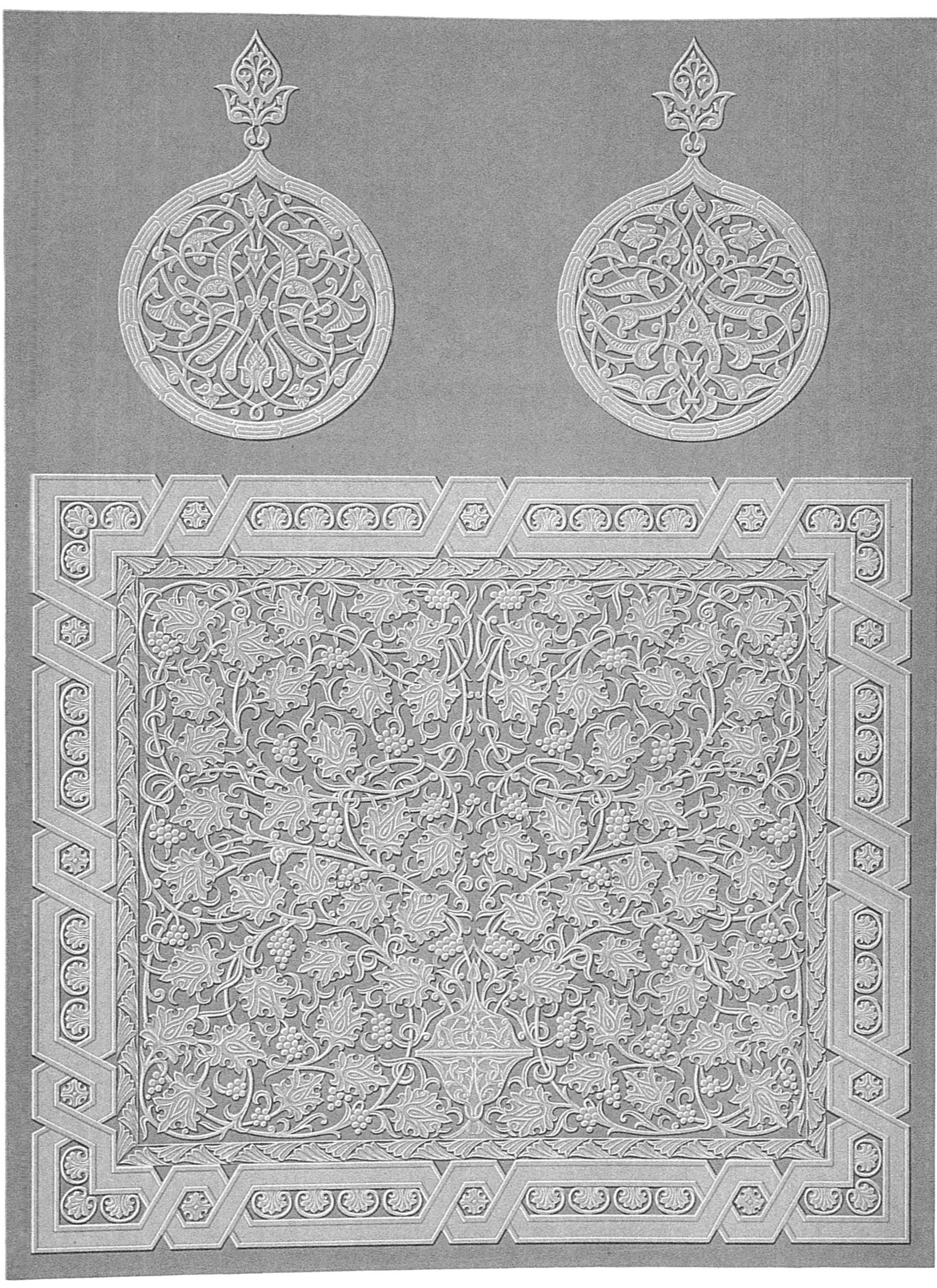

Plates XLVIII to LXVII
COVERINGS AND TILINGS

We feel it superfluous to preface the most beautiful plates in this group with detailed descriptions, only to repeat the work covered in the special chapter on this subject, concerning mosaics and inlays.

Tomb of Sultan Qansu al-Ghuri. Marble Panelling (Pl. LIII, LIV and LV).—This handsome panelling throughout the sepulchral room is formed of a series of marble panels in the manner common to most mosques of this period. A band of white marble approximately 0.08 metres wide runs all around the room and borders a long panel of black marble, 1.7 metres to 2 metres in height, covered in gilded intaglio engraving. Most of these arabesques are formed of interlaced letters and express short sentences taken from the Koran or the *hadith* of the Prophet. The black panel alternates with other assorted marbles.

The panelling is crowned in the enclosure of the tomb by an epigraphic frieze in Neskhi characters, recounting a chapter of the *Book*; in two recesses, it is surmounted by a small frieze of golden merlons, engraved in the same way as the ornaments, as may be seen in the first plate.

Several panels show most elegantly constructed calligraphic arabesques, and often include inscriptions in both ancient and more modern scripts within the same frame, thus lending even more variety to the composition. The ornamentation is of a style quite unlike anything seen elsewhere, making a most unusual piece of this covering.

During repair work on the dome in 1859, this handsome panelling was brutally taken down from the wall, broken in many places and then resealed with neither symmetry nor order.

There are only ten different panels; alternately placed at varying intervals with an occasional simple variation in inscription, the loss of the missing panels is perhaps less regretted.

Floor mosaics (Pl. LVI).—The various specimens composing this plate are arranged to show the floor mosaics of the Dorqa'ah and other oblong rooms. This typical arrangement was selected to group symmetrically diverse items collected here and there, and thereby give an idea of decorations much more varied than is usually seen. In the Mosque of al-Bordayni, there is a plat band which has several similar parts; this part is more complete, however, and comes from a house which gives it particular importance. The ligature linking the nine parts of the quadrilateral to make a whole is charming. It is found on the covering of a tomb, laid out in the same way.

Stucco Inlays (Pl. LVII and LIII).—In these various specimens, the grounds or designs carved in the marble are, whether they be wholly or partially full or inlaid, formed by stucco or coloured cement.

The origins of this type of mosaic made of coloured inlays lie in the Orient; in Italy, it is commonly known as "scagliuola".

This type of decoration, so widely used in Egypt yet barely known in France, deserves to gain recognition. The varied specimens found in Arabic Art will perhaps serve to increase appreciation for these fine arabesques, so elegantly drawn on the marble that they seem part of it.

When ornaments are large and swollen, instead of stucco, the Arabs use pieces of marble or artificial stone. The plat band taken from the Diwan of Adami, like many others, is composed of a strip from a large panel; this method employed by Arabic artists gives a disjointed and incomplete look to the decoration which is often shocking.

There is a plat bande formed from the same interlacing in the mihrab of the Mosque of Ibrahim Agha but the colours of the marbles are less evenly arranged, creating confusion in the mosaic.

Ornaments engraved in marble and filled with different-coloured stucco are quite common in the interior of edifices from the 16th century on. They are the result of an inlay process similar to that used in Paris today, where all sorts of designs are executed in marble panels with pieces of different coloured crumbled marble. Here, stucco, instead of crumbs of marble, fills the engraved patterns.

The stucco used by the Arabs is a sort of cement made of marble dust and lime, capable of a high polish. It hardens litle by little, becoming stronger than plaster and holding fast the colours given to it.

Ornaments made with this process are easily done anywhere; morover, they have the advantage of being far more economical than the same arabesques inlaid in marble or as mosaics.

Mosque of al-Bordayni. Various Mosaics. (Pl. LIX to LXV).—The Mosque of al-Bordayni, once entirely decorated in mosaics, has been dilapidated by the local inhabitants; among others, Abd-Allah-Bey, nephew of a Minister of War, brutally stripped the Mosque of its most beautiful mosaics to decorate his palace. We have not returned to the Mosque since the appearance of these vandals, and so cannot say whether the three specimens represented here are still in place at this time.

The first is of no particular interest, but the second offers one of the finest examples of a calligraphic mosaic. The interlacing forming the main part of this precious scene reveals, in rectilinear Kufic script, the names of the Prophet and the prinicipal caliphs, his successors.

The third example, also found in the mihrab of the Mosque of Ibrahim Agha, is a mosaic in mother of pearl whose sheen competes with the glitter of stained glass pastes.

In order to give a more exact idea of the handsome mihrab in the Mosque of al-Bordayni, decorated like the rest of the edifice, we have had to present its geometrical development (Pl. LXII) so as to display the regular lines of this mosaic in marble, mother of pearl and stained glass pastes. The interlaces are laid out in mother-of-pearl tongues whose opaline hues sparkle harmoniously over the main compartment.

Mosque of Qa'uam al-Din (Pl. LXIII to LXVI).—The tomb enclosed within this mosque of uncertain age presents unusual and rarely encountered forms. Like a souvenir of the Crusades, it could well have been the vision of some architect with delusions of Jerusalem.

Built in black and white marble, the sculpted ornaments on and about the tombstone alternately display well-matched Arabic and Persian motifs. The arabesques are not very pure and would seem to indicate the end of the second period; but all things considered, the disposition of the tombstone is delightful.

The frieze running around the tomb portrays the 256th verse of the second *sura* of the Koran, an admirable profession of faith: "God is the one God; there is no other God but God, the Living One, the Eternal one, etc."

The stone beneath which lies the deceased bears the following inscription in front of the sepulchral slab: "The just will live among fountains and gardens, in the abode of truth, near the all-mighty king." (Koran, *sura* 54: the Moon).

The entrance of a tomb near Mosque of Sisarieh (Pl. LXVII) is adorned in marble sculpted with highly decorative arabesques.

WALL MOSAICS
(12th and 14th centuries)

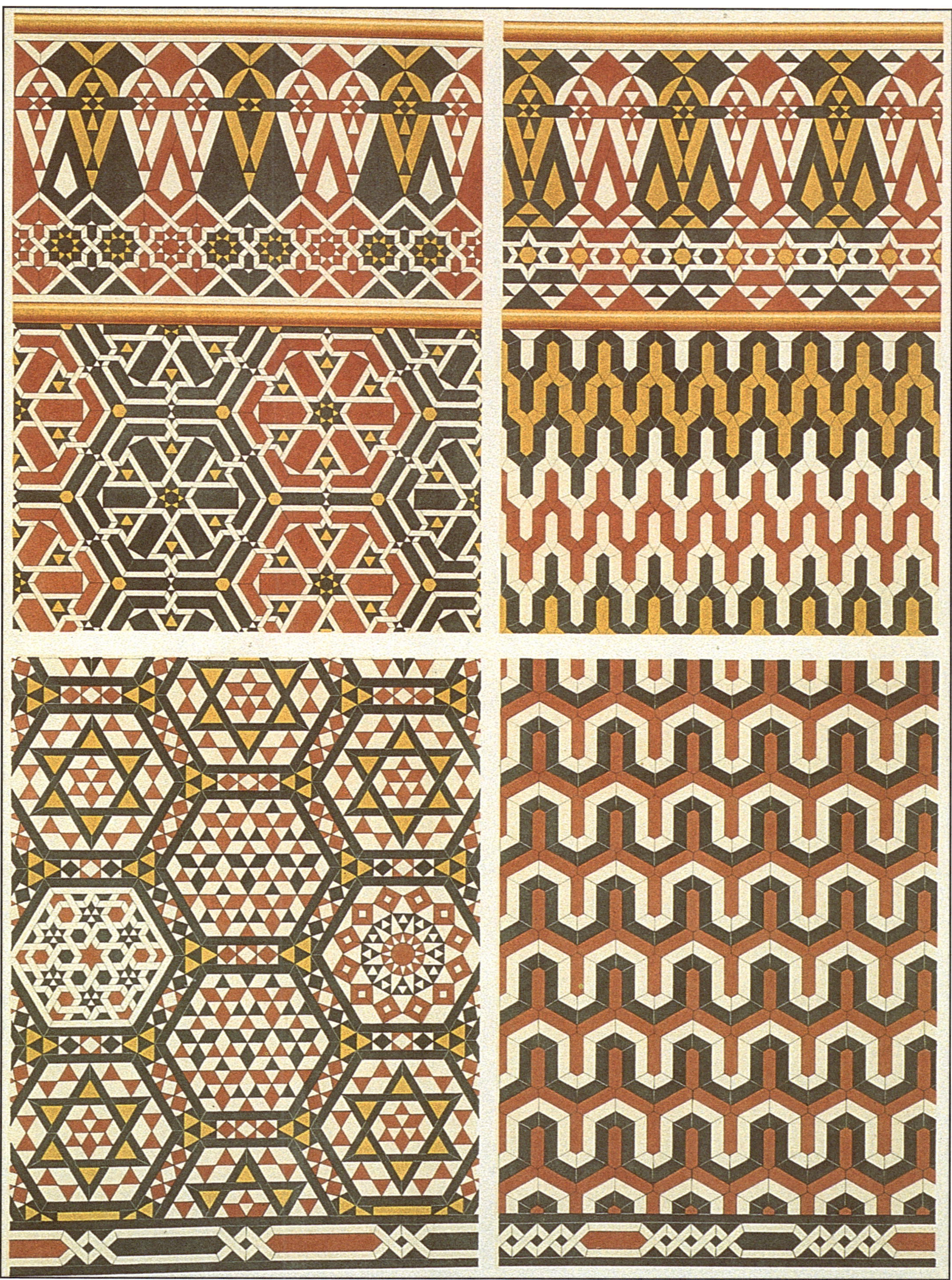

MAUSOLEUM OF SULTAN BARQUQ

Details of the Minbar (14th century)

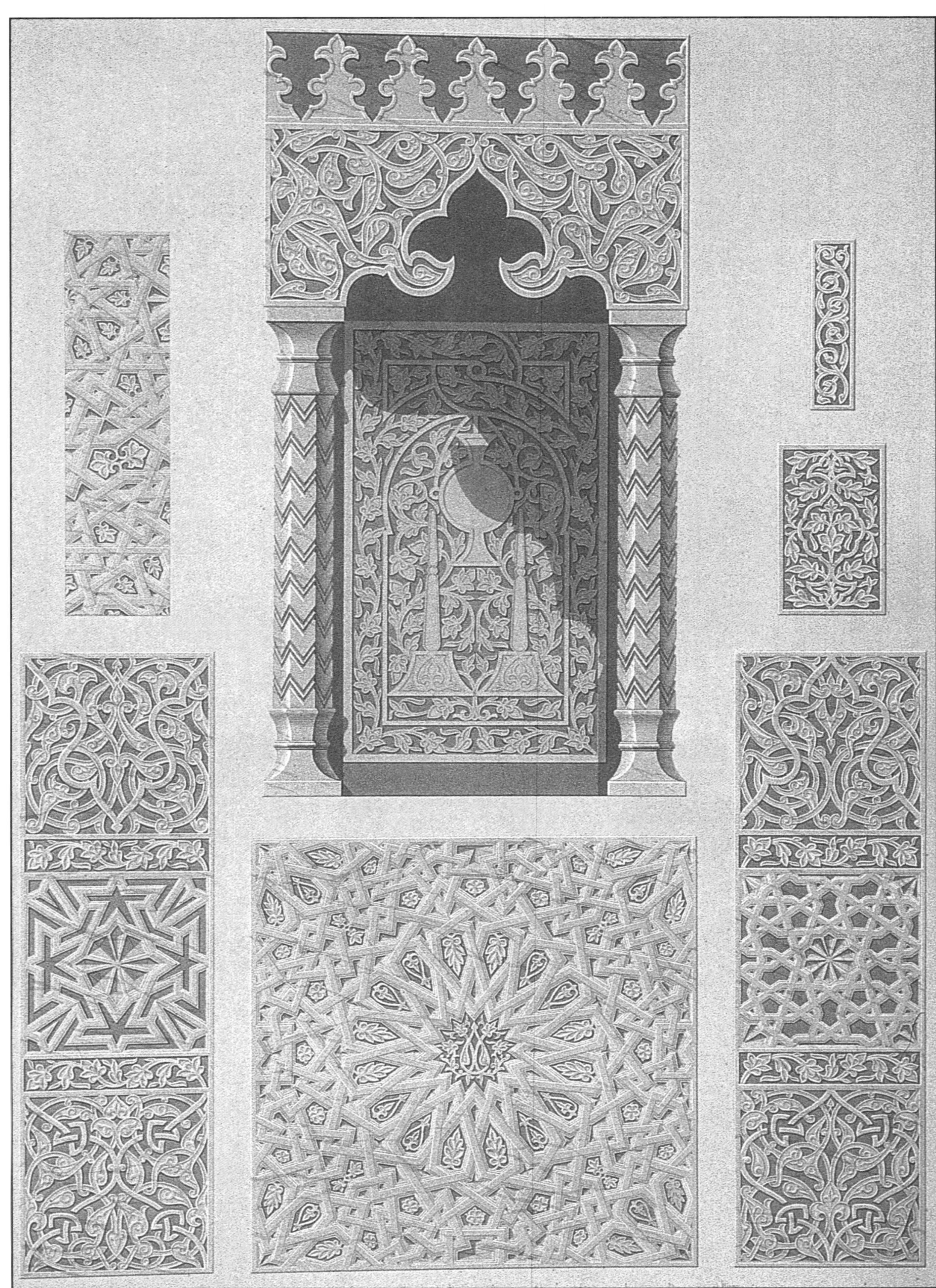

PANELS ON THE TOMB OF BARSABAY

Details of the Mosaics (15th century)

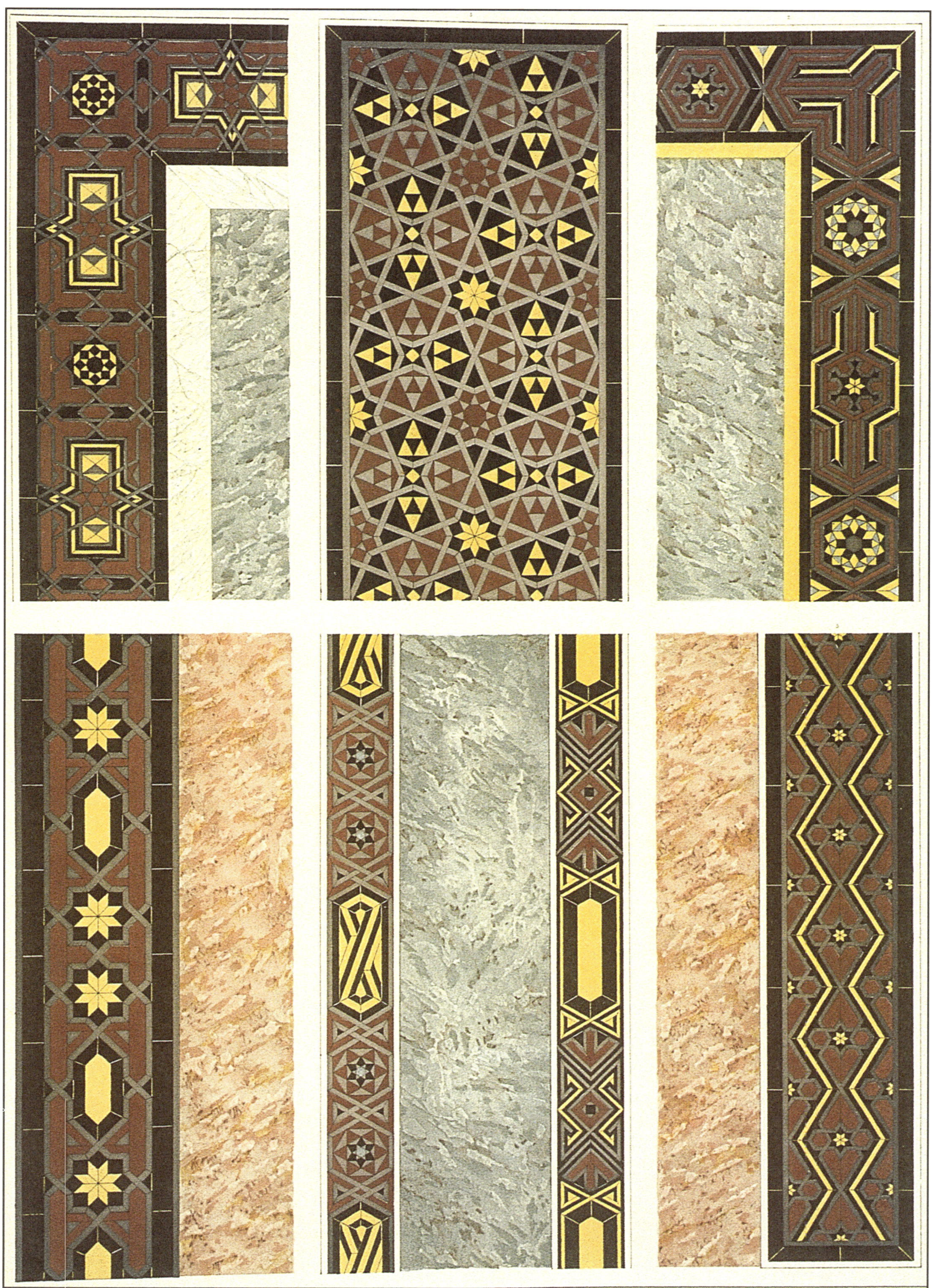

Plate LI

WALL MOSAICS
(15th and 16th centuries)

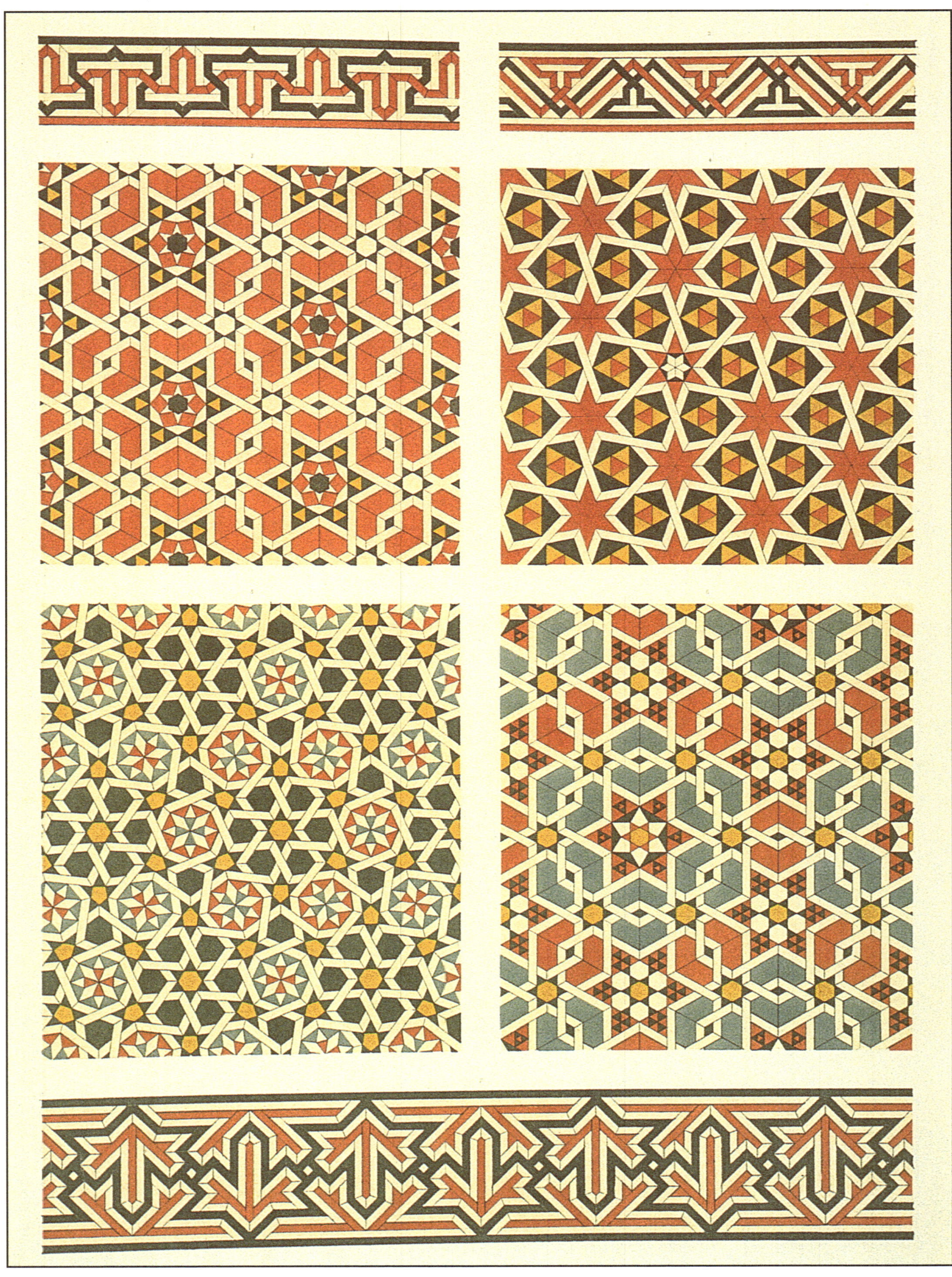

MOSAICS

Fragments from Wall and Floor Decorations (15th to 18th centuries)

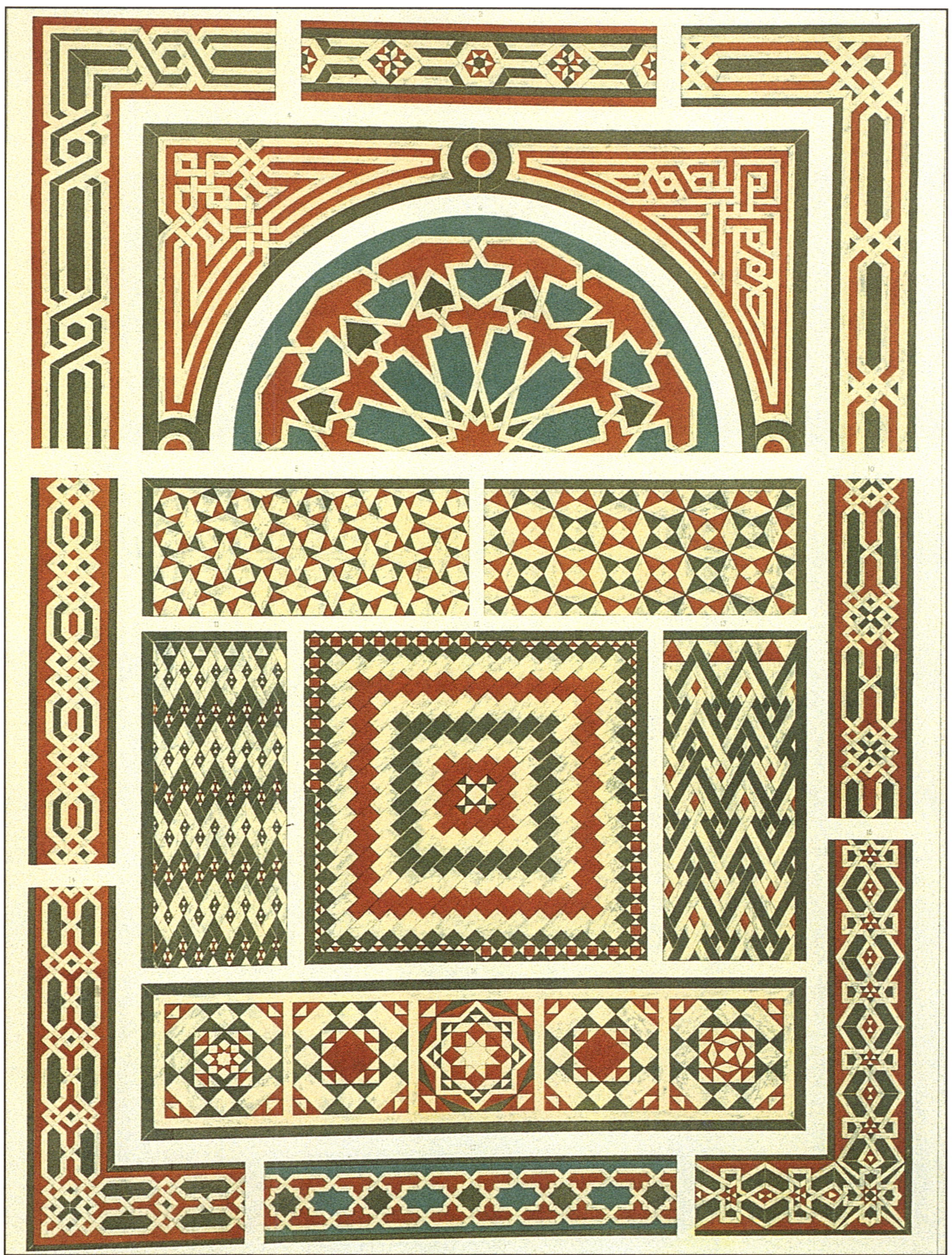

Plate LIII

TOMB OF SULTAN QANSU AL-GHURI

Marble Panel (16th century)

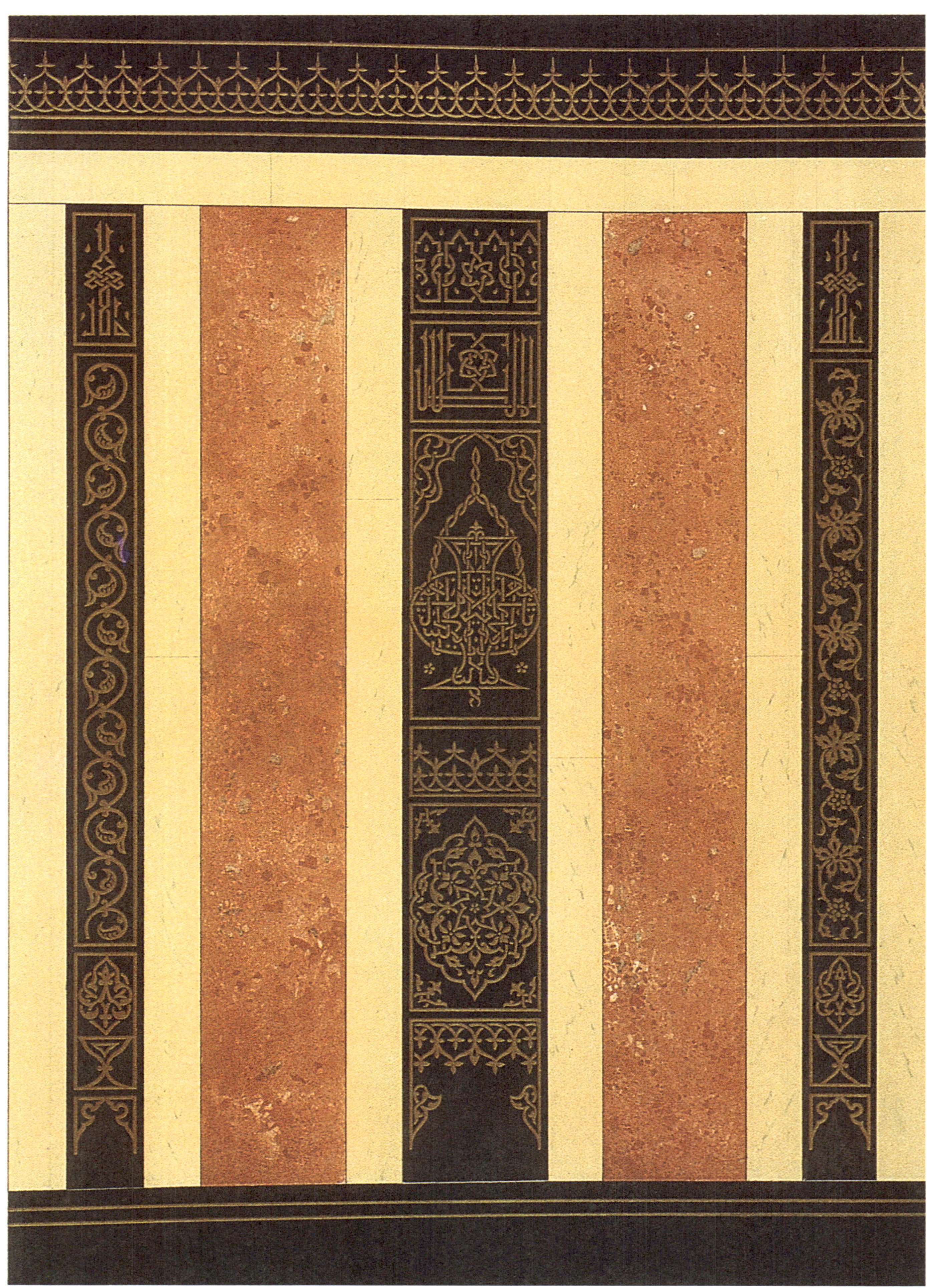

TOMB OF SULTAN QANSU AL-GHURI

Details of the Panels (16th century)

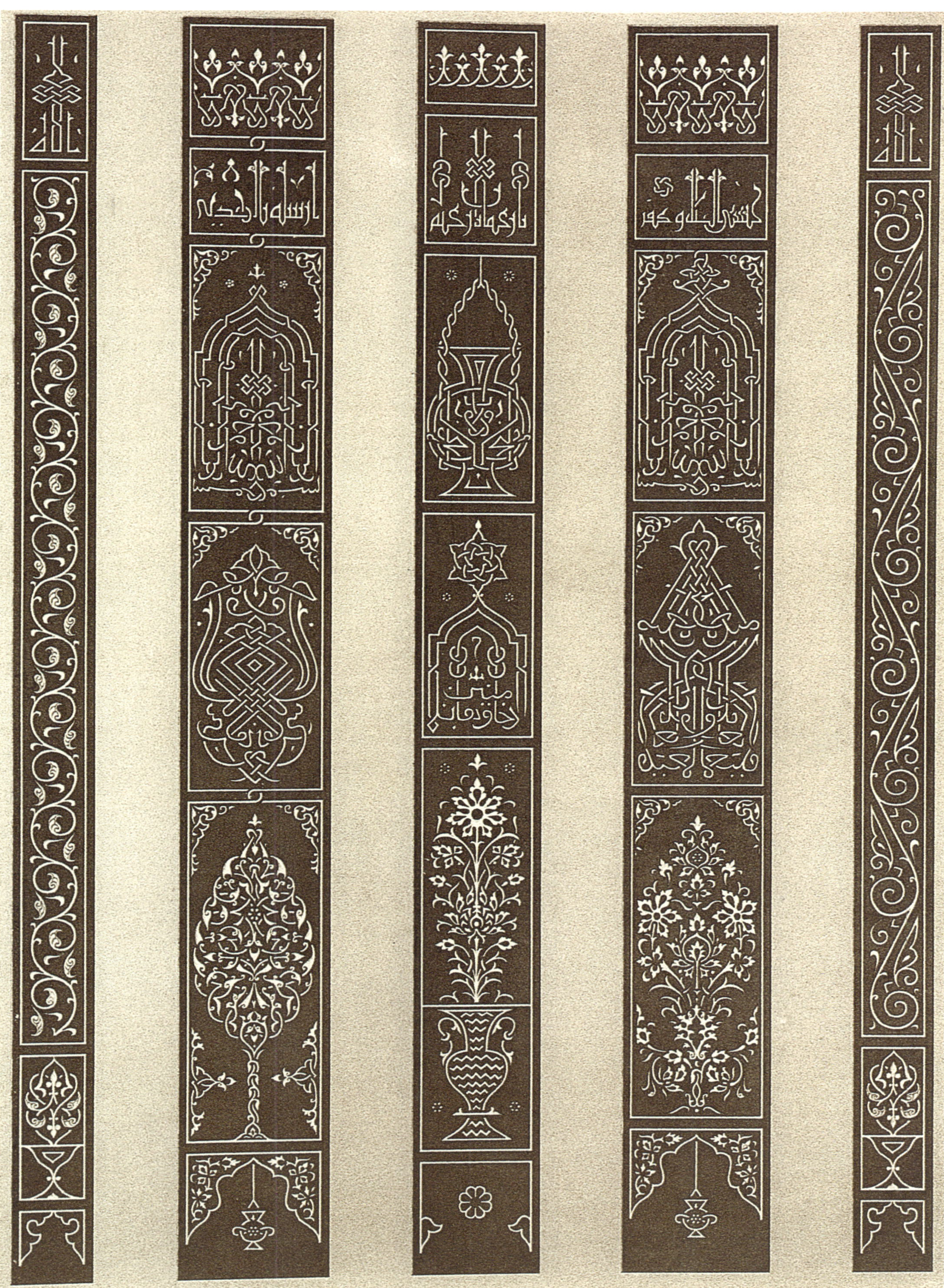

TOMB OF SULTAN QANSU AL-GHURI

Details of the Panels (16th century)

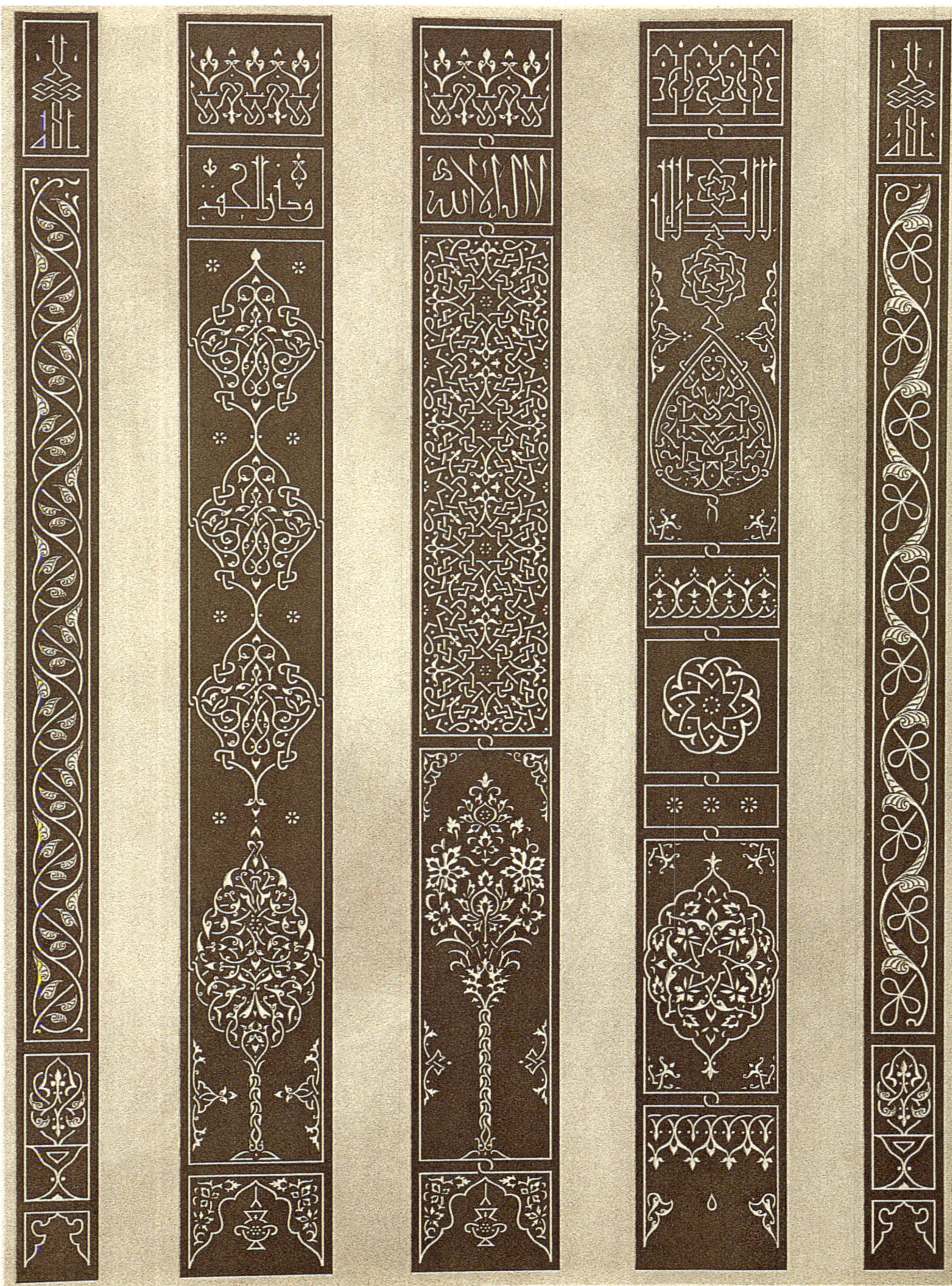

MOSAIC FLOOR

Fragments Laid Out on the Plan of the Dorqa'ah (16th to 18th centuries)

Plate LVI

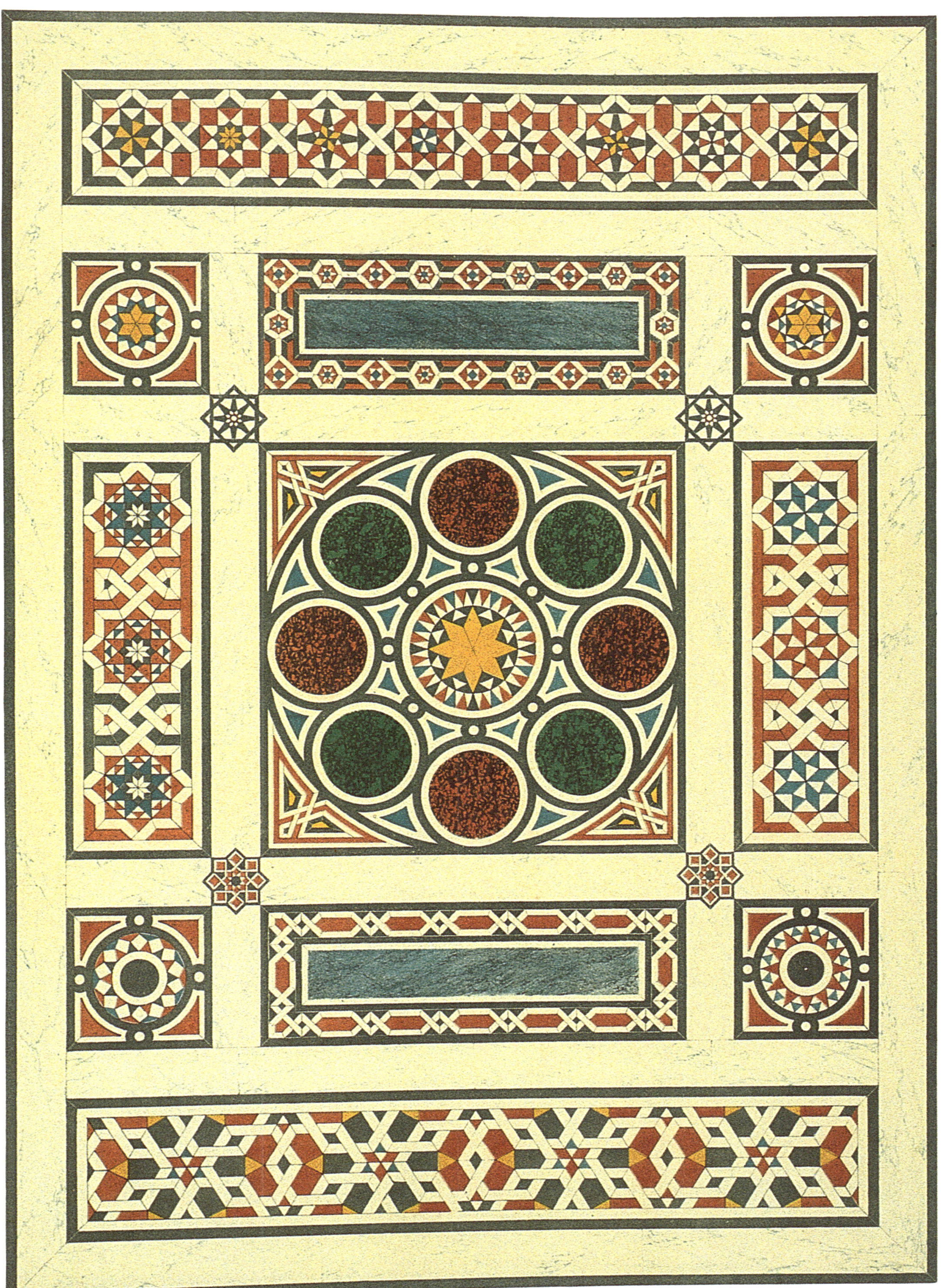

Plate LVII

STUCCO INLAID ON WHITE MARBLE
(16th to 18th centuries)

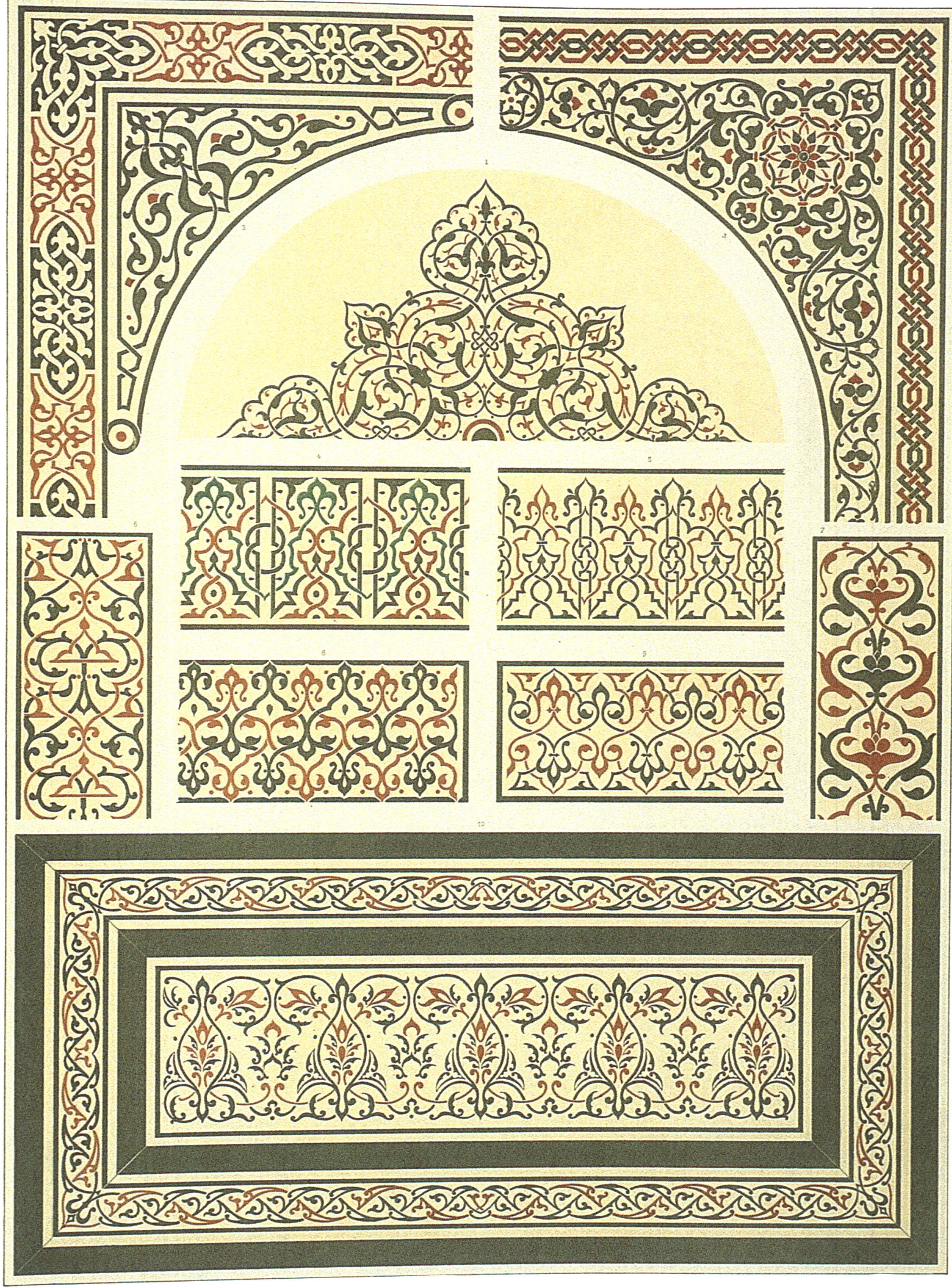

STUCCO INLAID ON STONE
(16th to 18th centuries)

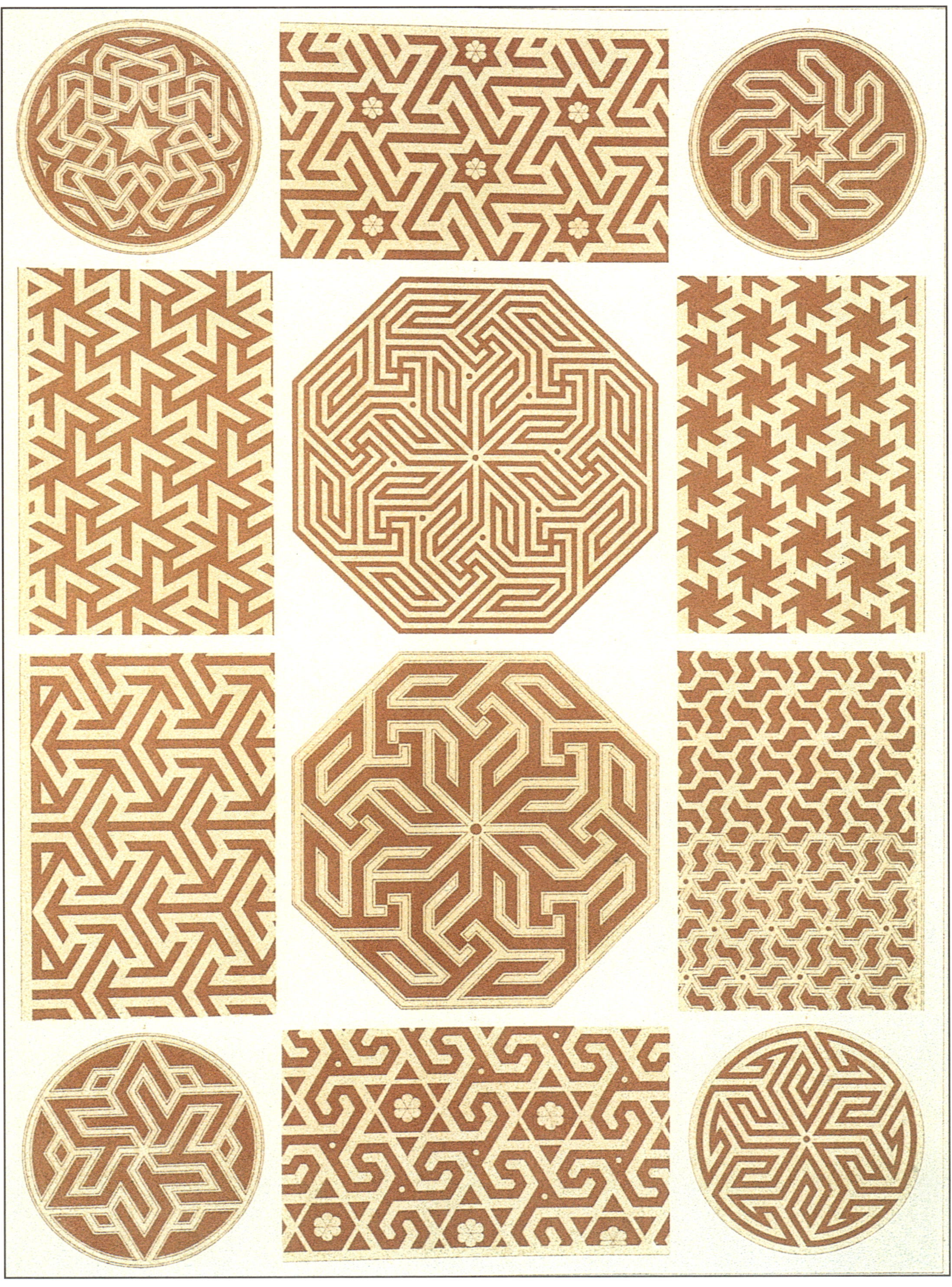

Plate LIX

MOSQUE OF AL-BORDAYNI
Interior of the Main Hall (17th century)

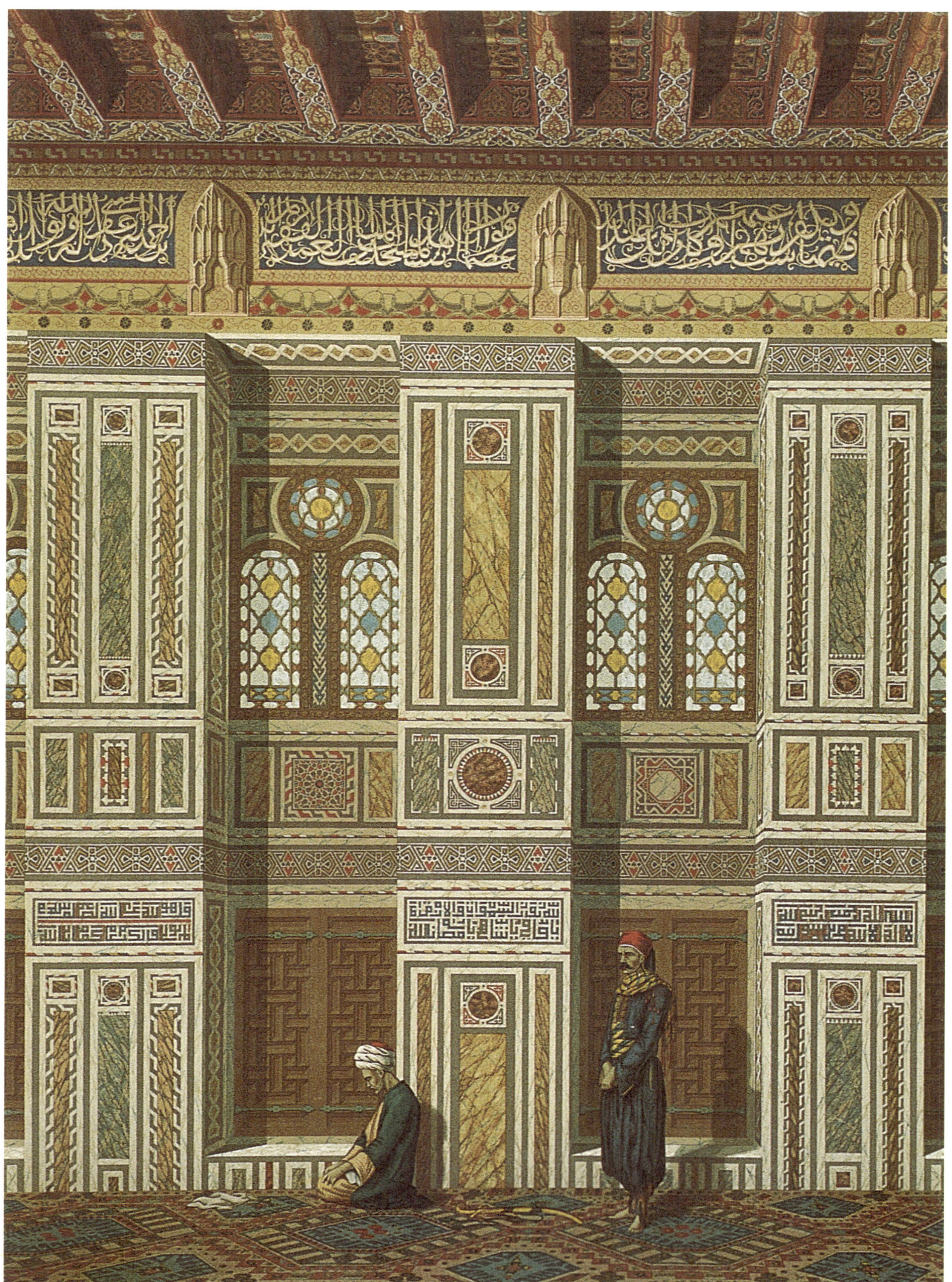

MOSQUE OF AL-BORDAYNI
Details of Mural Mosaics (17th century)

Plate LX

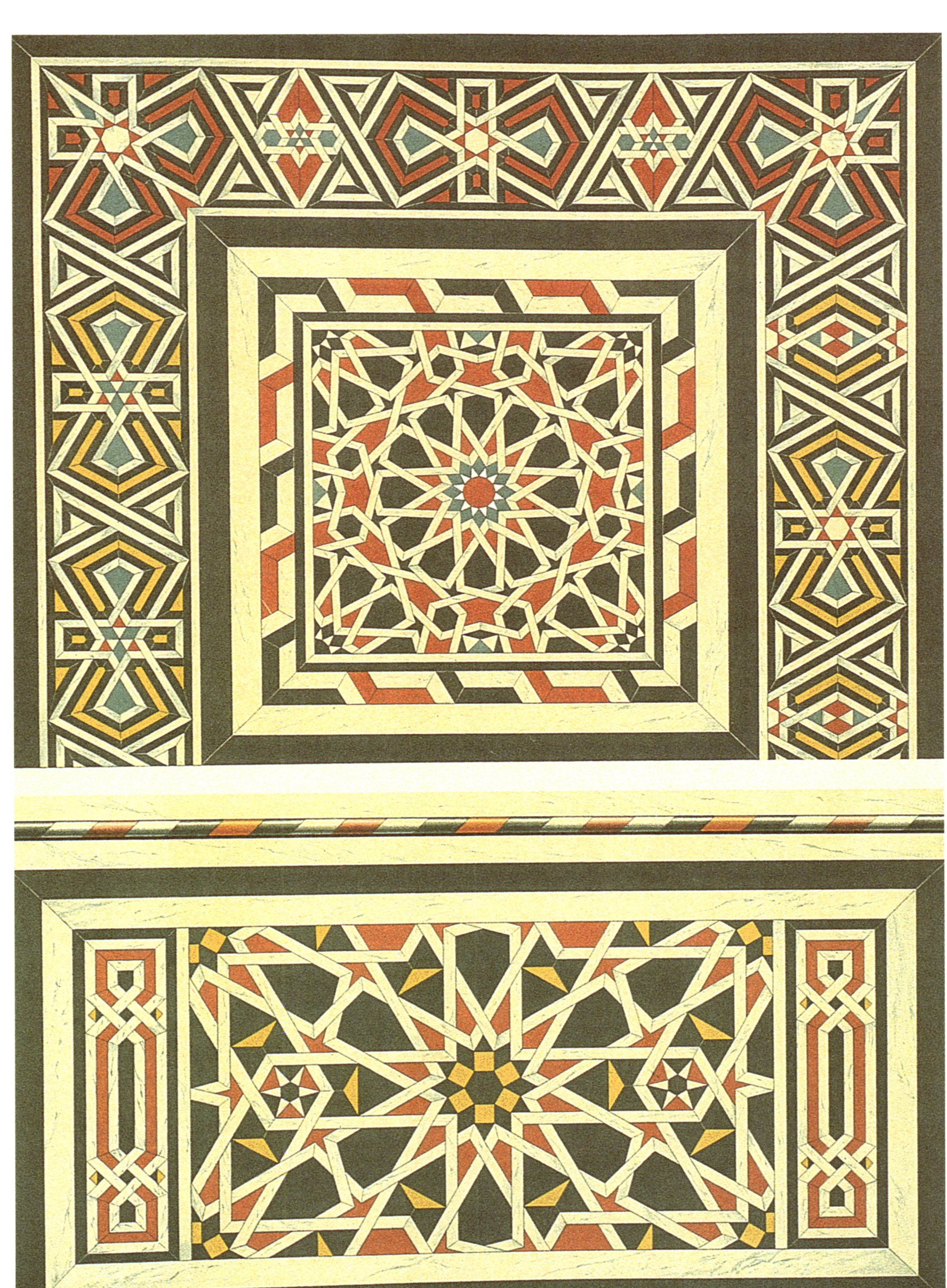

MOSQUE OF AL-BORDAYNI

Details of Mural Mosaics (17th century)

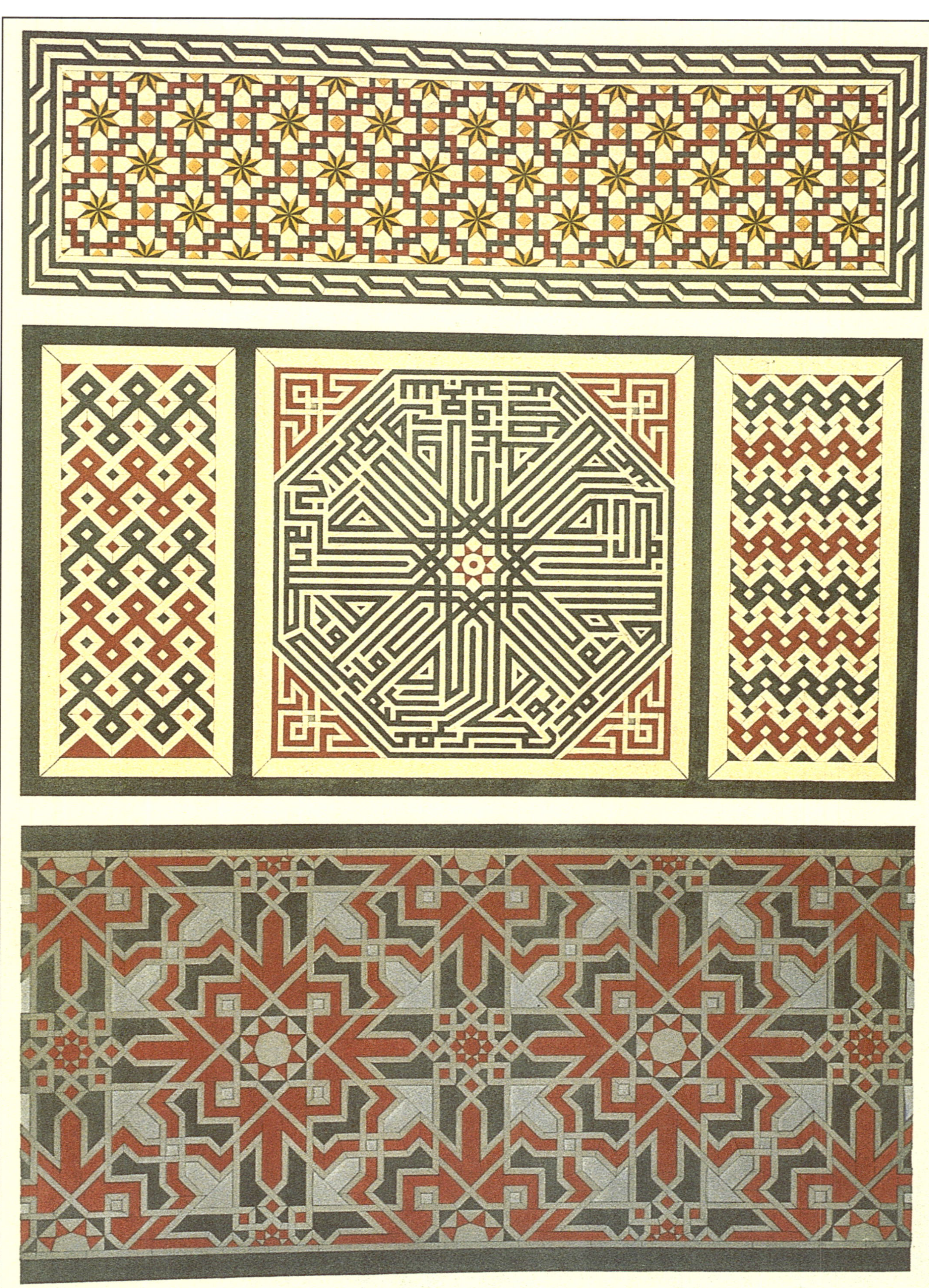

MOSQUE OF AL-BORDAYNI

Development of the Mosaic on the Mihrab (17th century)

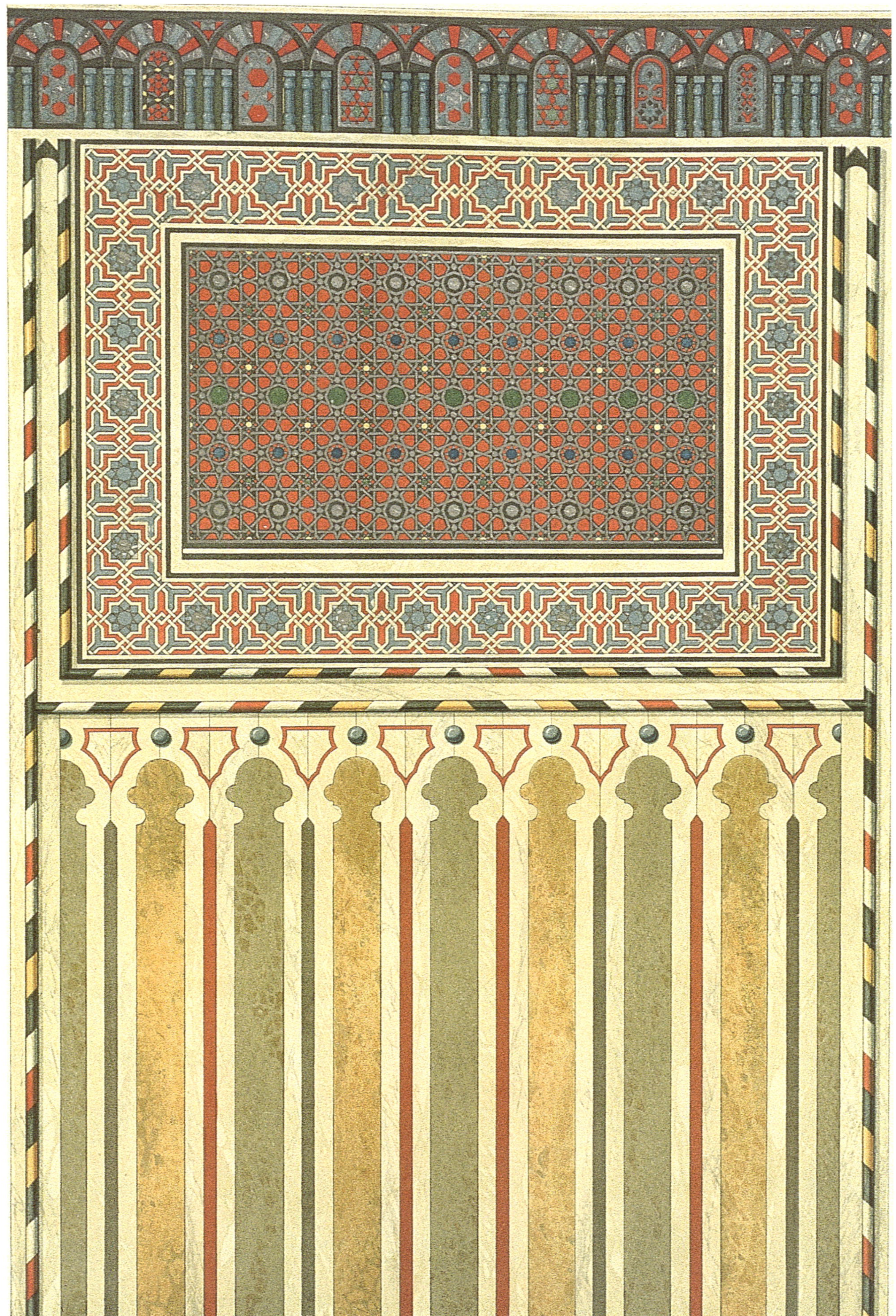

Plate LXIII

MOSQUE OF QA'UAM AL-DIN

Details of the Tomb (18th century)

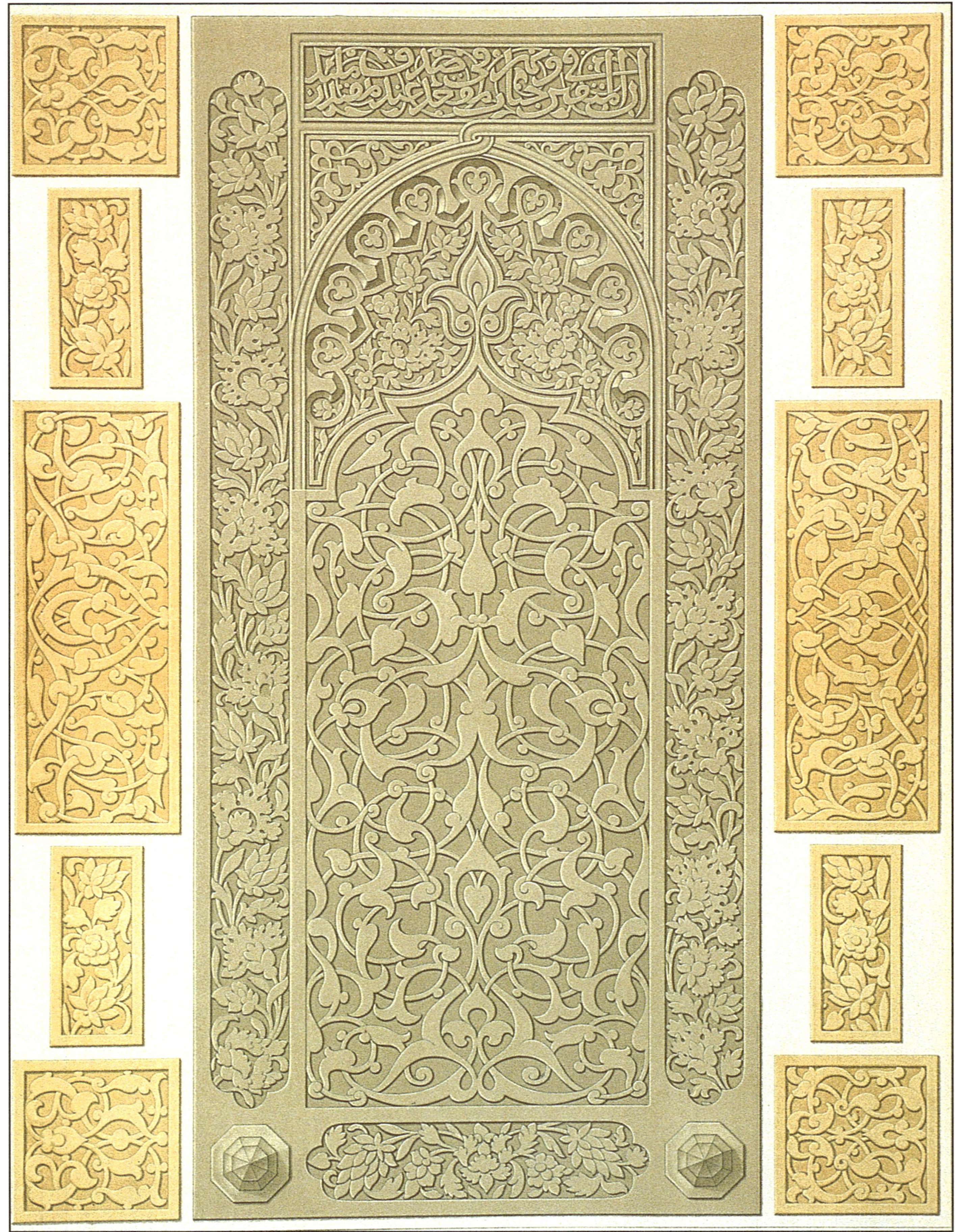

MOSQUE OF QA'UAM AL-DIN

White Marble Floor (18th century)

Plate LXIV

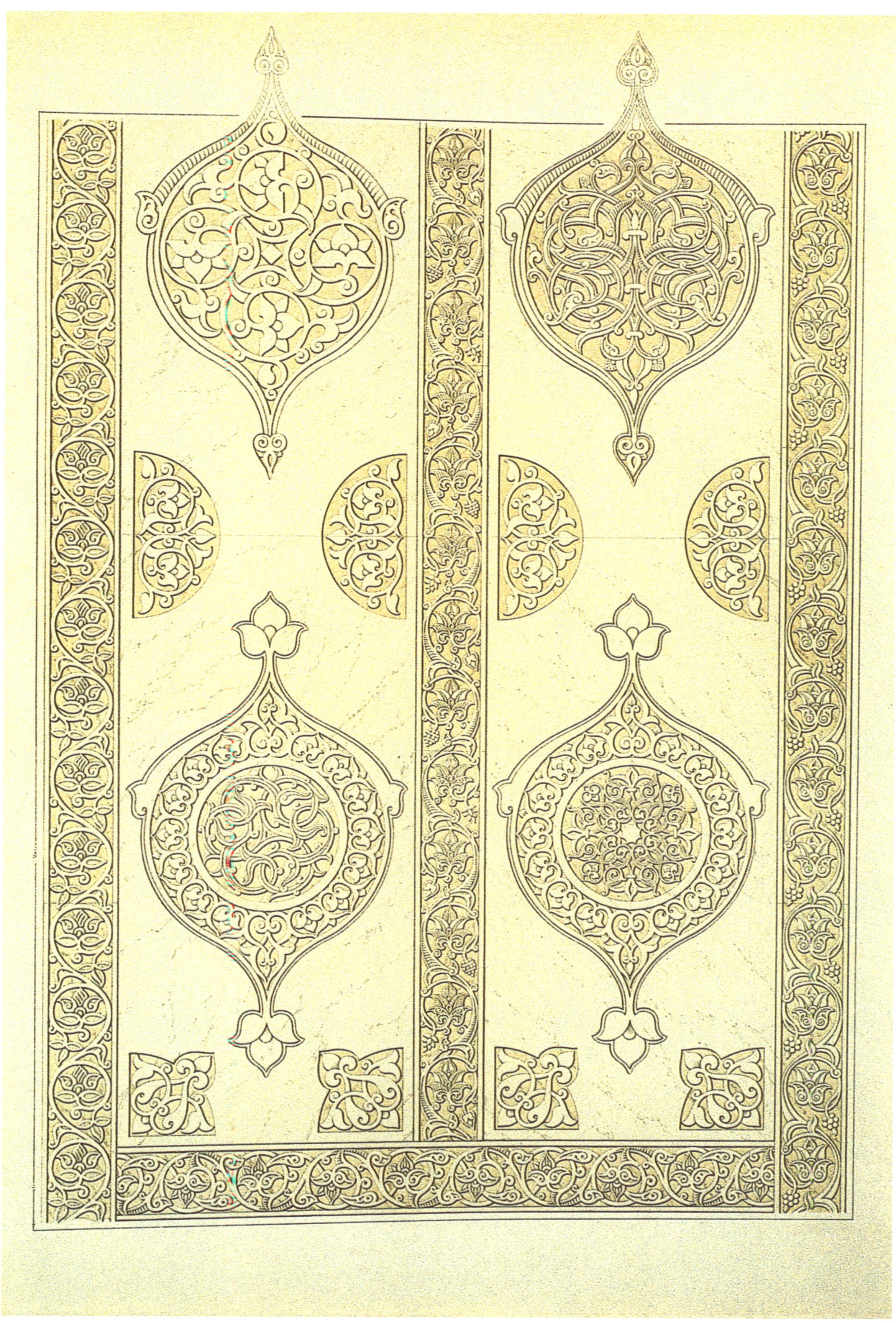

MOSQUE OF QA'UAM AL-DIN

Friezes and Rosette in Marble (18th century)

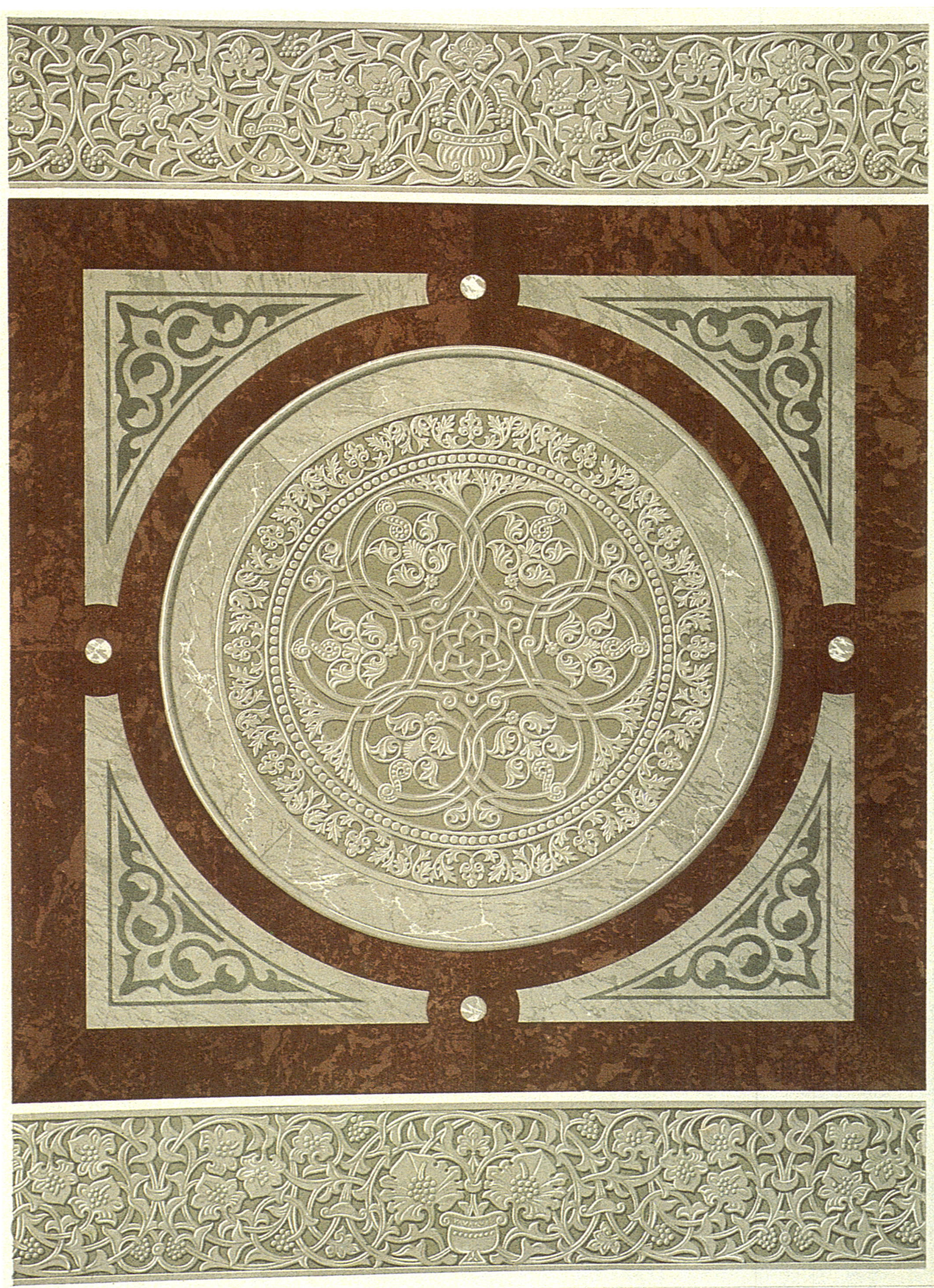

MOSQUE OF QA'UAM AL-DIN

Marble Panel (18th century)

Plate LXVI

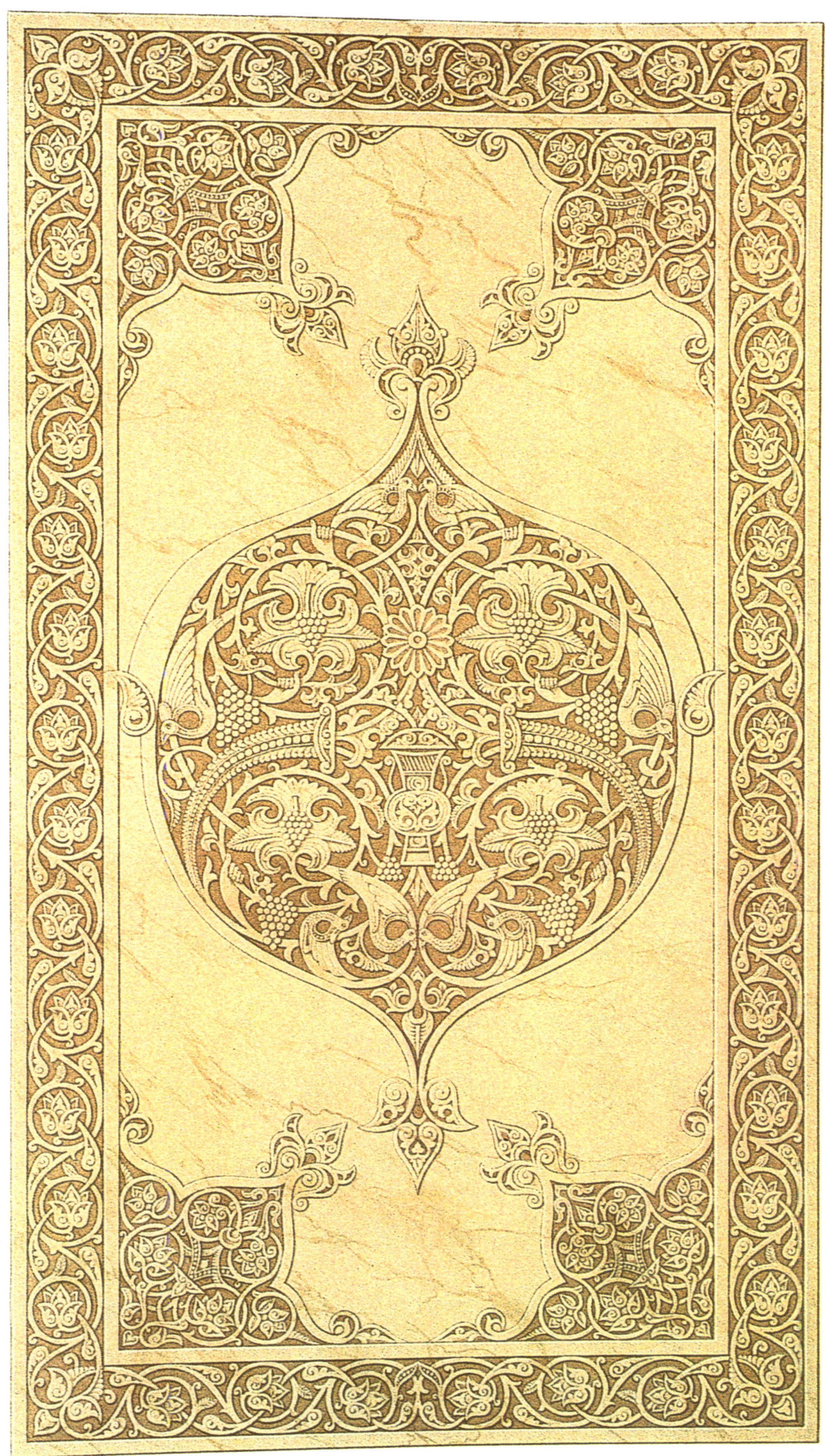

Plate LXVII

ENTRANCE TO A TOMB NEAR MOSQUE OF SISARIEH

(18th century)

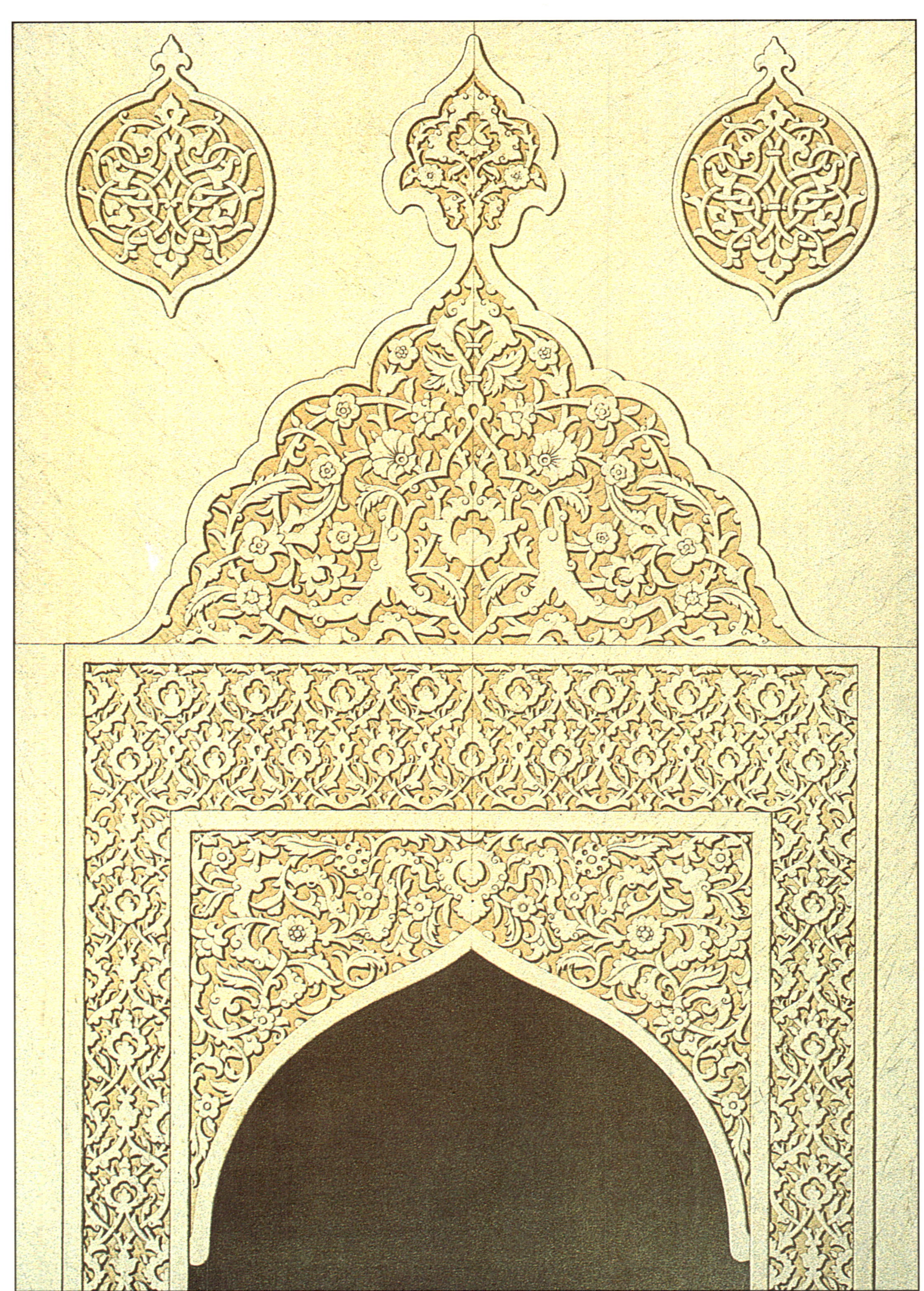

Plates LXVIII to LXXV
CEILINGS

Most interlacings seen on ceilings are composed of intersecting or continuous regular polygons. Regular dodecagons are the most frequently used since they provide the richest combinations and the widest variety. We leave it to the reader to appreciate the drawings in Plate LXXIV, representing dodecagonal, decagonal, and even octagonal stars (Pl. LXXV). Finally, other ceilings of various shapes have been given for comparison. We have tried to give special emphasis, in Plate LXXIII, to a splendid specimen of a Moresque ceiling, and then to the following detailed description of the four plates of the al-Bordayni Mosque.

Mosque of al-Bordayni. Arabesques (Pl. LXVIII to LXXI).—The small ceilings of the al-Bordayni Mosque decorate the soffits of doors and windows. We have lined them in such a way as to enable the eye to grasp easily this ornamentation in its entirety and to set off its beauty.

The first is seen on a window to the right of the mihrab. The rosette, 0.8 metres in diameter, gives the proportions of the rest.

The second is at the top of the window to the left of the mihrab. It resembles a long frieze of a very original style.

The third, cut out in an irregular trapezium, forms the ceiling of the large door.

Black lines are outlined in white and red; the gold, first in vermillion, then in black—it is by error that this last line was not outlined as well.

As in the two preceding plates, flat gold has been replaced by yellow in order to restore some part of the original effect to the drawing.

The al-Bordayni Mosque is built quite painstakingly, with regular courses 0.31 metres to 0.32 metres in height including the mortar, or an average height of 0.315 metres. This, along with the photographed view, gives an indication of the height of the edifice. The ornamentation differs in its colouring and in some details at the far end of the ceiling, near the door of the courtyard. This part has neither knobs at the centre of the sun, nor a white star around it, and all grounds are in pure gold, on which ornaments are drawn in red and in blue. The other part is much more beautiful: knobs are found only in the centres of the stars, and in consequence, only around the octagon.

The centre of the knobs forms another octagon, surrounding the first octagon and intersecting it at its corners; it intersects the large star, which shares a common line with the other, in the same way.

The gold is so thick that it forms a relief of 2 millimetres.

The ornaments painted on both this and the large ceiling are not Arabic in character; their Persian style leads us to believe that these decorative paintings are the work of foreign artists, similar to ornaments of the same type painted in the palace of Kourchyd-Pasha and elsewhere.

Plate LXVIII

MOSQUE OF AL-BORDAYNI

Ceiling and Frieze of the Dikka (17th century)

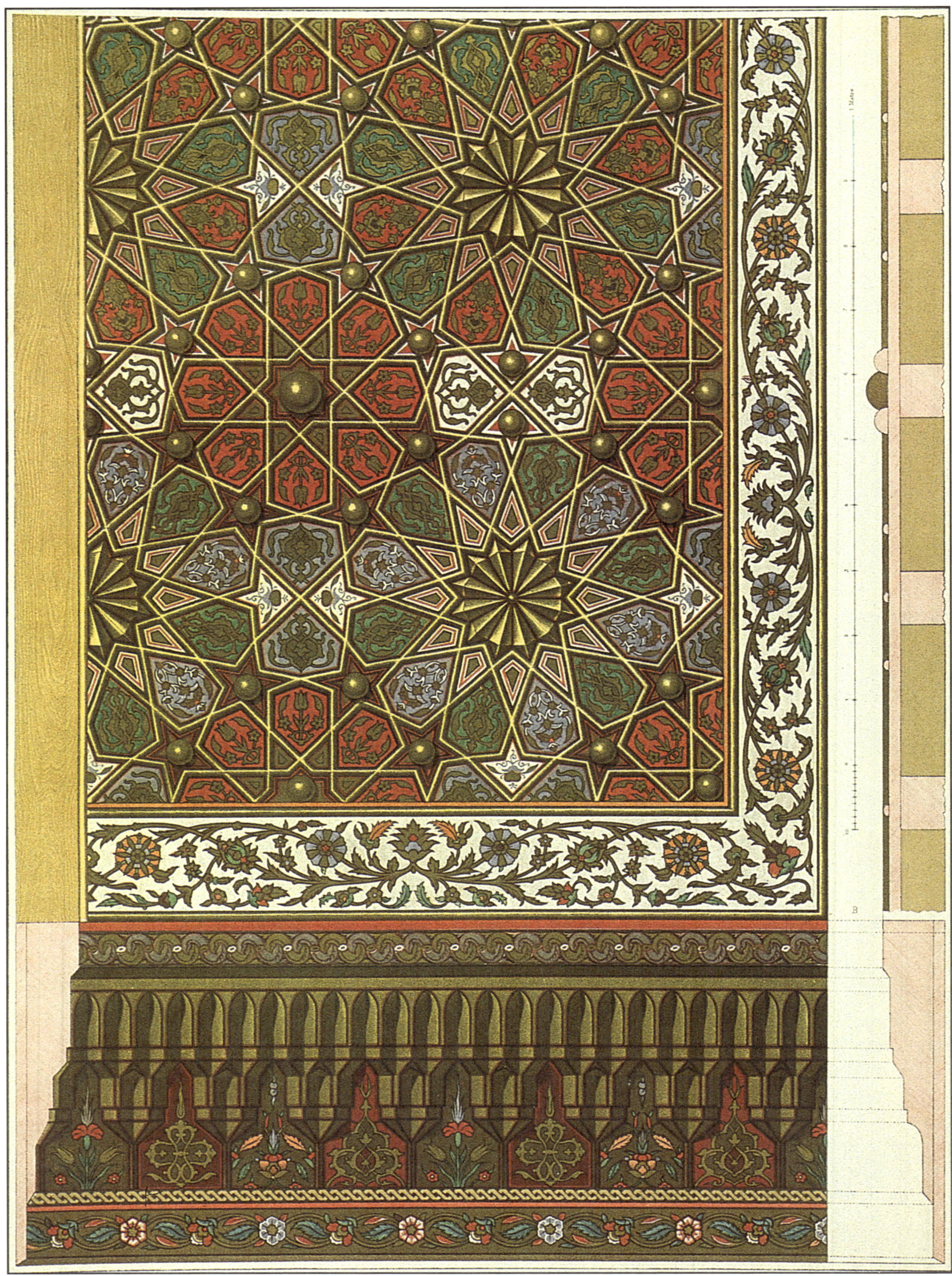

MOSQUE OF AL-BORDAYNI
Details of the Large Ceiling

Plate LXIX

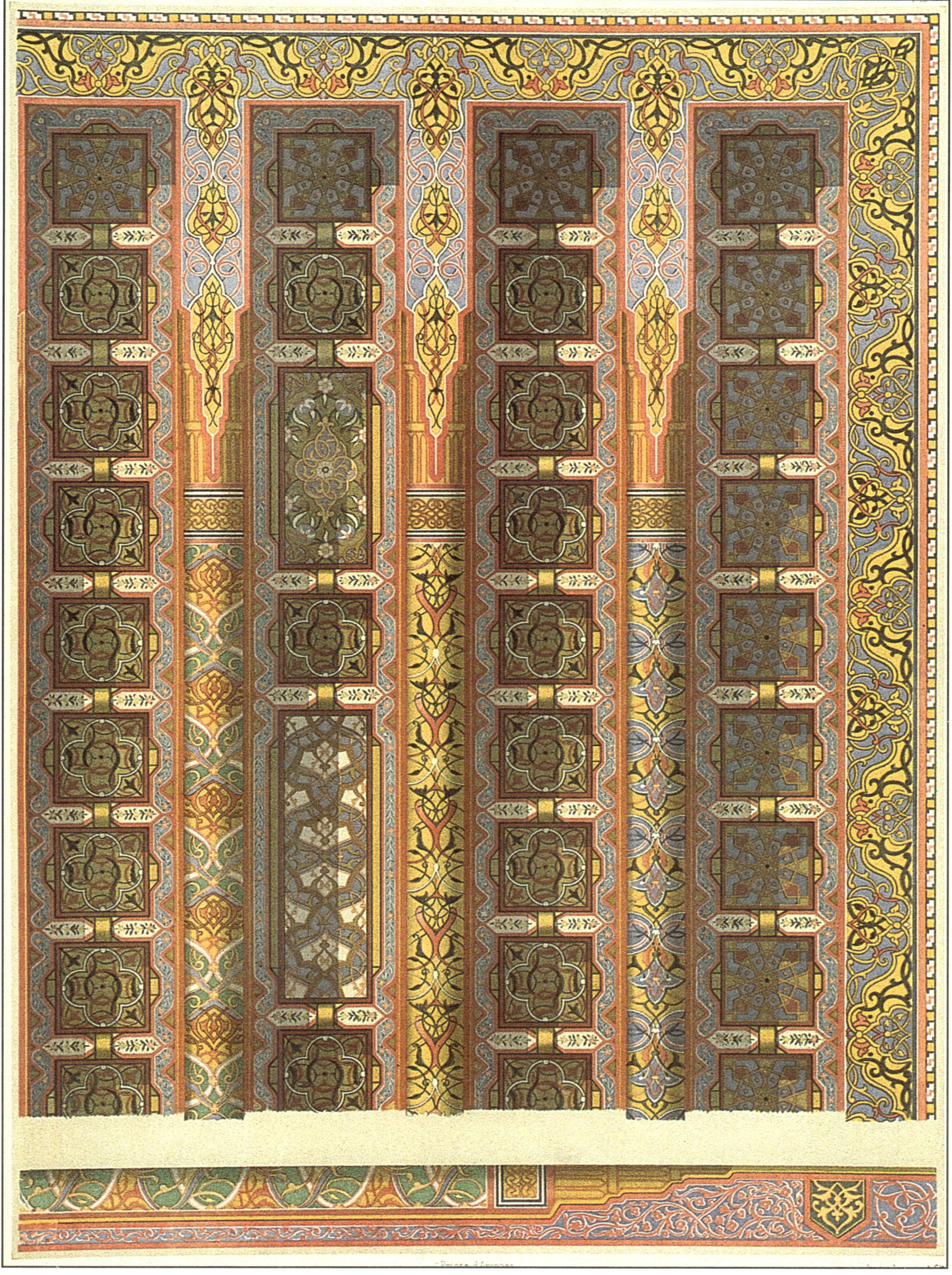

Plate LXX

MOSQUE OF AL-BORDAYNI

Friezes and Borders of the Small Rooms (17th century)

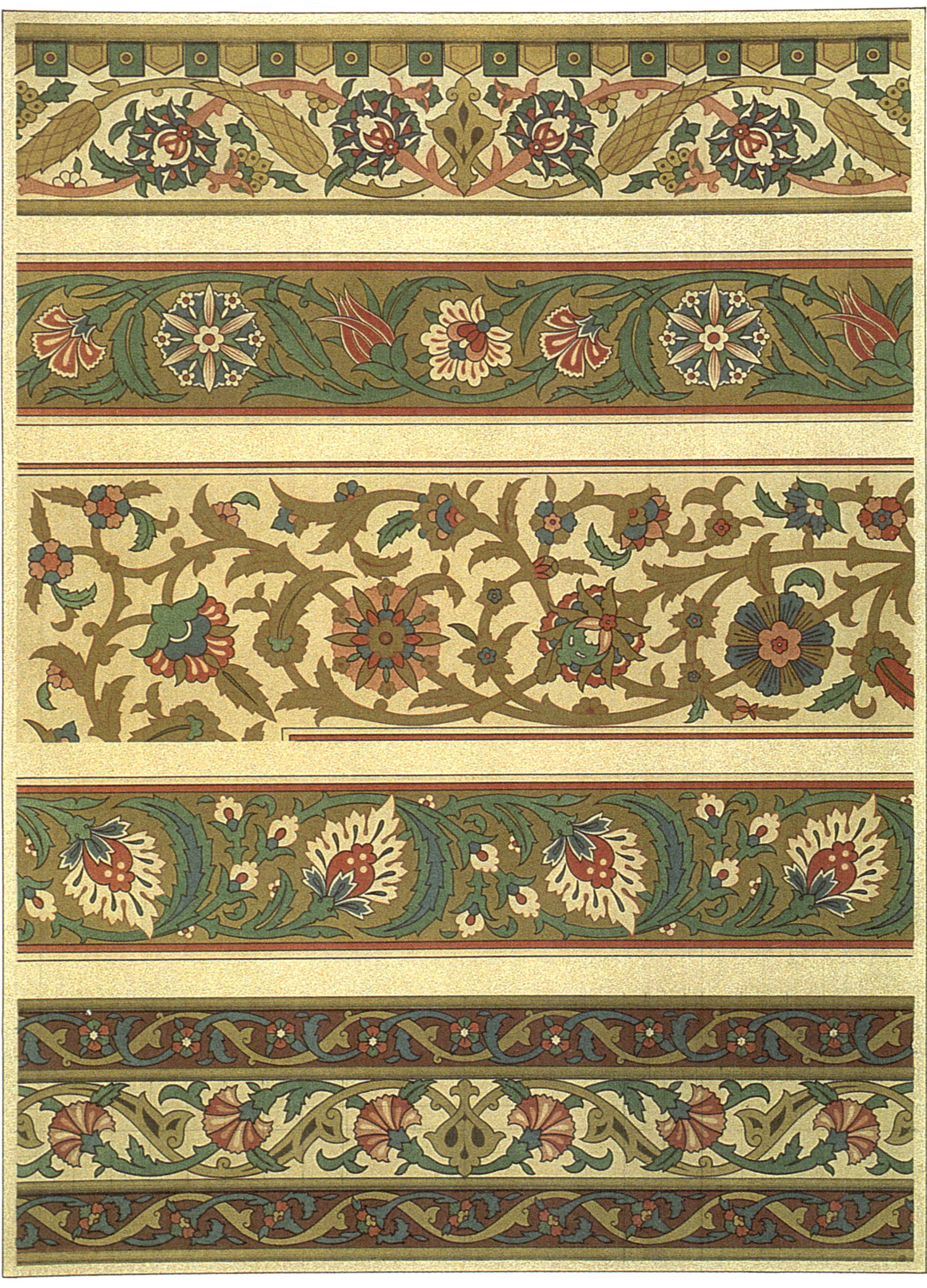

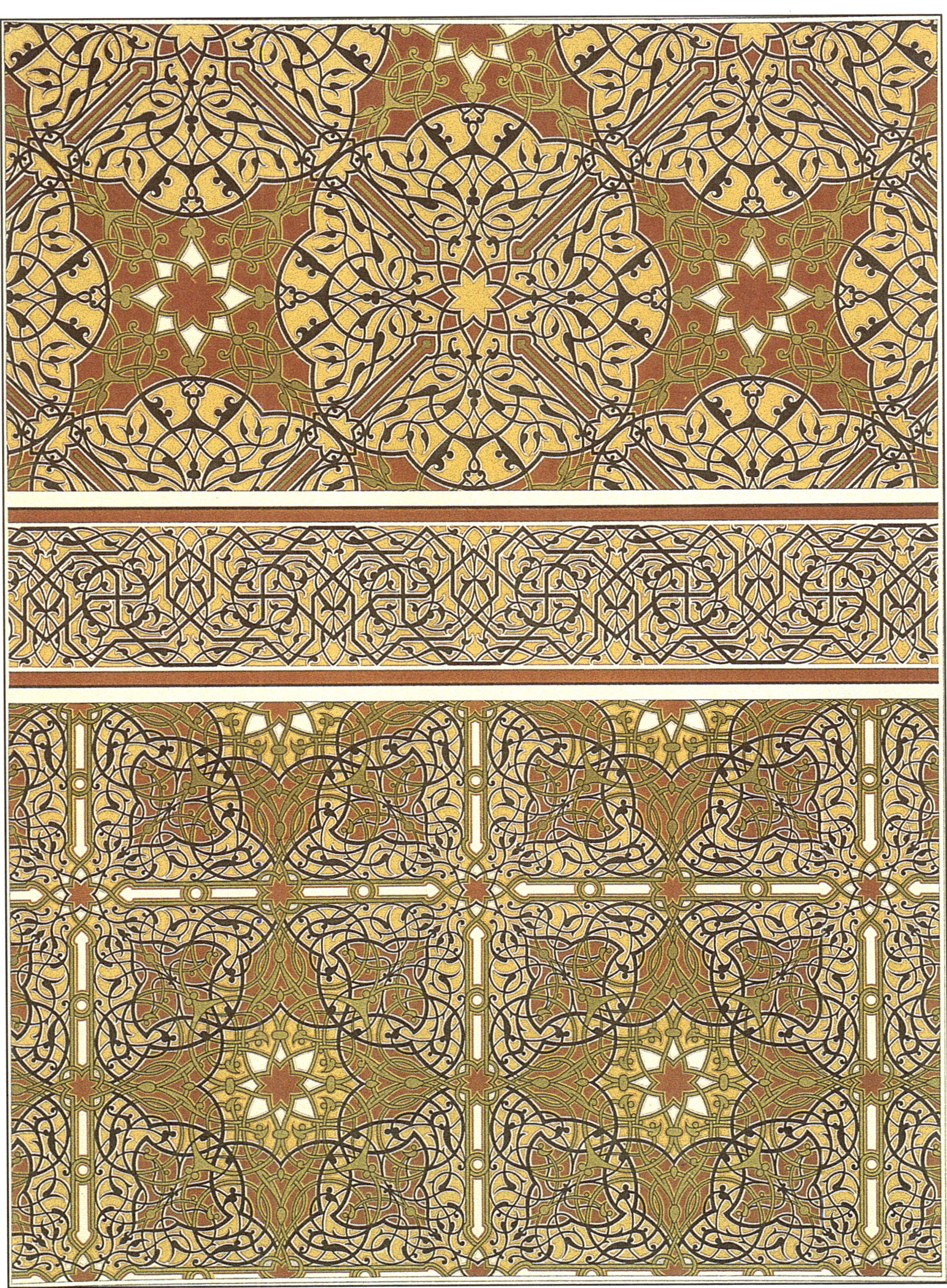

Plate LXXII

HOUSE KNOWN AS BAIT AL-SHALABI

Ceilings (18th century)

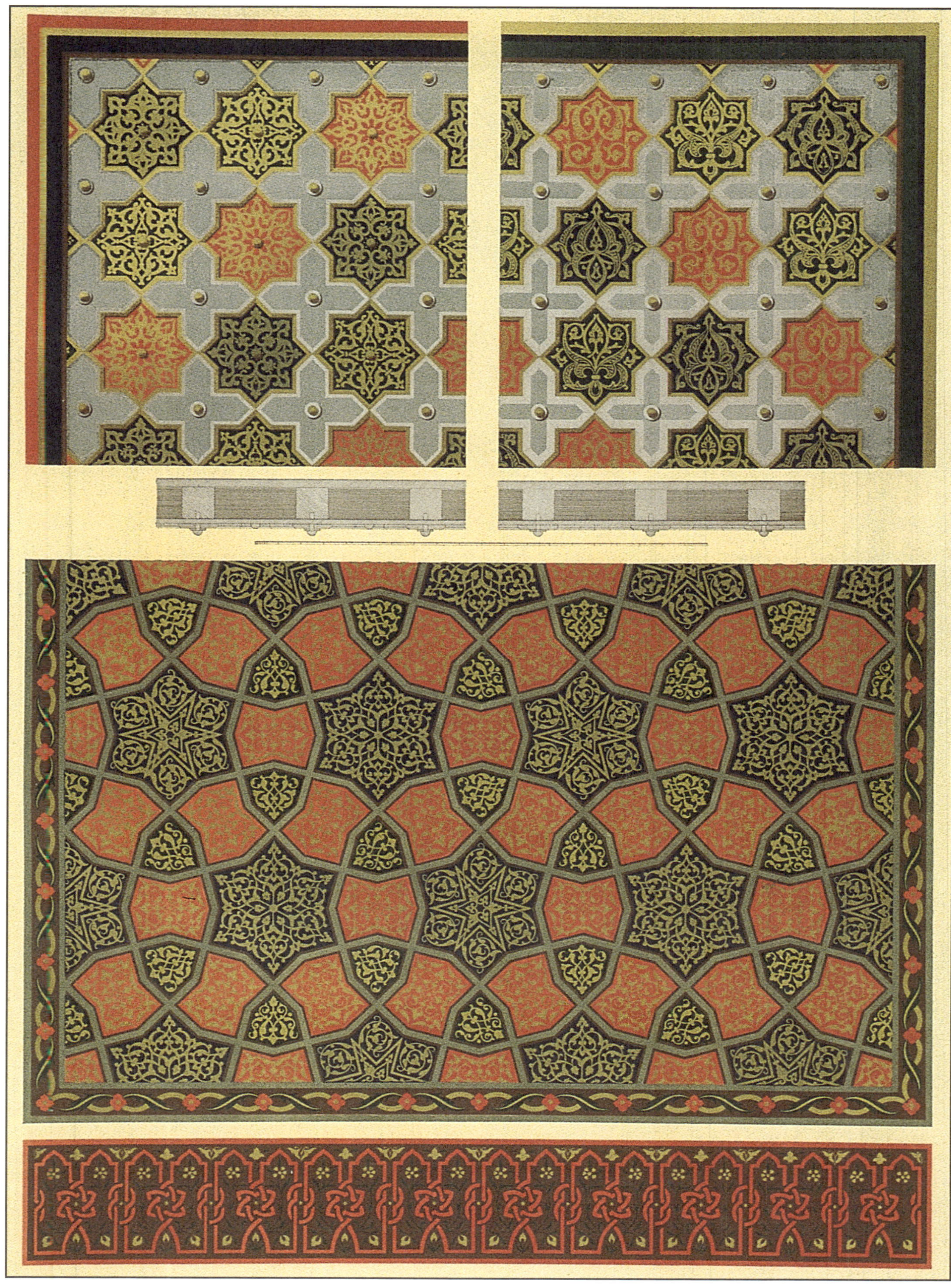

MORESQUE CEILING
(18th century)

Plate LXXIII

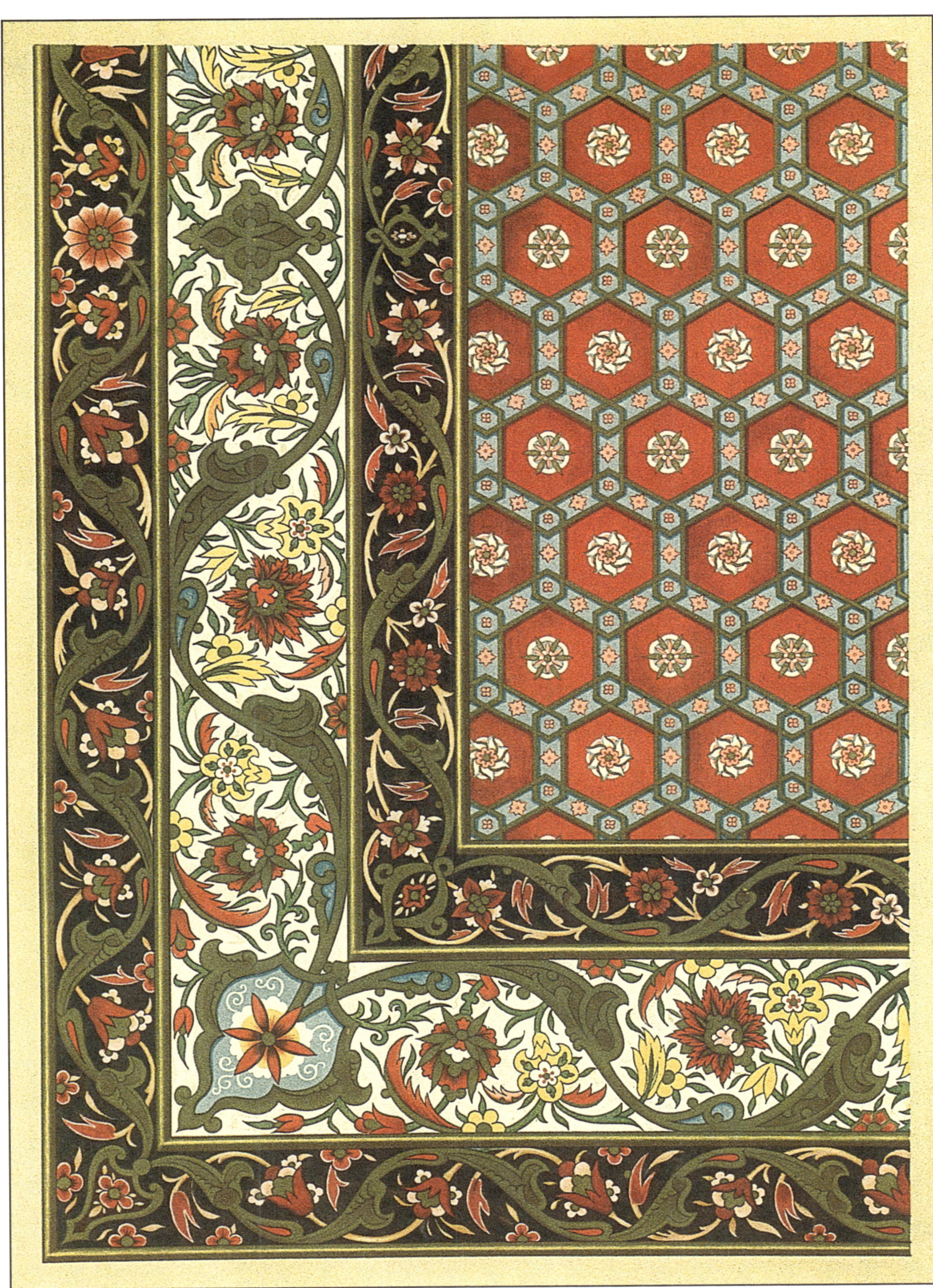

CEILINGS

Dodecagonal Stars

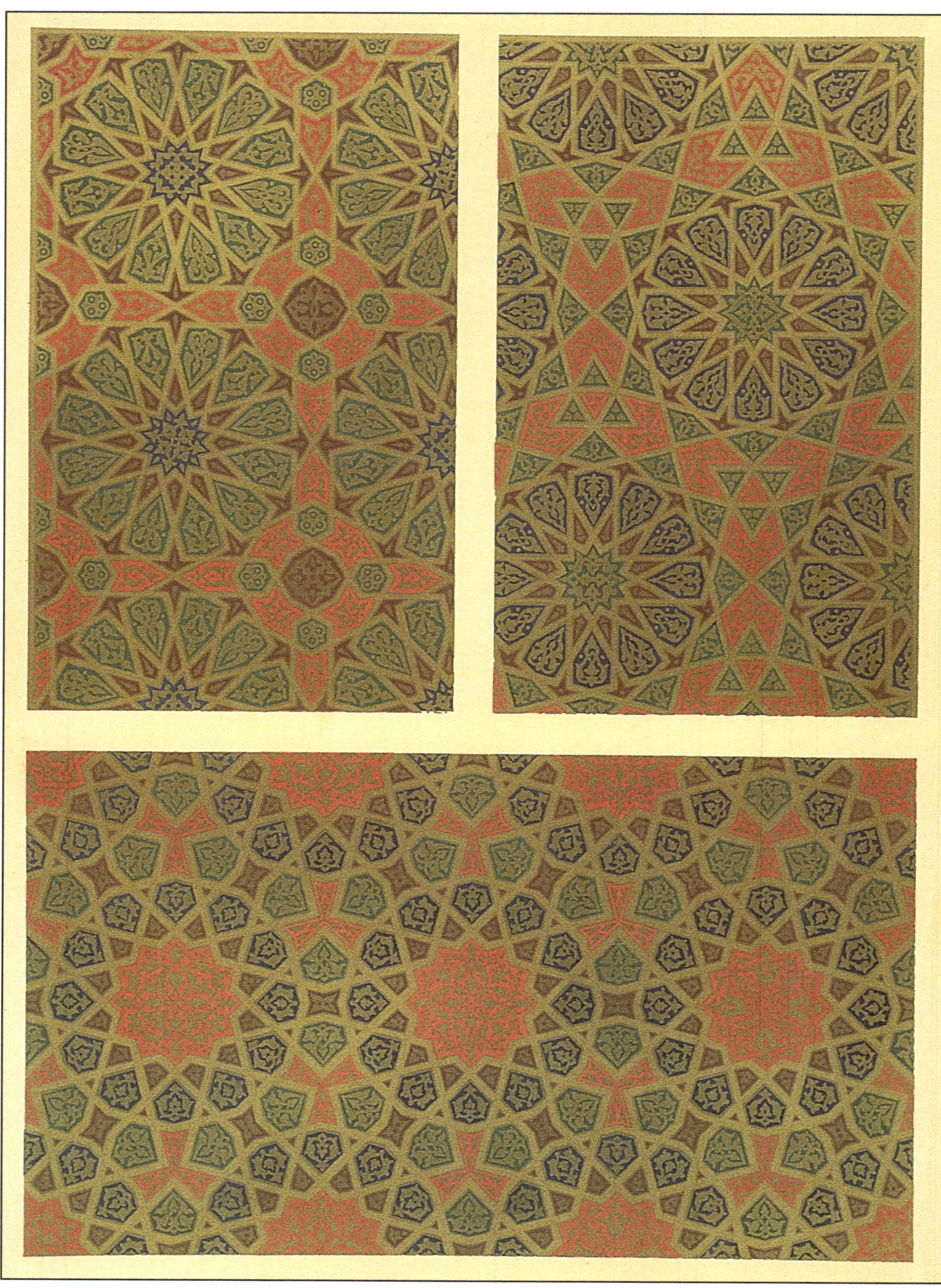

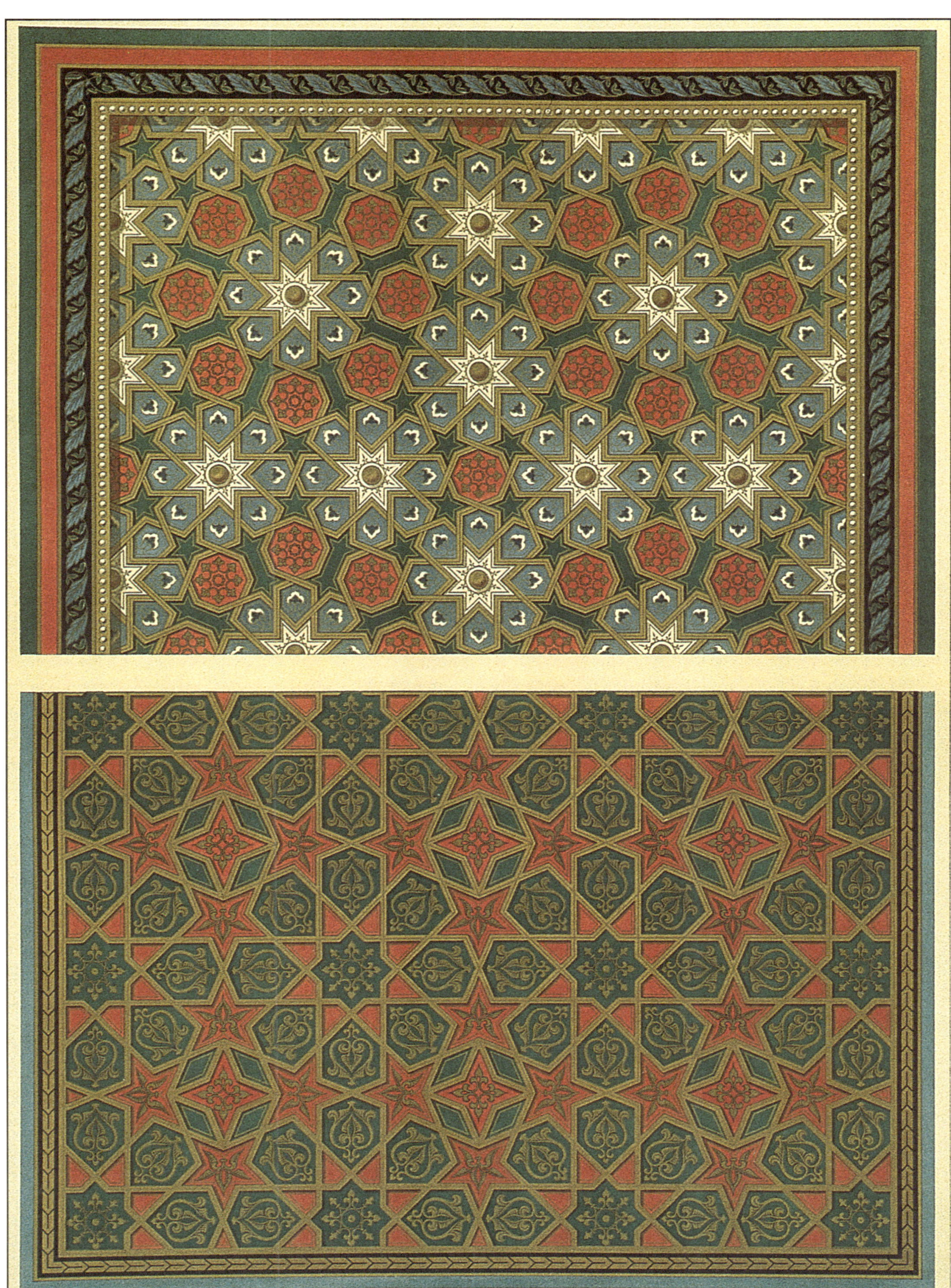

Plates LXXVI to XCIV
PANELLING
Ensembles and Details

Cathedral Mosque of Qus. Details of Panelling of the Minbar (Pl. LXXVI to LXXXII).—These pieces belong to the backrest, façade and uprights of the chair crowning the minbar of Qus, as well as different parts of this pulpit; they represent very pure fragments of this handsome piece of furniture.

Although not one of the monuments of Cairo, the Mosque of Qus has been considered by us as a monument of this city. It was built in effect under the inspiration of Arabic civilisation, particular to this city.

Moristan Hospital (Pl. LXXXIII and LXXXIV).—The beams represented in Plate LXXXIII are from a small room off the women's ward. These fragments were not visible because they were flush with the ceiling, which is very high; in order to draw and stamp them, we took advantage of building repairs undertaken at the time, placing them within our reach. They offer the same type of decoration as certain panels of the entrance door to the courtyard of this edifice and to one of the sick wards.

The Moristan Hospital is a most curious edifice which has never been reproduced with the care it deserves.

We will only draw attention to the median part of the panels of sculptures on the large inner door (Pl. LXXXV); the carving here is on a level just above the frame, while the rest is deeply carved so as to stand out, light against a dark background, and thereby enhance the effect of the sculptures.

Minbar of the Mosque of Qaysun (Pl. LXXXV to LXXXVIII).—Minbars are always in the shape of staircases, as prove those of the Mosque of Qaytbay (Pl. LXXXIX) and the Mosque of Qus. A side of this one has been extended to make a regular surface of it. These fragments show the backrest and the façade of the pulpit set atop the minbar.

Mosque of Talai' Abu Rizk. Details of the Minbar (Pl. XC to XCII).—This minbar, dating from the same period as that of the Mosque of Qus and built under the orders of the same ruler, the governor of Thebaid at the time, is not the work of the same sculptor. The work is equally fine, but different, with a more sculptural effect. The arabesques of Qus more closely resemble point lace and appear somewhat inspired by the Alhambra.

The workmanship of the arabesques of one portion of the grille of the maqsura offers a particularity in that it was largely made following the whim of the chisel, without a preliminary sketch or, at the very least, without a regular and mathematical design. This is not very noticeable in the carving because the design has had to be regularised since, in order to be followed; so worm-eaten was the original that the grain of the sycamore wood showed as much as the arabesques.

Tomb of Sultan al-Ghuri. Leaves and Cupboard Frames (Pl. XCIII).—We have provided quite a large number of plates which, although all very interesting as examples of ornamentation, could perhaps seem uniform in colour. We have hence thought it necessary to give this one a different hue, in the double aim of relieving monotony and of providing a new example of what can be achieved with this ornamentation, simply by varying colours.

CATHEDRAL MOSQUE OF QUS

Minbar with Details (12th century)

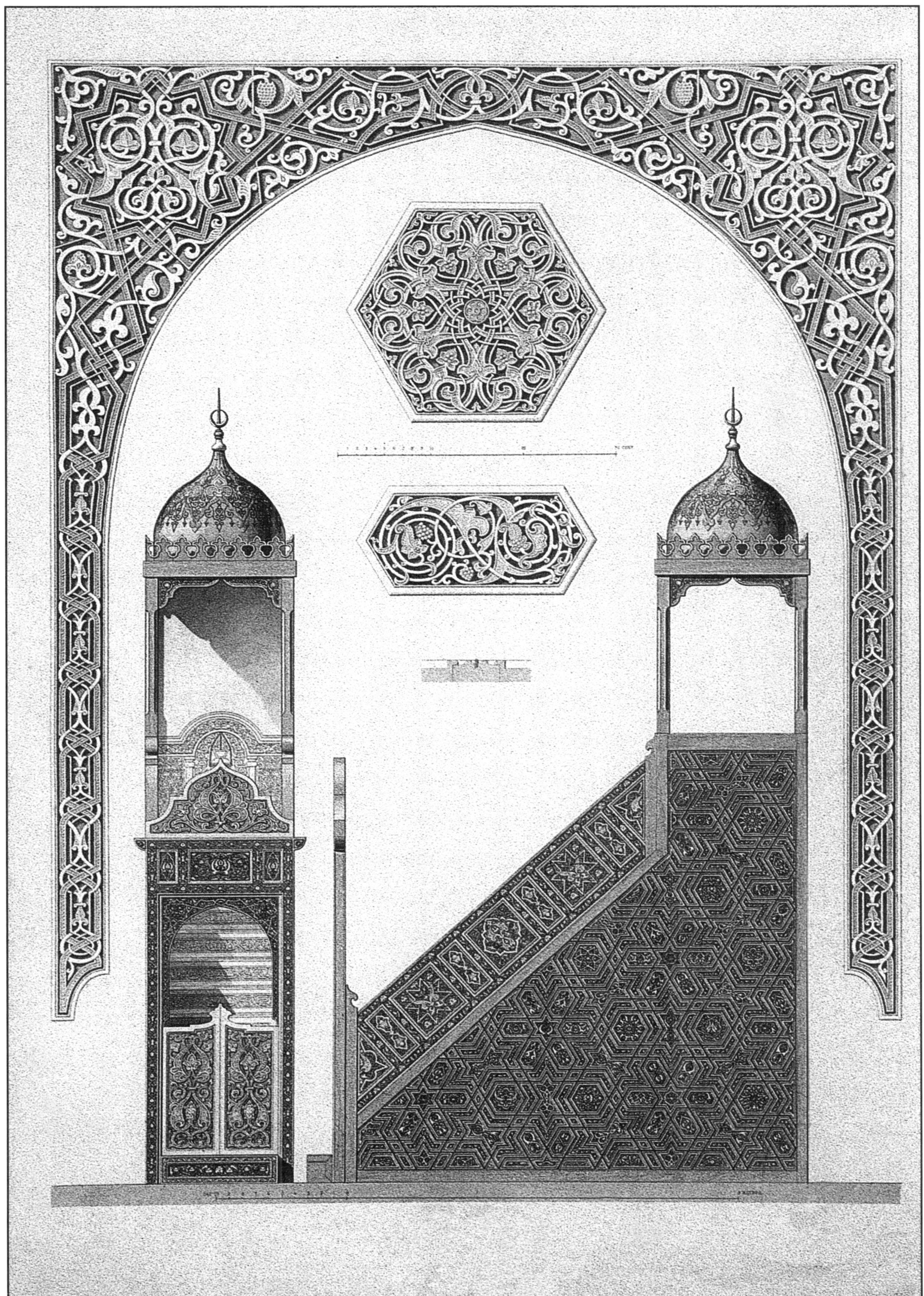

CATHEDRAL MOSQUE OF QUS

Minbar, Section and Details (12th century)

Decorative Sections of the Minbar (12th century)

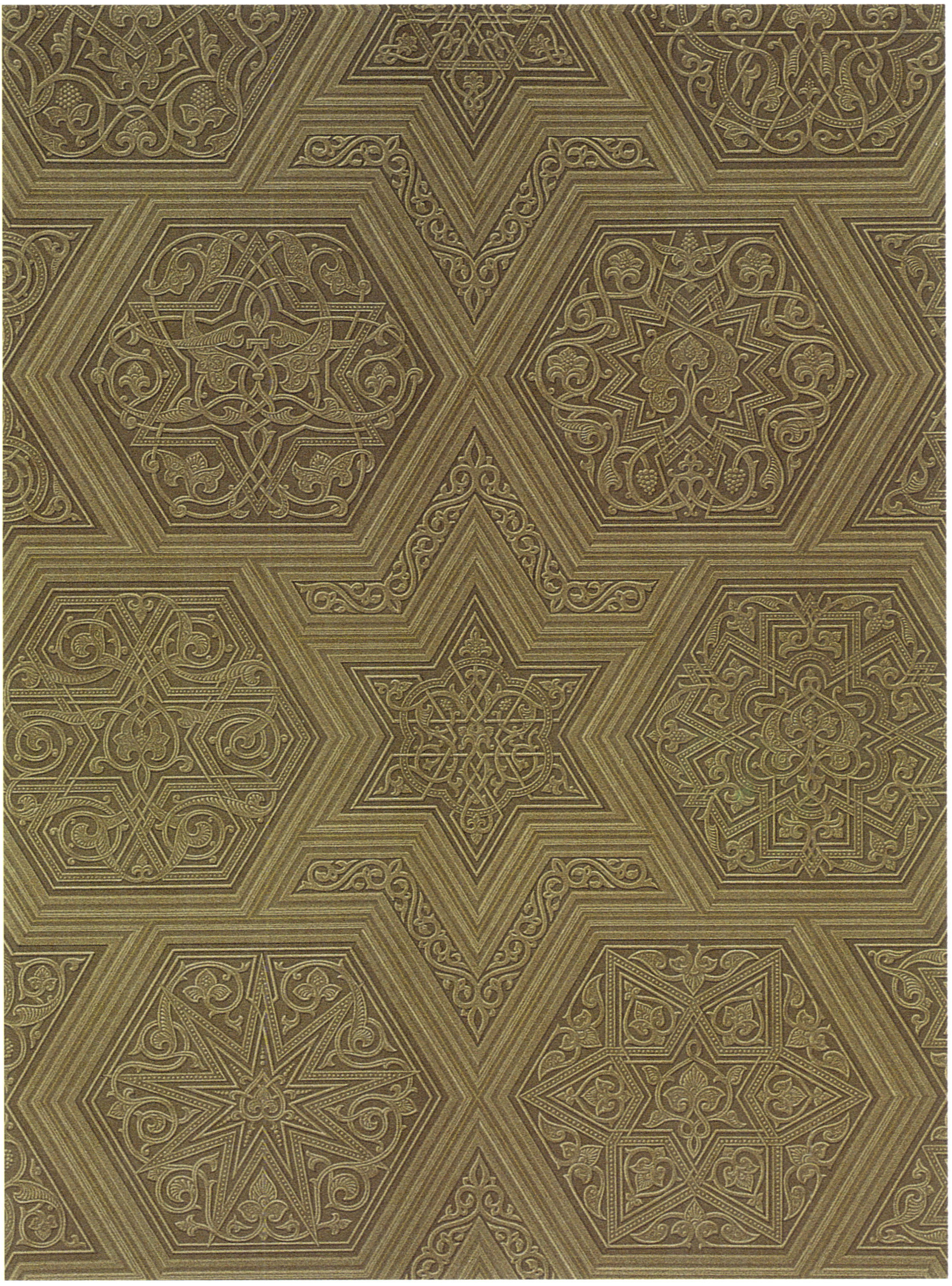

CATHEDRAL MOSQUE OF QUS

Minbar, Details of the Woodwork (12th century)

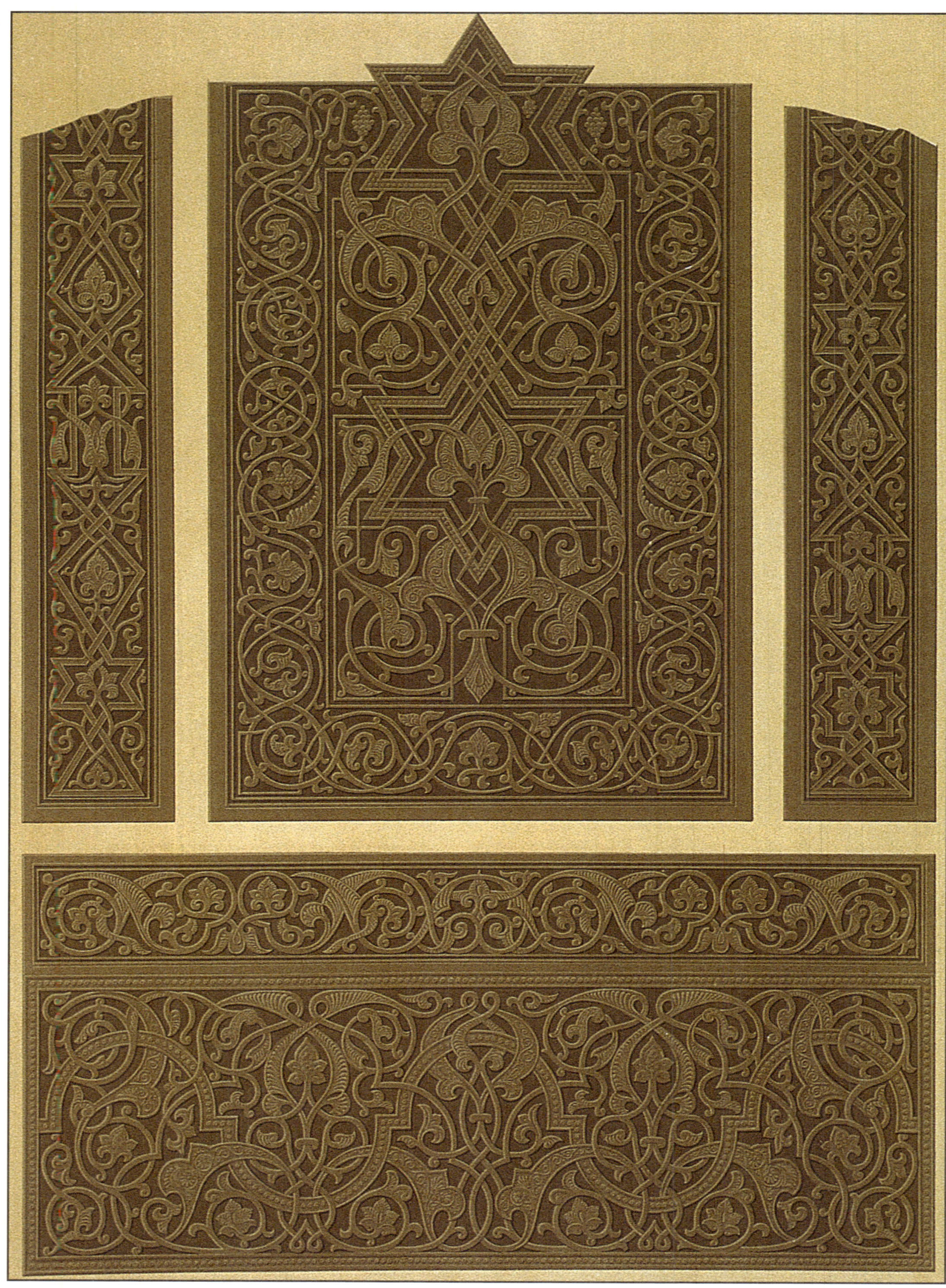

CATHEDRAL MOSQUE OF QUS

Door of the Minbar (12th century)

Plate LXXX

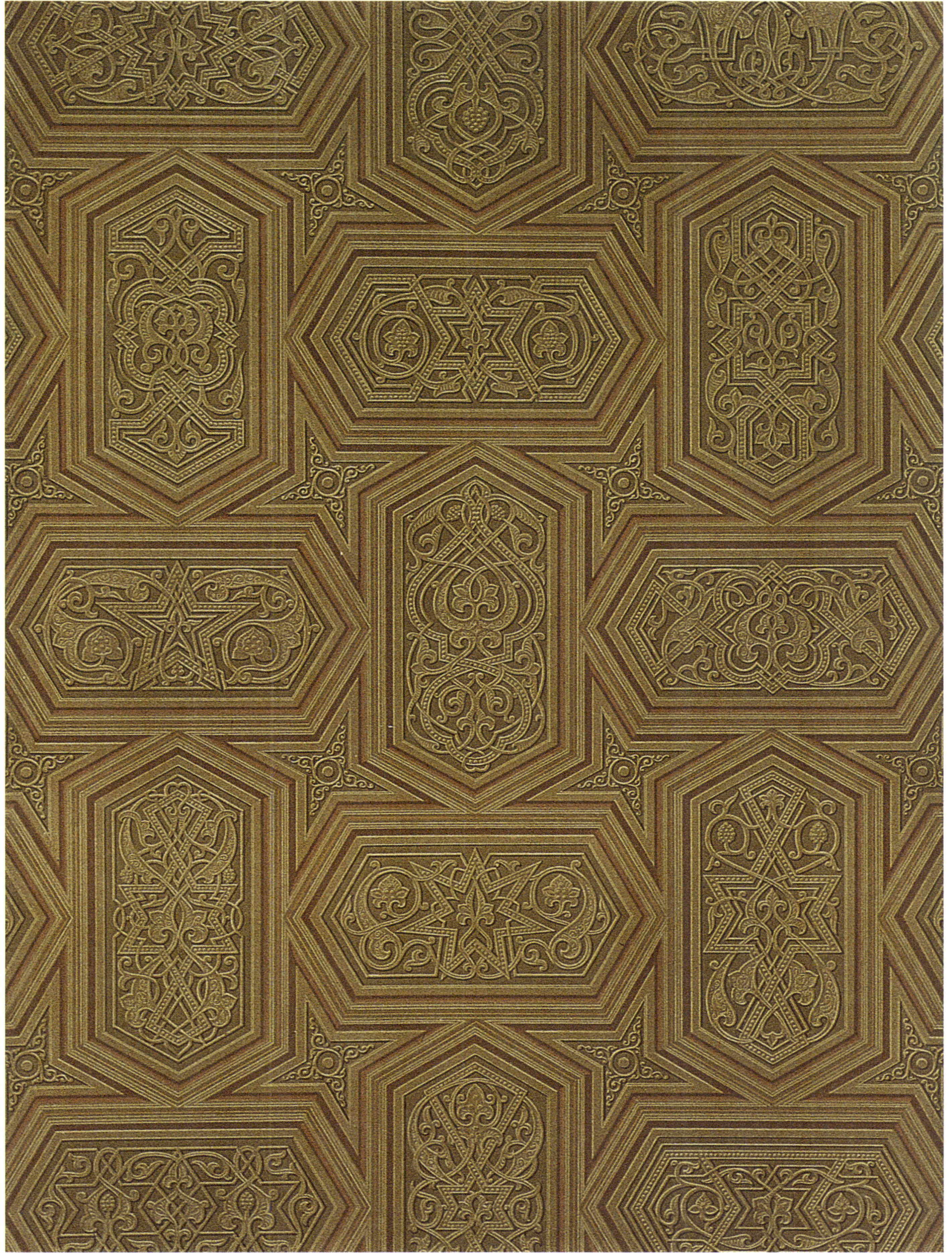

CATHEDRAL MOSQUE OF QUS

Details of the Minbar (12th century)

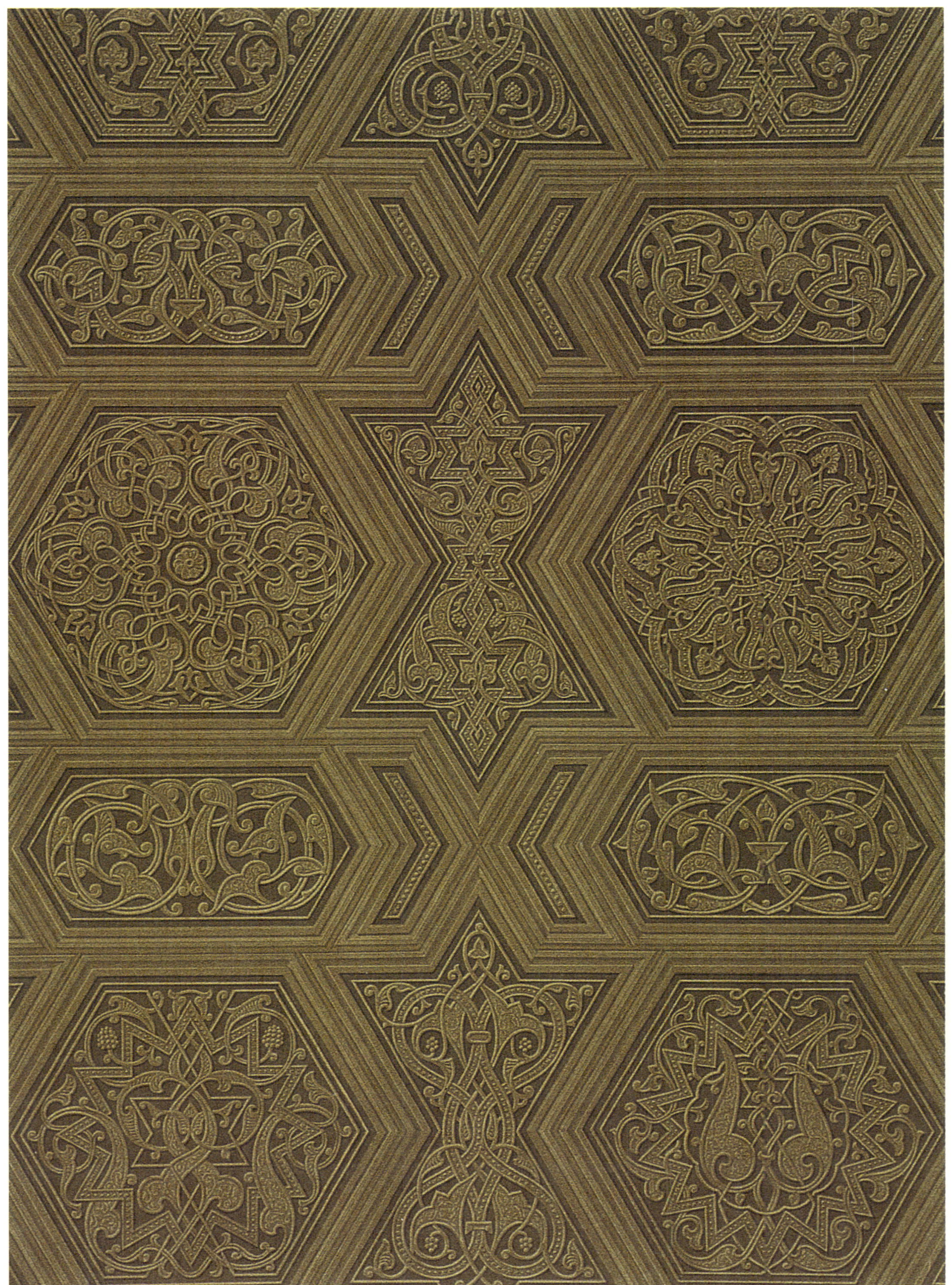

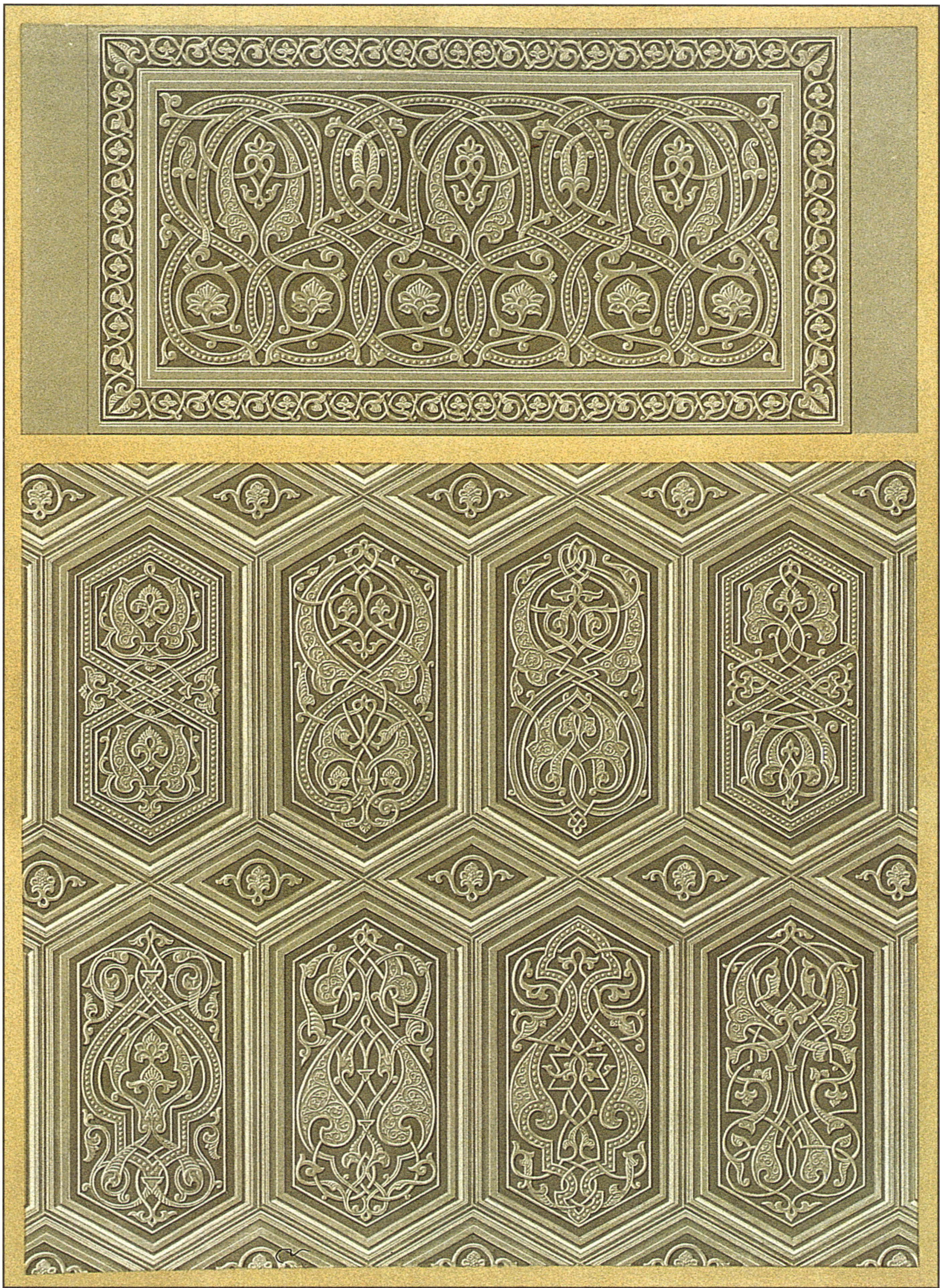

MORISTAN HOSPITAL

Details of Beams and Friezes (13th century)

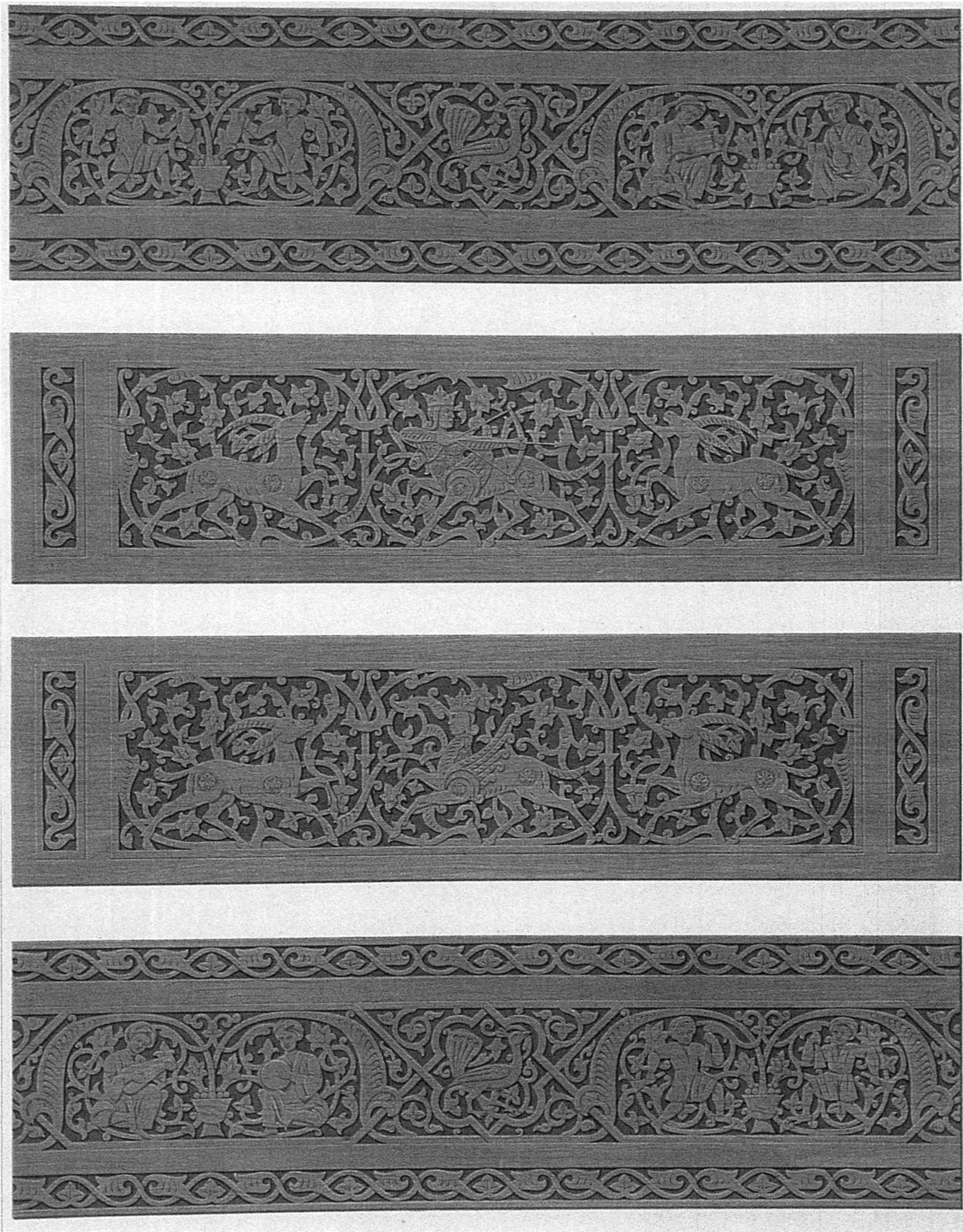

MORISTAN HOSPITAL
Carvings on the Large Inner Door (13th century)

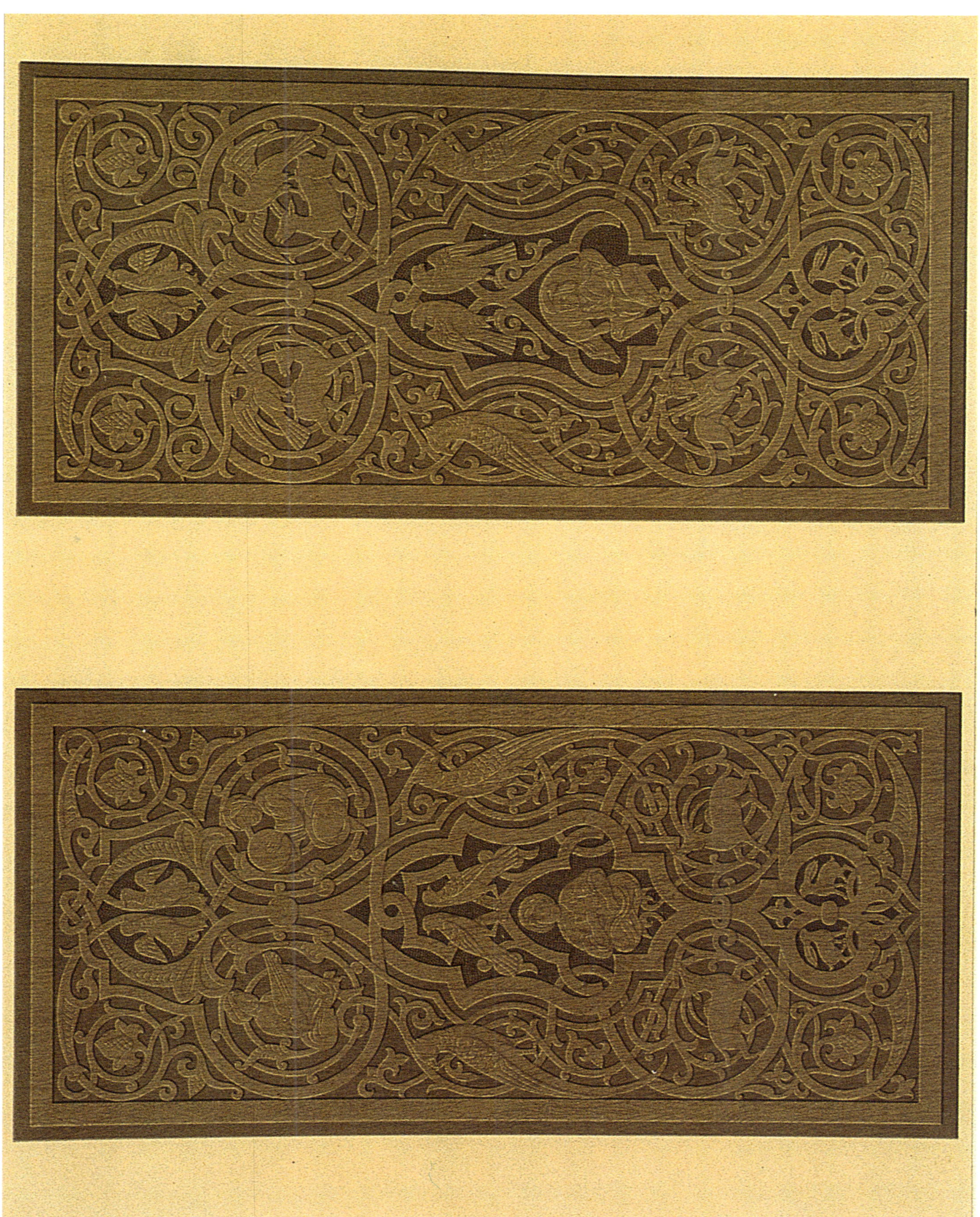

Plate LXXXV

MOSQUE OF AL-NEESFI QAYSUN

Ornamental Details of the Minbar (14th century)

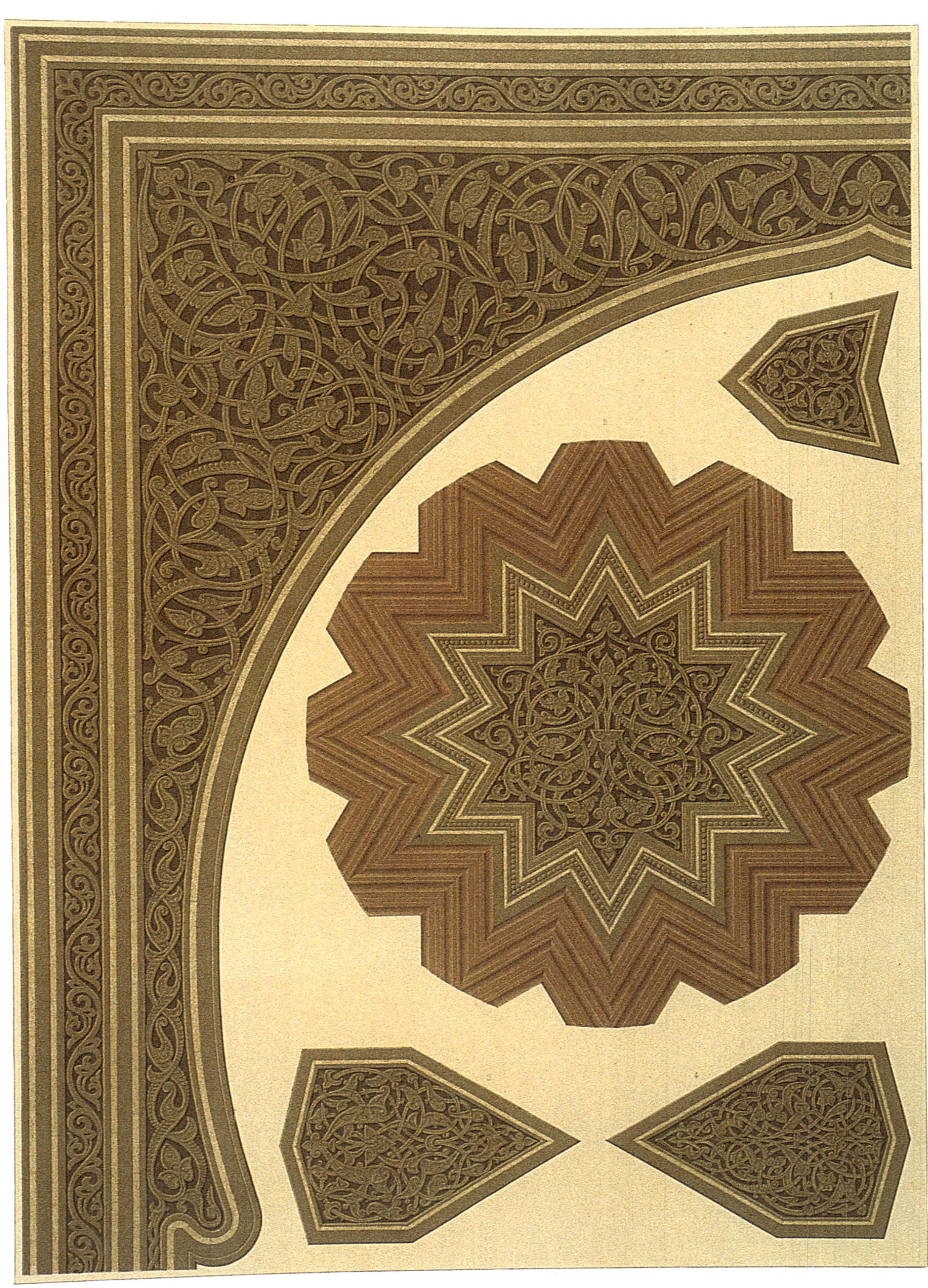

MOSQUE OF AL-NEESFI QAYSUN

Ornamental Details of the Mihrab (14th century)

Plate LXXXVI

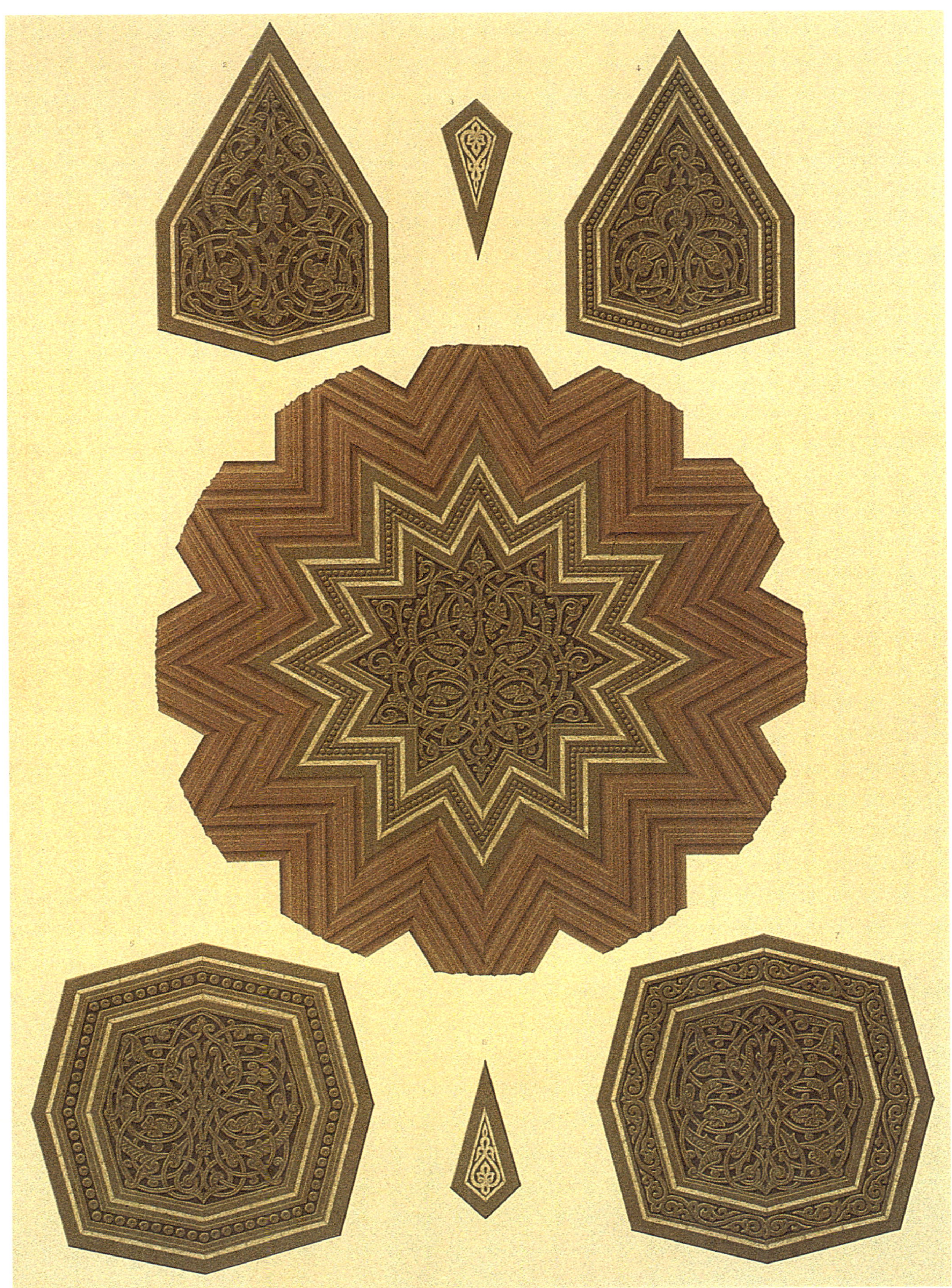

Plate LXXXVII

MOSQUE OF AL-NEESFI QAYSUN

Ornamental Details of the Minbar (14th century)

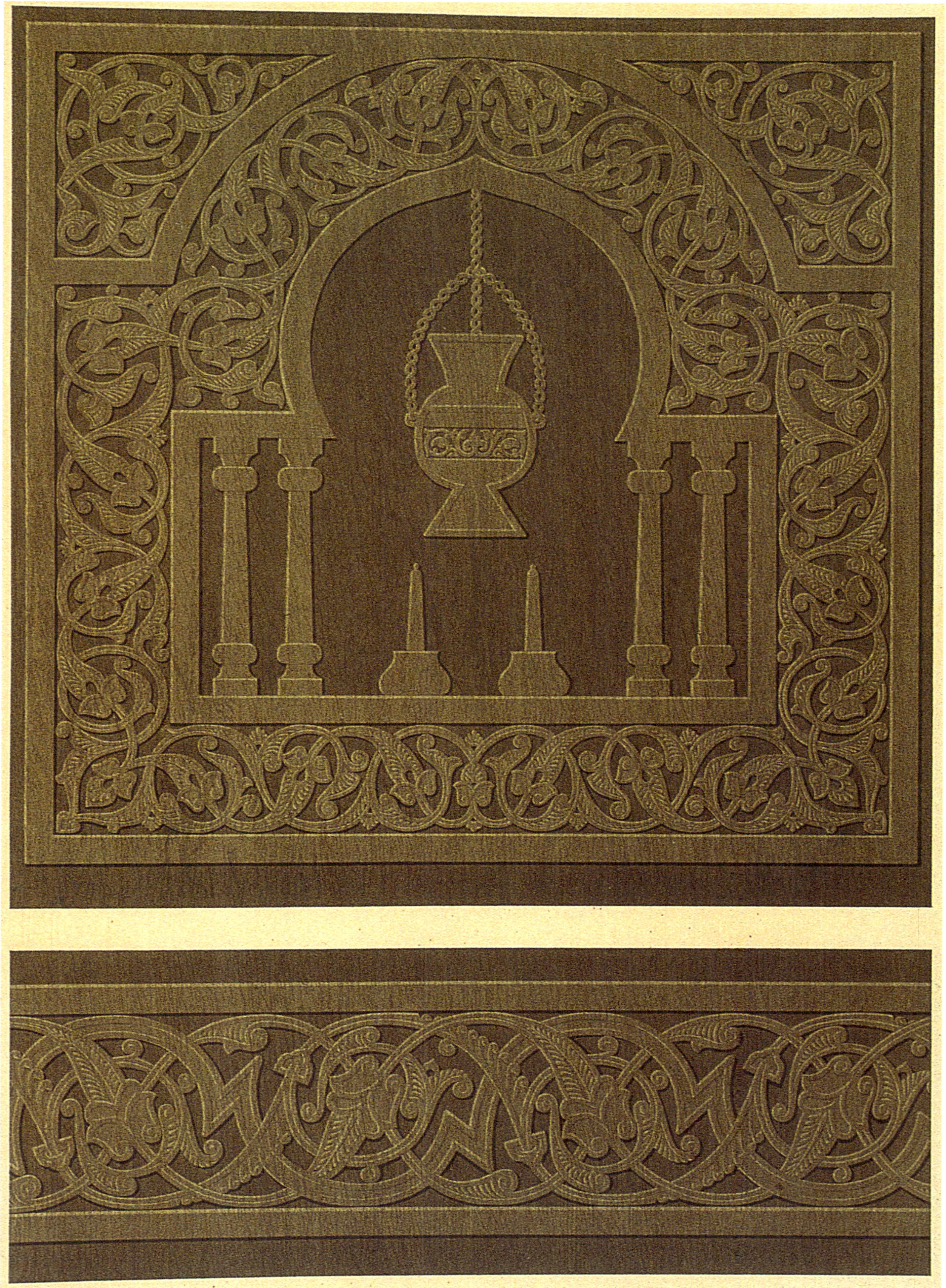

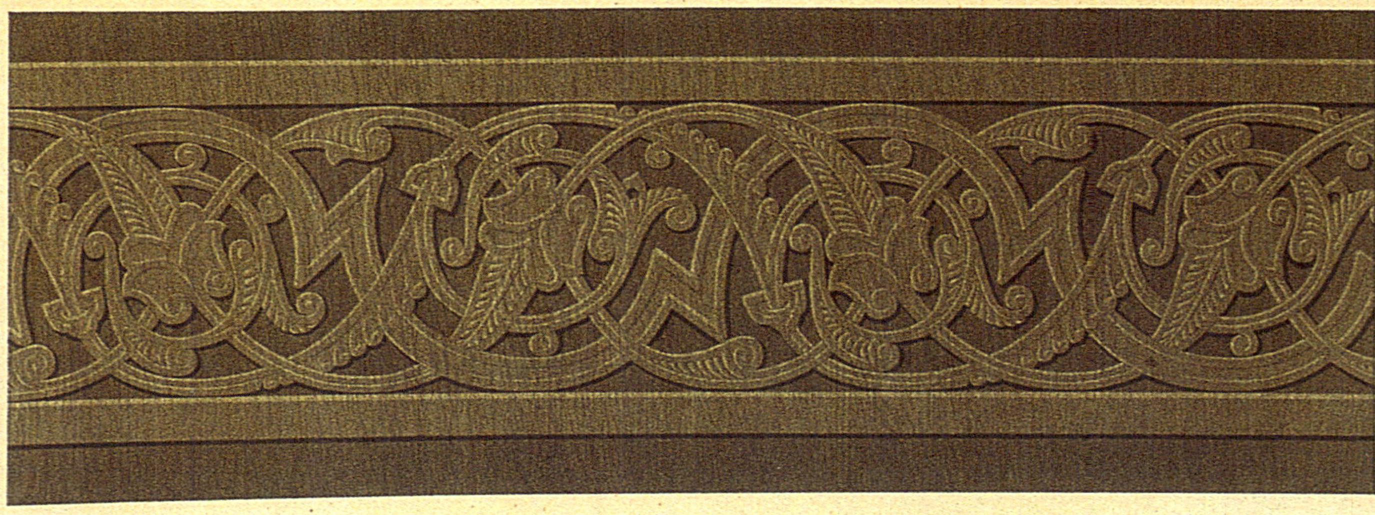

MINBAR OF THE MOSQUE OF QAYSUN
(14th century)

Plate LXXXVIII

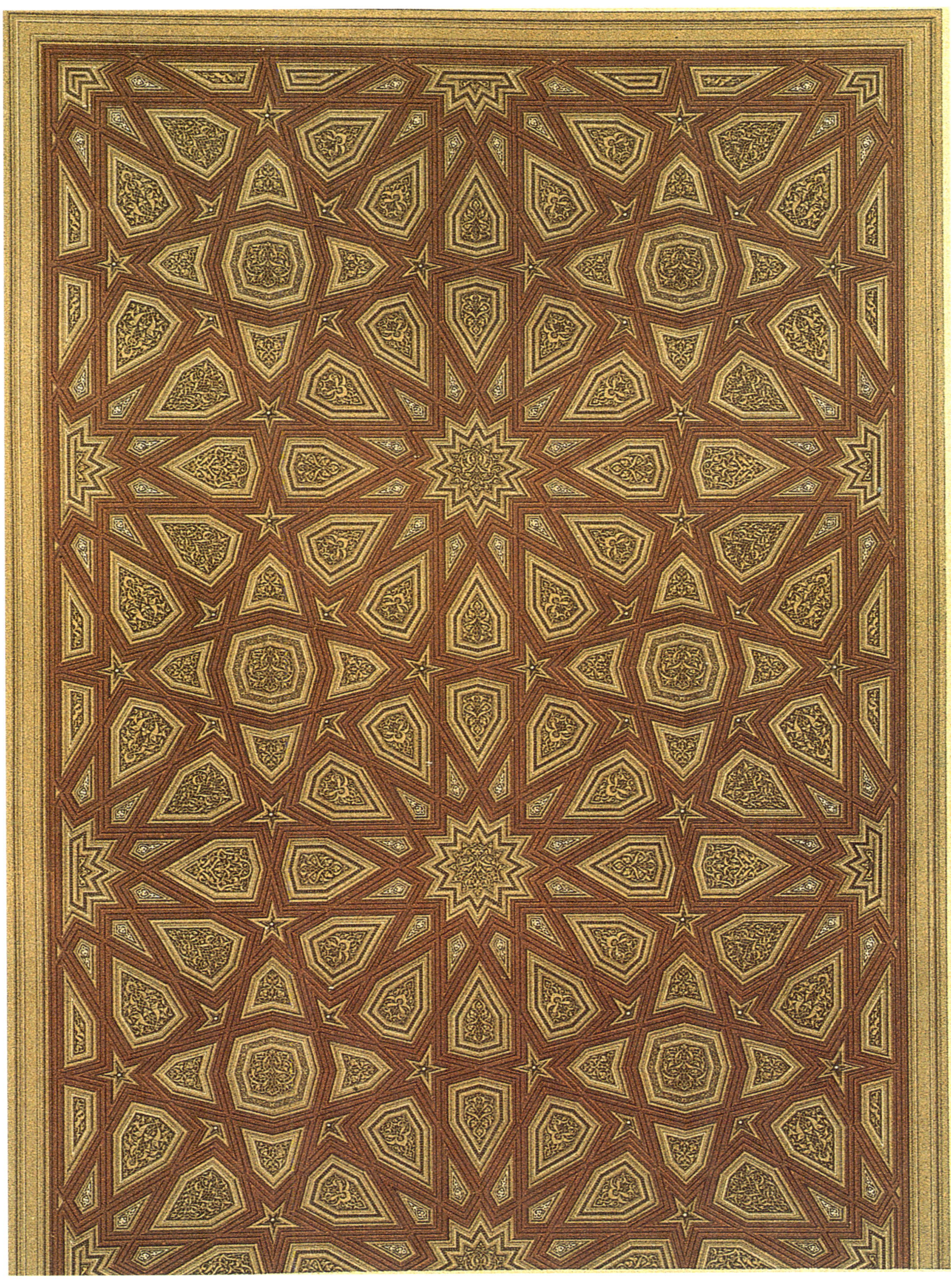

Plate LXXXIX

MOSQUE OF QAYTBAY

Elevation of the Minbar. Door. (15th century)

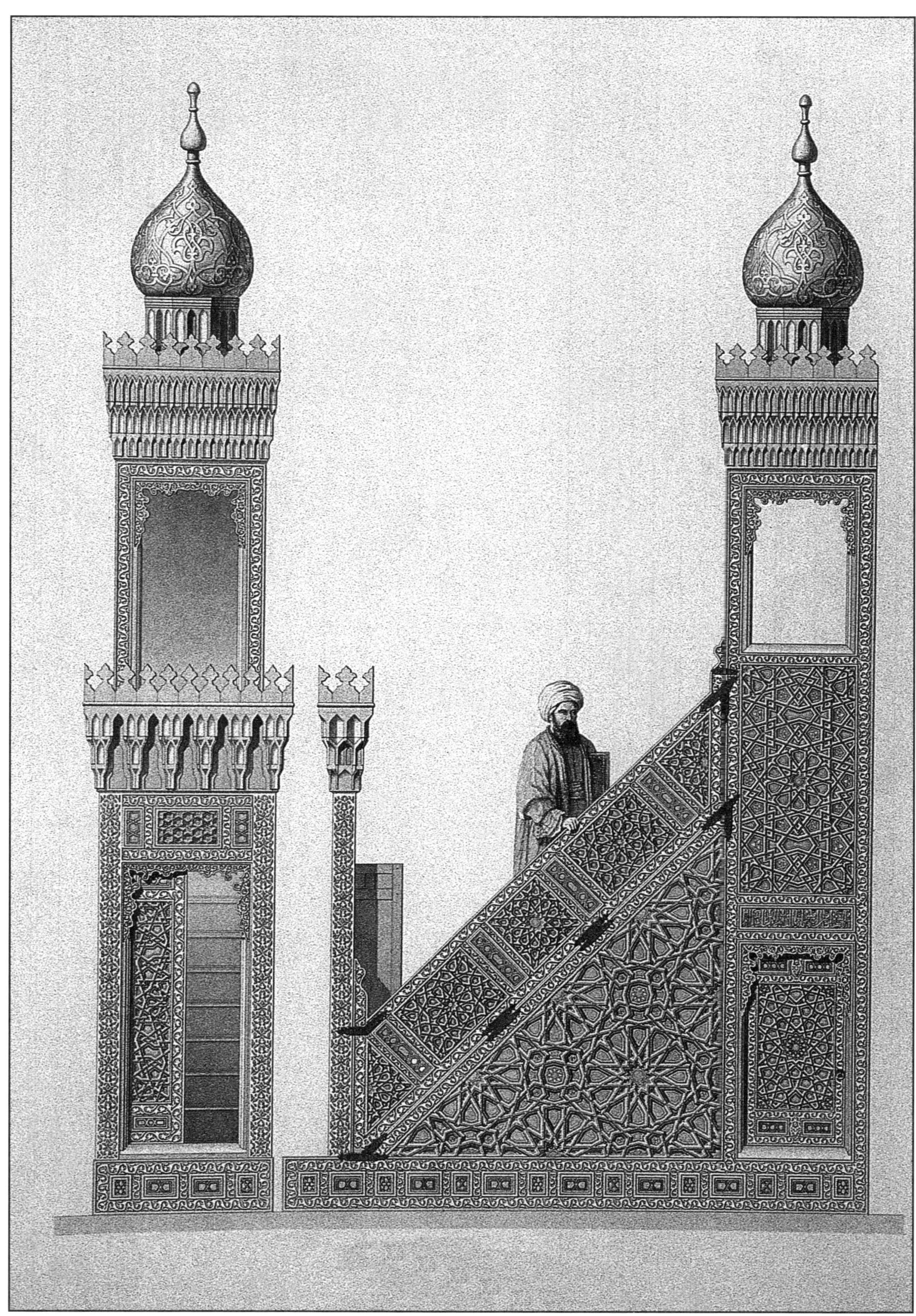

MOSQUE OF TALAI' ABU RIZK

Details of the Minbar (15th century)

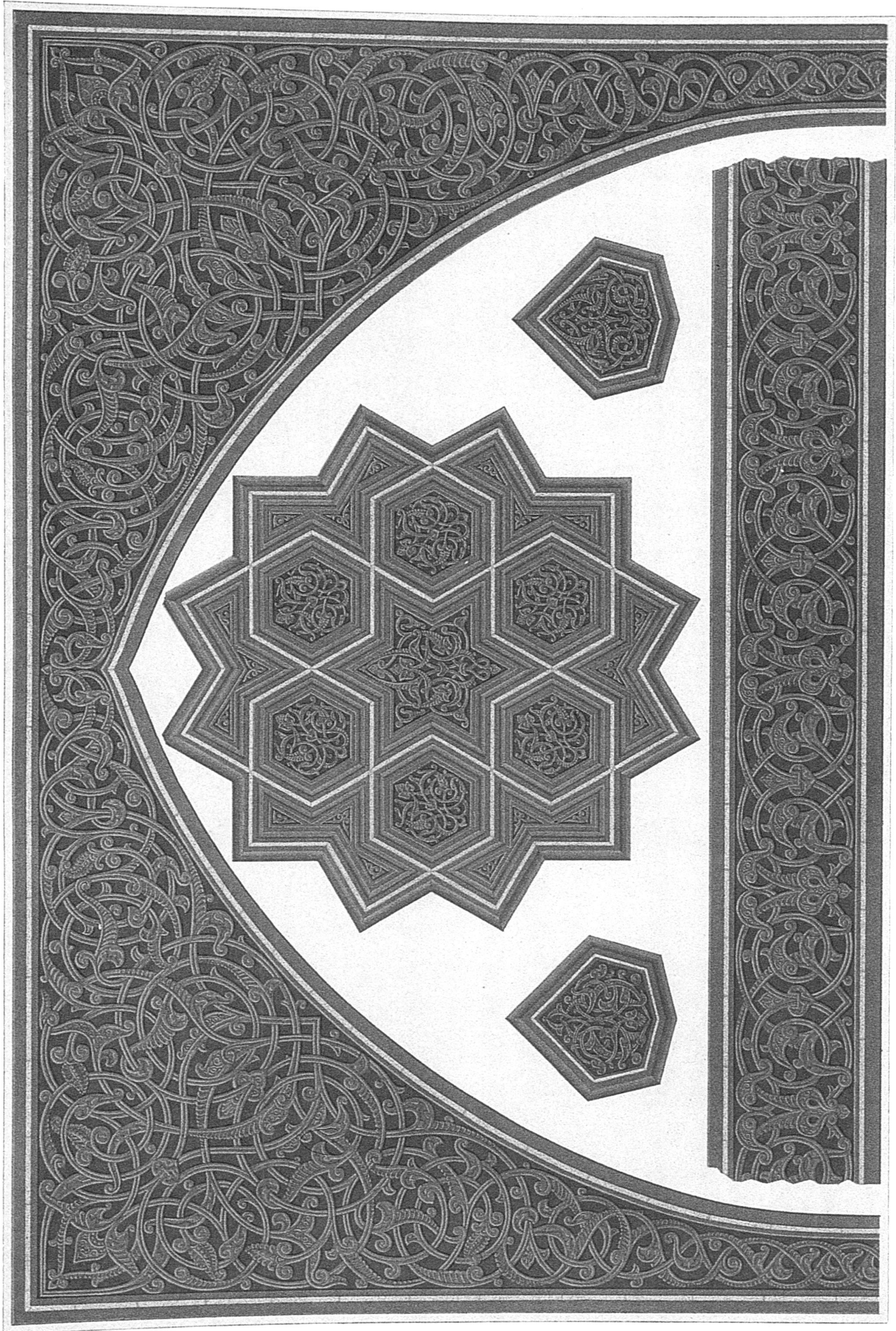

MOSQUE OF TALAI' ABU RIZK

Details of the Minbar (15th century)

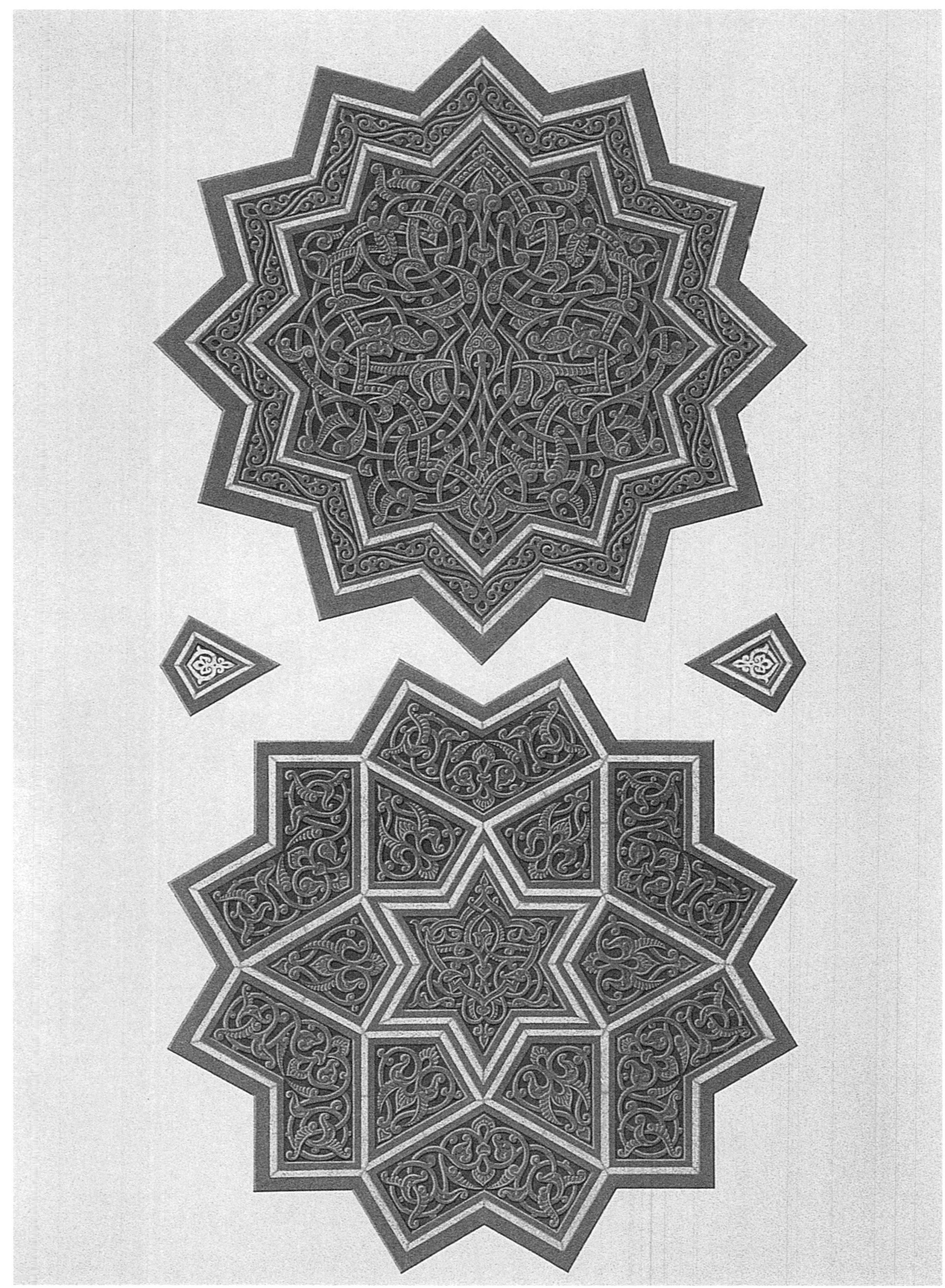

MOSQUE OF TALAI' ABU RIZK

Details of the Minbar (15th century)

Plate XCII

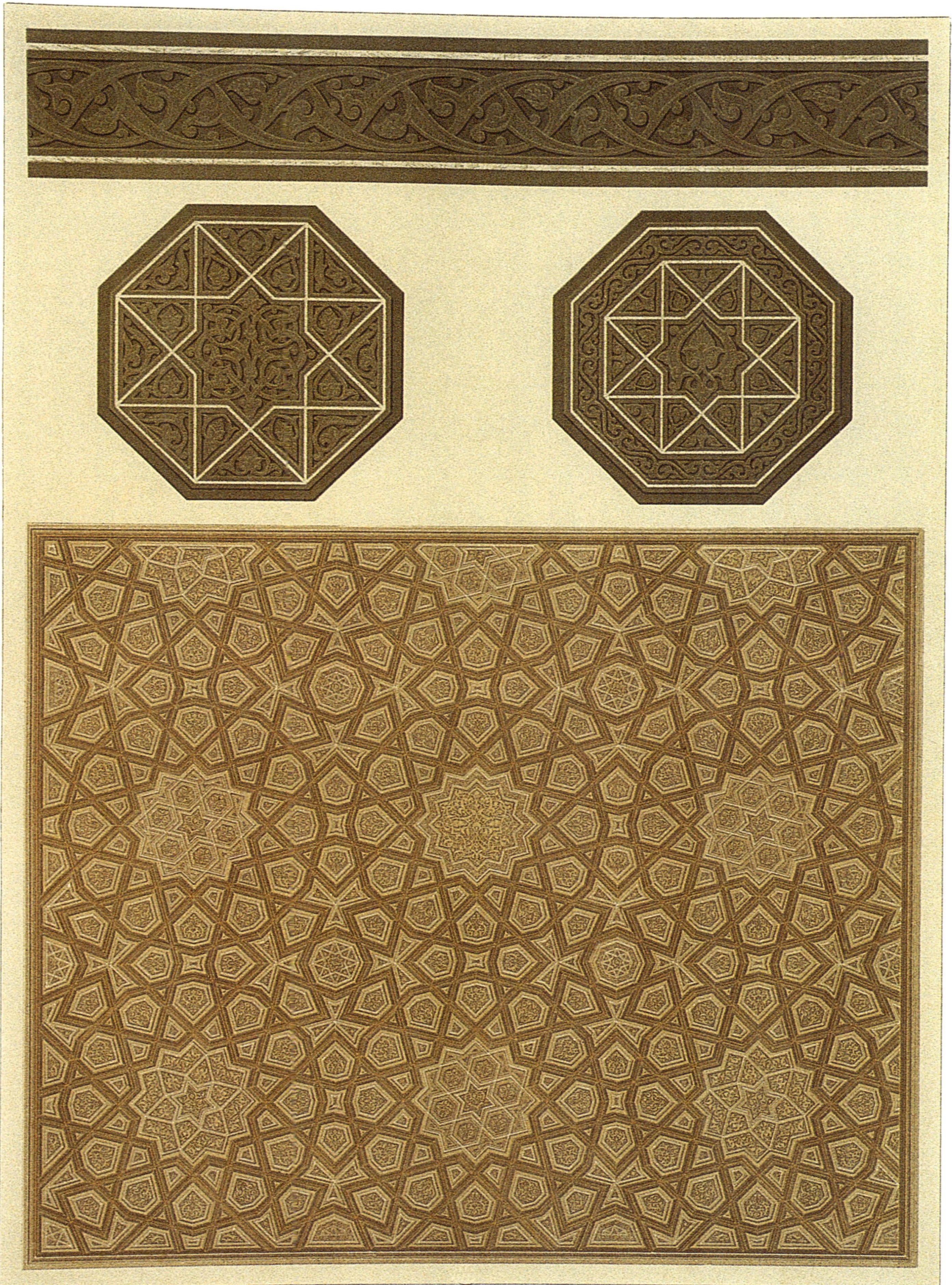

TOMB OF SULTAN AL-GHURI

Carved Wooden Cupboard. Door Leaves and Borders. (16th century)

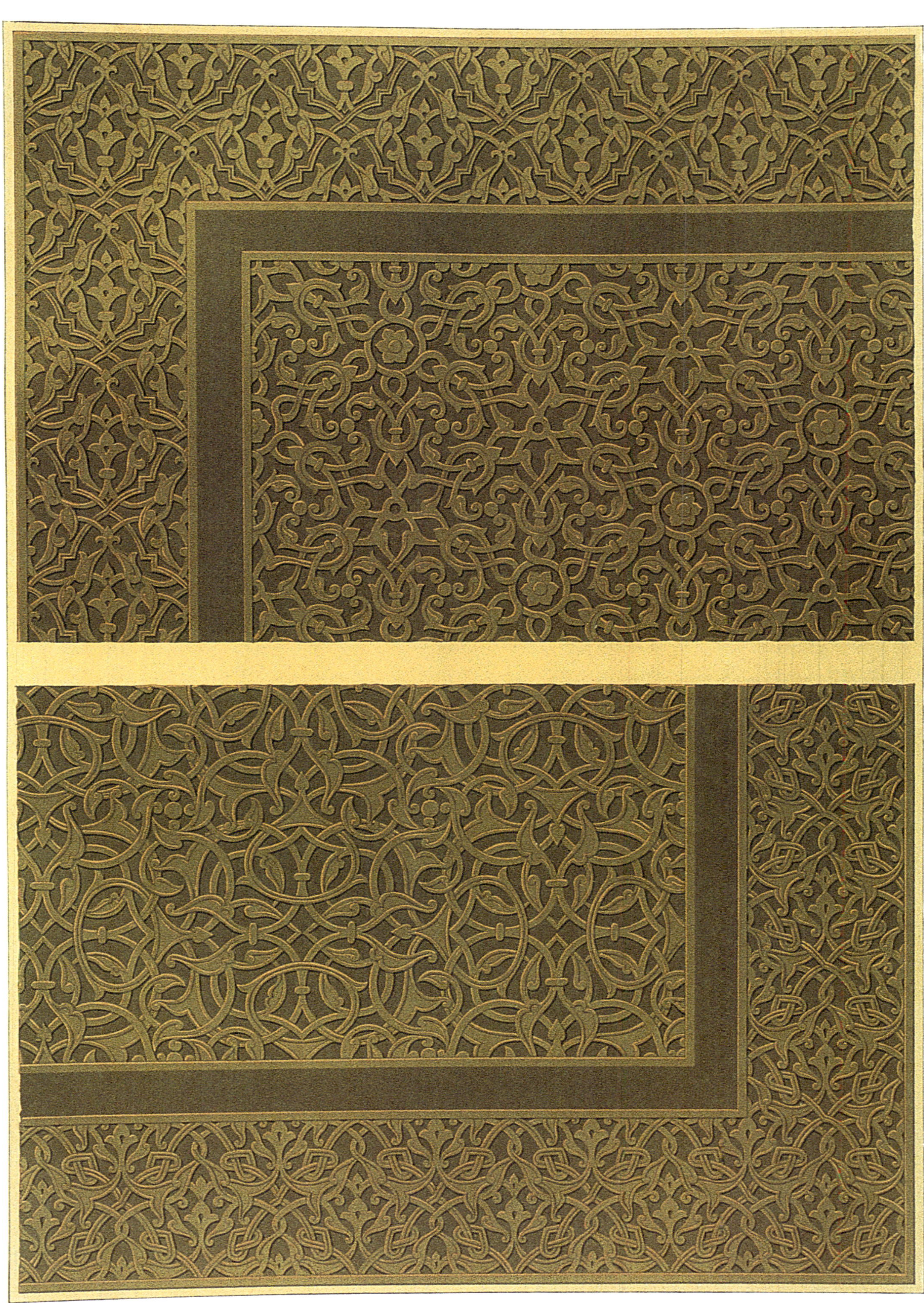

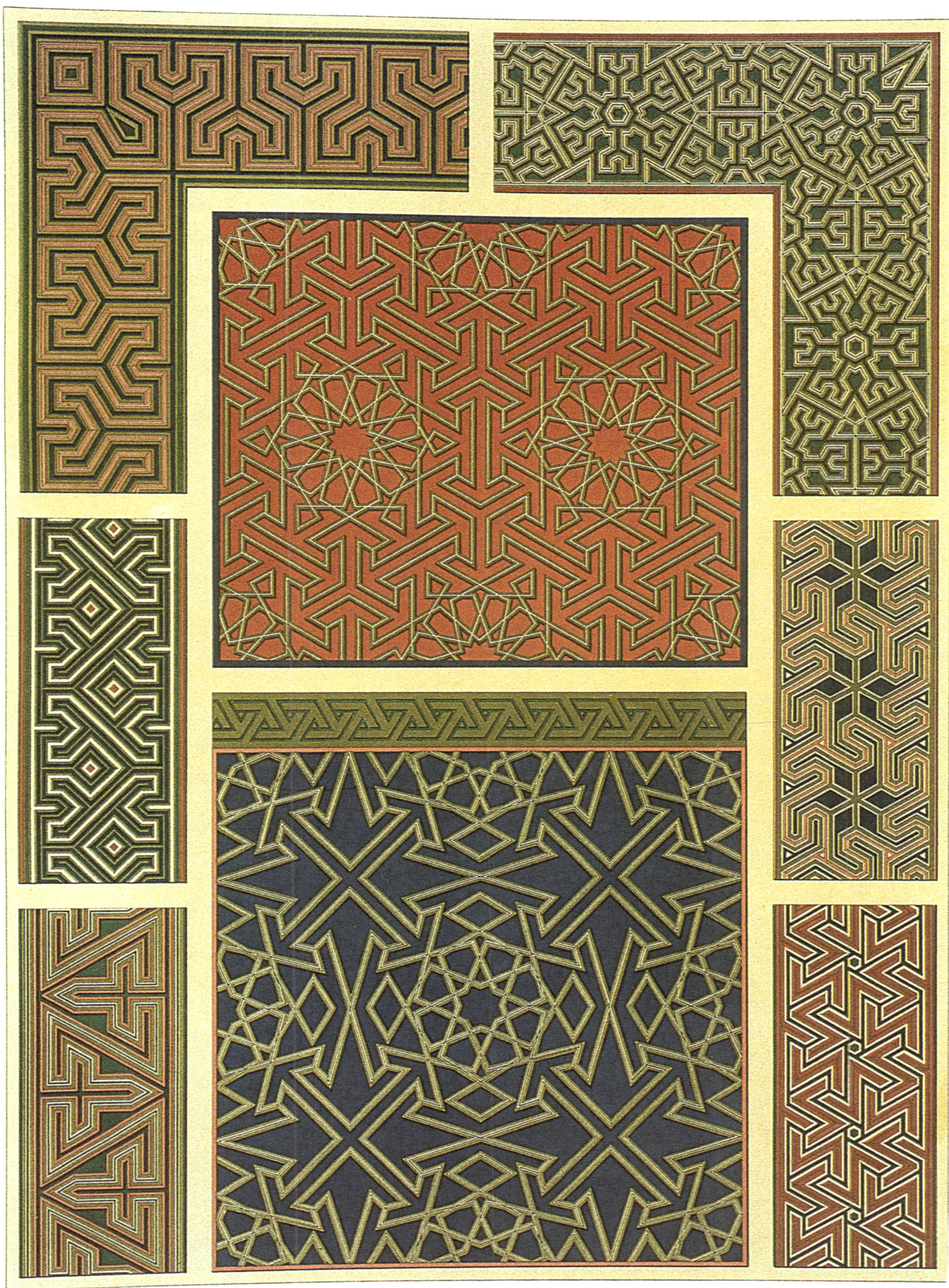

Plates XCV to CVII
DOORS

In order to protect the interior of mosques and to close off certain areas, Islamism imitated both the ancients in their temples and the Christians in their churches by making use of leaves of various forms, numbers and dimensions as a system of door-closing; the front and back sides of these leaves could be, according to circumstances, more or less richly decorated.

To all appearances, the nature or constitution of these leaves was quite varied. Not only of carved, painted and gilded wood, or with partitioned additions, they were also made in metal, that is to say, iron or bronze.

To acknowledge the existence of Arabic door-leaves in bronze is to advance that the smelting of this metal was practiced by the Arab people. The setting of a specific date to the works produced by this industry demonstrates the progression of this art through diverse phases. Indeed, any study destined to seek out, define and to classify such transformations could be considered a sort of history of this branch of technique.

The history of Arabic metallurgy would be quite an interesting subject to pursue, and would doubtless result in the reporting of new ideas and facts of all kinds. These, in order to be suitably treated, would require nothing less than the thorough examination of all metals ever in use throughout the ages.

Those works giving some idea at least of the period of their making provide irrefutable proof that the melting-down of metals, but more especially that of bronze, was practiced and cultivated by the Arabs.

There are few mosques in Cairo whose main doors are not decorated with bronze appliqués, nielloed or damascened in gold or silver. We have represented a large number of varied doors, some dating back to distant times. The most elegant and complete ones are those of the al-Yusufi Mosque, whose damascening has disappeared but of which some traces yet remain. Those of the al-Kanqah Mosque, which we have also reproduced, contain animal figures subsisting in one of the corners; these figures were probably designed by the artist, but they have been obliterated in the other compartments by an over-scrupulous sculptor.

The arrangement and ornamentation of these doors hardly varies. All the elements respect a general given rule as the same constituant parts always take the same place. Apart from the inscriptions, the arrangement is the same as that of certain marble or enamelled tile panels, as well as most tapestries of this period.

The bronze doors that adorn the mosques of Cairo are not cast in solid bronze, but are made of bronze-plated wood. The doors of the Church of St. Sophia, transported from Constantinople to Venice where they decorate the Church of St. Mark, are cast in solid bronze.

In the Mosque of Cordoba, there are five doors either in bronze or plated in bronze; there were formerly twenty-one.

Mosque of Talai' Abu Rizk. Front and Back of the Main Door (Pl. XCV).—This door is of a more recent period than the edifice to which it belongs, and appears to us to date from the restorations done after the earthquake, by order of Sultan Muhammad ibn Qala'un.

The same plate shows the ensemble and details of the double ornamentation of this beautiful door. It is decorated with a cutout and carved bronze covering. The geometric design, instead of being set in relief by a bulge or moulding, appears on the contrary to be intaglio, as if the decoration were incomplete; but there is no trace of the nails which would have been used to secure the beading, and it is certain these were never used. Moreover, the door of the Mosque of al-Maz presents the same singularity. Certain parts of the decoration of the Alhambra are also made of small compartments jutting out from the background in such a way as to render intaglio the entire geometrical pattern.

On the back, the door is decorated with arabesques carved on the five wooden panels framed by a bronze cutout which form the leaf.

Mosque of Sultan Barquq. Bronze Door (Pl. XCVI and XCVII).—Instead of arabesques, this outer door is covered in symmetrical gadroons, to very fine effect; it bears no trace of damascening and everything seems to indicate that the covering was of uniform bronze, with no other effect than the relief itself.

Leaves from the Tomb of Salah Salah al-Din (Pl. XCIX).—The 1867 Great Exhibition in Paris gave quite a false idea of Arabic architecture, and in particular of doors. Apart from those of the Salamlik, decorated with cast bronze appliqués on the entrance to the Sibil Kiahya (Pl. CV), all the wooden doors were poor pastiches. These were made in Cairo by a Piedmontese cabinetmaker who, inspired by the plates of the Alhambra, inserted several authentic panels within arches, frames and small columns in a hybrid fashion, so successful that onlookers and artists alike were fooled.

Arabic doors are much simpler, and their main lines more regular. Those that we publish here, dating from the 14th century, are of a most admirable style. It would be difficult indeed, with so few lines, to produce a finer effect.

This cupboard door leaf, with its ornaments which simulate or bring to mind Kufic characters, and its hinge-cover adorned with arabesques of exquisite taste, is most attractive.

The leaf of a shutter, taken from the same tomb, is less original; but, with its panels adorned with inscriptions, it is as severe as it is elegant.

It would perhaps be interesting to compare these two specimens to the doors of the Mosque of Sisarieh (Pl. CIV), which are more recent but inspired by the same artistic sentiment.

Mosque of Qaytbay. Decoration on Doors and Cupboards (Pl. CI).—These painted ornaments, applied to doors and cupboards and brightened by the use of an egg-white varnish, are handsome and varied. They seem to us to have been reproduced on walls for the most part, so as to make an immense wall decoration up to the mosaic ceiling.

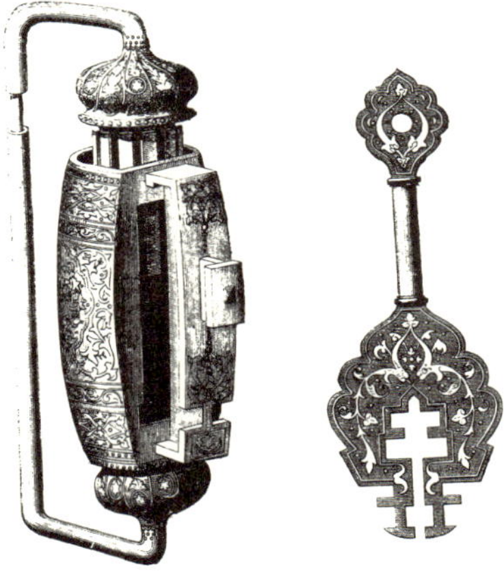

Fig. 1

Doors of the Mosque of Sisarieh (Pl. CIV).—These two doors, decorated with geometrical designs represented by mouldings, count among the most handsome of this period, at the beginning of the decadence introduced by the Turkish conquest.

The interlace on the shutter shows irregular stars although it would have been easy to find one of greater symmetry. The cupboard door leaf is of the monotony so often encountered in modern panelling; but the two borders and the bronze paintings give it some value. The median striking plate received the corresponding element fixed to the other leaf, and the door was locked with a padlock whose long stem completed the effect of a vertical bolt (Fig. 1). This fairly primitive system of locking was succeeded by padlocked bolts.

Doors of houses and furniture were most commonly locked with a wooden lock such as the specimen given on the next page (Fig. 2).

Door of the Sibil of Abd al-Rahman Kiahya (Pl. CV)—This door at the entrance to Djemelieh was broken to pieces by accident during the Cairo revolt under Napoleon. At the signing of peace, the general-in-chief, having engaged himself to repair all damages, wanted to have the door to the fountain restored; finding no one capable of this, Mr Dutertre, the illustrator of the expedition, was put in charge. After having all the pieces gathered up, he assembled them as best he could, and made up an ensemble which was melted-down with broken bits of canons by French soldiers and then put back in place, without any Arabs noticing the transformation; the door

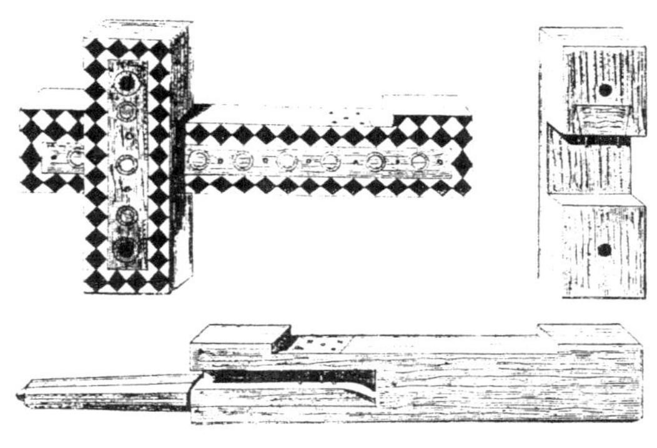

Fig. 2

has passed for the original ever since. Our drawing teacher, Mr Dutertre, told us this factual account himself, as did J.-J. Marcel.

Details of a Door of the Mosque of al-Khanqah (Pl. CVI).—The bronze appliqués of this door seem to us to have been designed by a Christian architect; but, upon the fitting, the design underwent serious modifications. The part entrusted to the Coptic artist was carried out accordingly with the animals drawn by the architect, while the other parts, entrusted to the burin and file of the Muslim artists, were obliterated so as not to violate the laws of orthodoxy, much to the detriment of the thought lying behind the work.

Arabic Door knockers (Pl. CVII).—No. 1 on Plate CVII shows the most common form of bronze knockers found on house doors in Algiers. This is certainly the most finished of all those we have seen. It is enriched with a line of engraving which underlies and brings out the the details of the ornamentation. The shadowed part, on which stands out the rosette, is a round of red morocco leather whose colour matches the bronze patina marvellously. This detail, quite minimal in appearance, reveals the highly developed feeling for colour of the Arabic artist.

No. 2, also copied in Algiers from the door of a house neighbouring the Casbah, is of remarkable taste, and must come from an edifice of the finest era of Arabic art. It resembles sculpted ornaments on an ancient door of the Mahoud-al-Gaouly Mosque in Cairo which dates from the beginning of the 14th century.

The two other knockers have been copied on doors of private dwellings in the Teyloun Mosque quarter in Cairo. They belong to the finest period of Arabic art and go back to the 15th century.

It is quite rare to encounter door knockers of such pure taste, for most are very simple and rarely adorned, with the exception of those on doors of mosques; these are always linked to the ensemble of bronze arabesques decorating the entire surface of the door, over both leaves. Those that we publish here are affixed to unassuming doors, whose only ornamentation consists of a vast cartouche in the best Arab style, generally in red on a green background, and portraying the sacremental phrase: *Bism'Illah.*—"In the name of Allah", or a short inscription of the nature: "Allah is the best protector."

MOSQUE OF TALAI' ABU RIZK

Plate XCV

Front and Back of the Main Door (12th century)

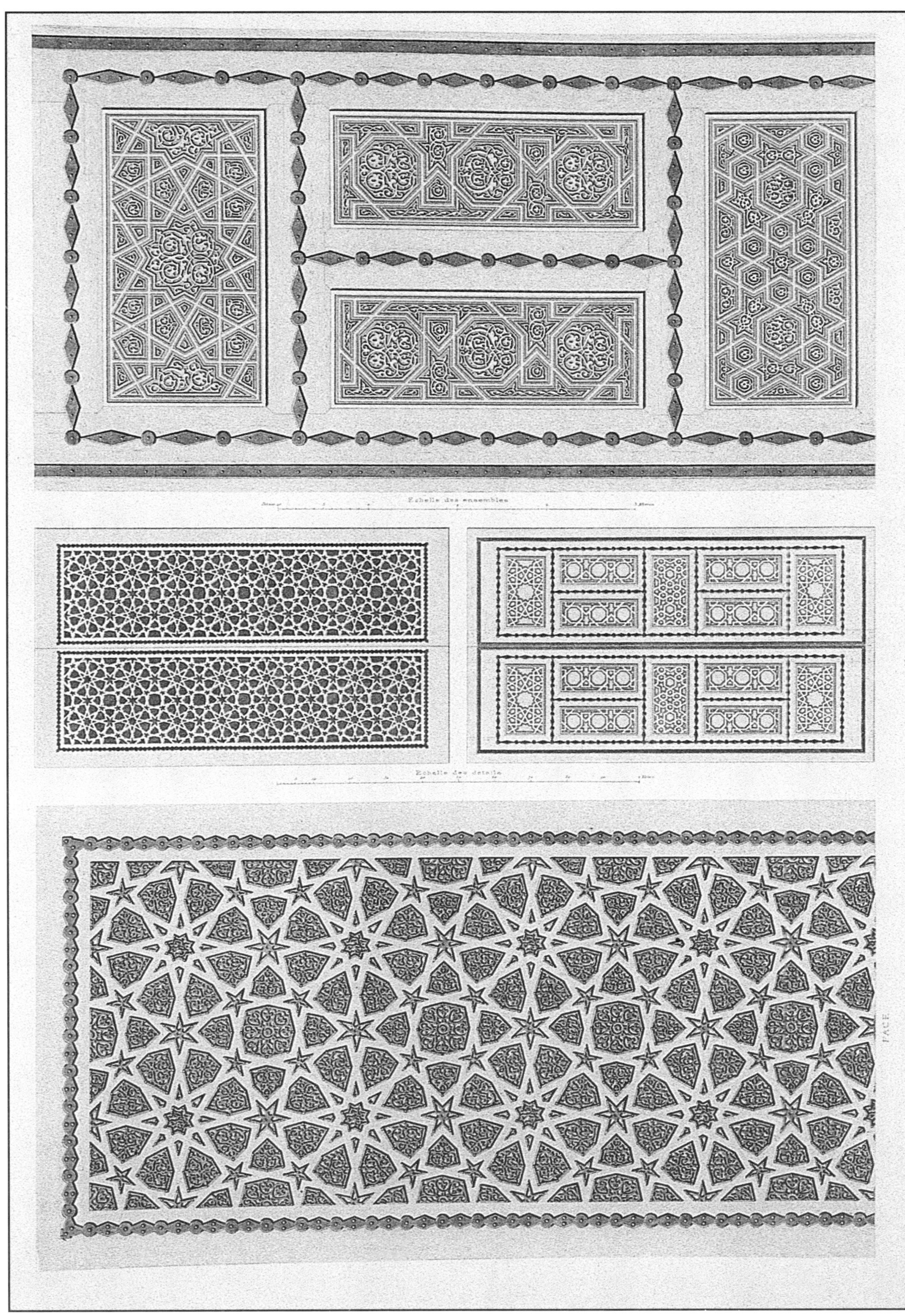

Plate XCVI

MOSQUE OF SULTAN BARQUQ

Outer Door (14th century)

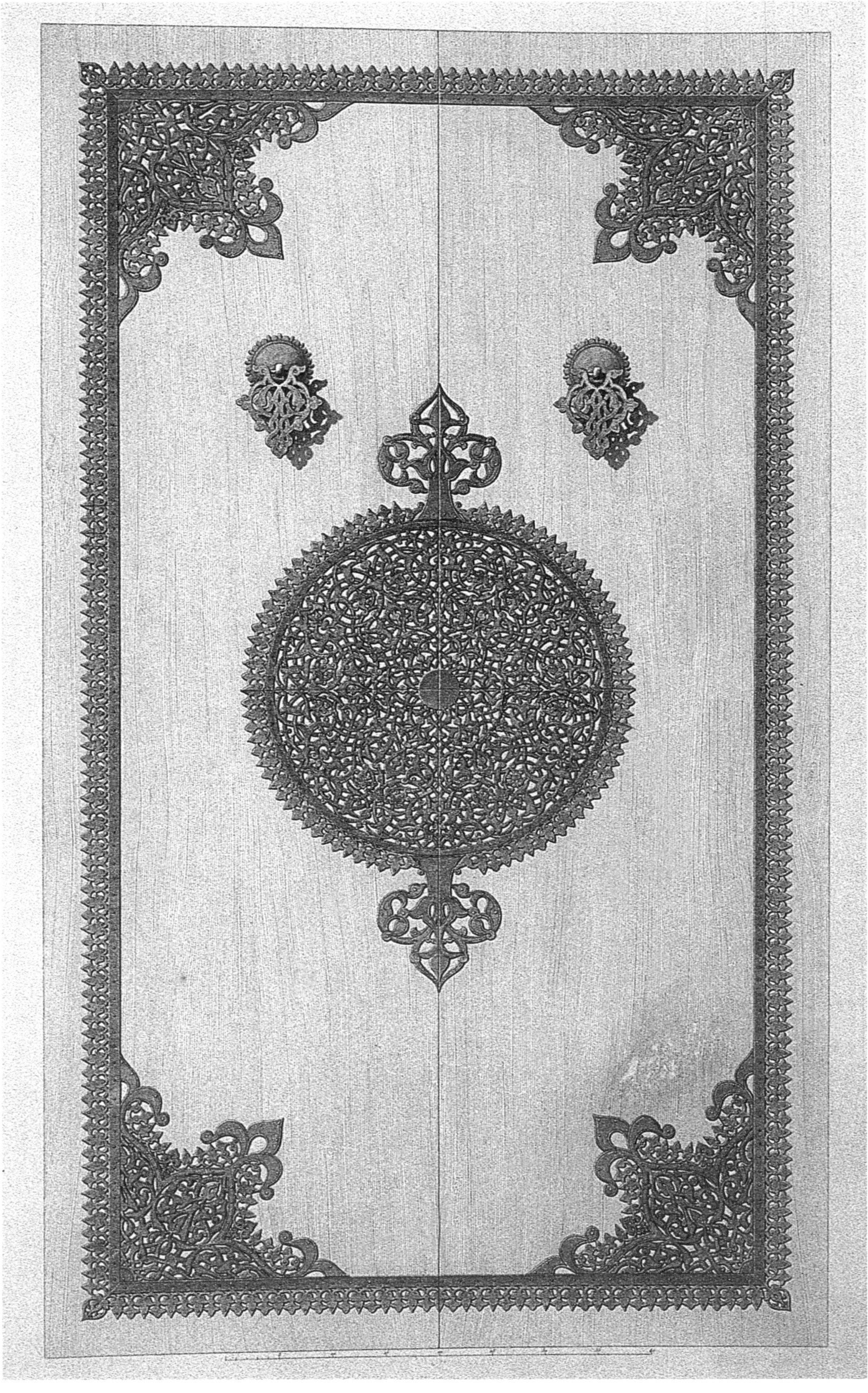

TWO BRONZE DOORS

Mosque of Barquq (14th century). Sidi Yusuf House (17th century)

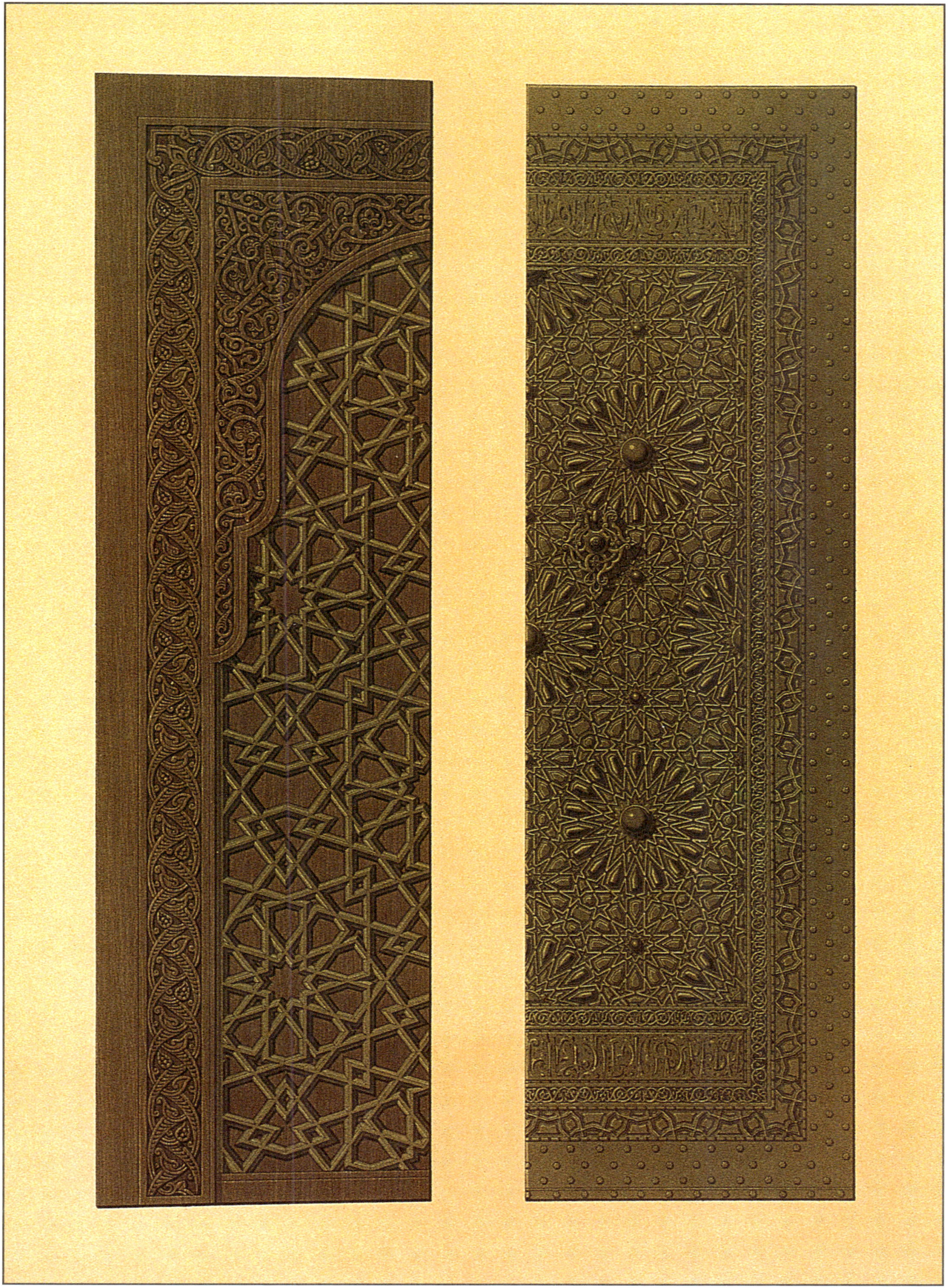

Plate XCVIII

MOSQUE OF OLGAY AL-YUSUFI

Exterior Portal (14th century)

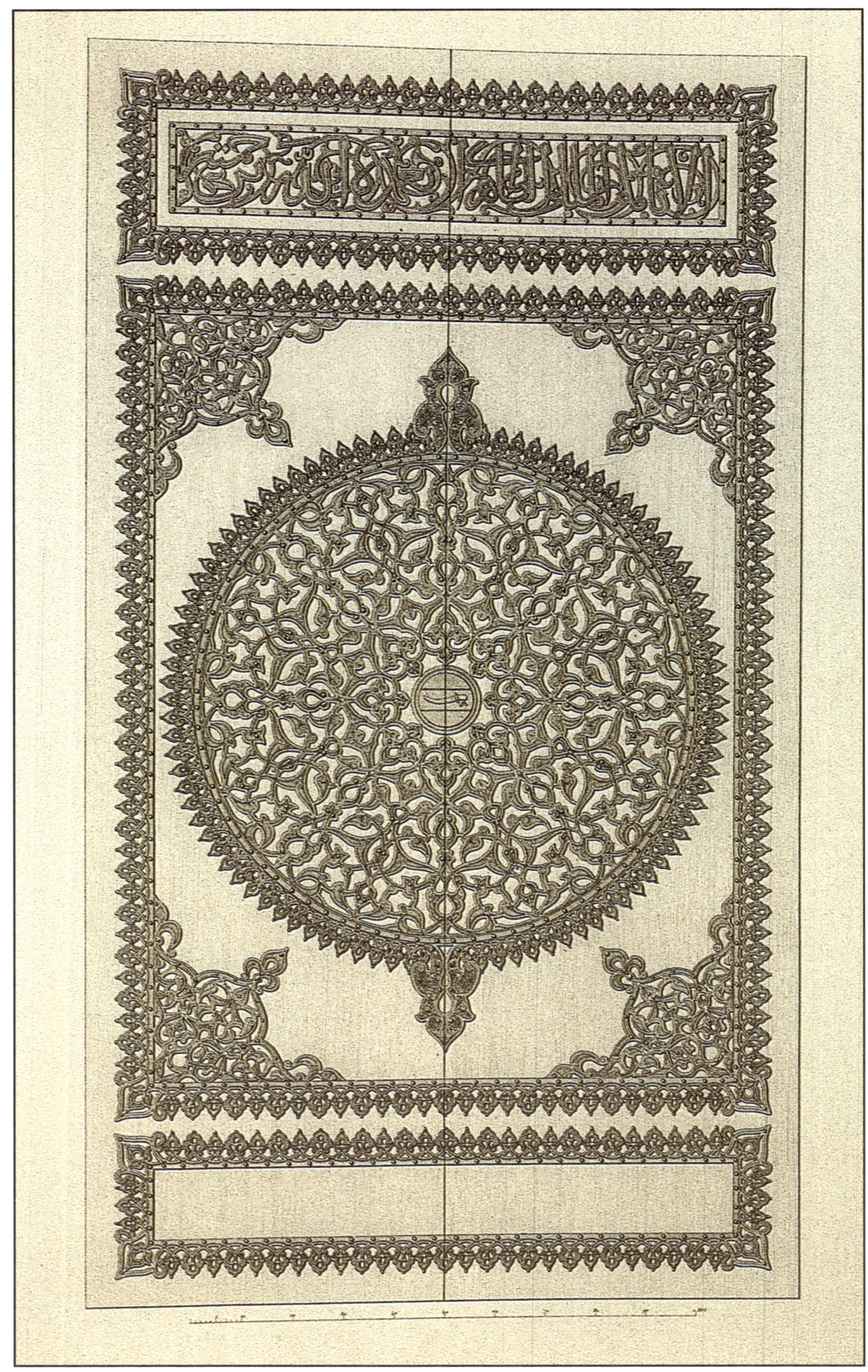

TOMB OF SALAH SALAH AL-DIN

Cupboard Door Leaf. Leaf of a Window Shutter (14th century)

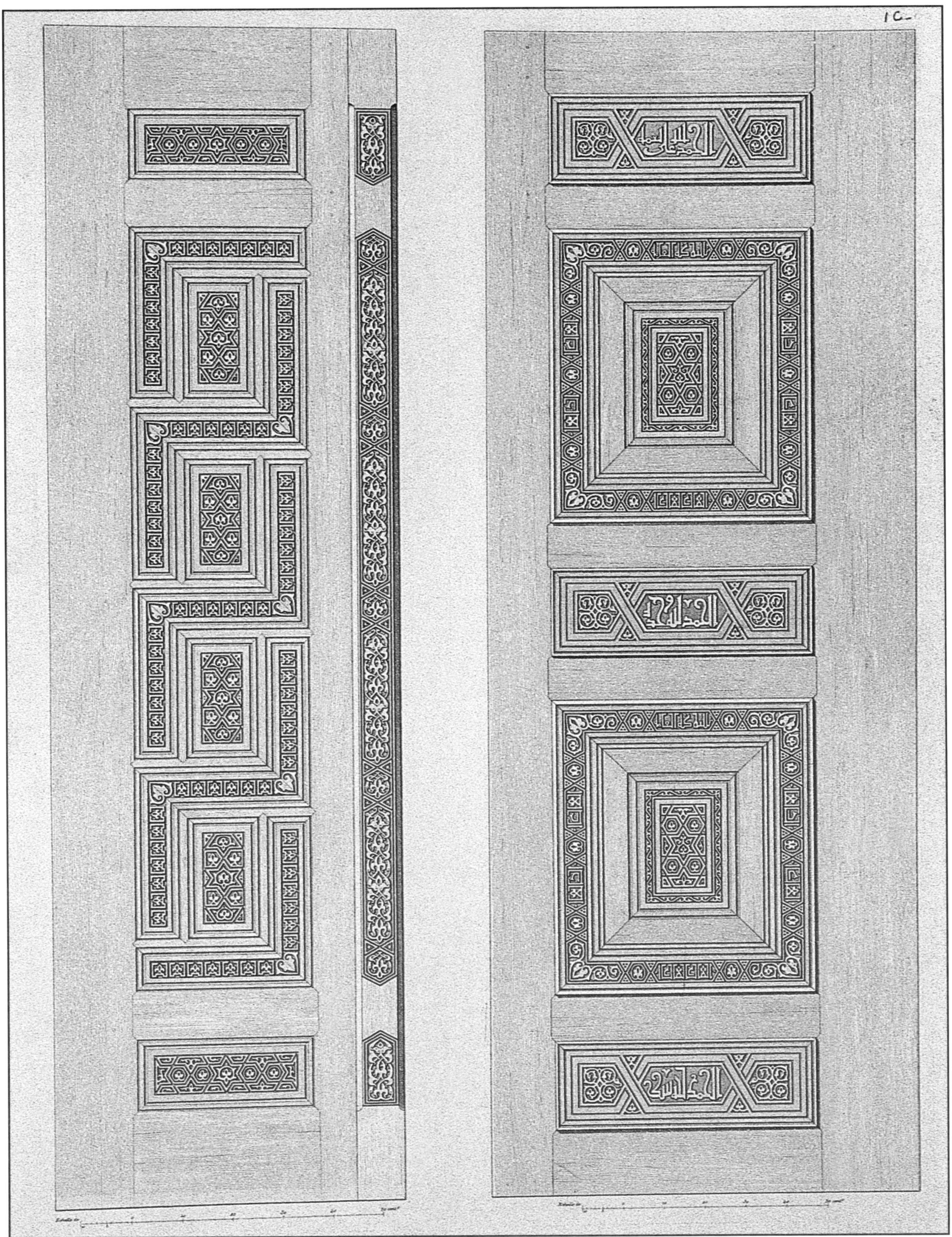

Plate C

MOSQUE OF SIDI YUSUF AL-MAZ

Main Exterior Portal (15th century)

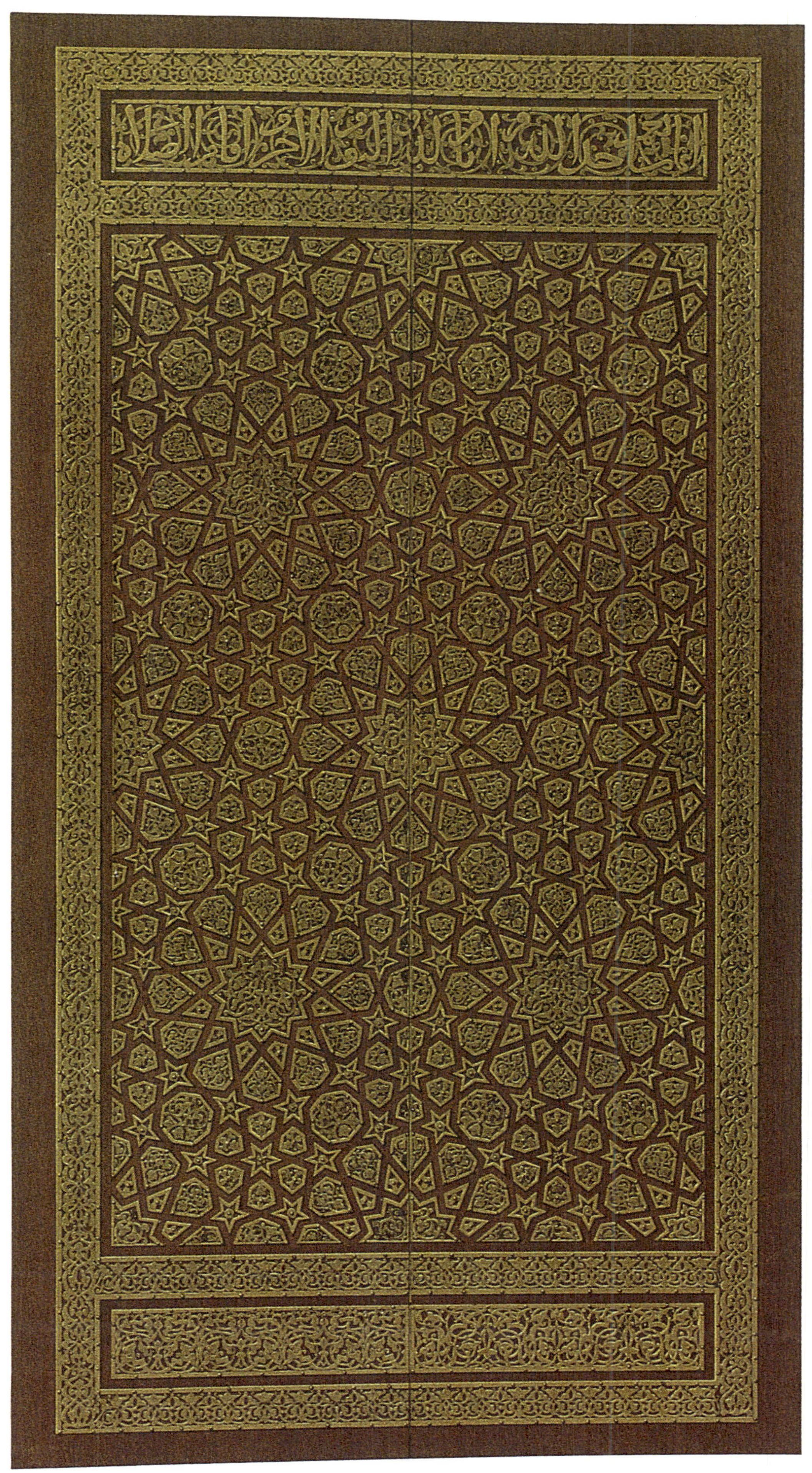

MOSQUE OF QAYTBAY

Plate CI

Decoration on Doors and Cupboards (15th century)

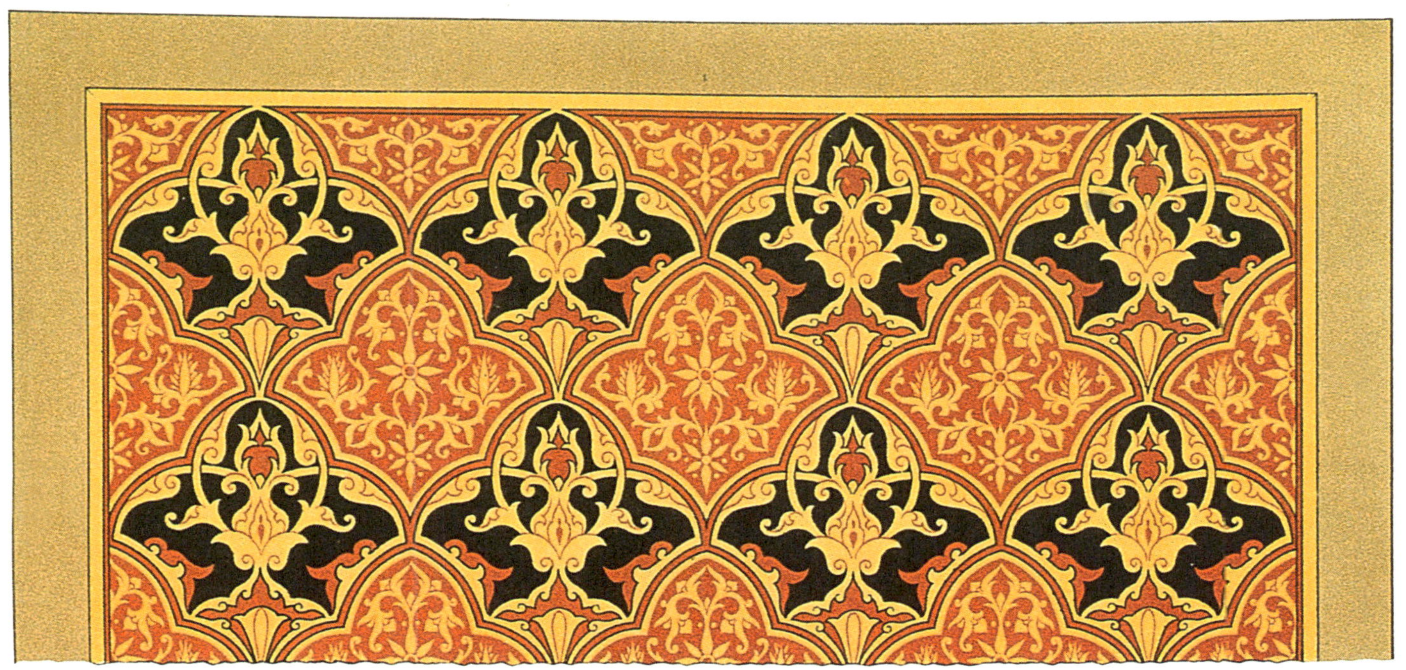

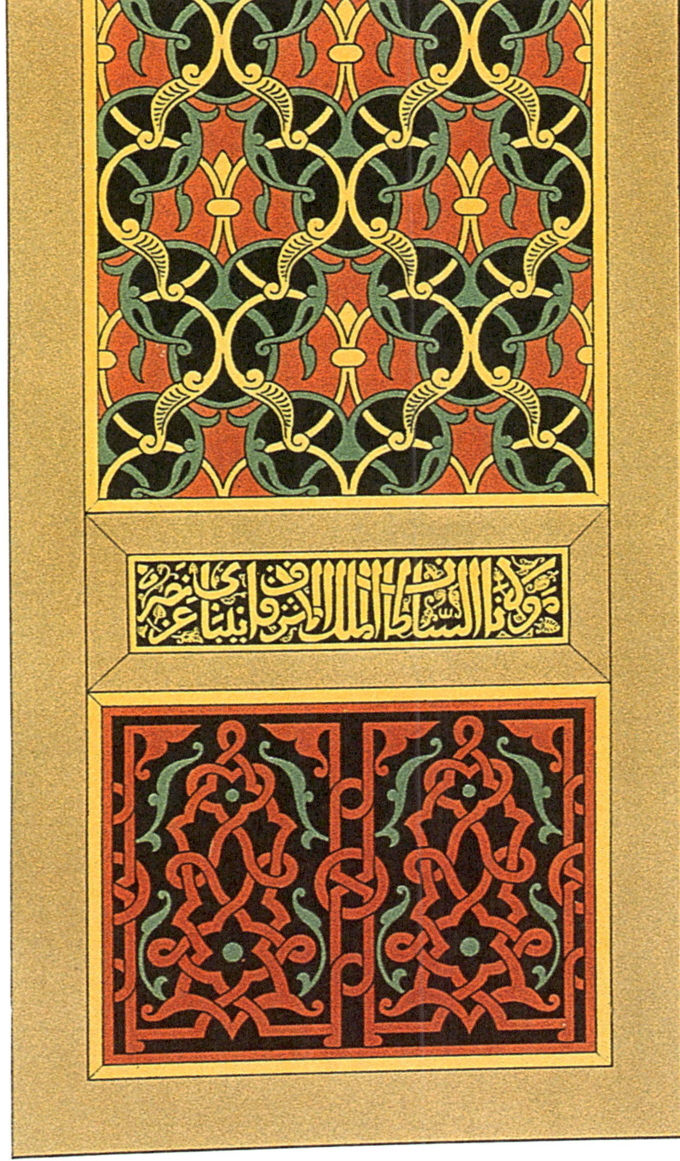

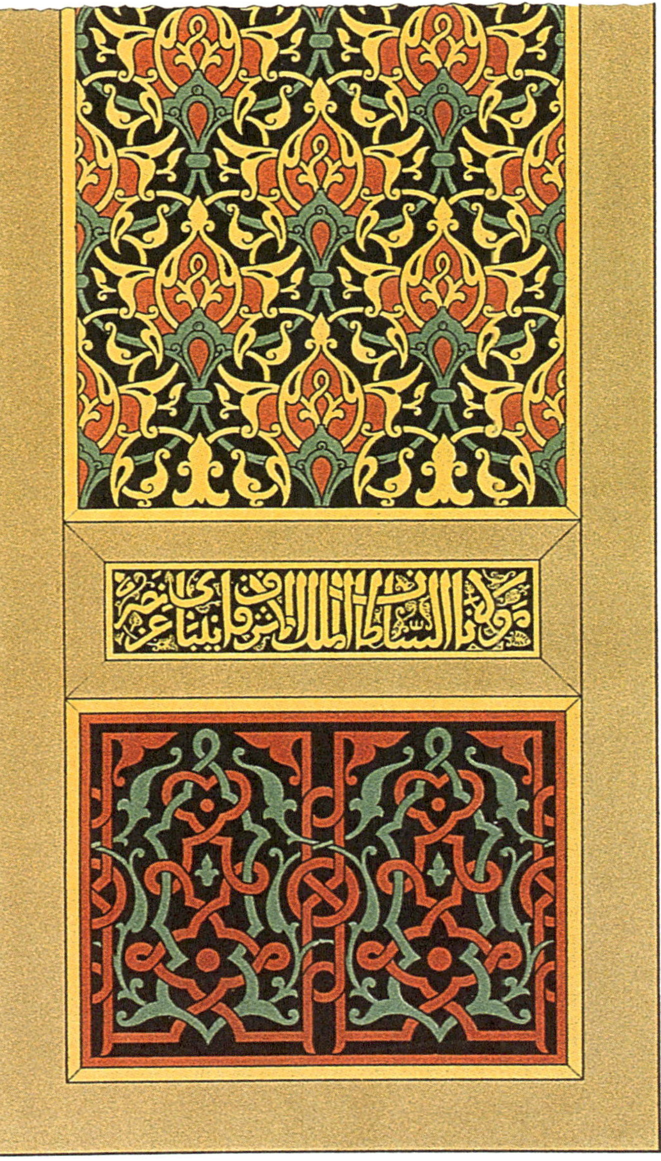

TOMB OF SULTAN QANSU AL-GHURI

Inner Door (16th century)

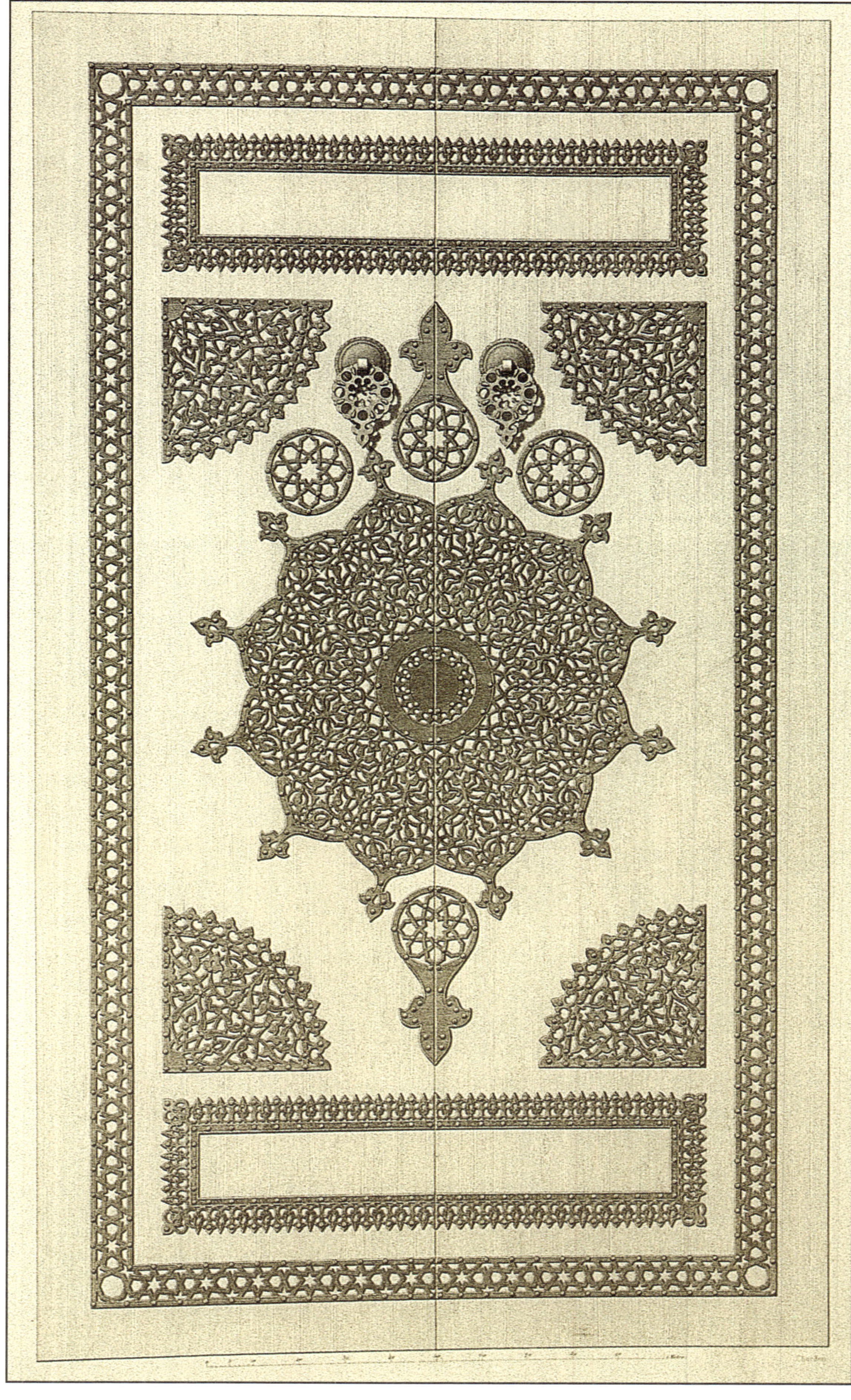

BAIT AL-AMIR

Plate CIII

Small Door with Details (16th century)

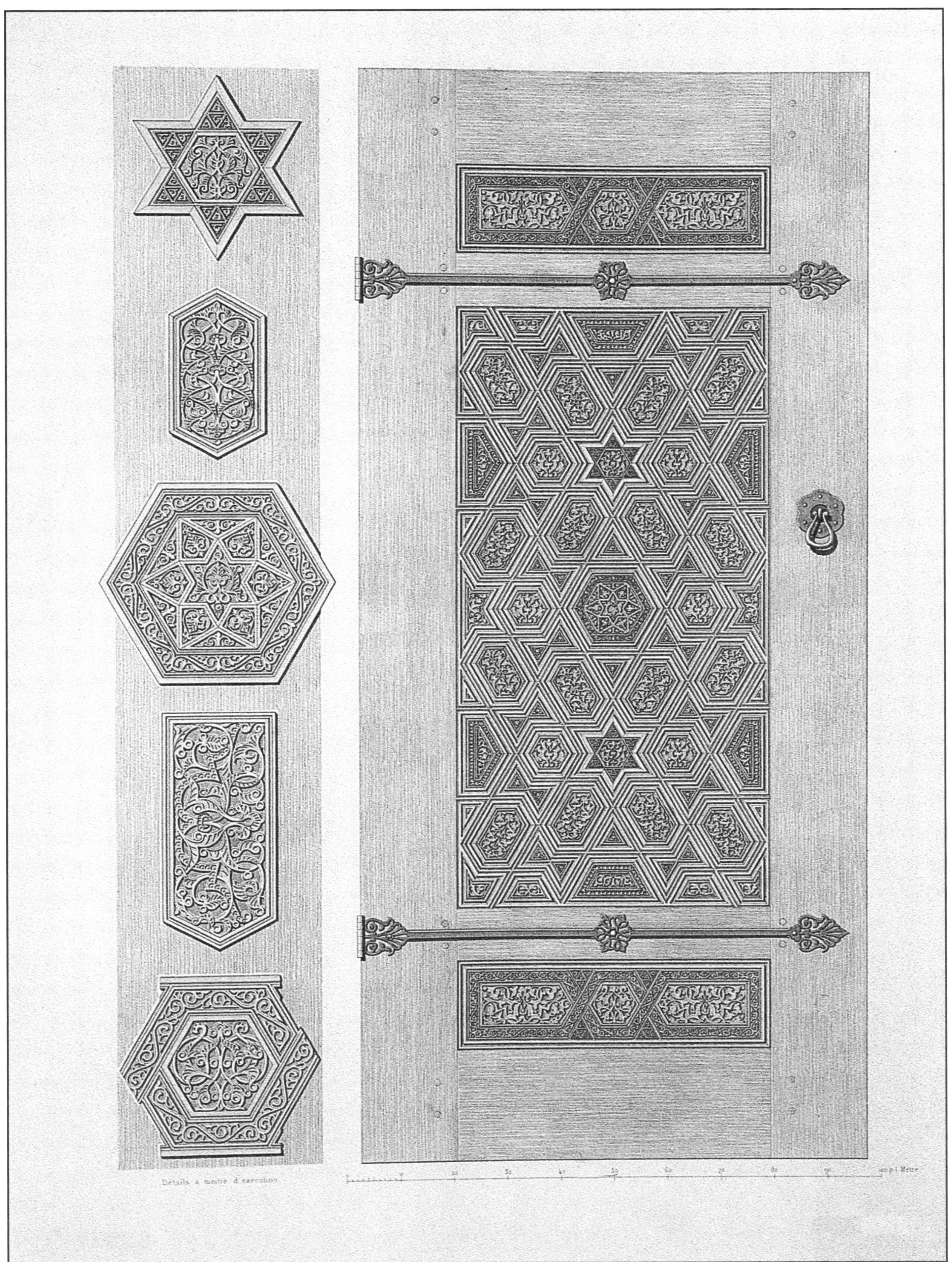

MOSQUE OF SISARIEH

Leaf of a Window Shutter. Cupboard Doorleaf. (16th century)

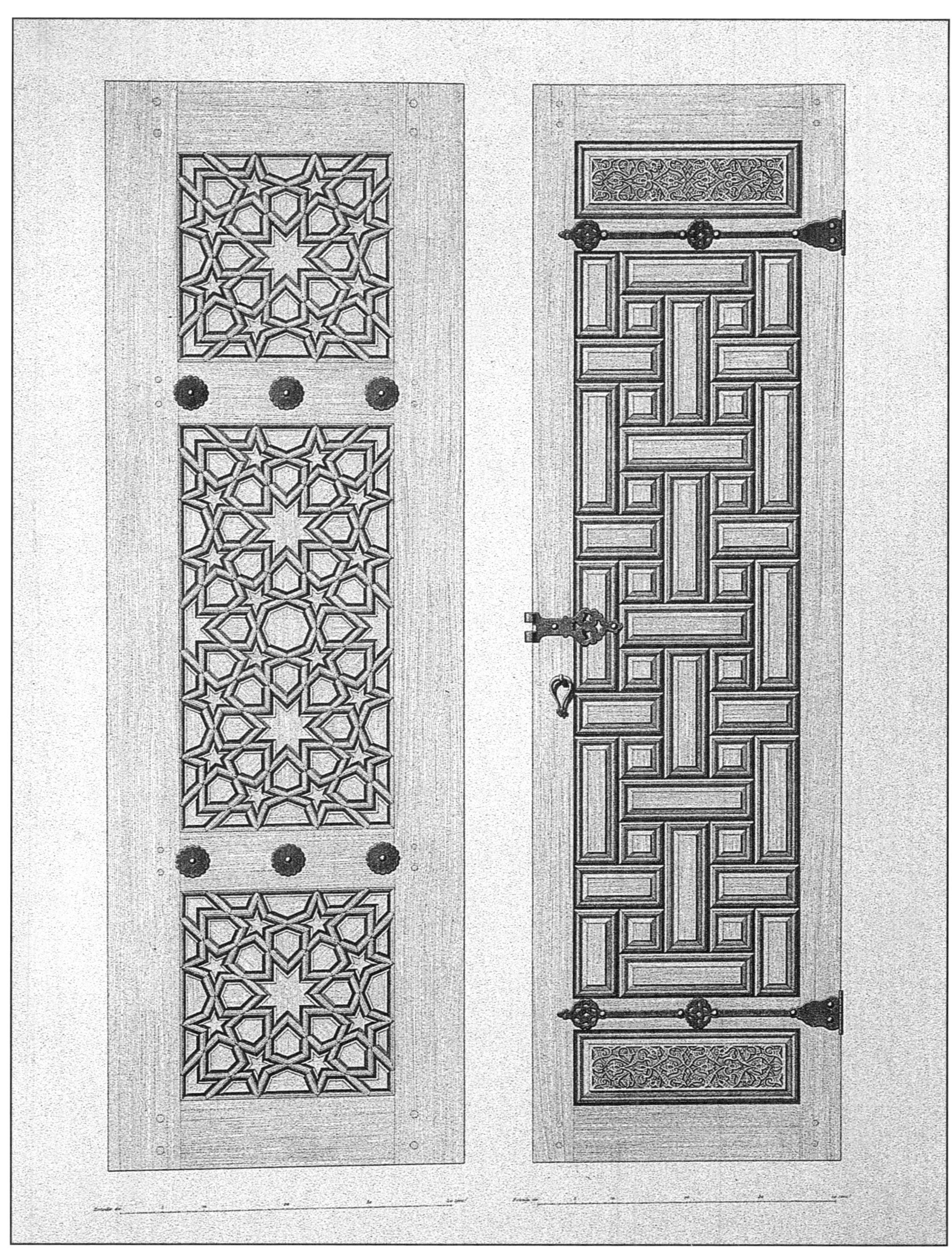

DOOR OF THE SIBIL OF ABD AL-RAHMAN KIAHYA
(18th century)

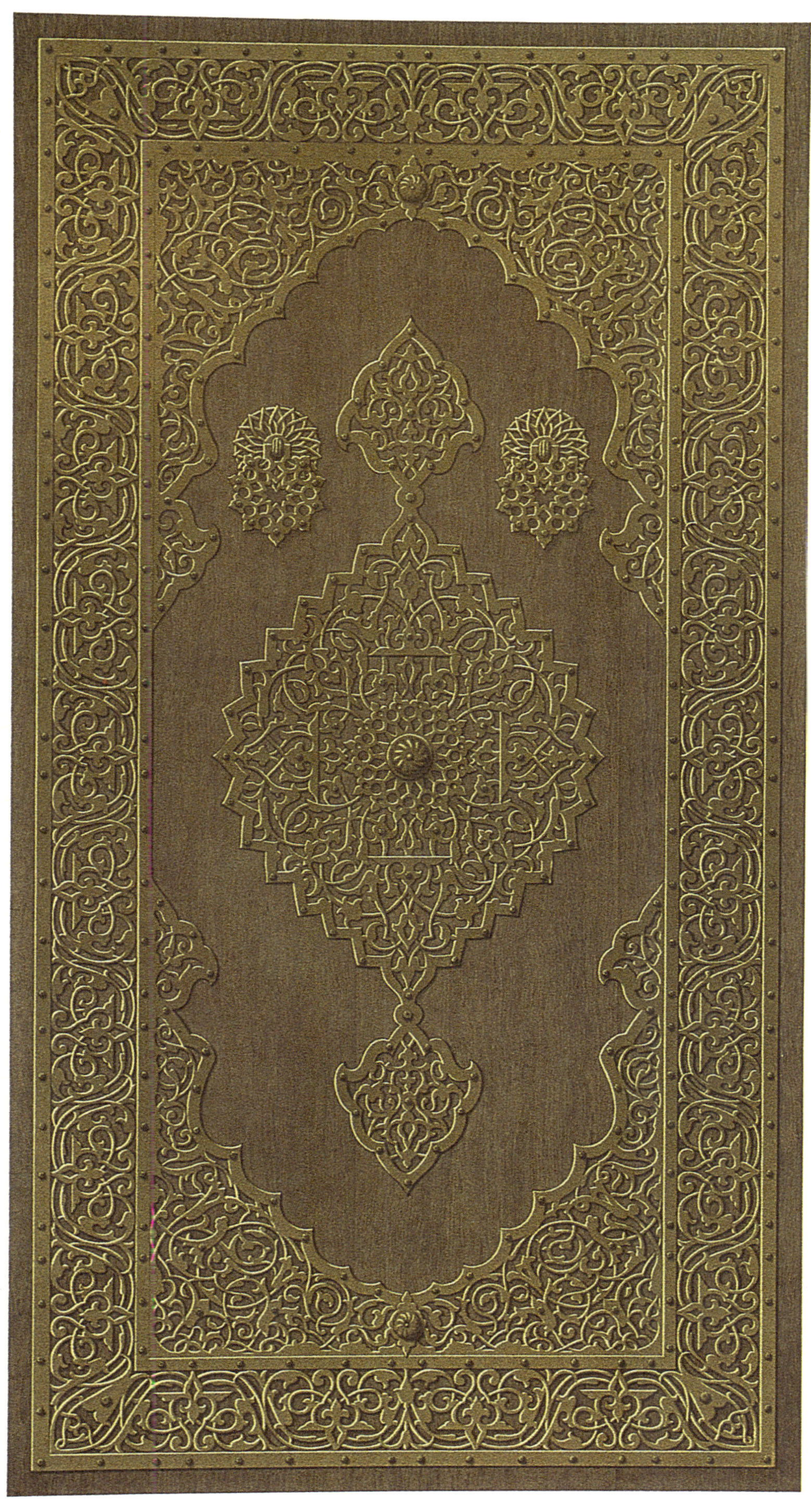

Plate CVI

MOSQUE OF AL-KHANQAH

Details of a Door (18th century)

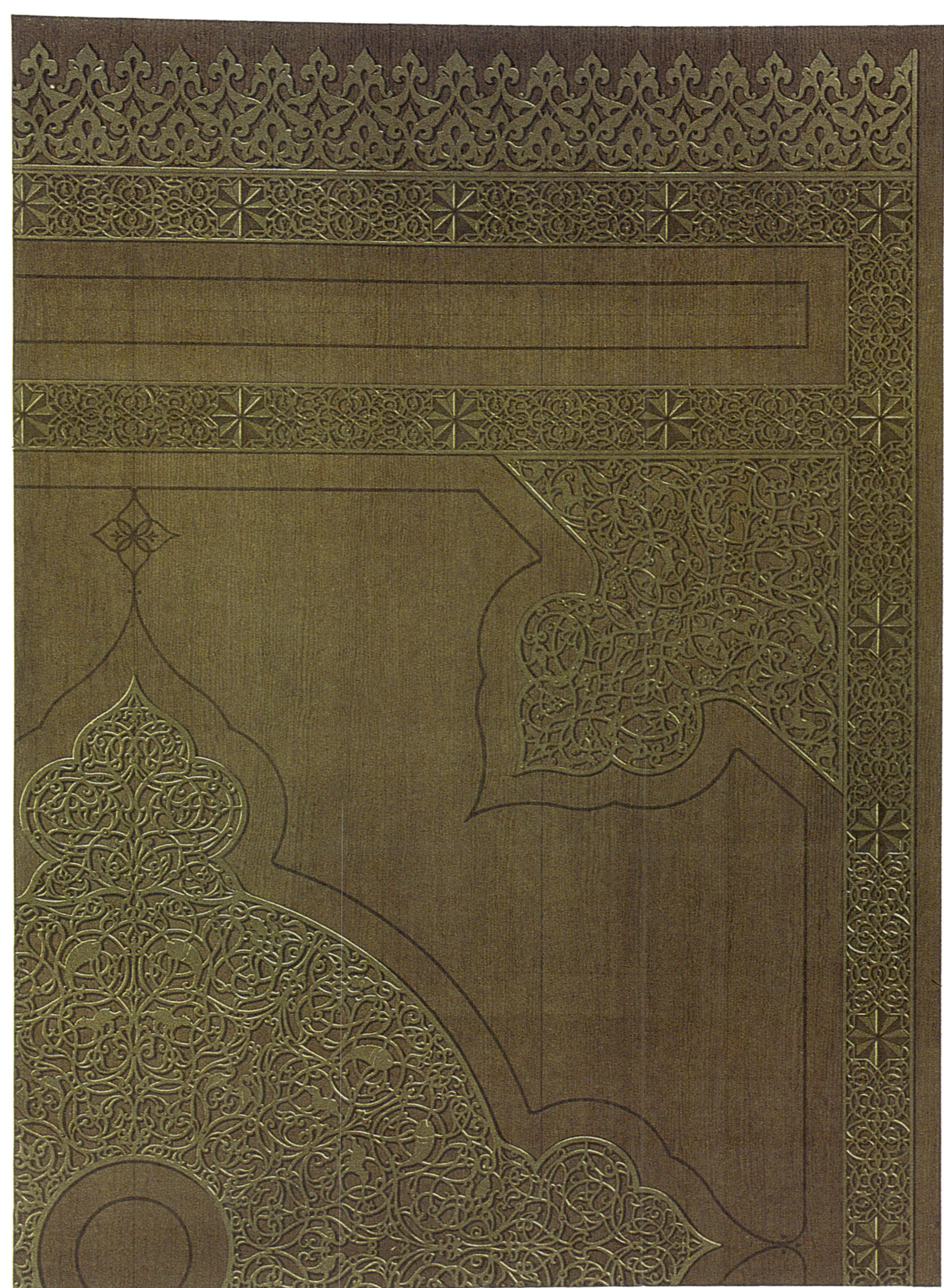

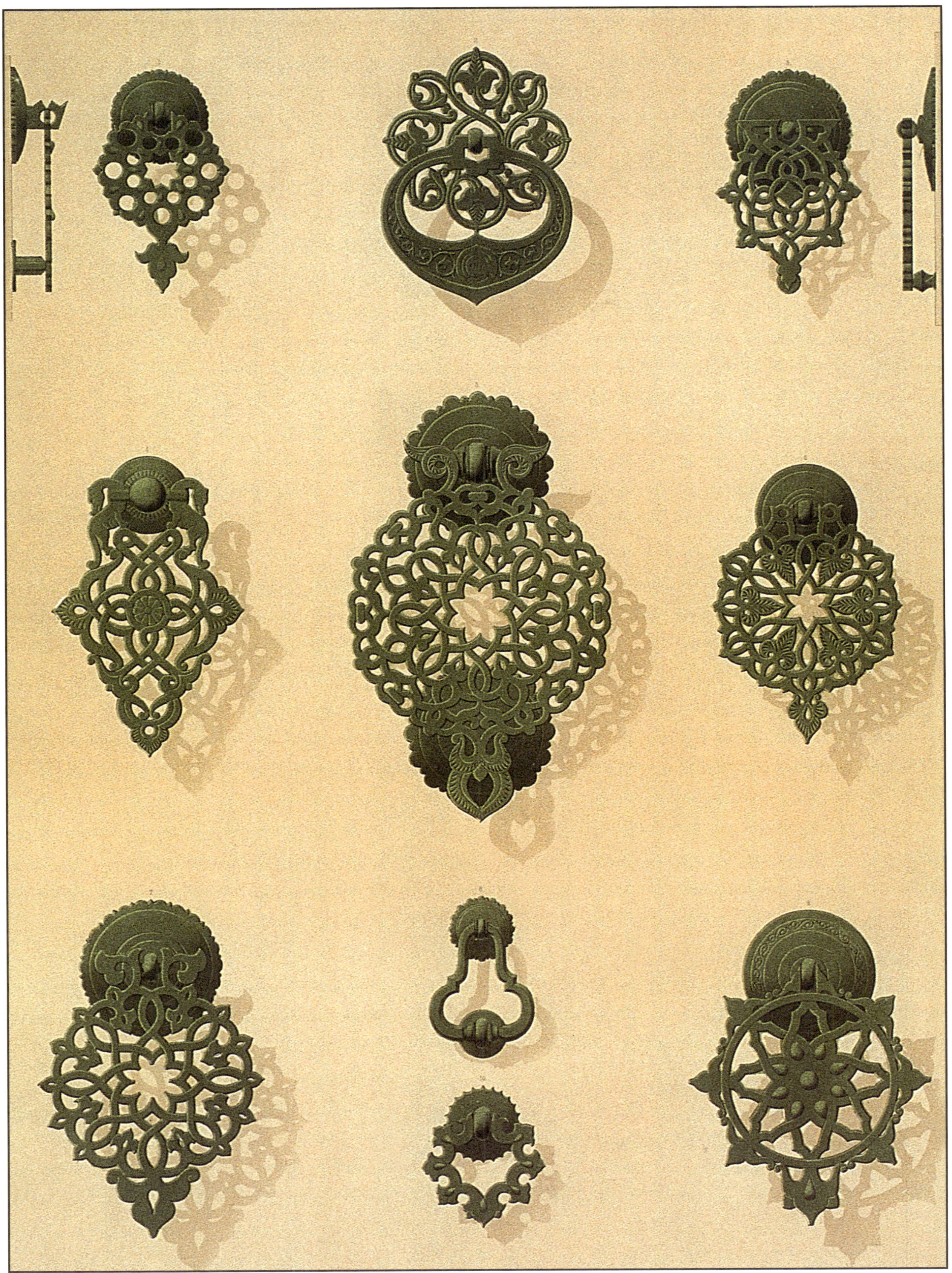

Plates CVIII to CXXXIII
PORCELAIN TILES AND IMITATIONS

Mihrab of the Mosque of Sheikhun. Tilework (Pl. CVIII and CIX).—These facing tiles certainly come from Andalusia because they resemble on all points tiles still produced in this province of Spain; these decorated the mihrab of the Mosque of Sheikhun, where they seem to have been laid during the period of construction of the mosque.

Panel representing the Ka'aba and its Surroundings (Pl. CXI).—This panel comes from the Diwan, or reception hall of the palace of Kourchyd-Pasha in Esbekieh; a similar one exists in the Sibil Kiahya and several others in various places in Cairo. As one of every faithful Muslim's favourite subjects, it is not unusual to see the Ka'aba represented on carpets and on Persian porcelain tiles, accompanied by Persian verse. This panel with a different frame is also found in the sanctuary of the Tekieh of the dervishes.

Cathedral Mosque of Qus. Tilework decoration (Pl. CXIV and CXV).—Plate CXIV represents a tiled tympanum framing a small tile of isolated arabesques. These enamelled tiles were, we believe, manufactured in Syria, where they were produced in great number.

Qus, the former capital of Thebaid, was, it is known, the sojourn of caliphs during the reign of the Ayyubites.

This porcelain decoration, of a rare simplicity, is especially remarkable for its frieze adorned with Kufic characters of a most beautiful style, running around the interior of the mosque. We have chosen the sacramental exhortation which prefaces every chapter of the Koran, in order to compare it better with others of the same tenor and which differ at each period.

Wall tiles from the Mosque of Ibrahim Agha (Pl. CXIX to CXXII).—These wall tiles were part of two magnificent pseudo-mihrabs, that we have reproduced in full on a much reduced scale and with a much more realistic tone.

Wall tiles from the Tekieh of the Dervishes (Pl. CXXIII to CXXV).—In Cairo, near the French quarter or *Moski*, there is a tekieh, or convent of dervishes, faced from one end to the other with glazed tiles pillaged or stolen from all quarters of the city; they carpet as best they can the outside walls and transform the small edifice into a ceramic museum remarkable for certain samples unfindable elsewhere today. We have examined its walls in depth and feel that there would be sufficient material to warrant the publication of a special album.

Glazed Tiles (Pl. CXXVII).—We have given them this name because the tiles may be laid either on the tip of the chevron or in the middle of it, forming two different patterns as seen in this edifice.

Tilework, Sibil of Abd al-Rahman Kiahya (Pl. CXXIX).—This tile covering decorates the spandrels of the three main ground floor windows of the cistern of Abd al-Rahman Kiahya. The tiles visible below are used as fillers on both sides.

To the left, above a tiled pseudo-mihrab, a tile painting portraying the Ka'aba and various stations of pilgrimage.

Study of Leaves and Floral Ornaments Painted on Tile (Pl. CXXX).—These leaves and fleurons being of a remarkable beauty and an admirable boldness, we have reproduced them in full, so as to allow a finer appreciation of the beauty of the small pseudo-mihrab represented in one of our plates.

Oval Tile Panel (Pl. CXXXI).—This unremarkable panel is of a heavy style, probably Turkish, taken from Asia Minor. We give it here only to show how the bareness of walls was adorned.

Tilework of a Hanut (Pl. CXXXII).—Hanuts are small edifices, composed of pools or basins used to wash and to enshroud the dead before carrying them to the cemetery. One of the most handsome hanuts is the one in annex to the sepulchral Mosque of Qaytbay; it is unfortunately half-destroyed today.

Door Crowning on the Door of the Minbar in the Mosque of Sisarieh (Pl. CXXXIII).—The Mosque of Sisarieh or the mosque of Geneyd, situated in the citadel of Cairo, dates from the year 933 (1526); it was built under the orders of Soliman-Pasha by Turkish workmen, and offers little of note apart from various details of ornamentation which seem to date from an earlier period.

The one featured in this plate is painted, probably to imitate enamelled tile facing, on the door of a small minbar in white marble. Never finished, its rather rough arabesques testify to the decadence of art under the Ottomans.

MIHRAB OF THE MOSQUE OF SHEIKHUN
Tilework (14th century)

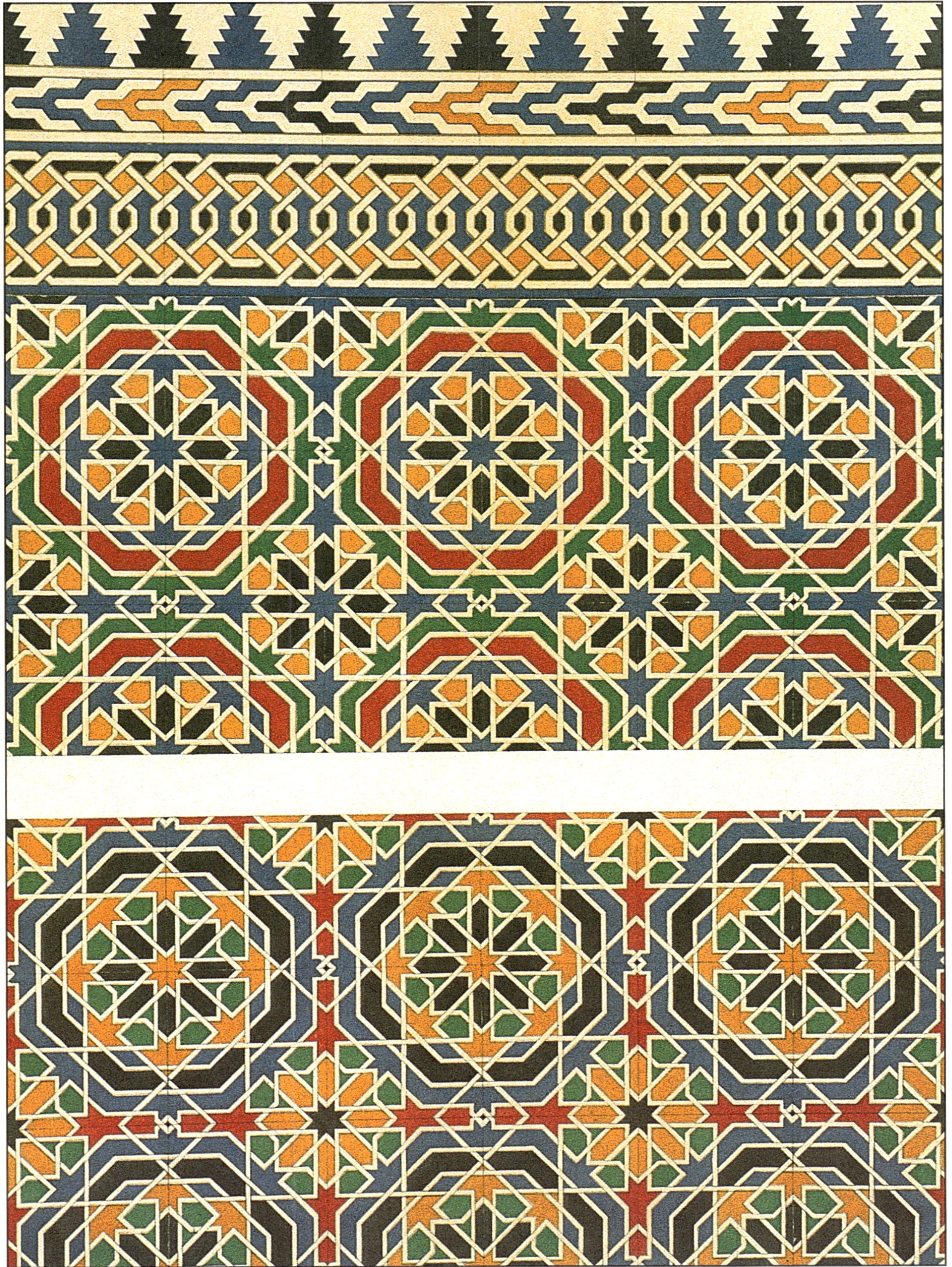

Plate CIX

MIHRAB OF THE MOSQUE OF SHEIKHUN

Tilework (14th century)

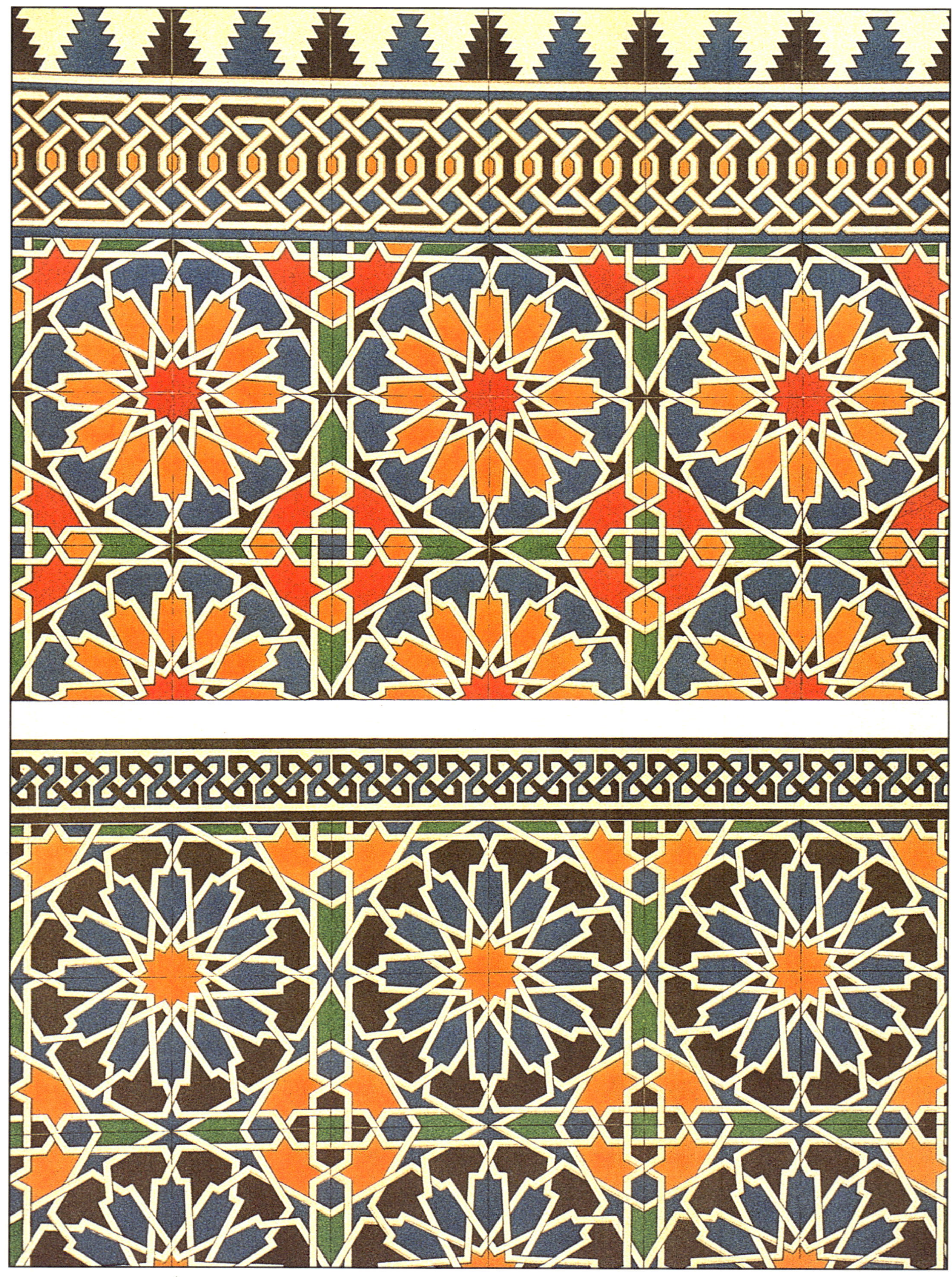

TILEWORK

Borders (16th century)

TILEWORK

Panel Representing the Ka'aba and its Surroundings (16th century)

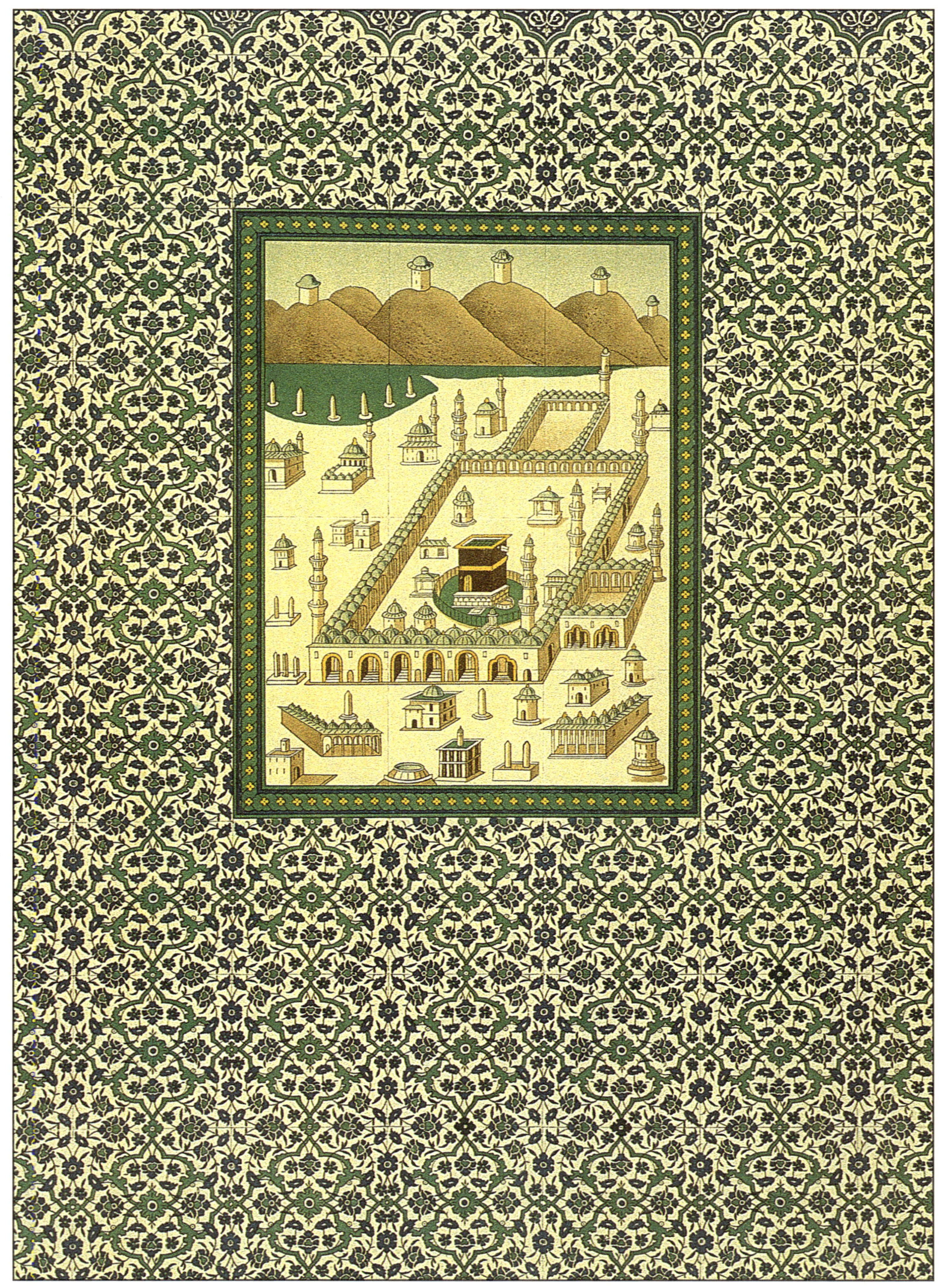

KIOSK TILEWORK
(16th century)

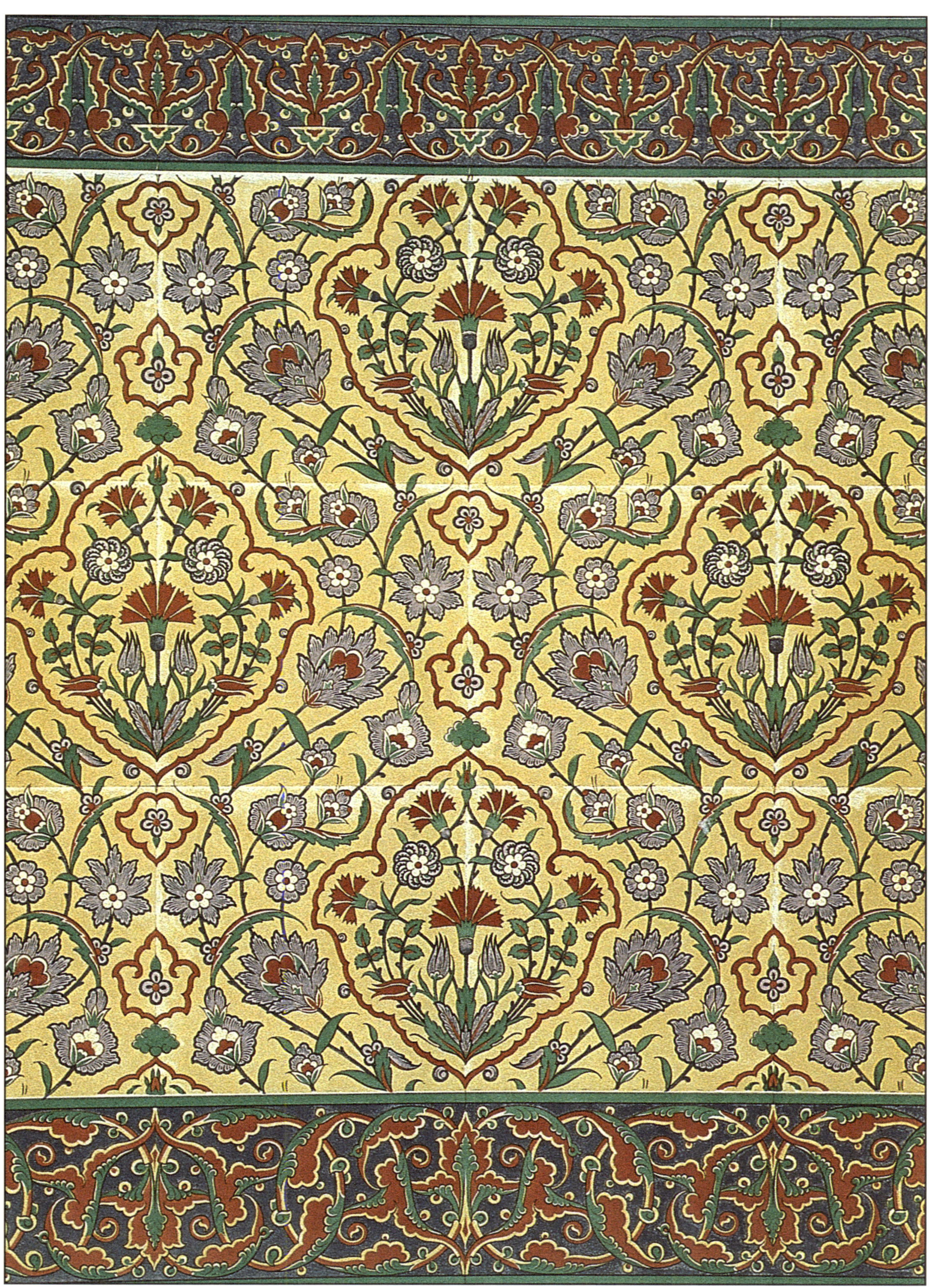

KIOSK OF MAHU BEY

Tilework (16th century)

CATHEDRAL MOSQUE OF QUS

Tympanum and Corner Piece in Tilework (16th century)

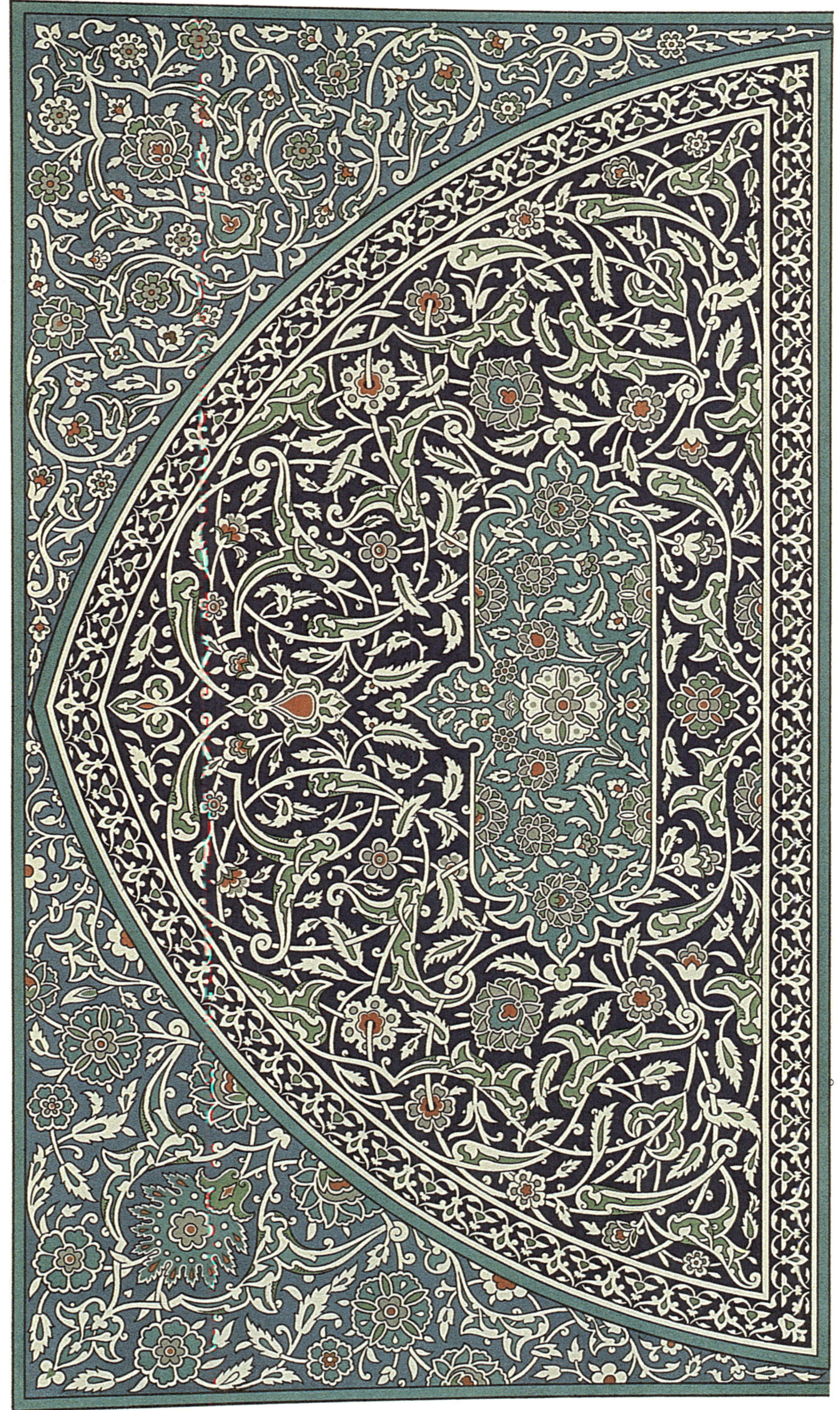

CATHEDRAL MOSQUE OF QUS

Tilework (16th century)

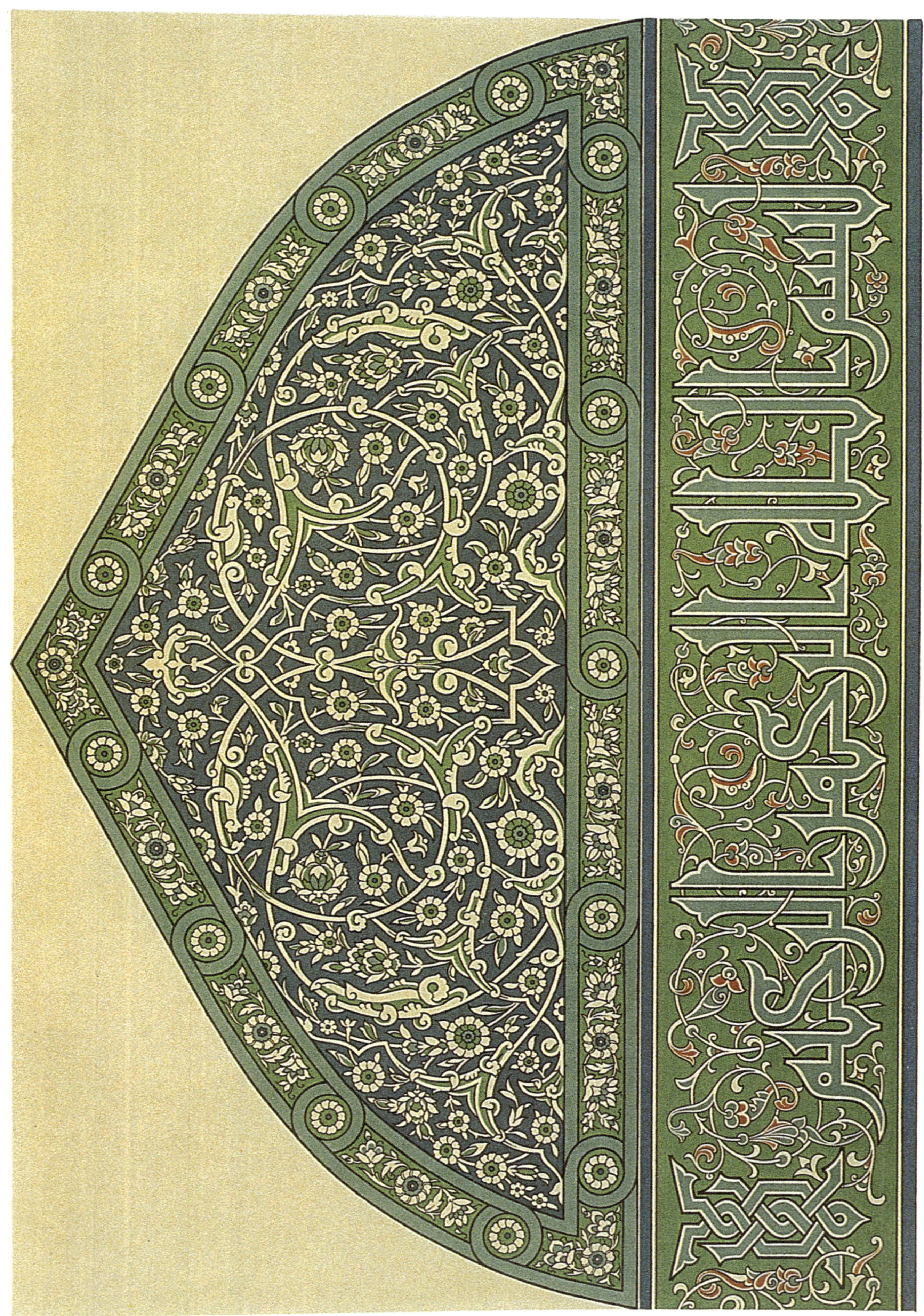

PALACE OF ISMAIL BEY

Tilework (16th century)

QASR RODUAN

Tilework (16th century)

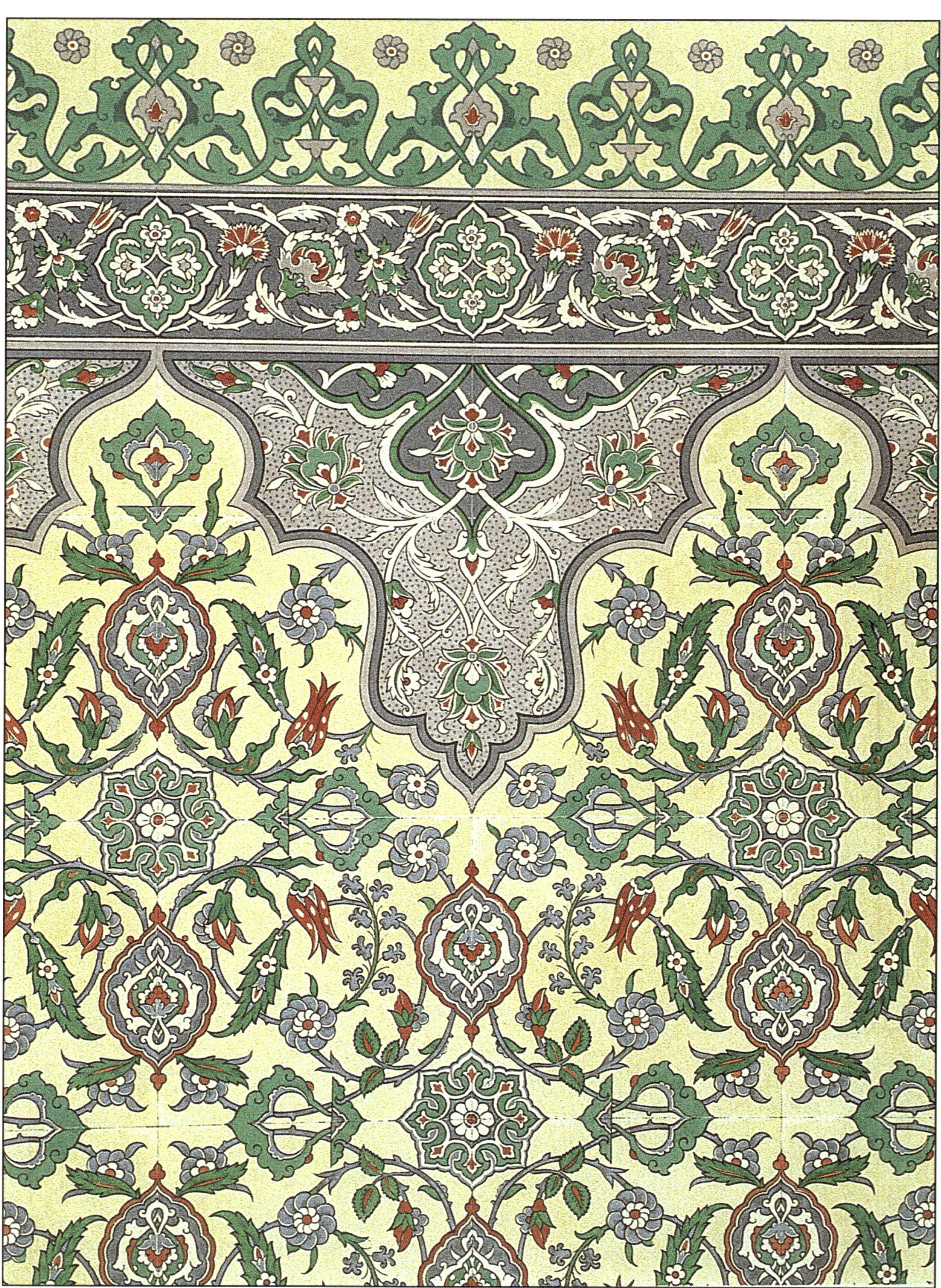

QASR RODUAN
Tilework (16th century)

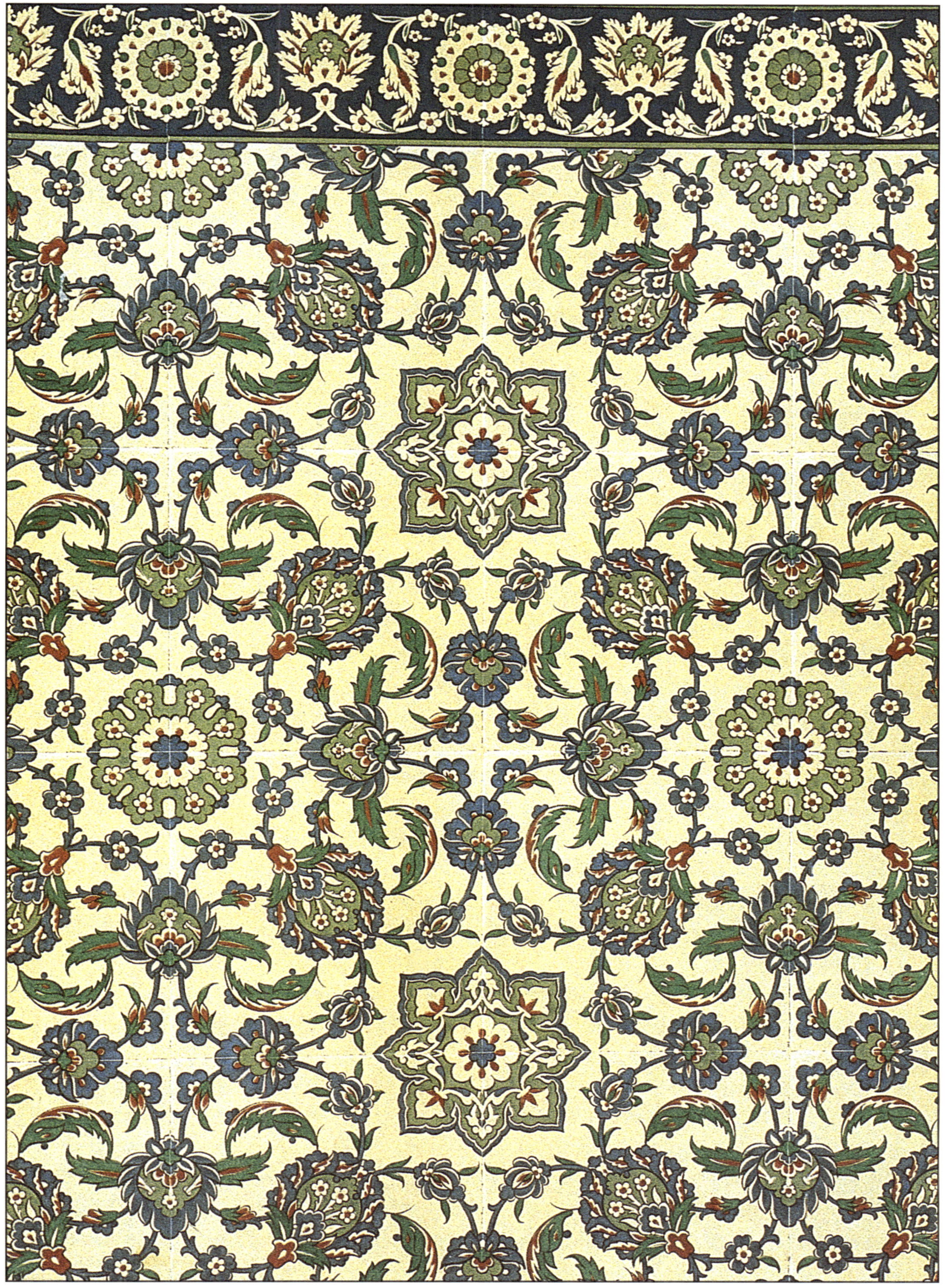

MOSQUE OF IBRAHIM AGHA

Tilework (16th century)

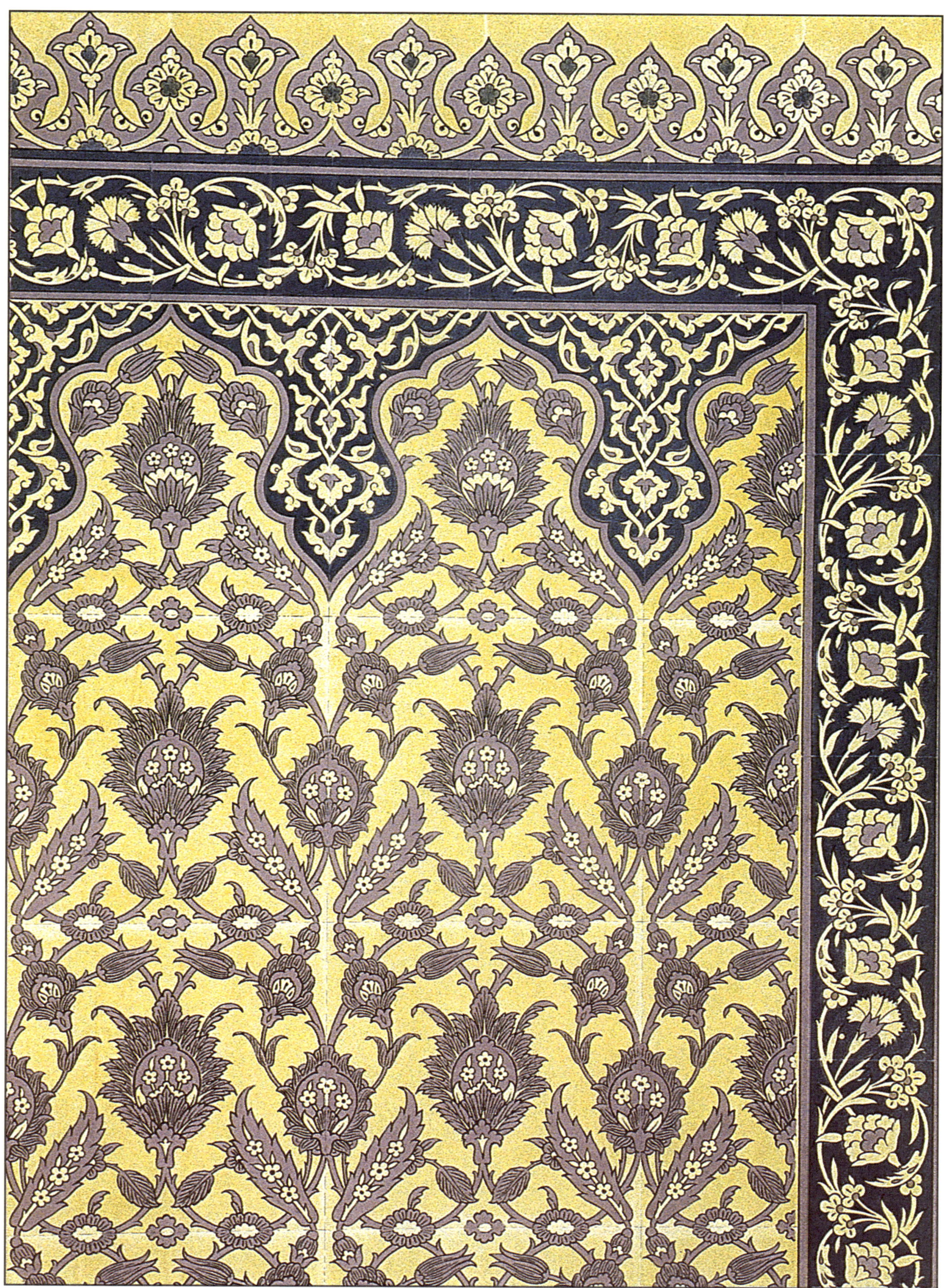

MOSQUE OF IBRAHIM AGHA

Tilework of Pseudo-Mihrab (16th century)

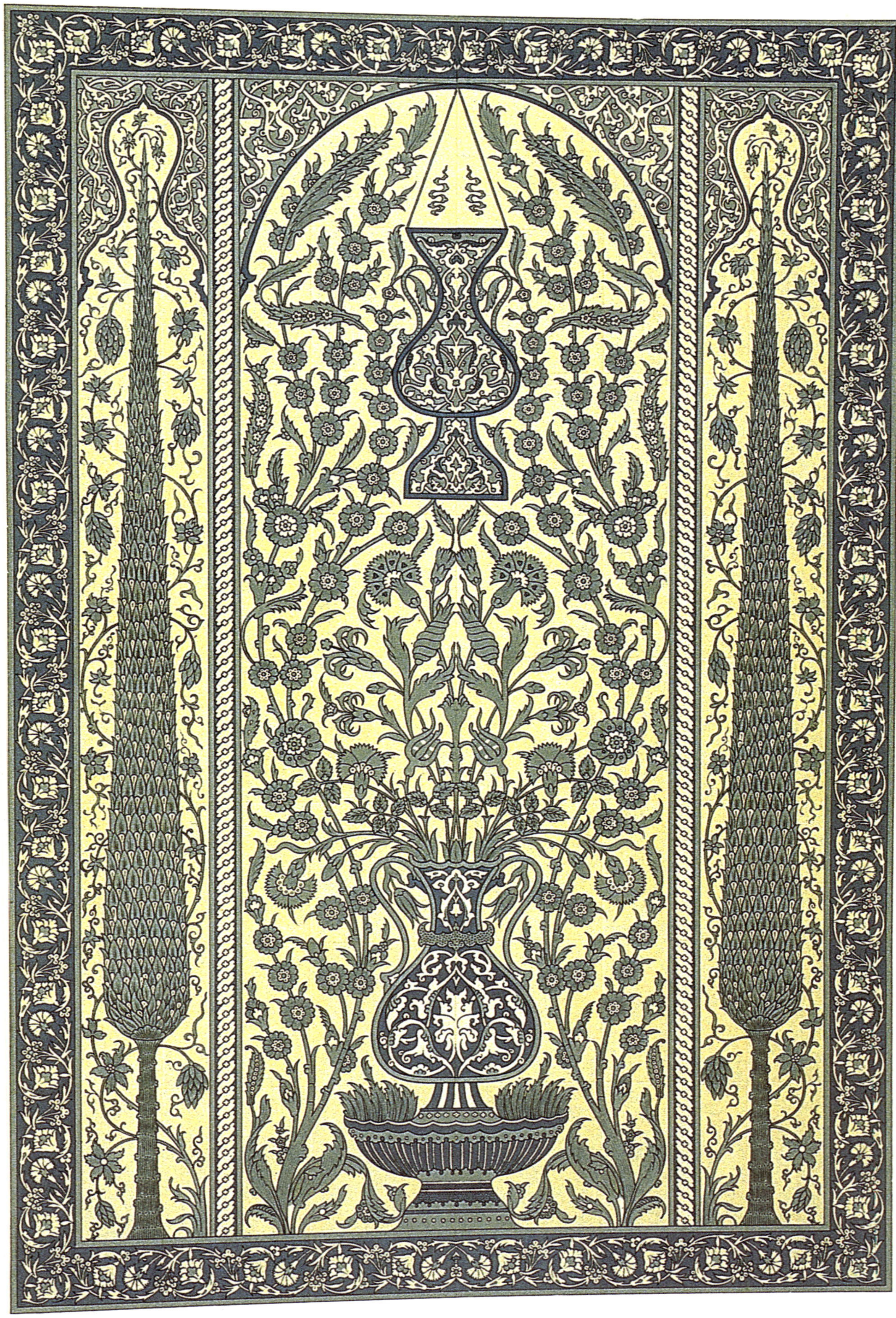

MOSQUE OF IBRAHIM AGHA

Tilework (16th century)

TILEWORK

Tekieh of the Dervishes (17th century)

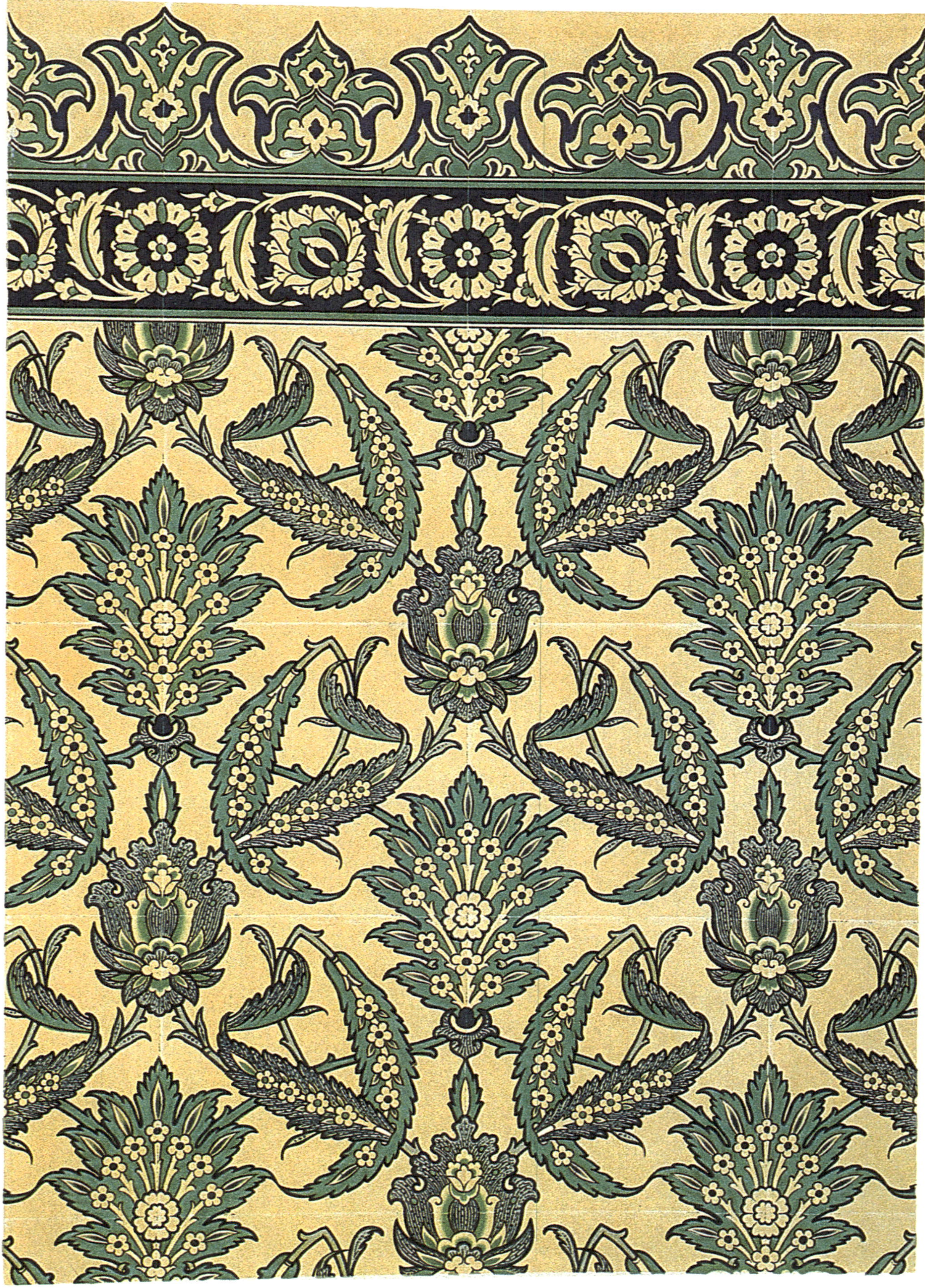

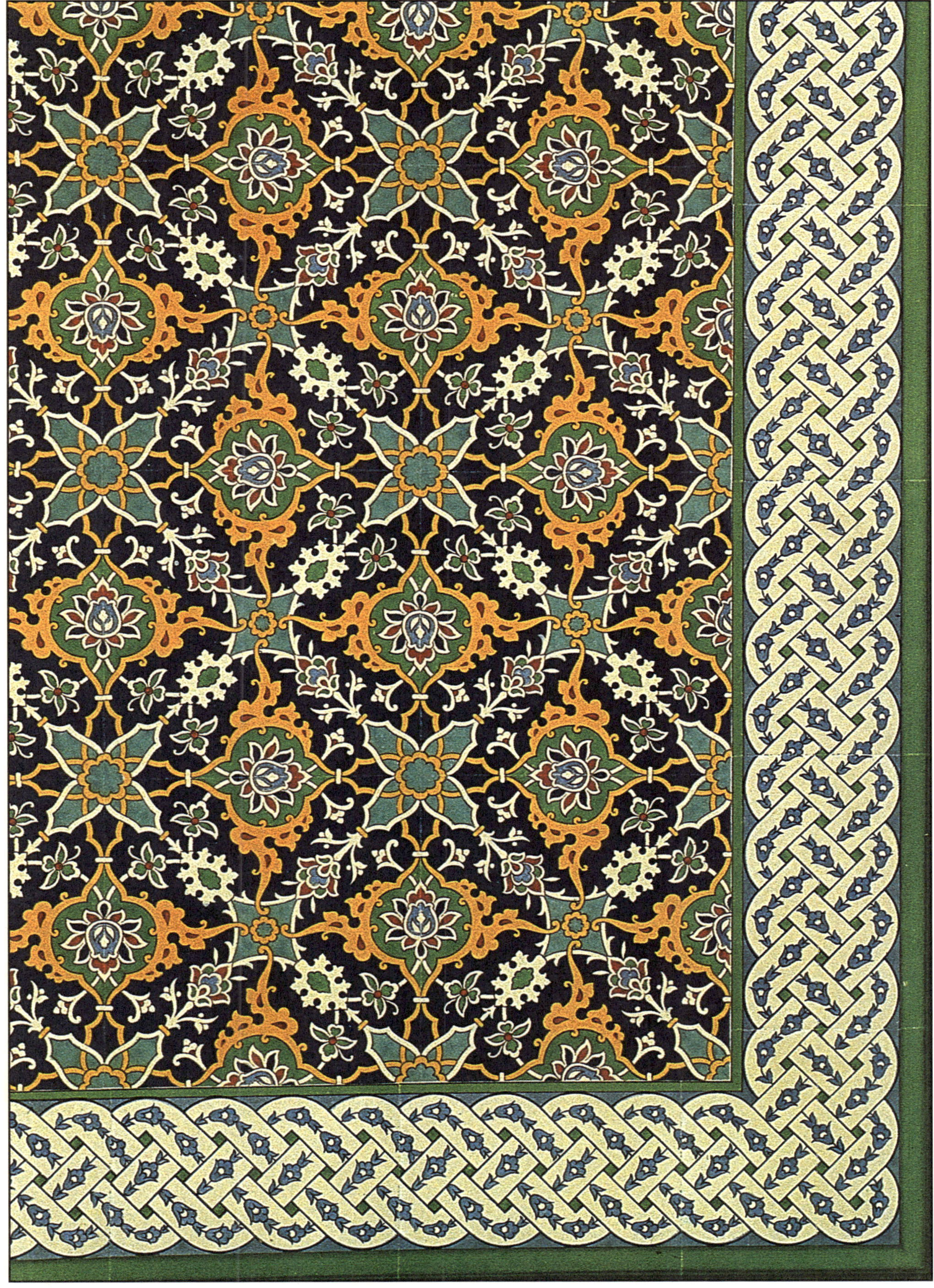

Plate CXXV

TEKIEH OF THE DERVICHES

Tympanum and Border of an Arcade in Glazed Tile (17th century)

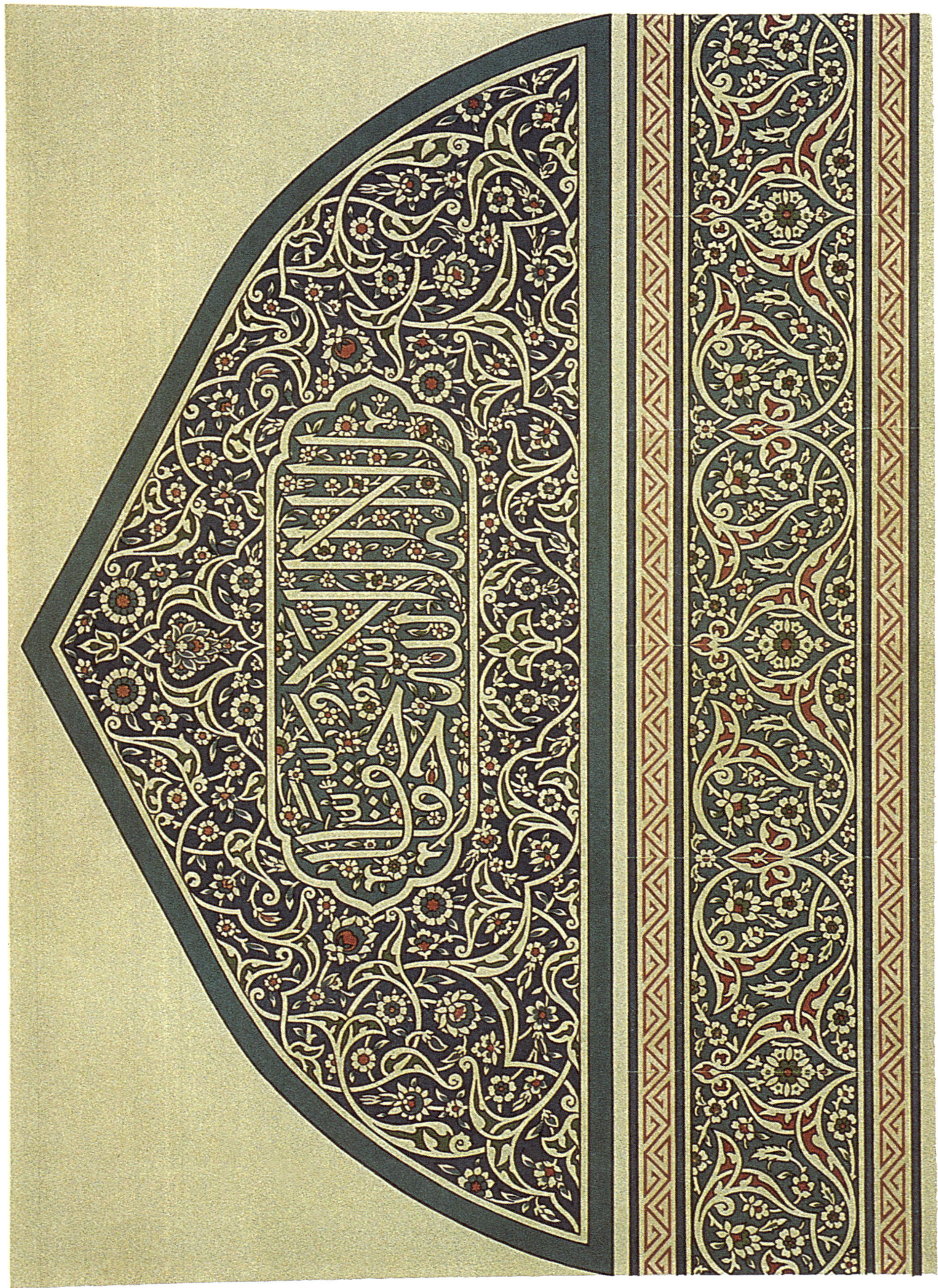

BAIT AL-AMIR
Tilework (17th century)

Plate CXXVI

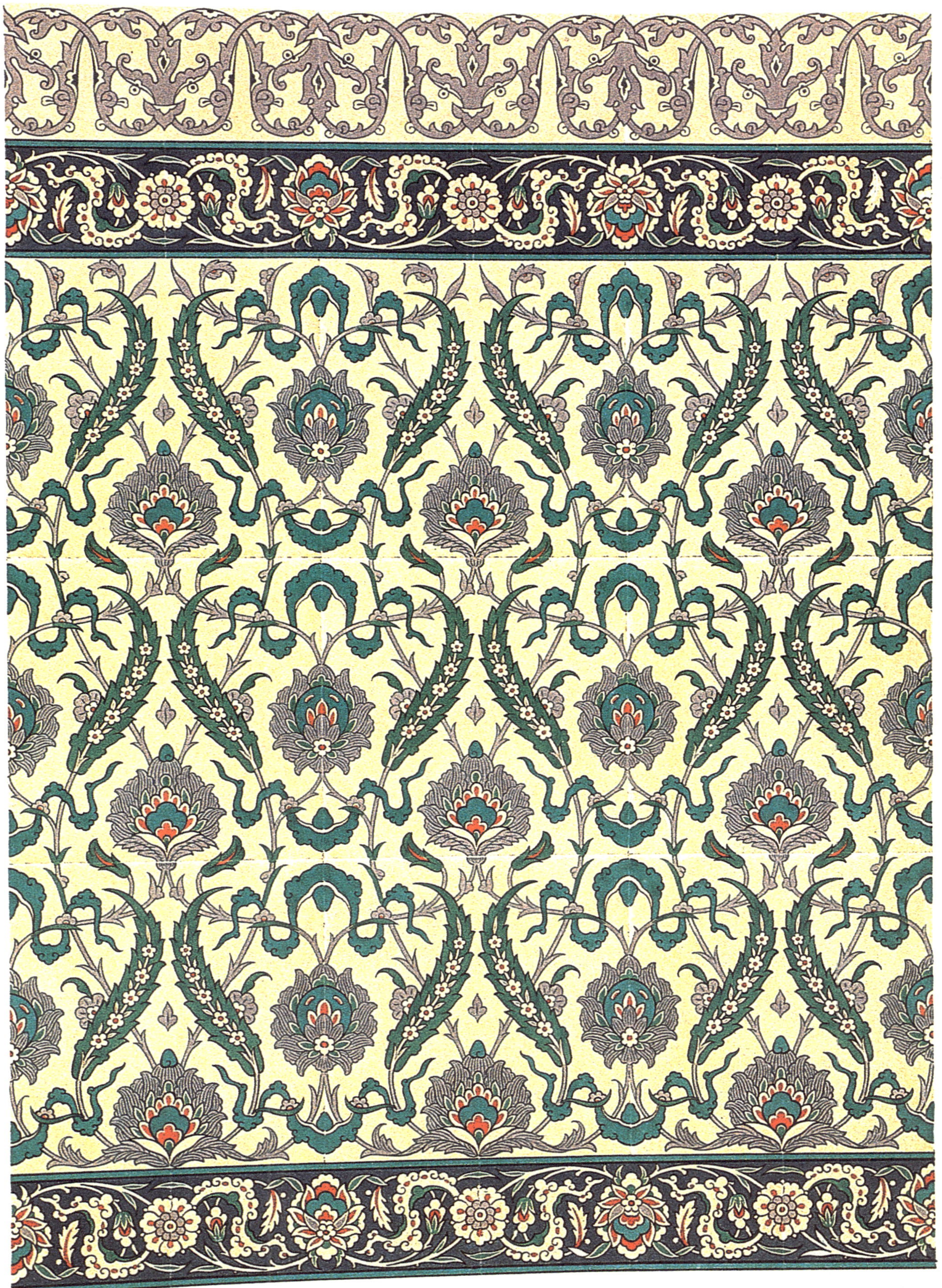

GLAZED TILES
(18th century)

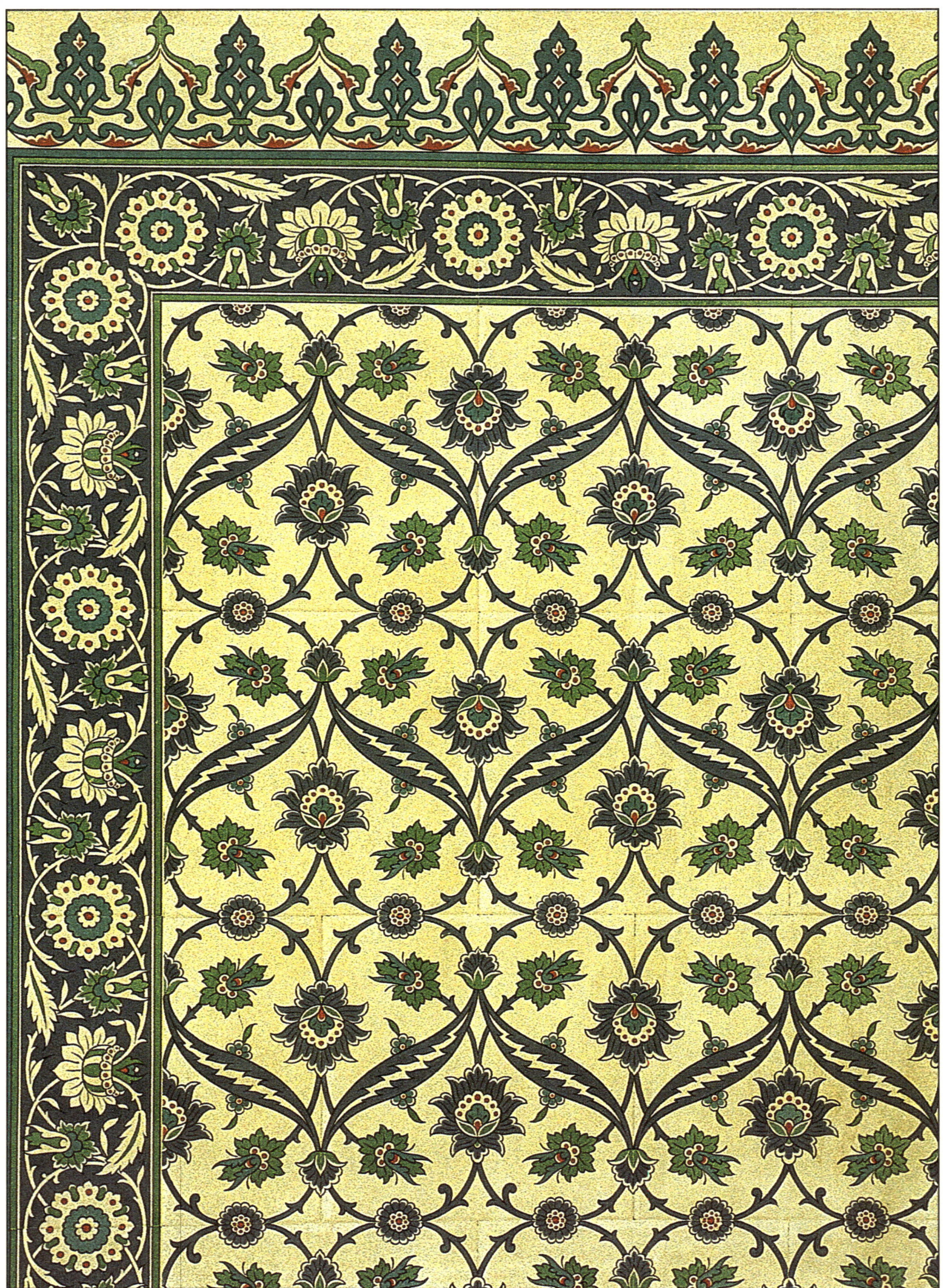

MOSQUE OF SHEIKHUN

Tilework (18th century)

Plate CXXIX

SIBIL OF ABD AL-RAHMAN KIAHYA

Tilework (18th century)

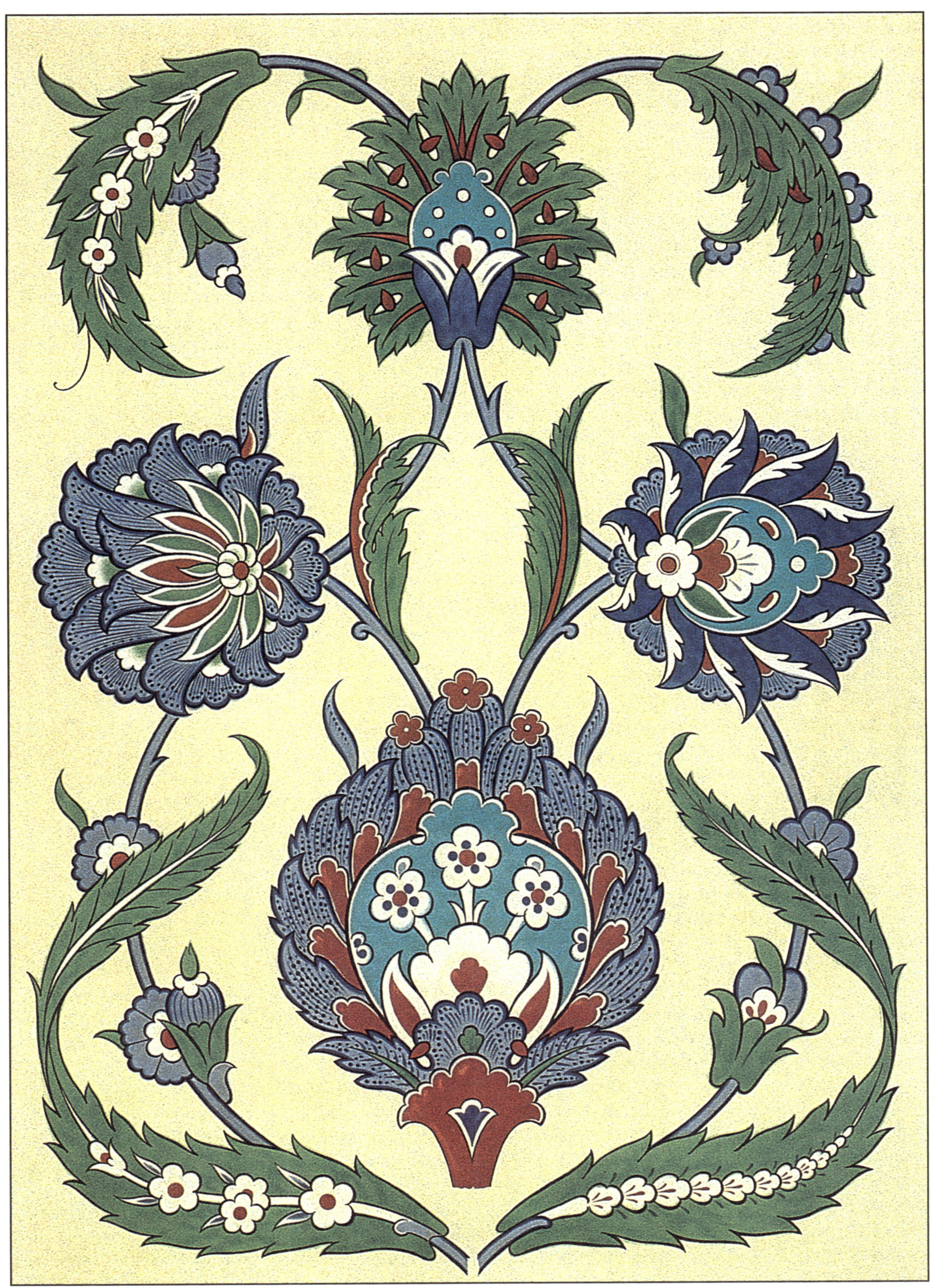

OVAL TILE PANEL

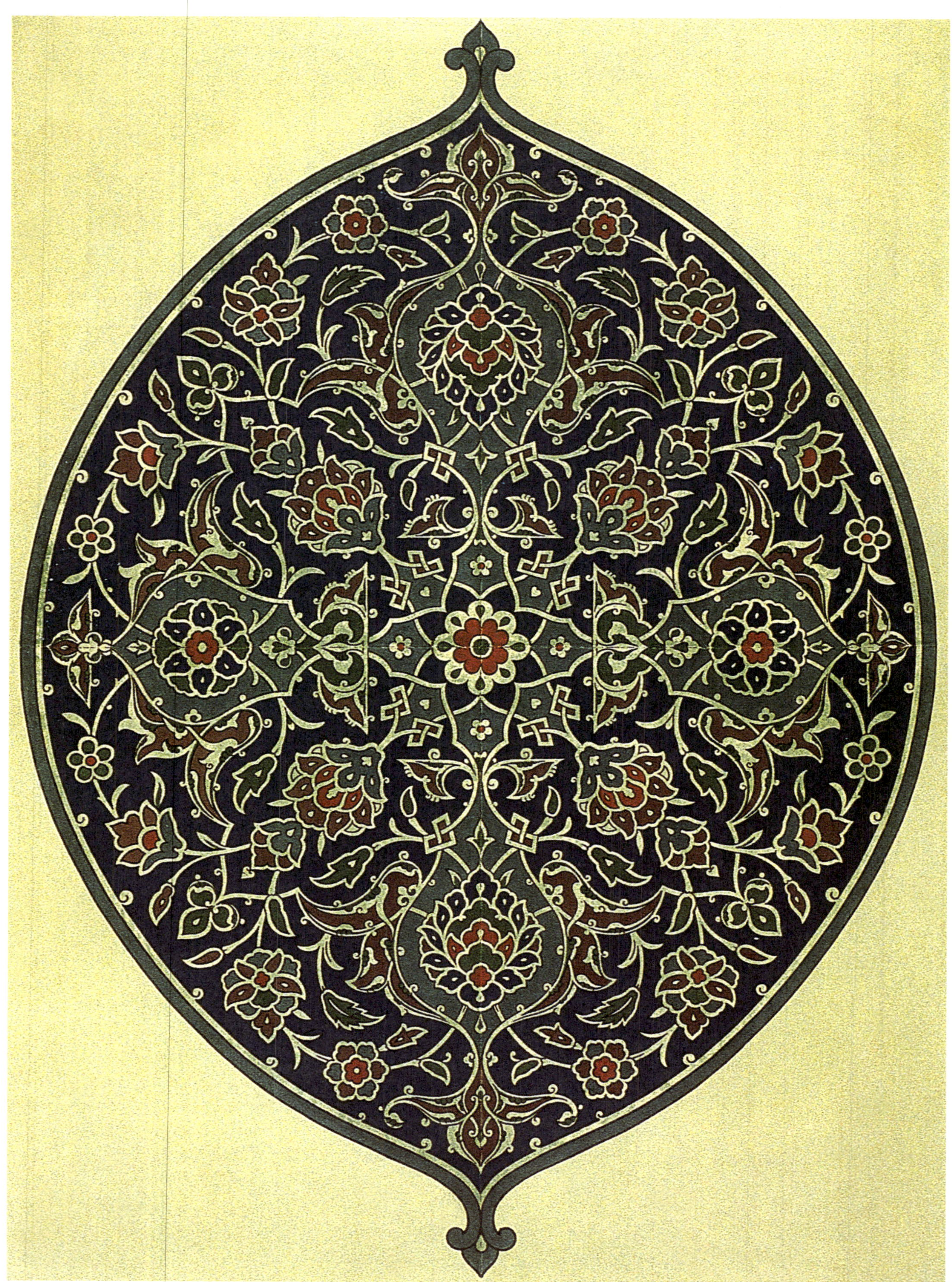

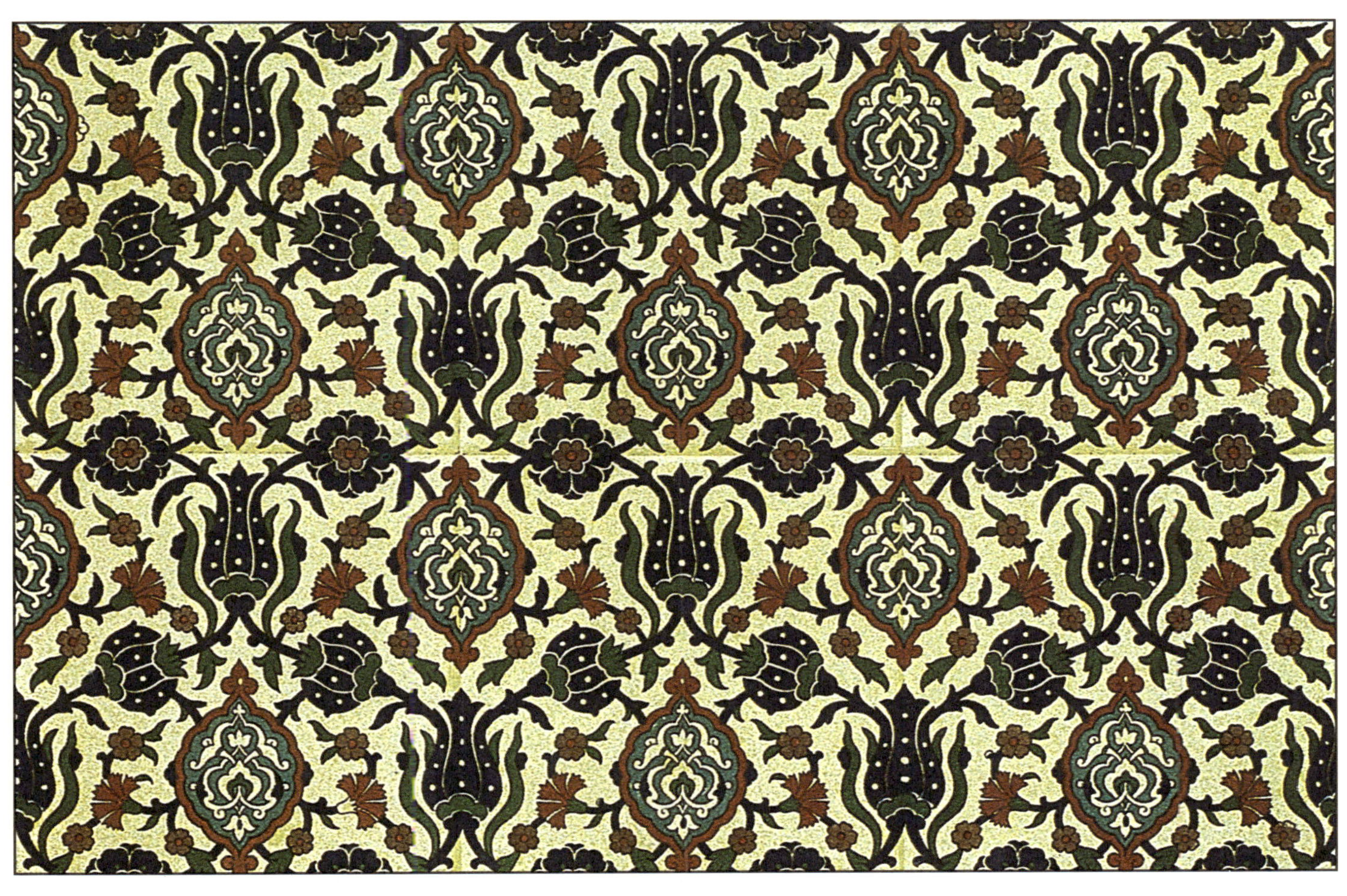

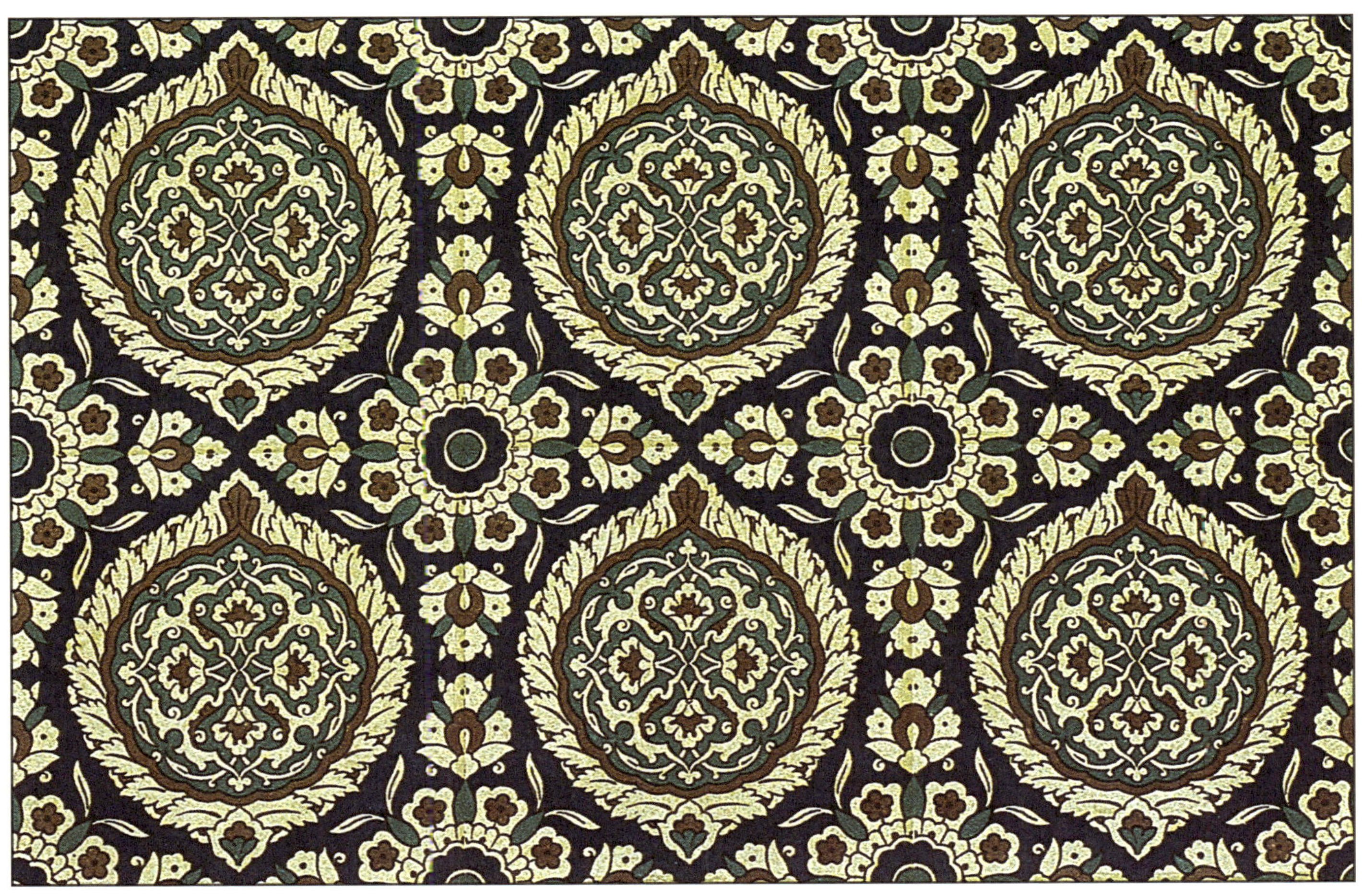

Plate CXXXIII

CROWNING ON THE DOOR OF THE MINBAR IN THE MOSQUE OF SISARIEH (18th century)

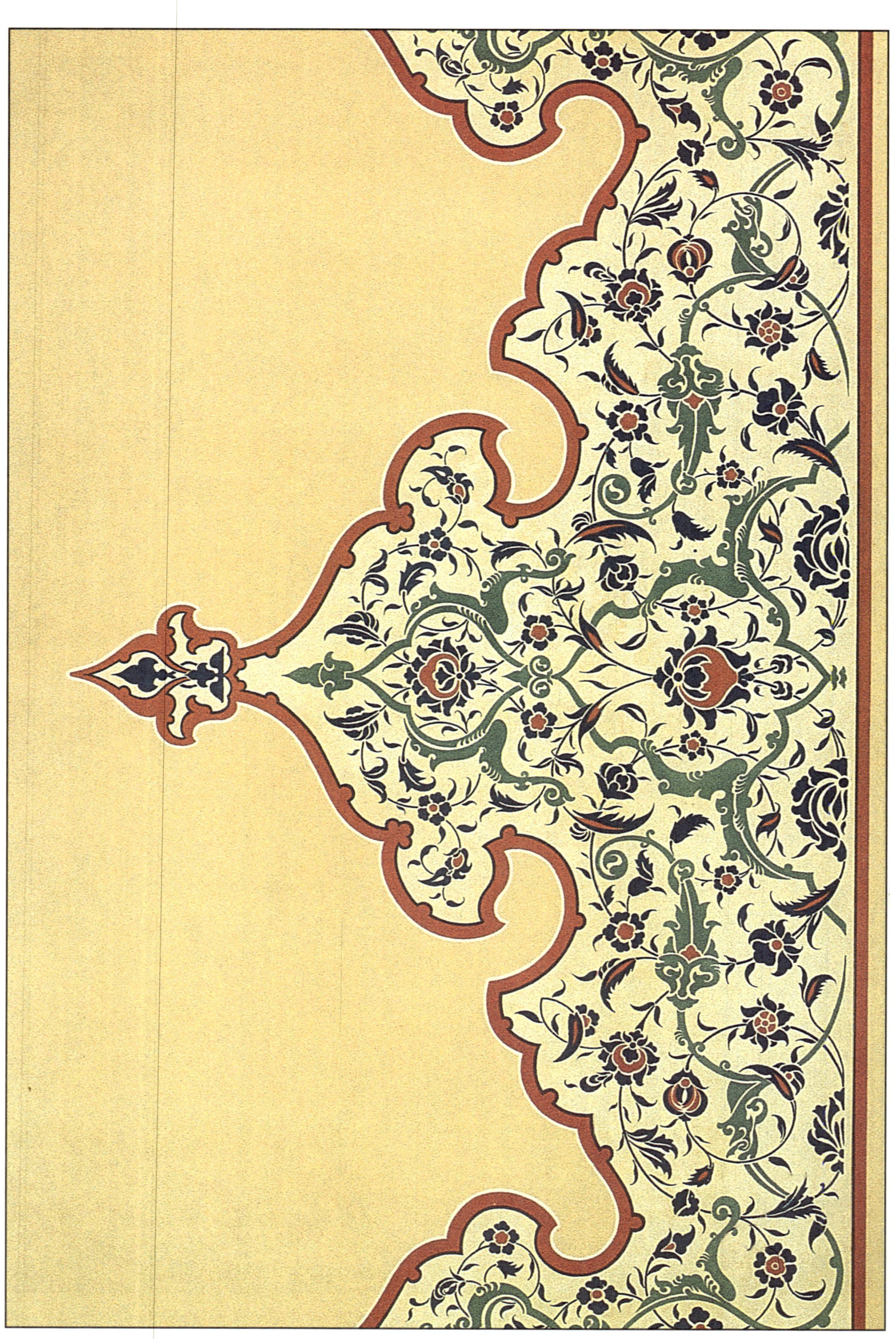

Plates CXXXIV to CXXXVIII
WOODWORK
Moucharaby and Wooden Grilles

In Egypt, as in most Oriental cities, the hot climate has made the circulation of fresh air within doors a necessity; thus, windows are ordinarily nothing more than openings closed by lattice work, very artistically rendered and allowing fresh air to enter while blocking the interior from the outside view, in such a way that people within the apartment can look outside without being seen. These latticed windows are called *chibbak*; they are charming works and quite varied, as can be seen in the specimens reproduced in our plates; often they are pierced by small openings featuring a movable grille, also in lattice work, which allows a head to pass out to look or call out if need be. There are few simple lattice work frames. These windows are also sometimes replaced by moucharaby of the same sort, but which offer the advantage of seating in order to enjoy the coolness and the view.

Bait al-Amir: Pentagonal Moucharaby (Pl. CXXXIV).—This elegant moucharaby, surrounded by its latticed windows, resembles an aviary hung upon a wall. It is adorned with climbing plants, whose greenery buffers the reverberation of the sun and whose flowers brighten the solitude of the harem. We have changed nothing and added nothing to this charming Arabic motif, contenting ourselves with the faithful reproduction of what we saw in the courtyard of an abandoned house, so decrepit that we dared not enter the pretty garden pavilion glimpsed through the window. It is the handsomest example of this type of woodwork that we have ever encountered – its turned lattice work furnishes every detail of its construction.

For an exact idea of this type of openwork window, a comparison can be made with the moucharaby of the house of Sheikh Sadat.

Grilles in Cut, Turned and Carved Wood, with Kufic Inscriptions (Pl. CXXXV to CXXXVIII).—The two inscriptions in rectangular Kufic characters, frequently used in the ornamentation of panelling and mosaics, read and translate as follows:

The one on top of the large window, No. 1: *L'illahi-el-amr min qabl ou min b'ad.*—"To God, the empire of the past and future" and that on No. 2, a fragment of a moucharaby: *Bism'illah macha'a Allah.*—"In the name of God, the will of God".

Plate CXXXIV

BAIT AL-AMIR

Interior Moucharaby (18th century)

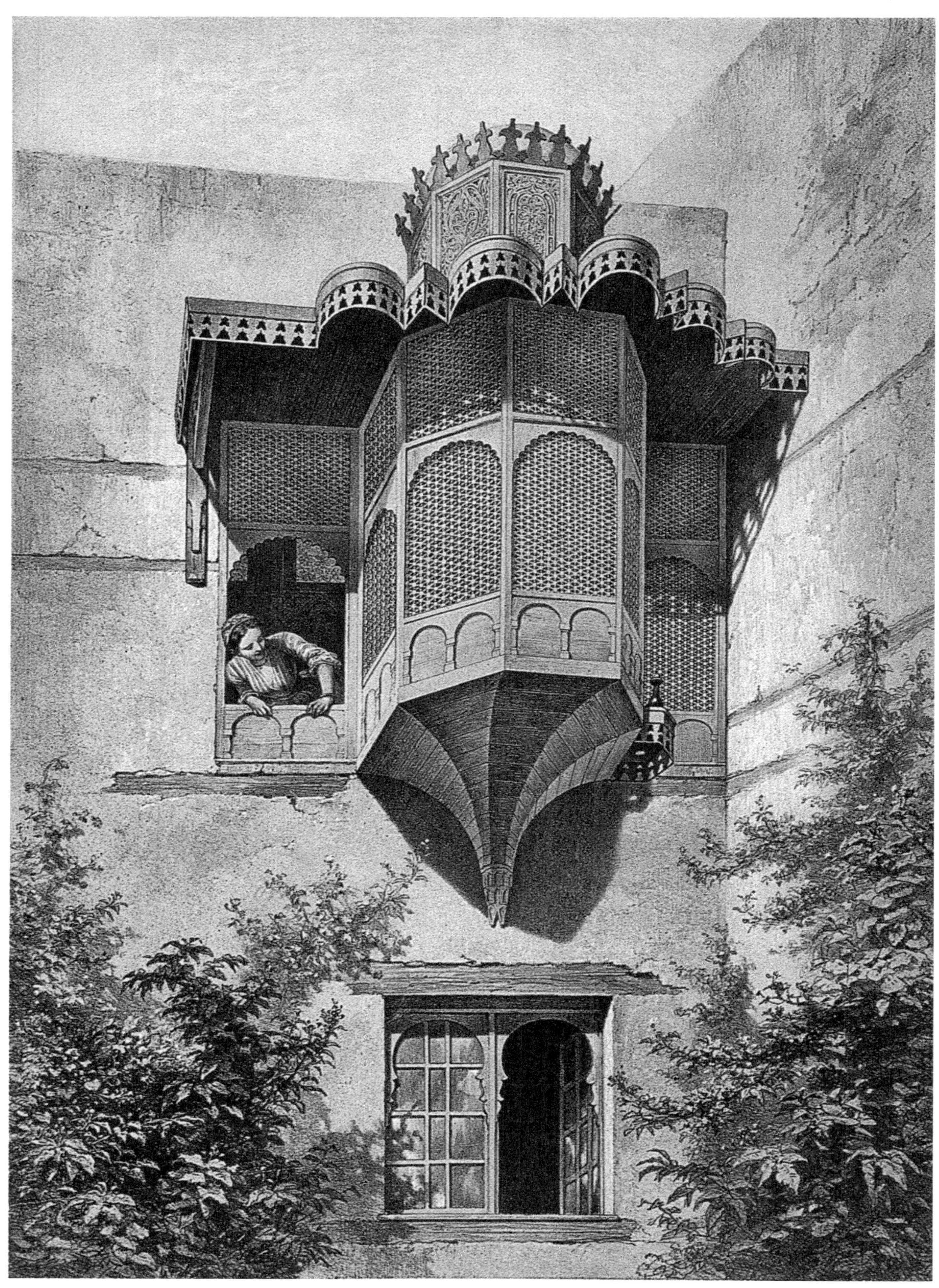

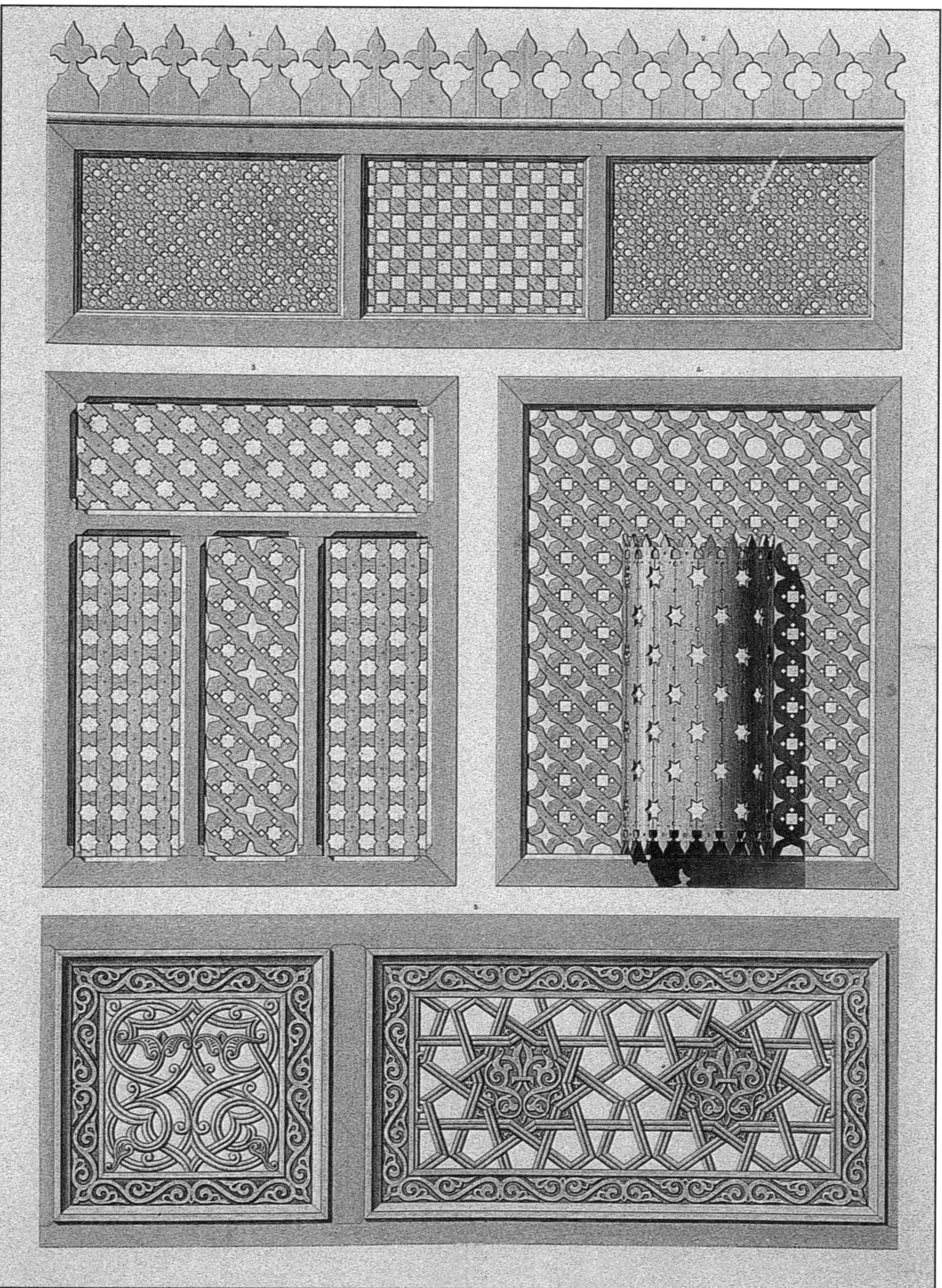

LATTICEWORK, TURNED WOOD
with Kufic Inscriptions

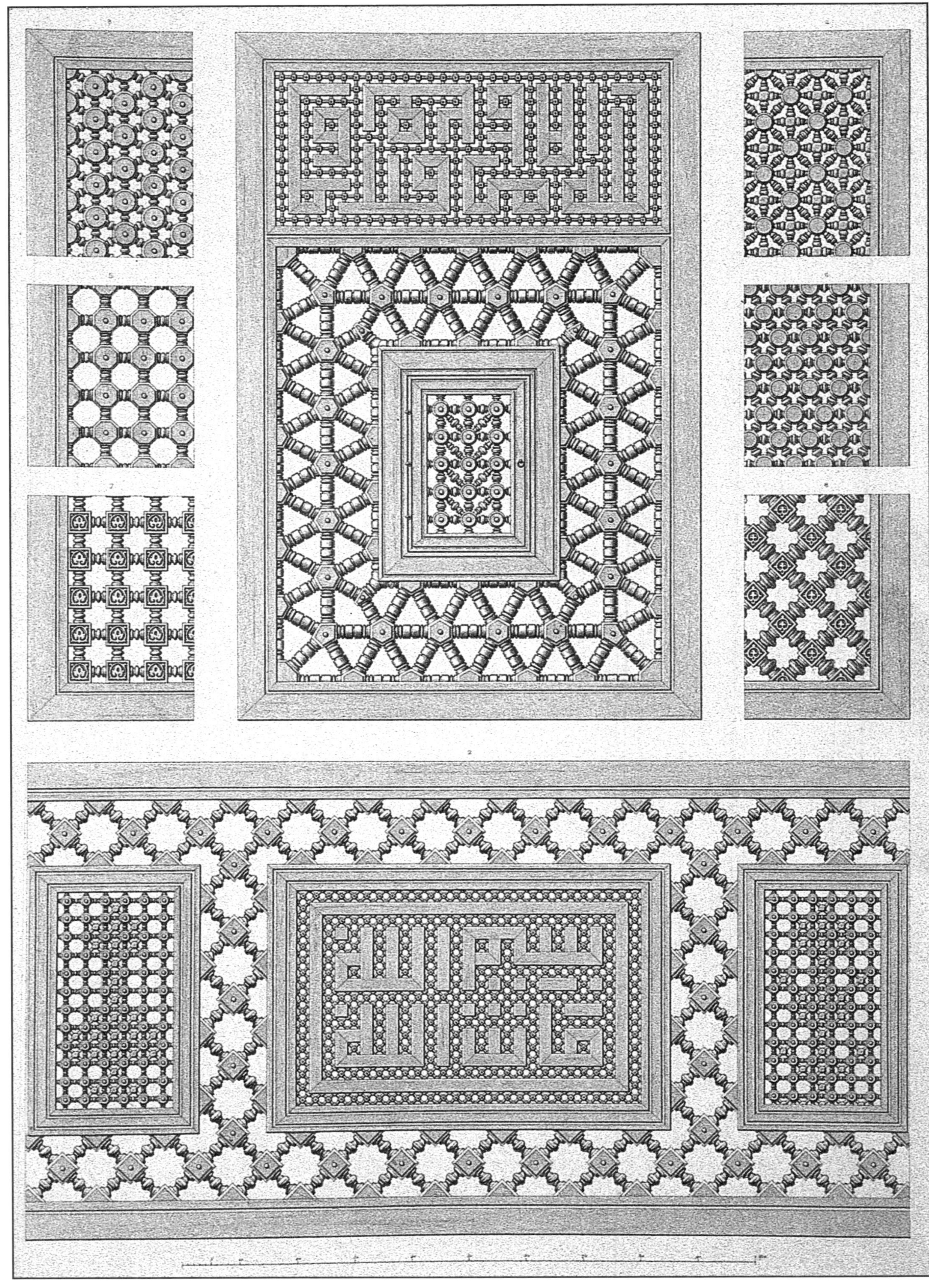

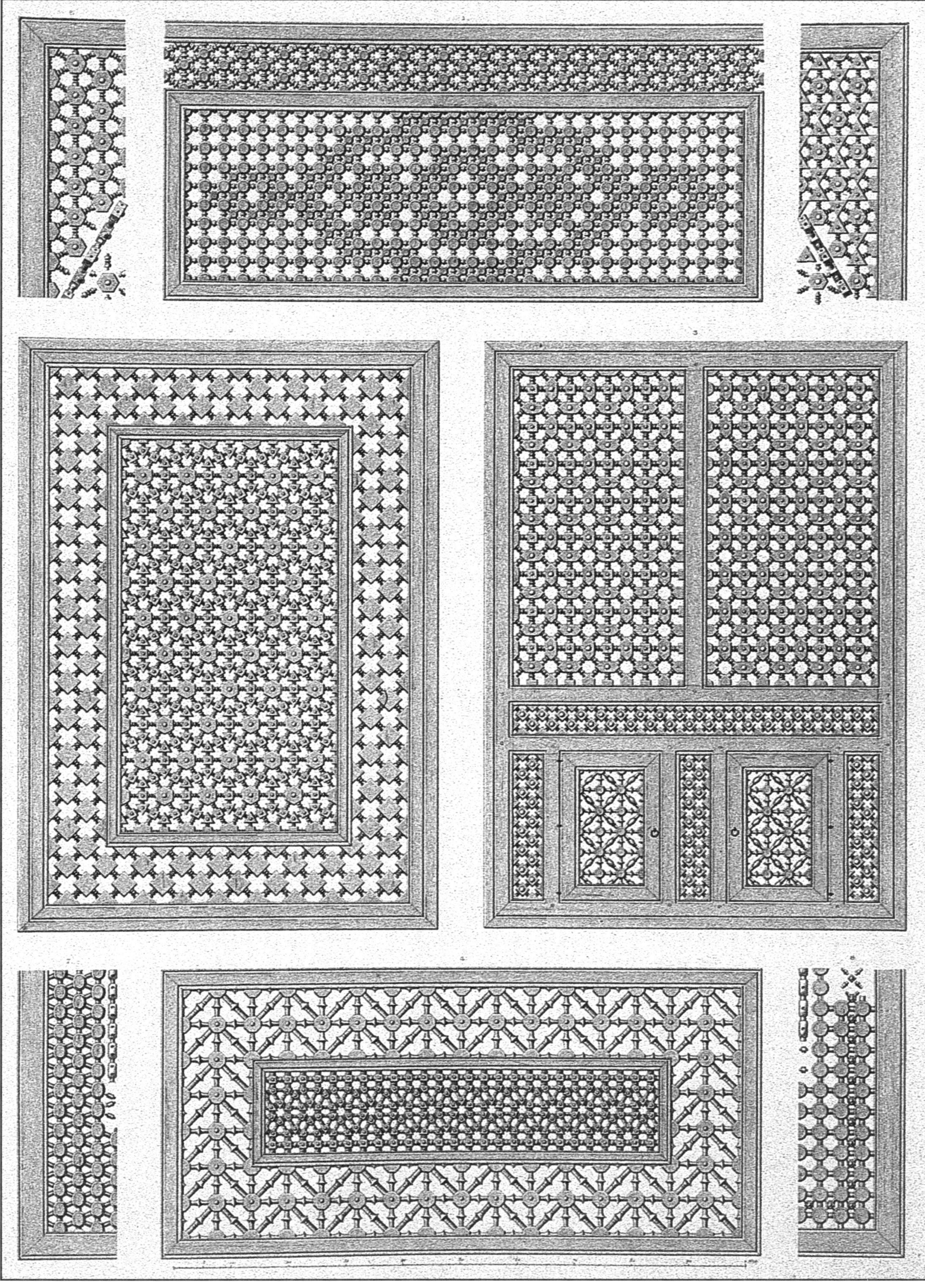

LATTICEWORK, TURNED WOOD

Whole and Details

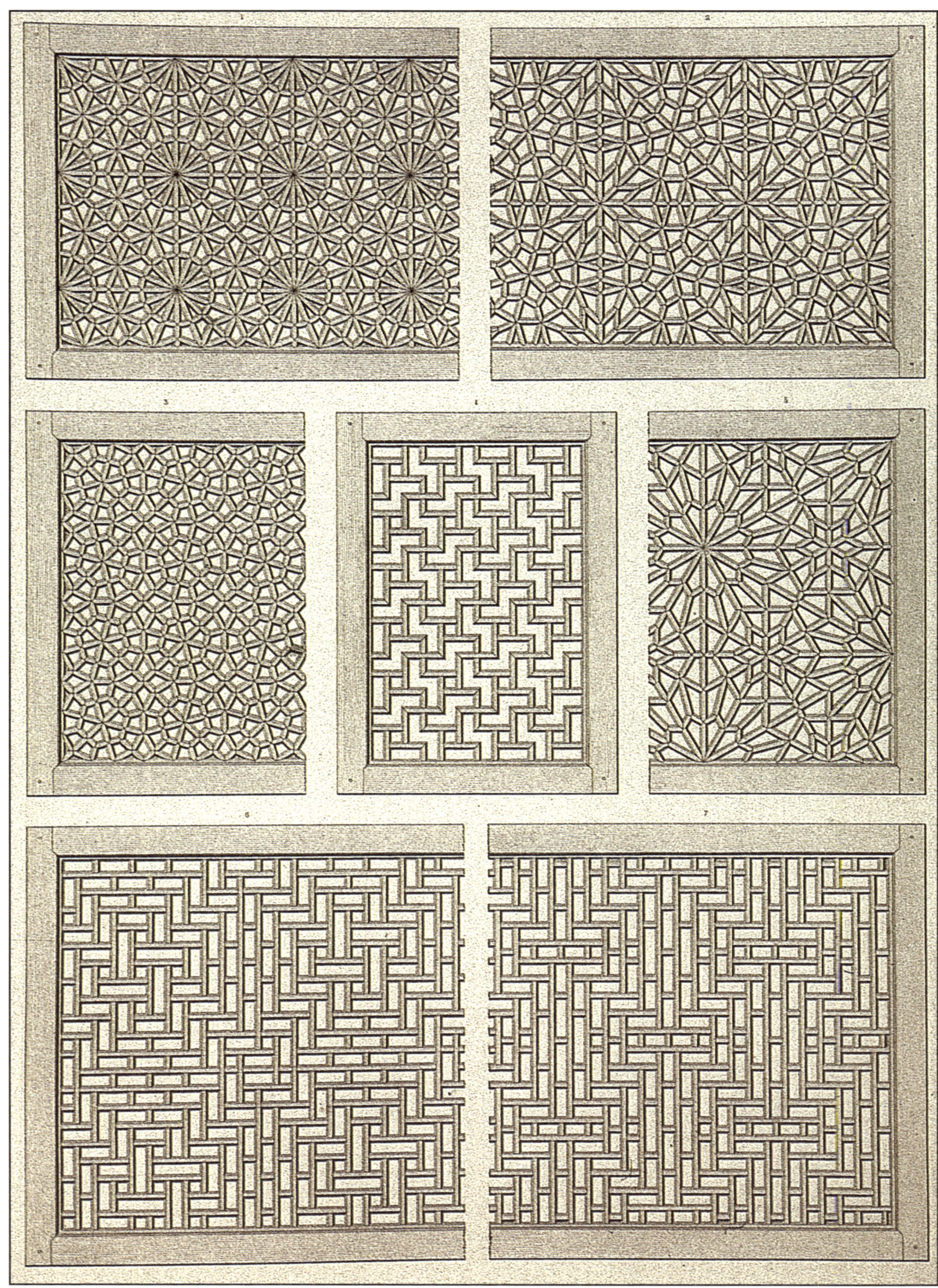

Plates CXXXIX to CXLII
INTERIORS

In the reproductions of one of the most remarkable houses of Cairo, Bait Sidi Yusuf Adami, we have wanted to give an idea of the inner apartments of rich dwellings at the height of Arabic civilisation in Egypt. We will try to detail successively their particularities and artistic beauty.

Reception room of Sidi Yusuf Adami (Pl. CXLI).—As in all the large reception rooms on either floor, this room was divided into two parts by a vestibule, separating the section reserved for women from that reserved for men. These sections, one slightly raised from the other, were covered with carpets, matting and cushions. The medial part, garnished with a suite of small arcades sculpted in marble, was used to place alcarazas and other small furnishings used daily. Above, near the ceiling, a suite of arabesques has been painted in counterpart to the stained glass windows, above the facing door, illuminating this room aired by vast moucharabies. A woman, leaning on the balustrade, gives an idea of the height of this part of the building.

The small room below the reception room is also decorated with niches sculpted in white marble, called *Kawarnakah.* This room, used by the wet-nurse, decked with household utensils, was also decorated with marble plaques (Pl. CXL). Moreover, the house is, like all Arabic homes, slightly westernised; it is difficult to easily gain entry to Muslim houses.

SIDI YUSUF ADAMI HOUSE

Upstairs Reception Room

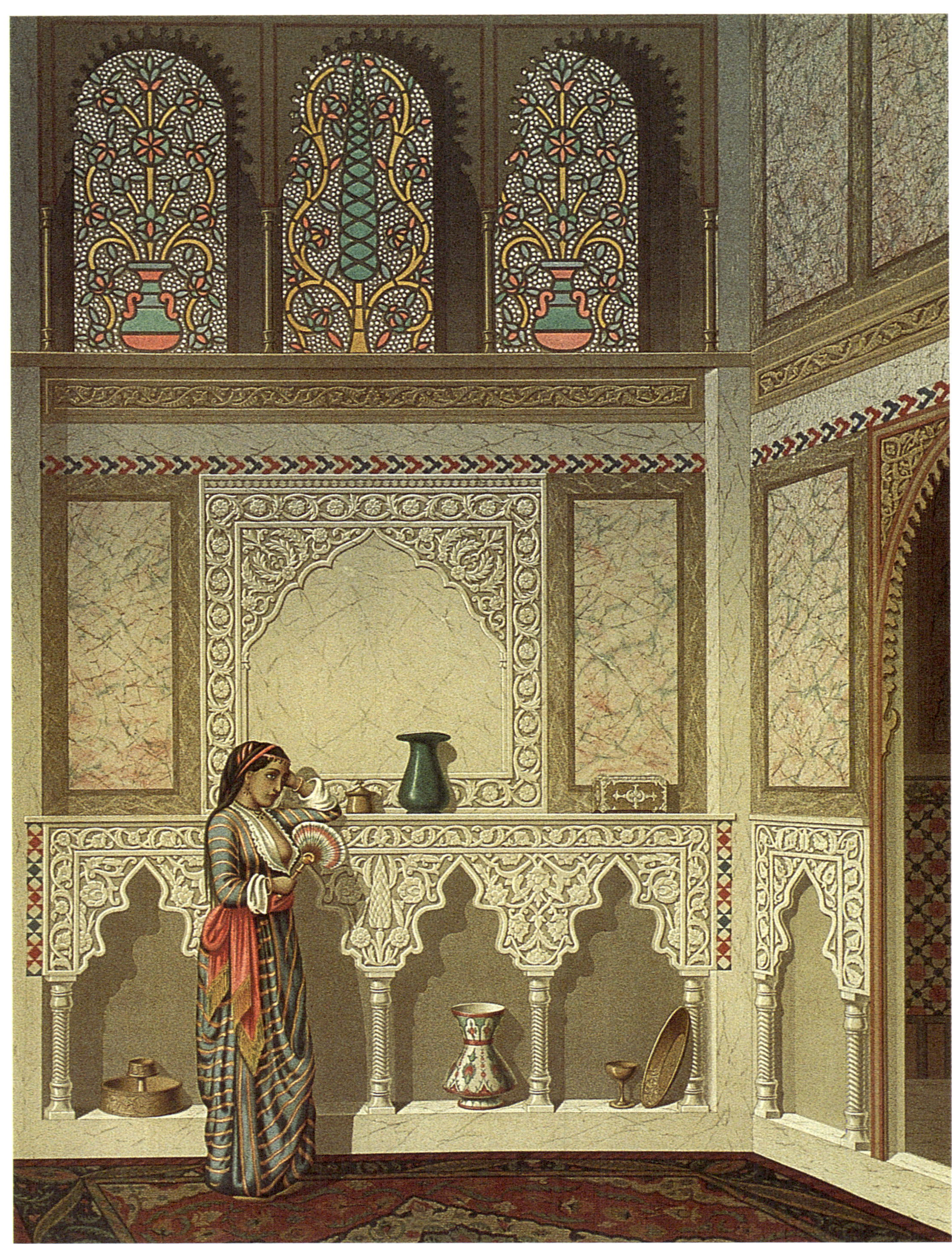

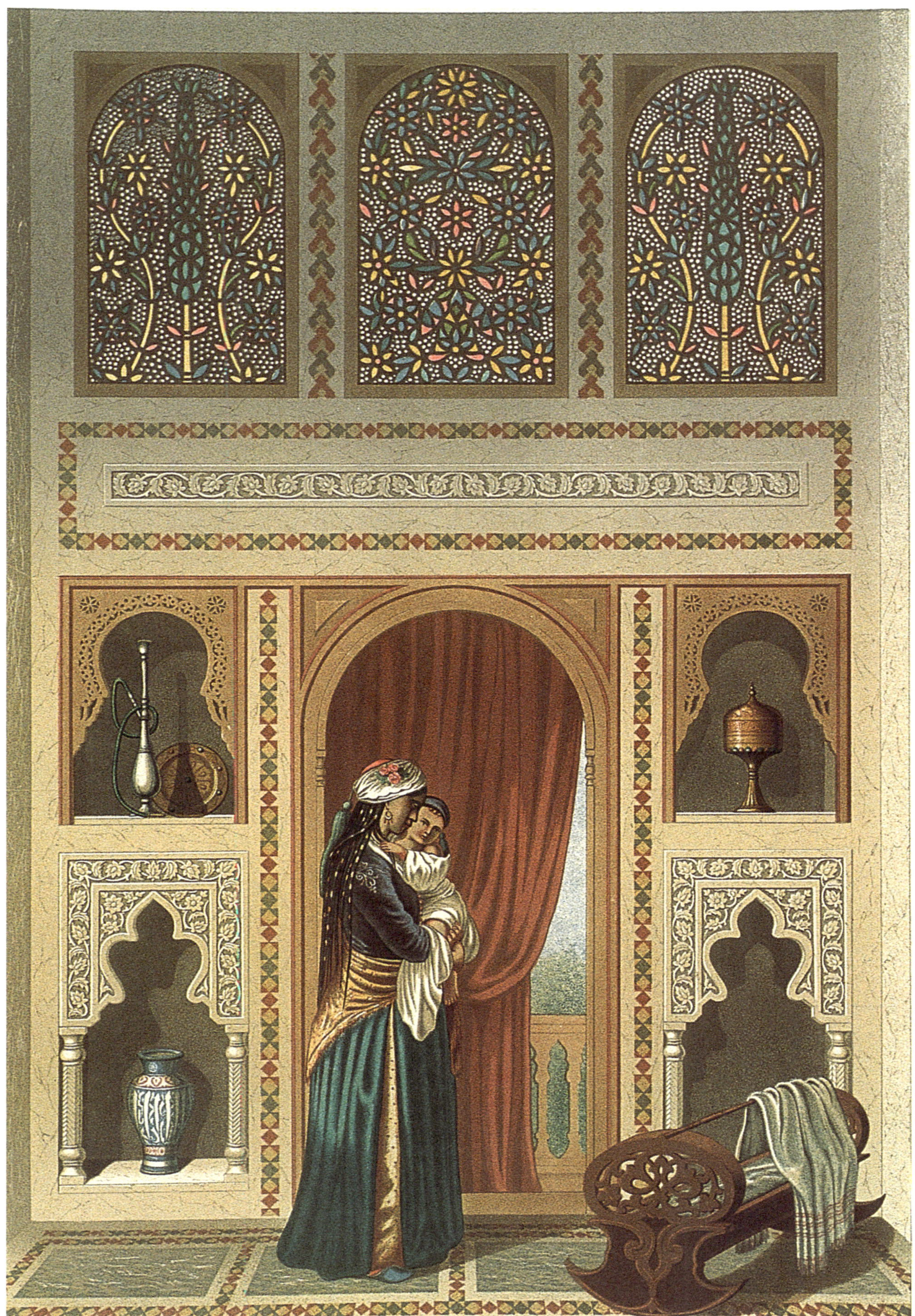

Plate CXLI

MANDARAH

Reception Room on the Ground Floor

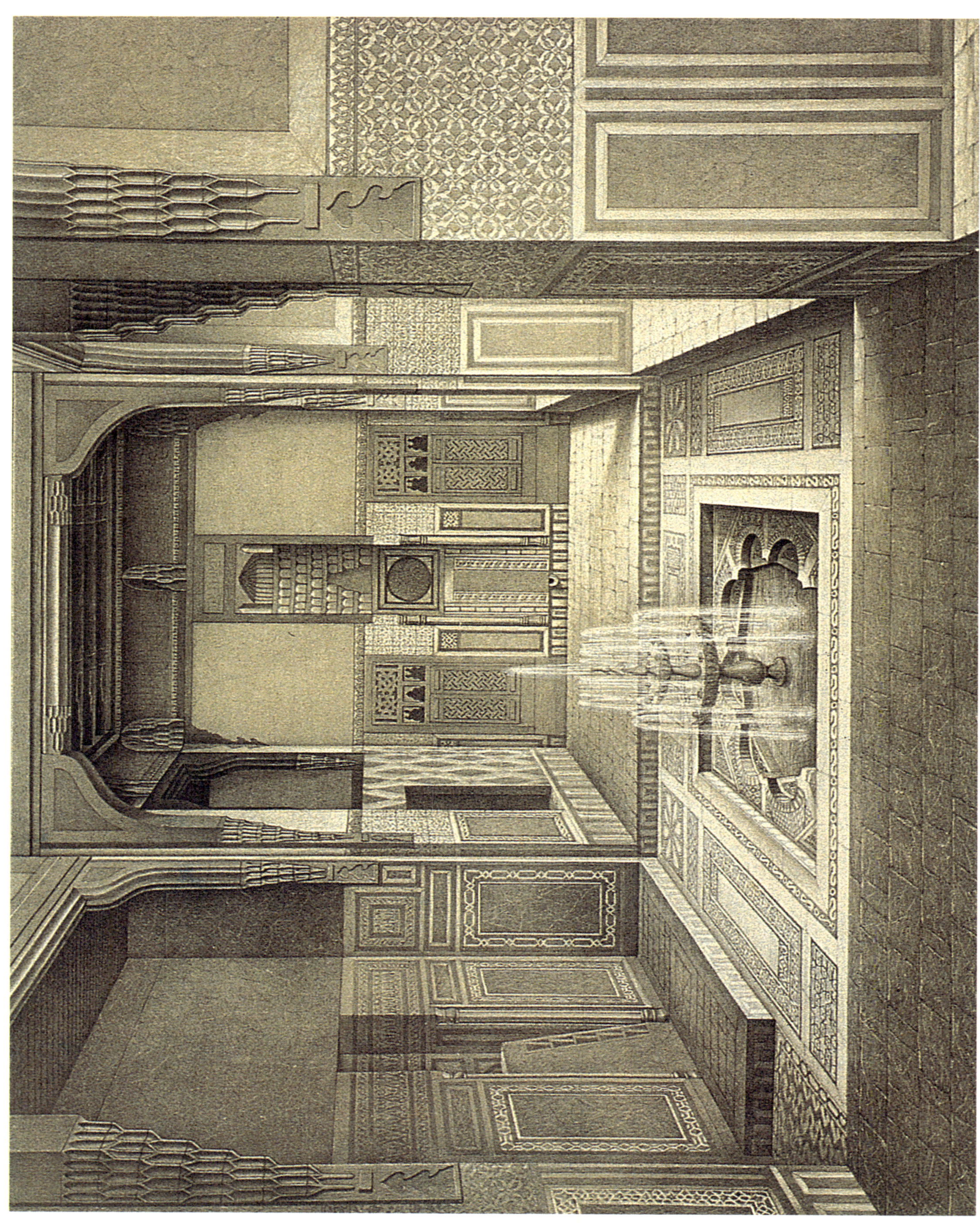

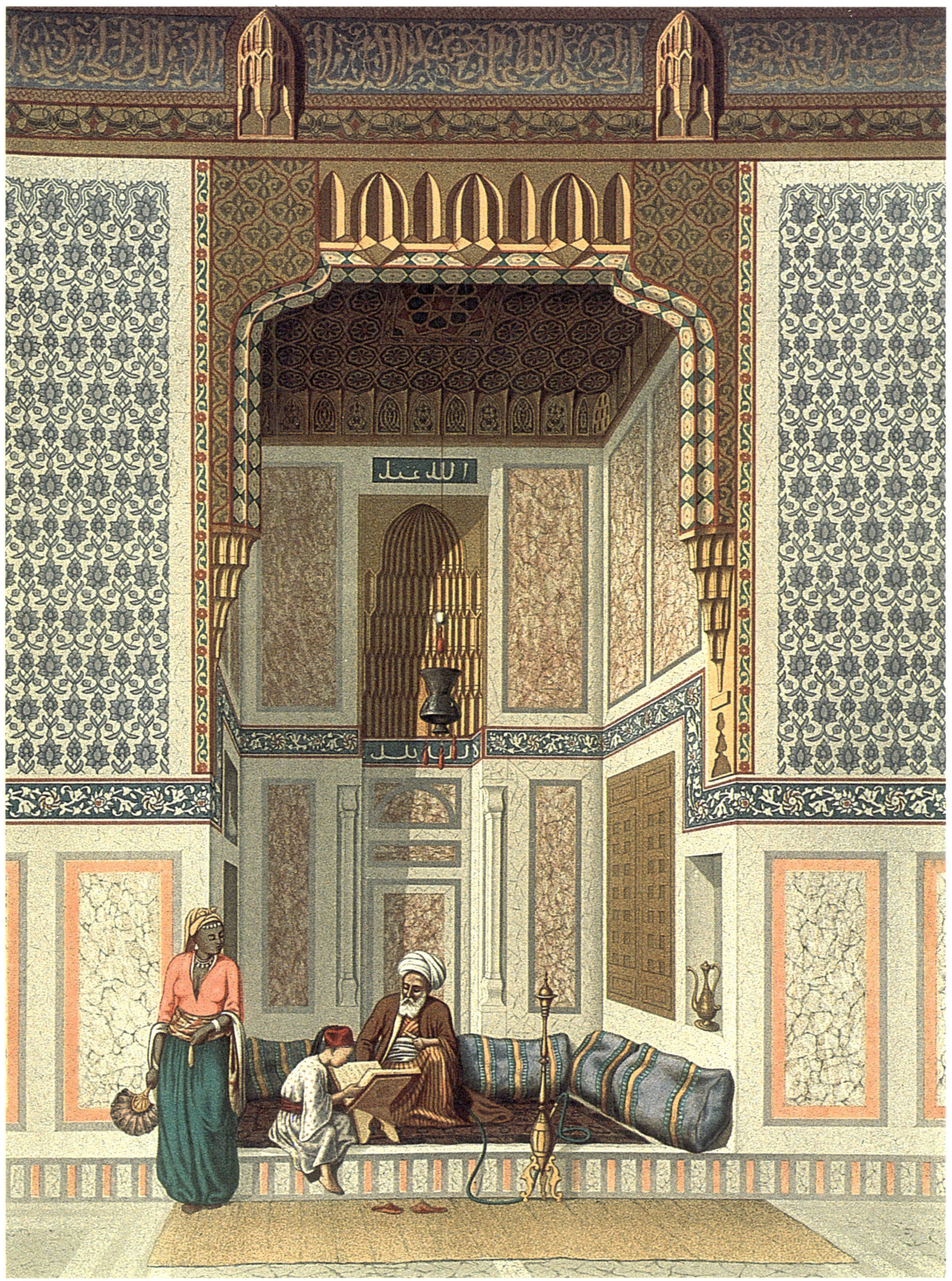

Plates CXLIII to CXLVI
STAINED GLASS AND GLASSWORK

Mosque of al-Saida Zenab. Shamsah or Stained Glass Window with Pierced Plaster (Pl. CXLIV).—We have indicated elsewhere how perforated plaster is garnished with bits of coloured glass to create ravishing windows of Oriental simplicity. The Arabs call them *Shamsah* or *Shamsiah*, and we have adopted the term to distinguish them from glassware *per se*.

The Mosque of al-Saida Zenab where we copied this attractive shamsah dates back to ancient times and was greatly venerated by the women of Cairo. Restored and embellished several times throughout the ages, the small room containing this lovely stained glass was recently redone.

From the style alone, we had no hesitation in dating this fragment of architecture back to the 14th century.

Mosque of al-Ashrafieh. Shamsah or Stained Glass Window with Pierced Plaster (Pl. CXLV).—We know neither the exact origin or date of this *shamsah* we drew in Paris. Shipped from Egypt for the 1867 Great Exhibition, it and several other stained glass windows from the same edifice arrived in pieces.

After estimating the damage for insurance purposes, the sender was about to throw the fragments away as rubble when we acquired them. Long hours of meticulous endeavour later, we were able to reassemble completely two of the six *shamsah*, too similar, alas, for both to be reproduced here. The seller, Mr Maynard, assured us that he had taken the stained glass from a mosque called al-Ashrafieh but could furnish no other details.

Several Mameluke sultans have been known under the name of "Melek al-Ashraf, the very noble king" amongst whom must be counted al-Melek al-Ashraf Schaban III and Barsabay, whose edifices are called: *al-Ashrafieh.*

In conformance with information received, we have attributed this *shamsah* to the Mosque of al-Ashrafieh, built by Barsabay in the 15th century.

Vessel with Enamelled Decorations (Pl. CXLVI)—This vessel is part of the superb collection of Mr Schefer, director of the School of Modern Oriental Language Studies. The colouring is smooth and harmonious; made in Egypt, it quite justifies the lasting passion over the years of the true amateur.

MOSQUE OF SULTAN BARQUQ

Lamp with Enamelled Decoration (14th century)

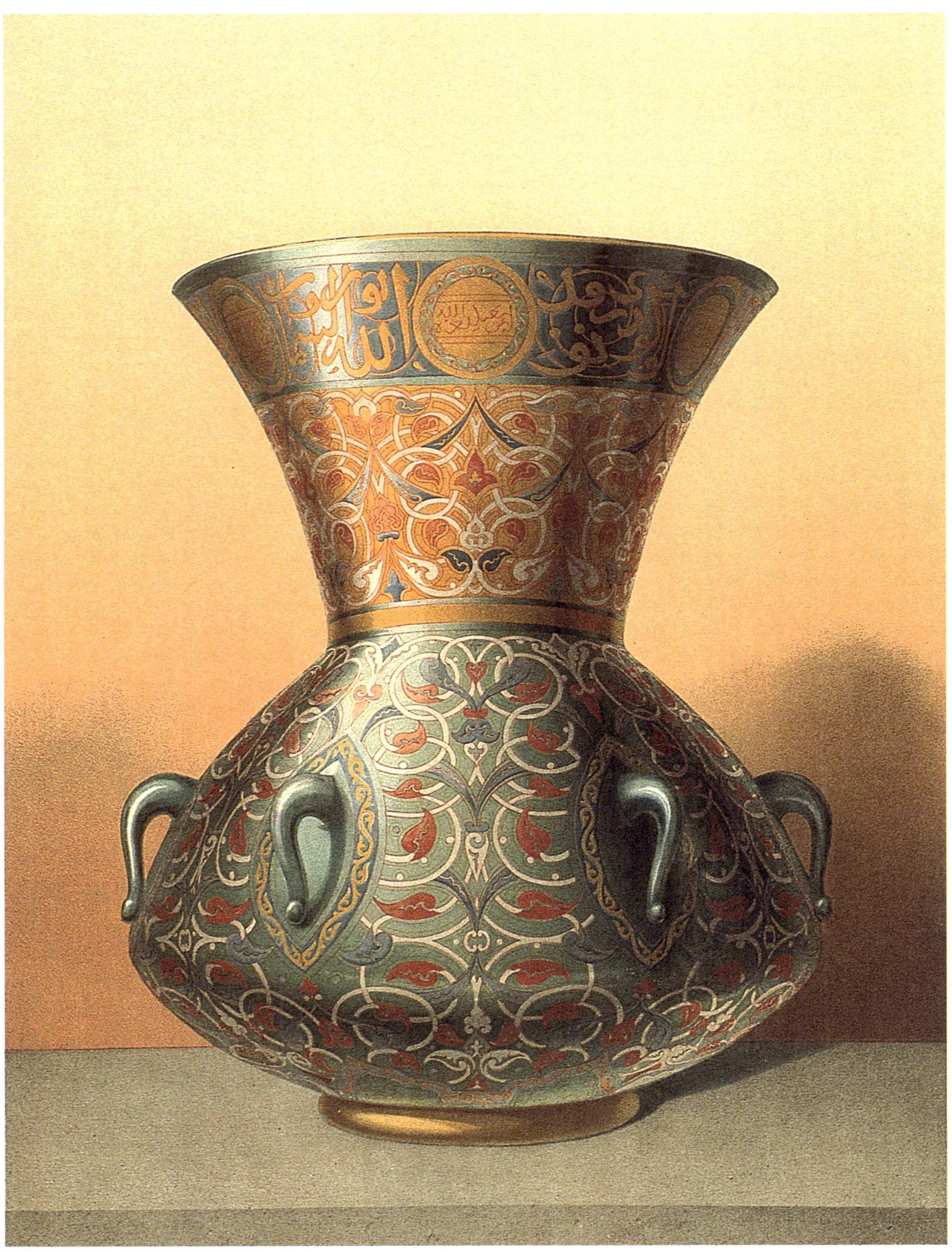

Plate CXLIV

MOSQUE OF AL-SAIDA ZENAB

Shamsah or Stained Glass Window with Pierced Plaster (14th century)

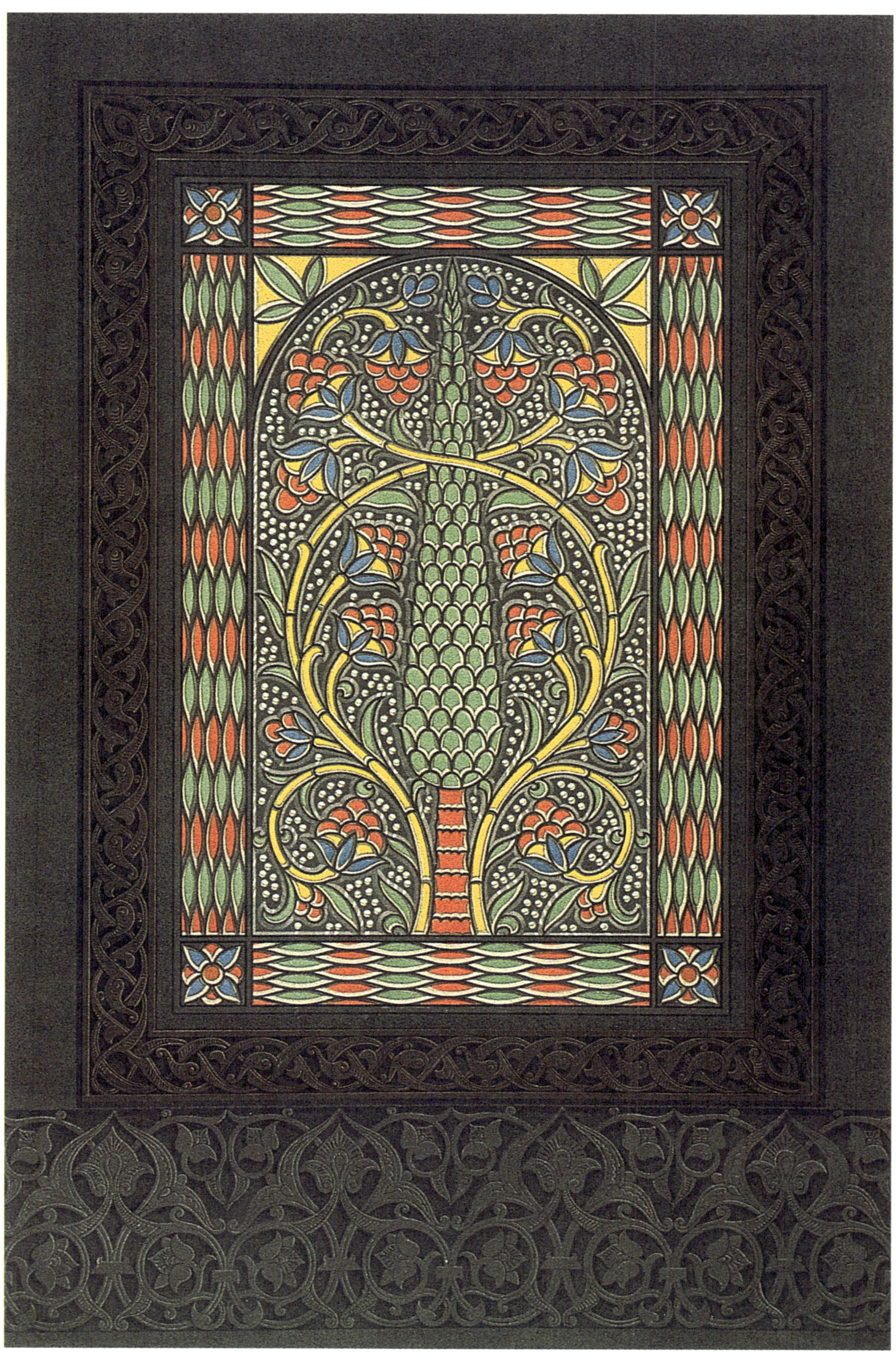

MOSQUE OF AL-ASHRAFIEH

Shamsah or Stained Glass Window with Pierced Plaster (15th century)

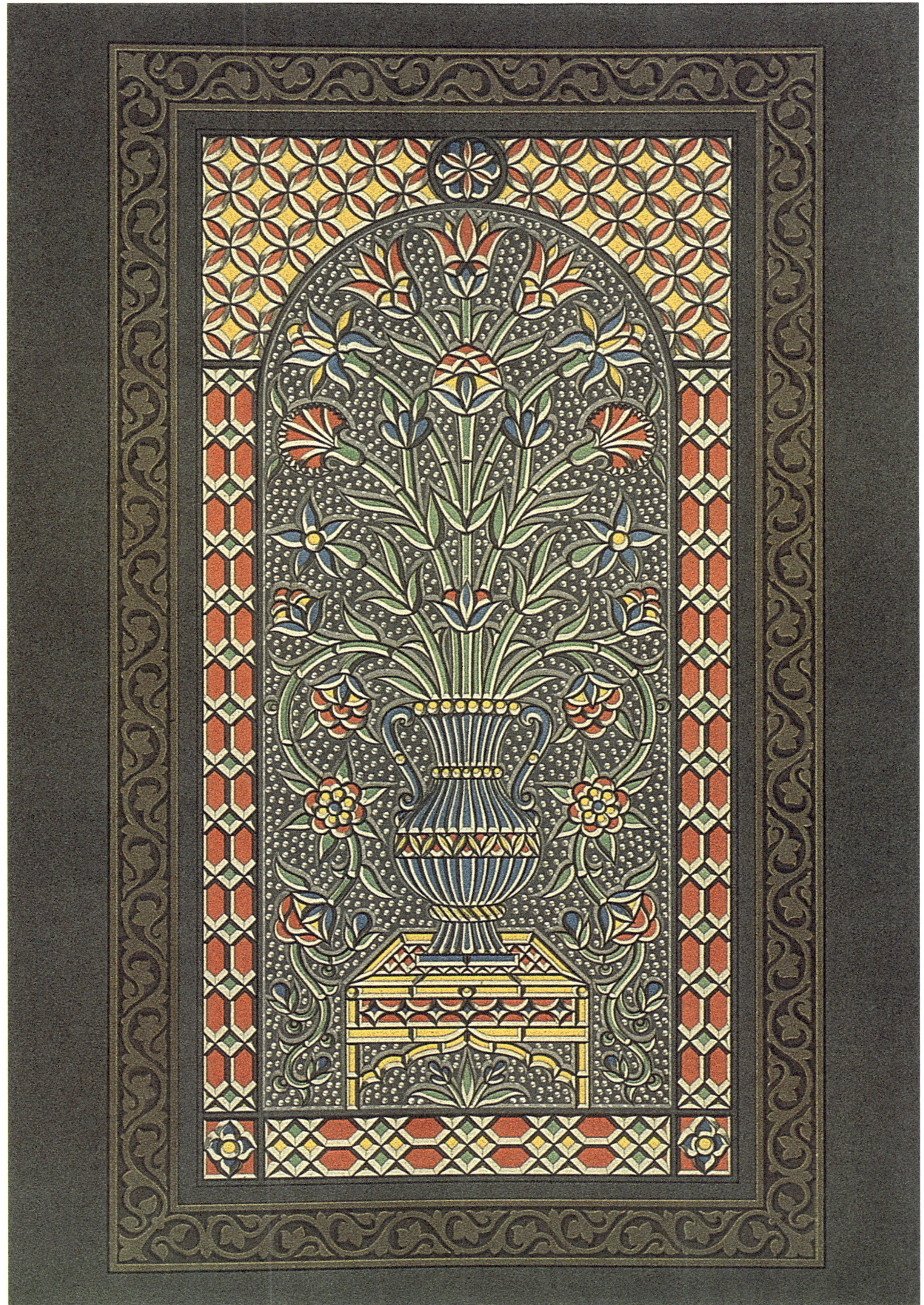

VESSEL WITH ENAMELLED DECORATIONS

(17th century)

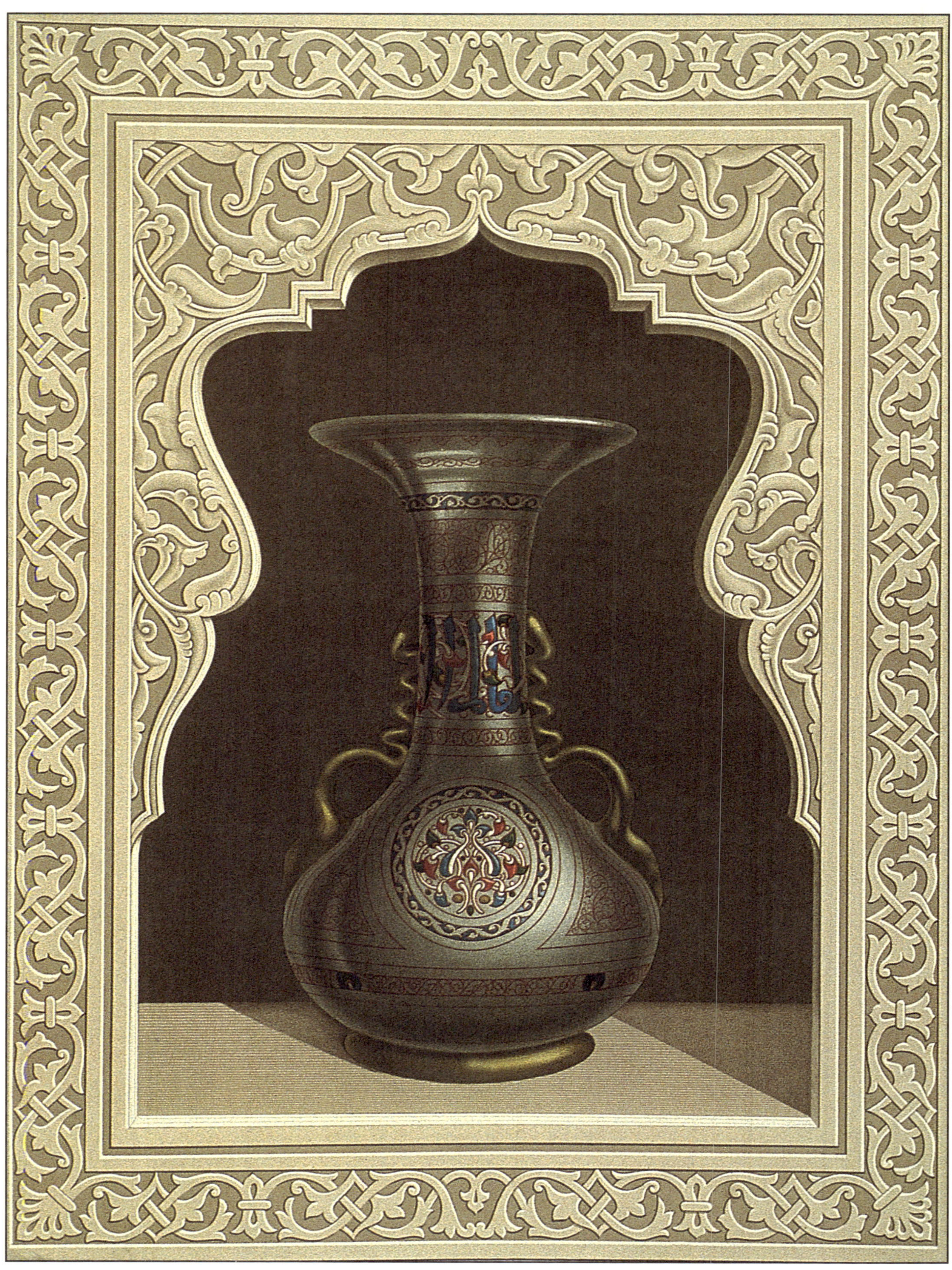

Plates CXLVII to CLIV
TEXTILES AND CARPETS

We have described at length, in Chapter XI, the processes used to manufacture tapestries of which Arabic art presents such remarkable specimens. We will confine ourself here to those few details which may have been omitted.

Fragment of a Tapestry Conserved in the Church of Nivelles (Pl. CXLIX).—We believe that this tapestry may be attributed to the Hispano-Moresque workshops of Andalusia at the beginning of the 14th century.

Small Velvety Carpet (Pl. CL).—This fine carpet, 3.22 metres long by 1.58 metres wide, seems to date back to the end of the 14th century. The Venetian painter Paris Bordone is claimed to have used it as the model for the carpet beneath the feet of the doge in his famous painting of the *Adriatic Fisherman Bringing Back the Ring of Saint Mark.* This can be confirmed by visiting the École des Beaux-Arts where a copy of this superb painting is hung.

Textile Conserved in the Museum of Utrecht (Pl. CLI).—Herring-bone pattern, light blue background with white, yellow, red and green design; strongly pronounced grain, as in samite. As can be seen, the pattern consists of three rows of peacocks facing each other with tails closed, set between white arabesques of remarkable elegance. Along the vertical axis, the bodies of the birds are alternatively green, red or yellow; their necks are white; the beaks, eyes, crest, feet and a single long tail-feather take on the body colour of the peacock in the row above.

The disposition, hues of dye and the style of this admirable fabric point to the same school as that of Nivelles; but its purer design and uncontestable originality denote an earlier period. It is most likely the classic example of a series of cartoons, of which the cloth of Toulouse is one variety.

We do not think ourselves bold in attributing the magnificent sample from the Museum of Utrecht to the flourishing period of Arab-Egyptian manufacturing.

Quiver and *Bow-case* (Pl. CLII).—These two cases, one for arrows, the other for the bow, seem to be the work of the same hand: they are both covered in crimson velvet adorned with an arabesque.

Tirkech means *quiver* in Persian; moreover the French word for it, *carquois*, is of Oriental origin.

Plate CLII represents a large velvety carpet from the 18th century. We give also Plate CLIV as a specimen of a textile for tapestry, *Hada.*

TAPESTRY TEXTILE
(12th century)

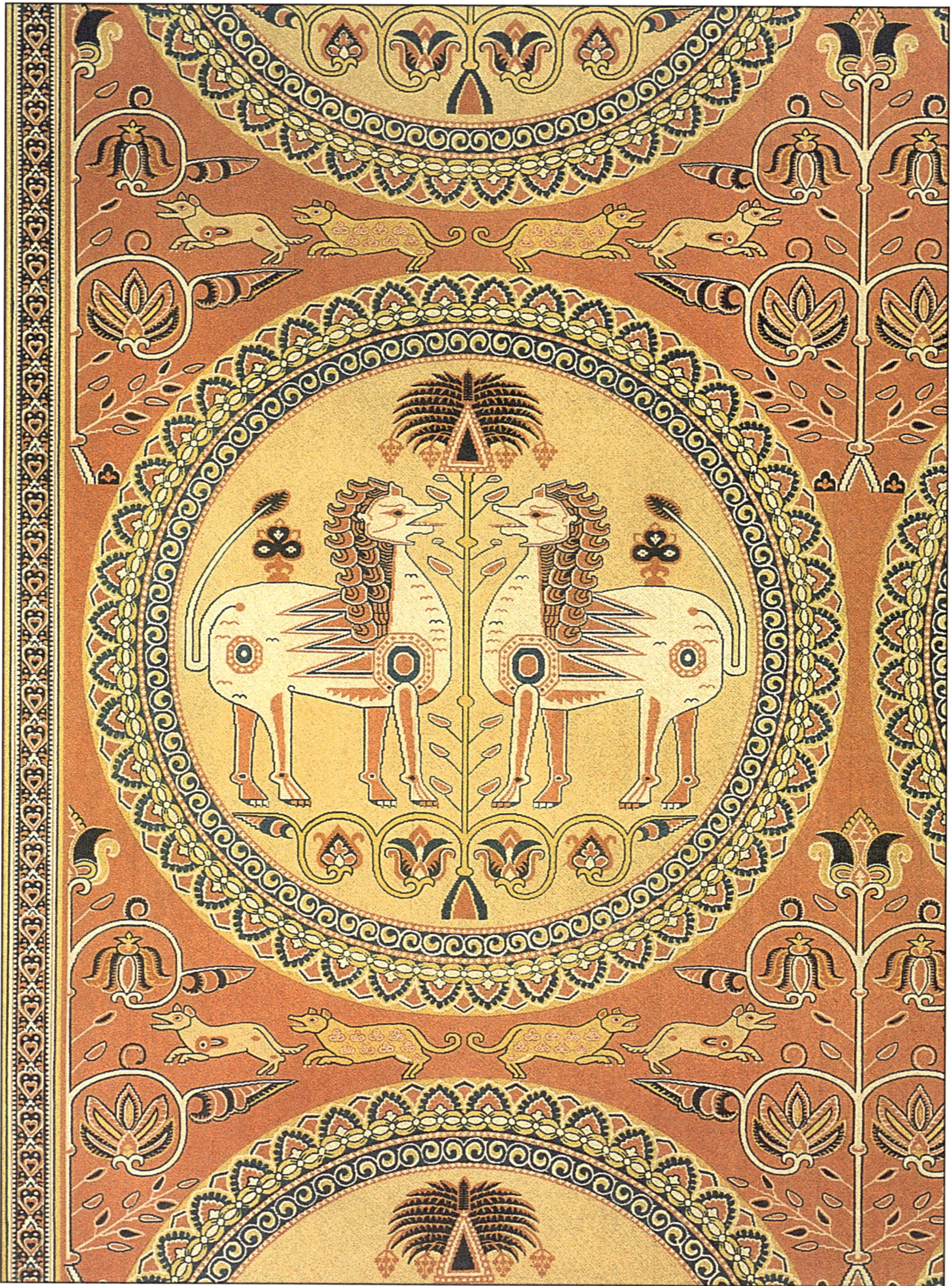

SILK TEXTILE
Conserved in Toulouse (14th century)

Plate CXLVIII

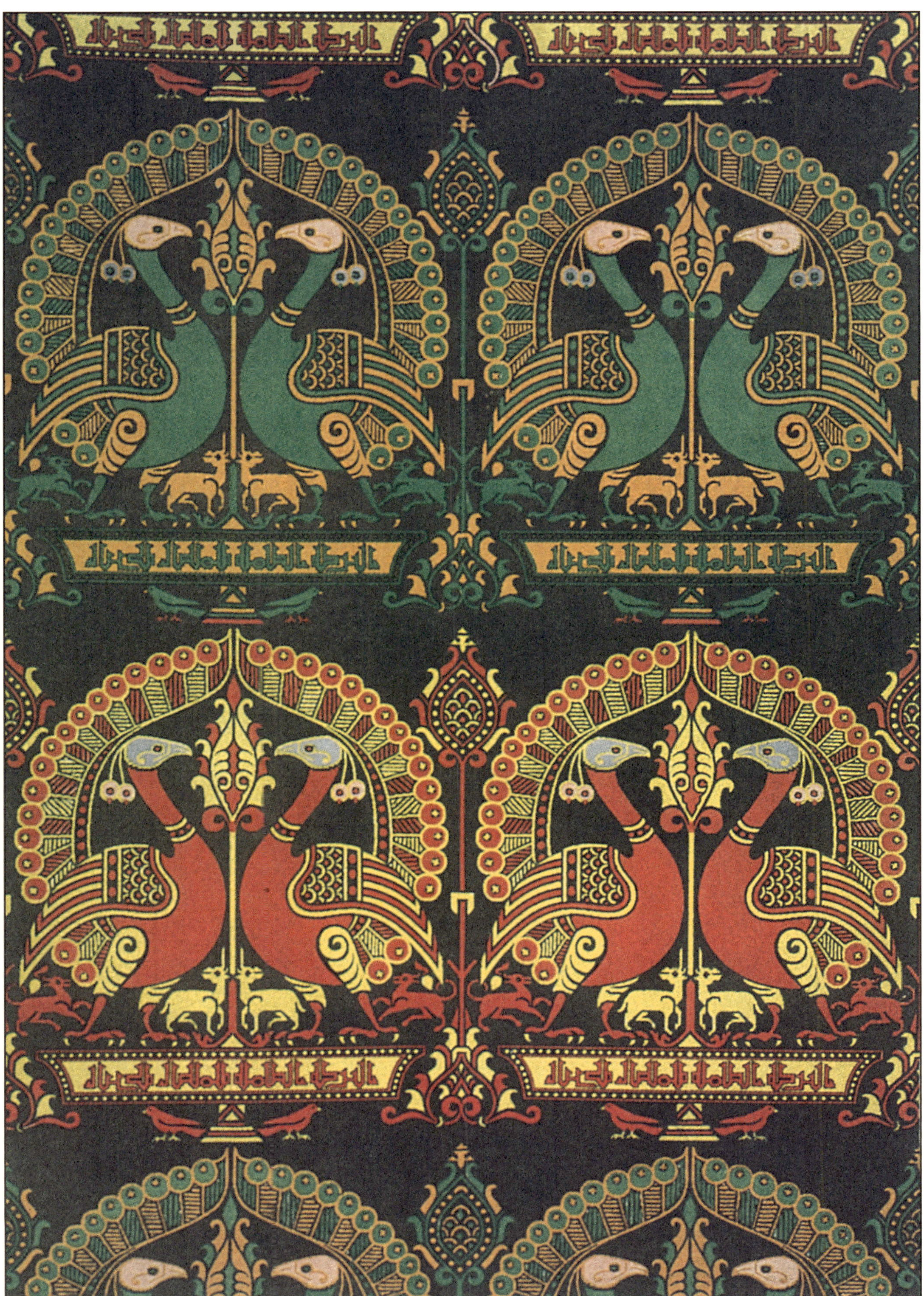

FRAGMENT OF A TAPESTRY

Conserved in the Church of Nivelles (14th century)

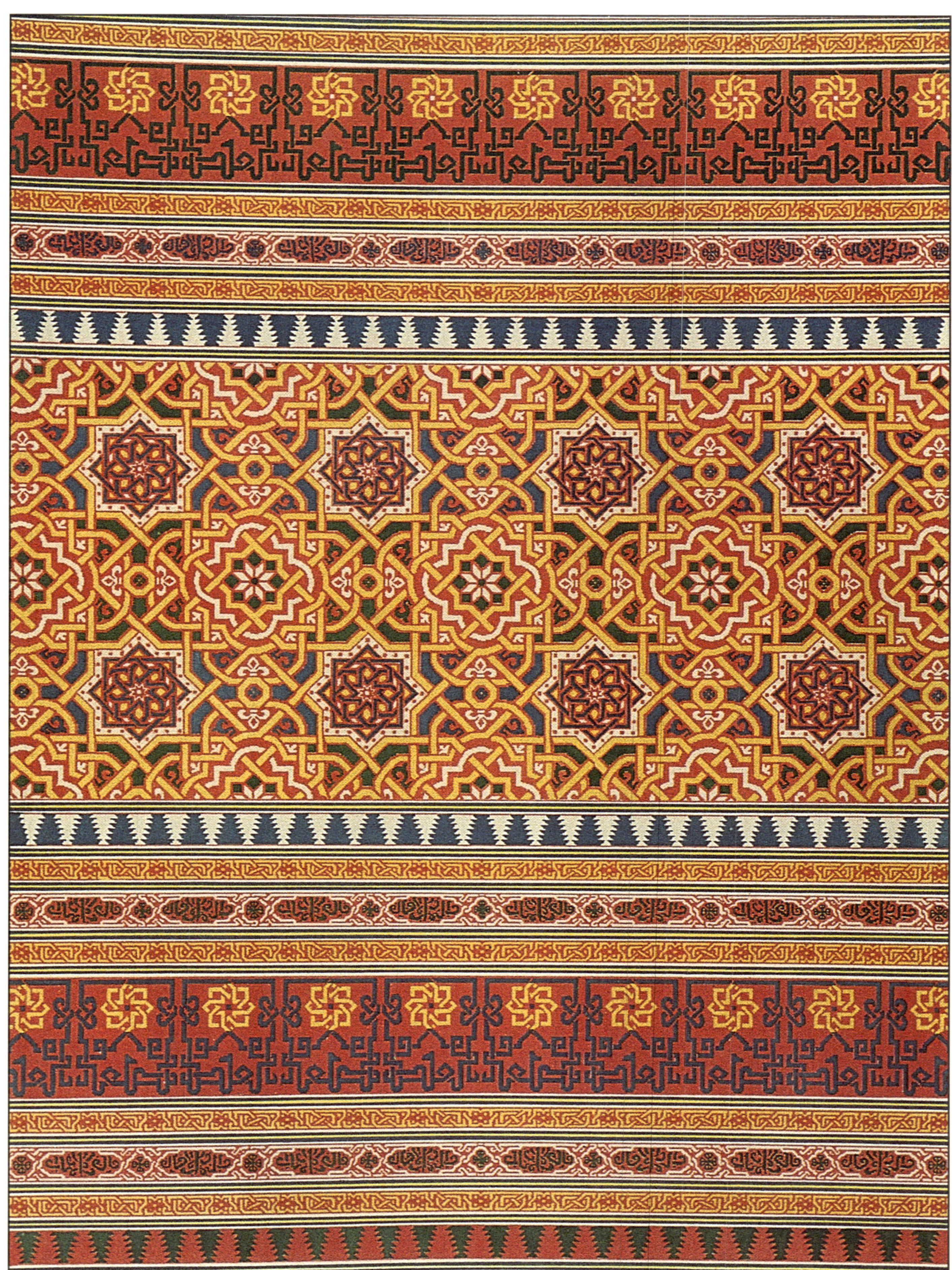

SMALL VELVETY CARPET
(14th century)

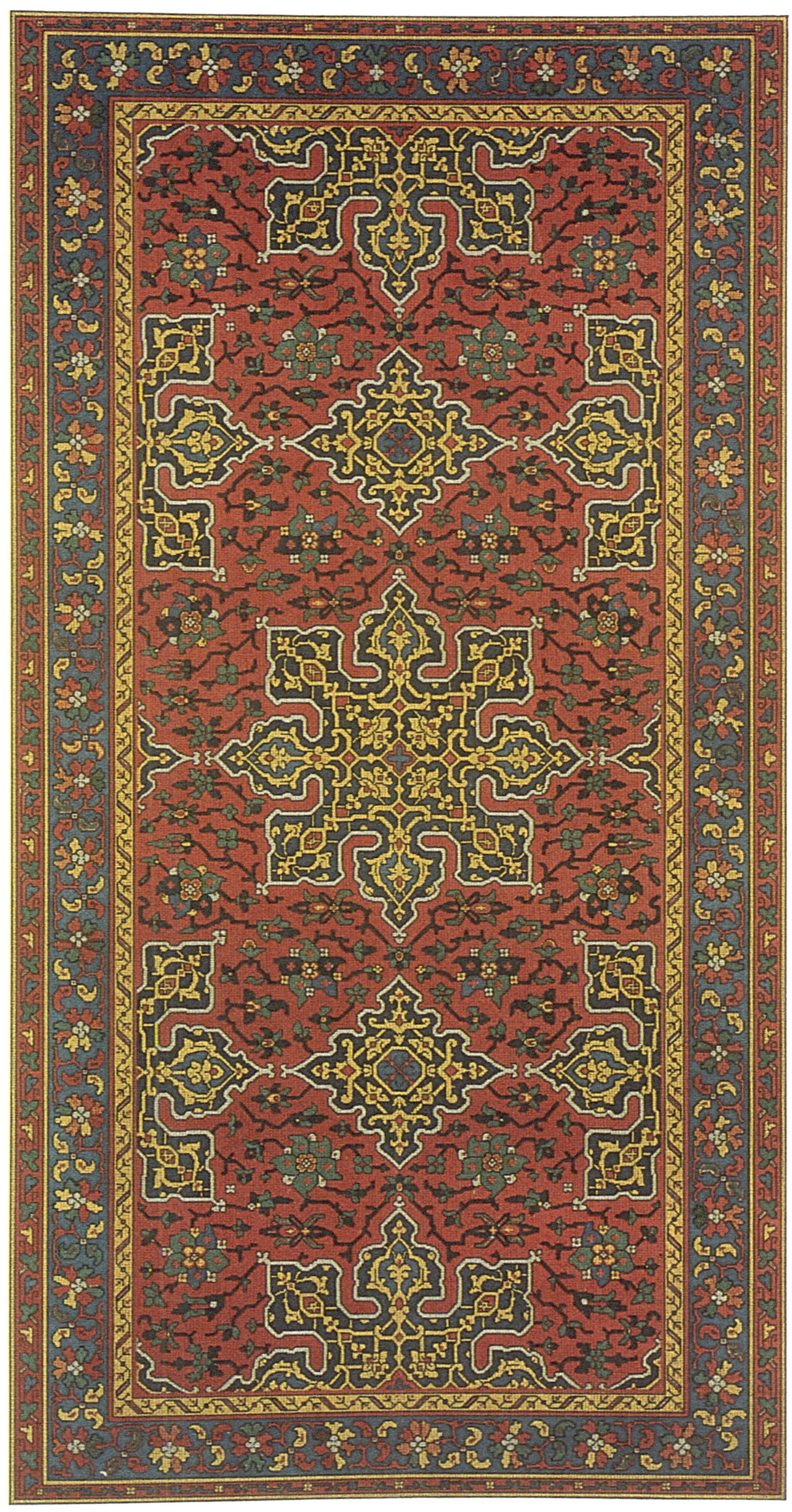

Plate CLI

TEXTILE

Conserved in the Museum of Utrecht (14th century)

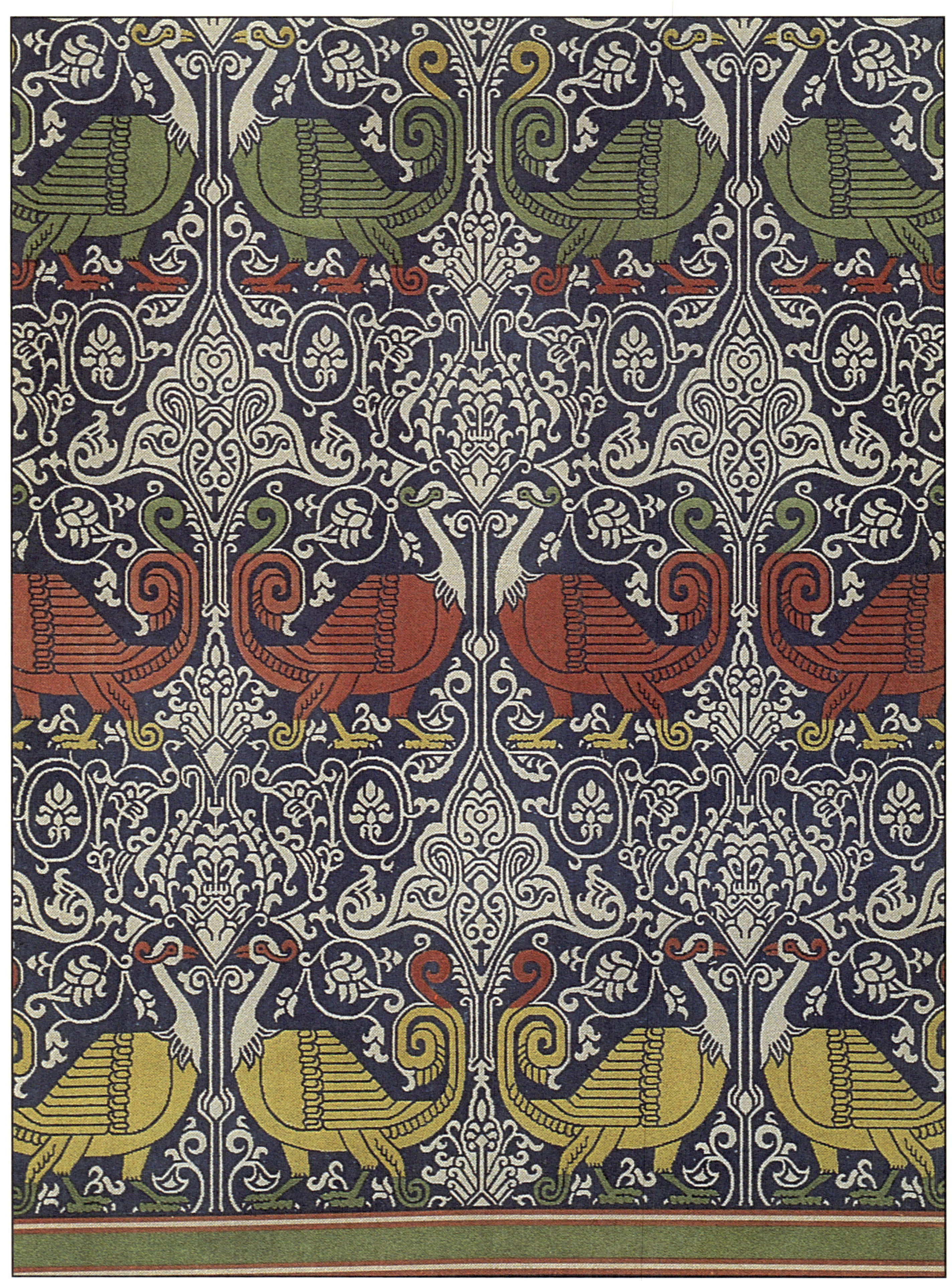

QUIVER AND BOW-CASE

(16th century)

Plate CLII

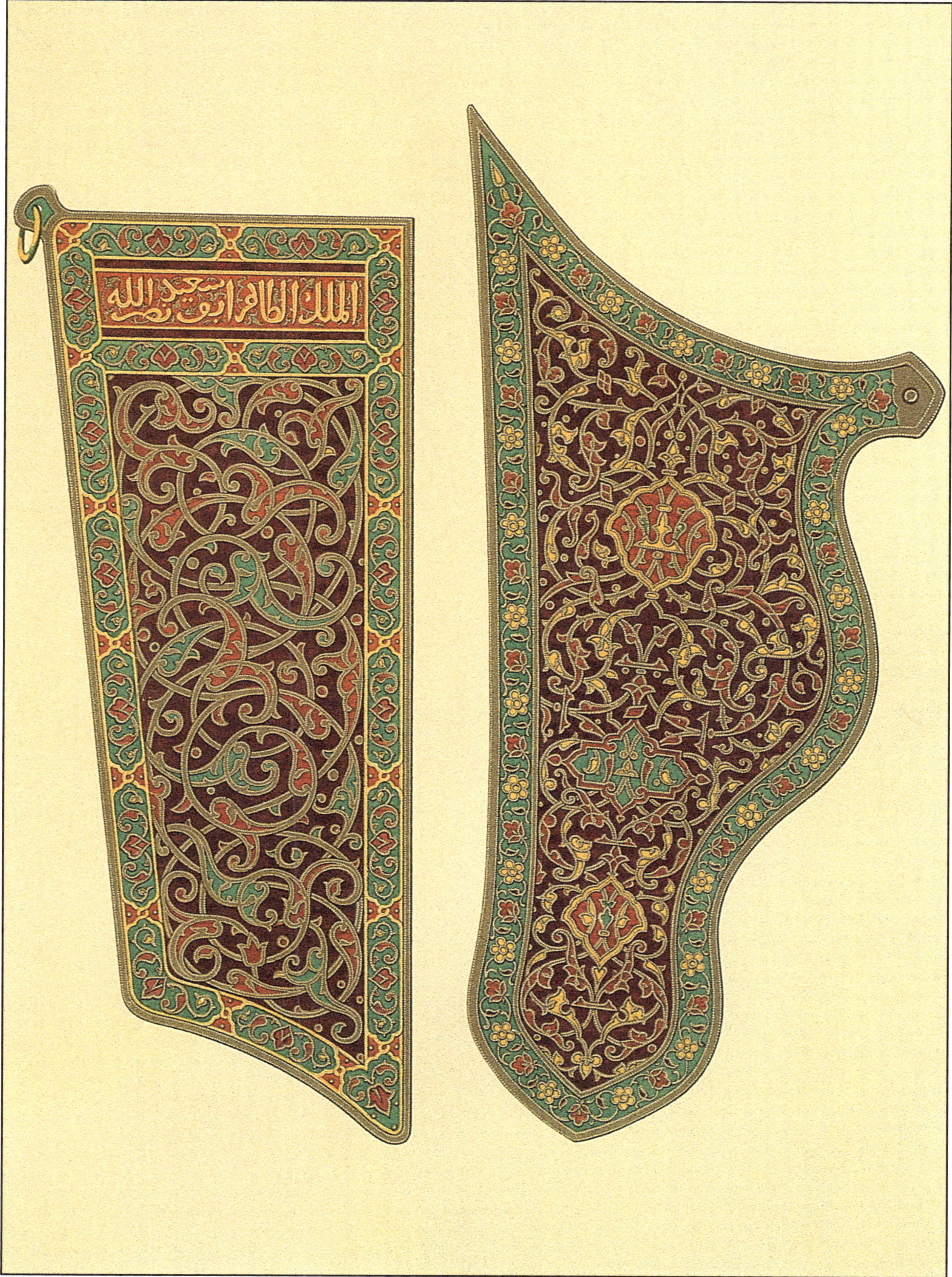

LARGE VELVETY CARPET
(18th century)

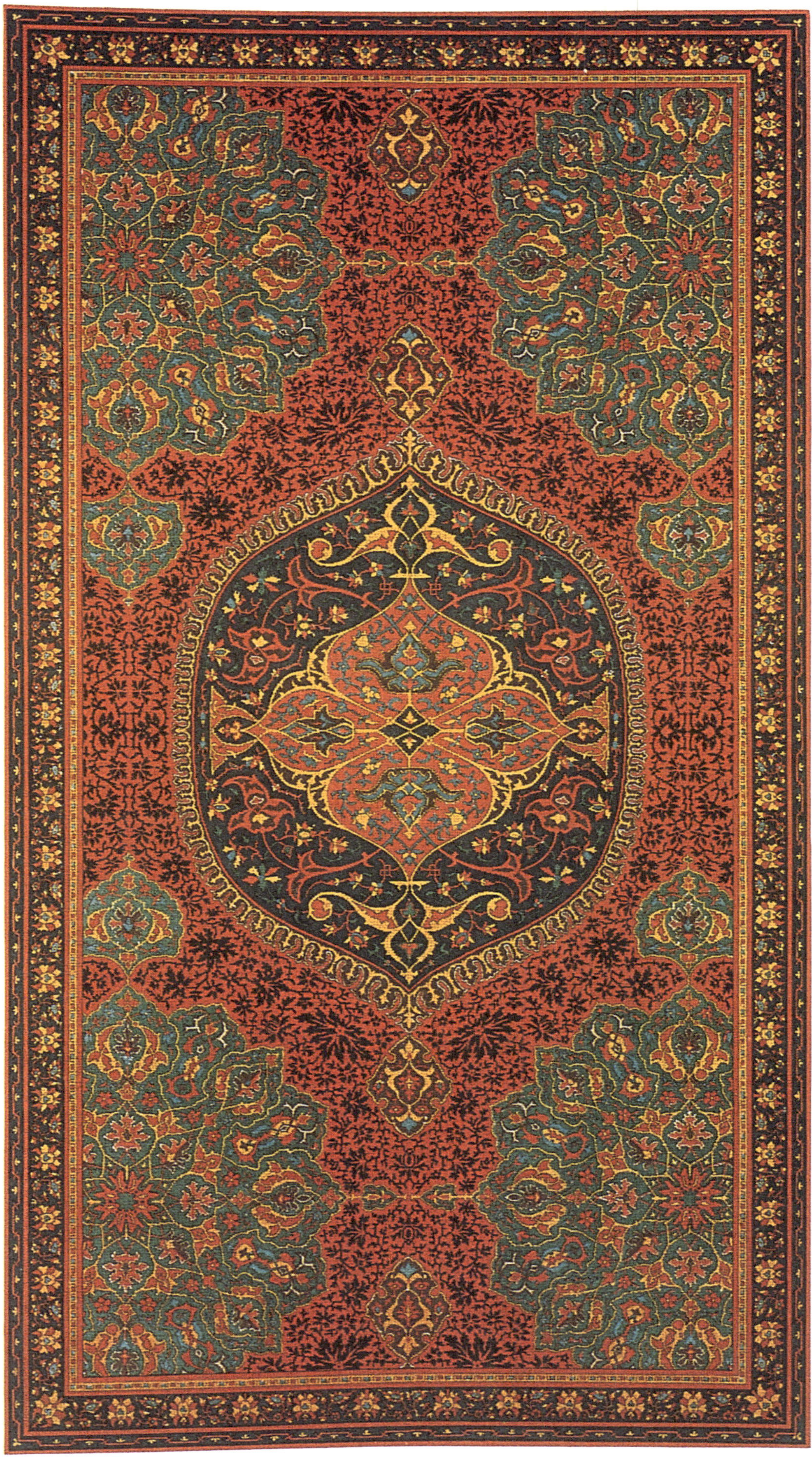

HADA

Textile for Covering Wall Panels (18th century)

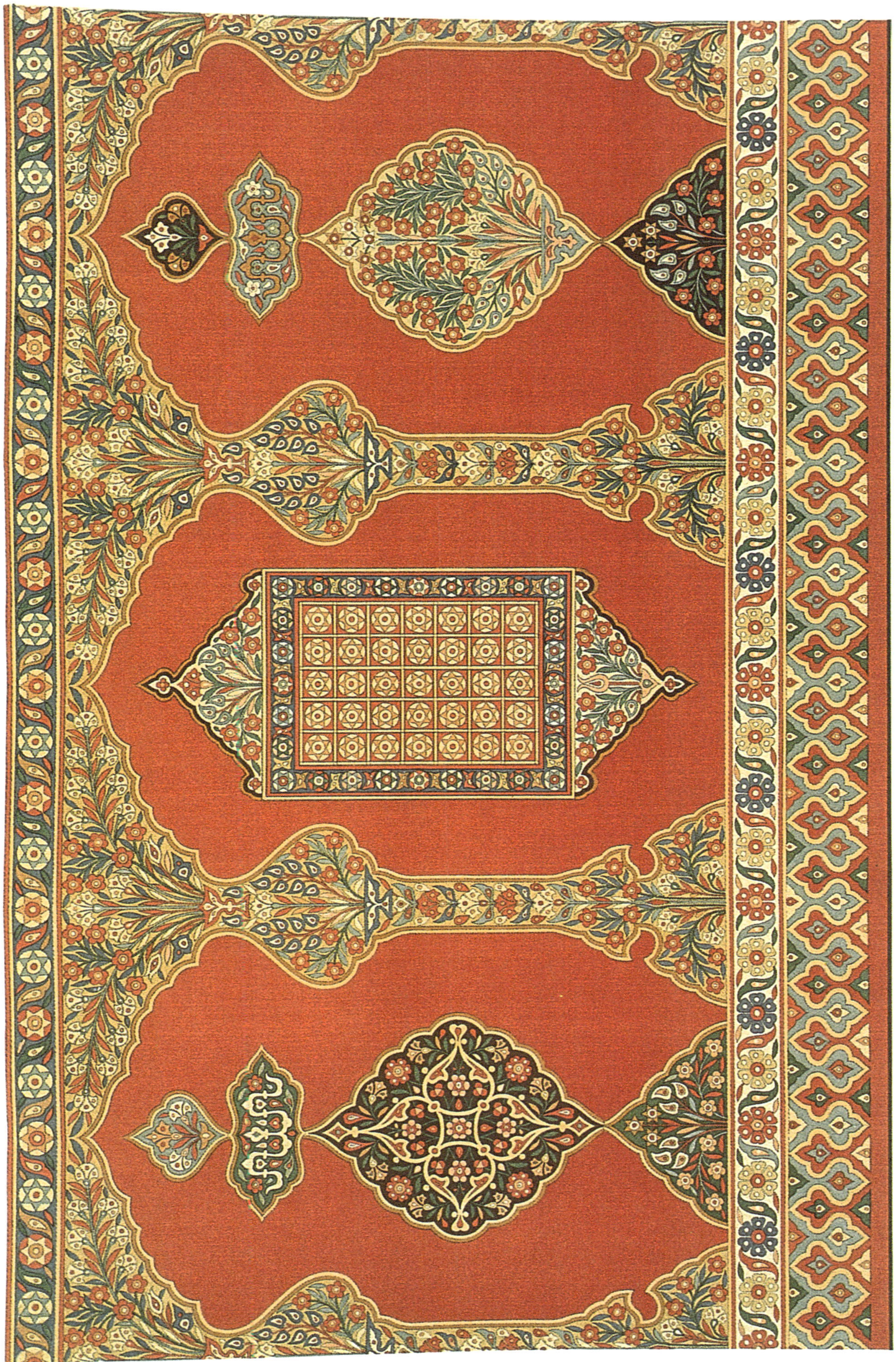

Plates CLV to CLVI
ARMS AND ARMOUR

The arms of Toman Bey al-Achraf (Pl. CLV) consist of his helmet, lance, dagger, axe, *djoukan* and mace. They all bear the name of the Sultan and the date, years 917 and 921 of the Hegira (1511 and 1515 of the Christian era). Made in Persian steel, known as *Khorassan*, they are very tastefully damascened in gold. The most common procedure for fixing these elegant arabesques on steel consists of engraving or rather striating all the ornaments with a smooth file; a thread of gold is then laid down and fixed in the groove with a hammer and burnisher.

The helmut, of Oriental form, which is to say rounded on top and visorless, is in Damascus steel, burnished and damascened in gold. On the front of the helmet, a small screw holds in place the steel tongue, which is lowered over the face to protect it from sabre blows. The rest of the head and neck are protected by a network of steel, of which only a few rings remain. The escutcheons adorning the band of the helmet display various passages from the Koran and pious phrases: "God: there is no other God than he. He possesses everything on heaven and earth. The greatness of his throne encompasses the entire universe, whose preservation and government do not disturb him. He is the high one, the majestic one, the vigilant one par excellence. Sleep and distractions never affect him. Oh, thee who brings matters to an end! Oh, judge of important things! give victory to the true believers, etc., etc."

The *djoukan* is a pointed staff with a curved palm used by the ancient Mamelukes to break chain mail. This hook also served to retrieve javelins or *djerid* falling to the ground short of the mark without requiring the horseman to dismount. The Mamelukes usually entrusted the dangerous task of retrieving lost javelins to their grooms, as they ran amongst the mounted combatants.

The mace or bludgeon resembles that of our ancient knights. The handle was trimmed with crimson velvet held in place by a steel tongue damascened in gold.

The axe is in good taste and of priceless workmanship. The two finely-chased designs decorating the lance indicate by their style that this arm was made in Persia. It bears no other inscription but these three words: "Allah, Muhammad, Toman", which is to say, the name of God, that of Muhammad, his prophet, and that of Toman, his possessor.

The dagger, whose handle is in agate adorned with semiprecious stones and whose undulating blade features chiselled ribs, bears two inscriptions: "I encharge thee with my revenge, God, who is the best master, the best protector and the best agent... My God, do not oppose what I undertake to do... Lord, complete thy blessings to good end."

The lance, which is of admirable workmanship and taste, resembles rather more a jousting lance than an arm of war. The entire shaft is covered in crimson velvet and a long green-and-white silk cordlet is wrapped around it. The small-columned structure which links the blade to the ferrule of the shaft represents the temple of Mecca, the eternal Ka'aba. The base bears the names of Allah, Mohammed, Ali and Toman on its four sides. The ball of silver holds a clod of earth from the tomb of the Prophet, and bears the legend: "We have made another conquest for us, in the name of God, lenient and merciful."

The small amulet hanging from the cordlet contains a piece of the coat of the Prophet; upon it is inscribed the profession of Islamic faith.

We have not deigned to figure the sabre of Toman Bey, whose design resembled every sabre in Persia.

The shield or rondache probably still decorates the ceiling of a harem in Cairo, from which these arms were taken to be sold at auction several years ago.

Armour for the Head of a Horse (Pl. CLVI).—Executed after a stamping by Mr Cournault, it is in steel damascened in gold. This piece, although belonging to the Turkish era and of a slightly heavy style, seemed to us to complete the panoply of arms of Toman Bey.

ARMS OF TOMAN BEY
(15th century)

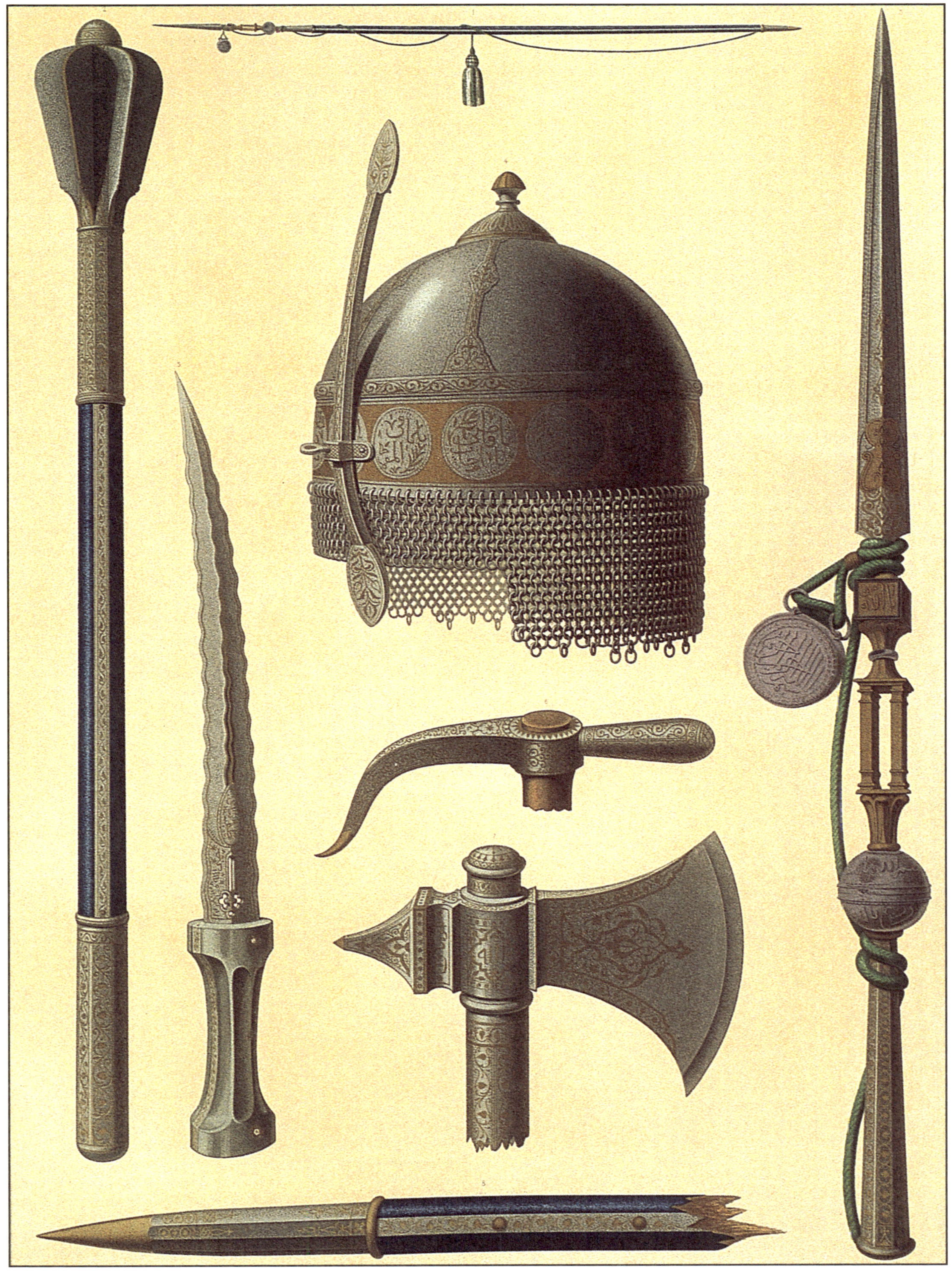

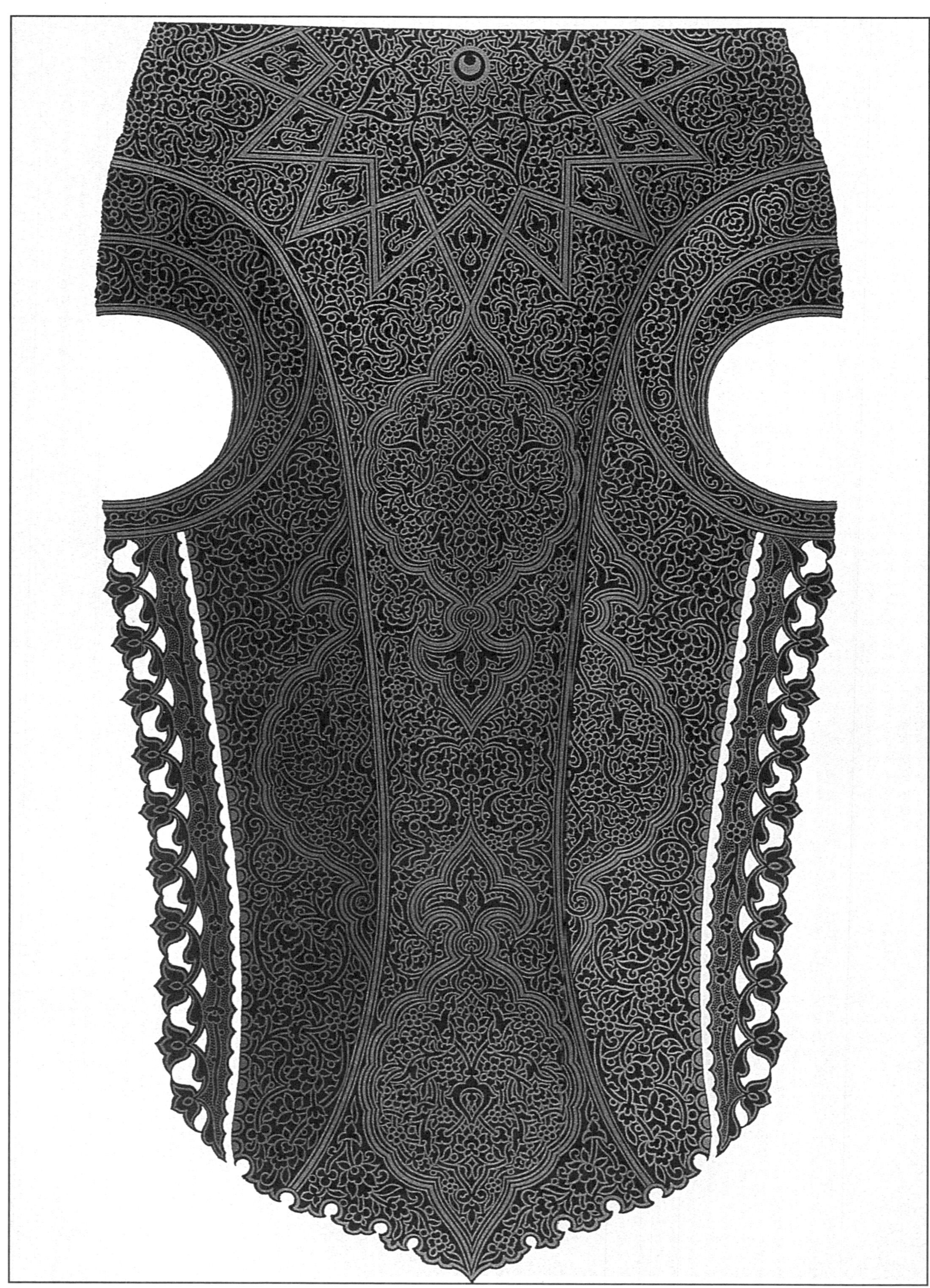

Plates CLVII to CLXXIII
CIVIL AND RELIGIOUS FURNITURE
Copper and Damascene

At the end of the meal in the homes or tents of rich Muslim families, a servant or slave appears holding a large metal basin in one hand, and an ewer in the other; each guest is approached in order of seating and invited to wash. Ablutions follow a certain order: first the hands, then the mouth and finally the beard. The servant wears a towel on his shoulder of varying richness, sometimes embroidered in silk and gold, and each guest in turn uses it to dry off.

The bottom of the basin is equipped with a sort of openwork tray, which allows already sullied water to be hidden from the gaze so as not to disgust the viewer. In the middle of the tray is a small cup to hold the soap. The basin is called a *Techt* and the ewer an *Ibrik*.

These small everyday furnishings are ordinarily in tinplated copper or brass in modest homes, in silver in the homes of certain more important personages, in enamel for the Shah of Persia, and in gold for sultans.

The one represented in Plate CLXI is in brass with dry-point engraving; it comes from Persia and dates from the 16th century.

Ivory Casket Decorated with Silver. Conserved in the Bayeux Cathedral (Pl. CLVII).—We have given a long explanatory note on this casket in Chapter XI[1].

Lamp from the Tomb of Sultan Baybars II (Pl. CLVIII).—This lamp in gilded bronze decorated the tomb of Sultan Baybars II, and was ordered by his eunuch to honour the memory of his master. It is indeed original and of admirable taste.

Ornamental Details of a Sedrieh (Pl. CLIX).—The curved vases known as *sedrieh*, widely used in all Arabian palaces, are well-enough known to dispense here with a detailed description, such as the one given of the sedrieh of Sultan Muhammad ibn Qala'un (Pl. CLXVII). We have limited ourselves, therefore, to reproducing its ornamental details.

Brass trays (Pl. CLX and CLXI).—We believed, in accordance with Mr Cournault, that this tray and another of the same type had been executed by Arabs of Egypt. After a more serious examination and in light of information gathered in Italy, we now think that they come rather from a small city near Venice, where Muslim workmen and captives were held prisoner and obliged to earn their keep.

All these works, although Arabic in reality, take on a special recognisable style as a result of a geometrical pattern particular to them. One of these is a tray in brass, completely covered with very fine interlaces showing traces of silver inlay.

Tinned Copper Tray (Pl. CLXII).—This tray or dish in tinplated copper, displaying an Arabic legend in its centre, is represented lying upon an exquisitely embellished tablet said to belong to Sultan Barquq. As it is of a more recent period than the tablet, it was probably left there inadvertently by some traveller.

Metal Hand-mirrors. Backs (Pl. CLXIV).—The backs of these mirrors are of exactly the same tone of metal as the fronts, a higher polish being the only difference.

They represent martichores singly or in groups, hunting scenes, etc. Most of these mirrors have already been reproduced by Mr Reinaud, in his work *Egyptian Monuments.*

Furnishings of Sultan Muhammad ibn Qala'un (Pl. CLXVI to CLXIX).—Many objects widely found in diverse European collections indicate, by their crest and the inscriptions embellishing them, that they were manufactured

1. See Prisse d'Avennes, *L'Art arabe d'après les monuments du Kaire,* volume of texts, same publisher.

for Sultan Melek al-Nacer Muhammad, son of Sultan Melek al-Mansour Qala'un, who reigned from 692 to 708 (1294 to 1309).

Plate CLXVI shows a bronze candlestick holder with ornaments and inscription damascened in silver and in gold from the furnishings of this sultan. It has three legs, like certain candlesticks from the Middle Ages, and still bears the point destined for the candle. On the medallion all that can be read is "Al-Melek-al-Nacer", a title common to several Muslim sovereigns, but the ducks from the Qala'un coat of arms, which form the border of this medallion, leave no doubt as to the sultan to which it belonged: Melek al-Nacer Muhammad ibn Qala'un.

We give again, in Plate CLXIX, two candlestick holders from the 14th century, most remarkable for the artistic richness of their decoration.

Vases in metal, brass or tinplated copper, very numerous in the homes of the different Islamic peoples, both in days gone by and the present, take on varied forms which imply diverse uses, and bear diverse names as yet unknown to us. They are generally adorned with inscriptions and arabesques which make veritable works of art of them, carefully crafted or damascened in gold and silver.

Most inscriptions only express a banal wish in favour of the owner, written by the manufacturer for the use of all and sundry: "Blessings, safety, health, affluence and lasting happiness to my owner!" But vases manufactured for sultans and emirs always bear their name and titles, allowing them to be dated precisely. Lastly, these vases are sometimes signed with the name of the manufacturer or damascener.

Several vases, like the mirror-backs, represent hunting scenes, animals fighting one another, musicians and revellers. Sometimes the twelve signs of the Zodiac, decorated with figures, are present.

In Egypt, vases of the rounded form seen in Plate CLXVII are called *sedrieh.* No longer in fashion today in noble dwellings, they are still quite common in the boutiques of Cairo food merchants where European amateurs buy them at all cost.

We know of three vases similar to the splendid *sedrieh* shown in this plate, all three of the same size and craftmanship. From the palace of Sultan Muhammad ibn Qala'un, two are still in his tomb in Moristan, and the third is in the British Museum.

A long and beautiful legend is inscribed on the belly of this *sedrieh,* in lovely Neskhi characters, damascened in silver and surrounded by arabesques featuring ducks, from the distinctive Qala'un coat of arms; it reads: "Glory and honour to our Master, the victorious king, the wiseman, the just, the warrior, supporter of the world and of religion, Muhammad Ibn Qala'un".

The three flowered medallions which separate the compartments display a small band damascened in gold in their centres; each repeats the following words: "Glory to our master, the sultan".

The bottom of the vase shows a lovely rosette, formed mainly by a series of fish, a type of ornament frequently encountered on *sedrieh.*

In Plate CLXXII, we have reproduced other, less important, *sedrieh* to demonstrate the wide disparity in richness; these were for sherbets and other refreshments. We also provide several drawings of vases and trays in copper (Pl. CLX, CLXII, and CLXV).

Penbox of Sultan Bahrite Shaban. Details (Pl. CLXX and CLXXI).—The *khatib,* or secretary to the sultan, used large and artistically wrought writing cases. When presenting himself to the audience of the prince, his writing case was carried by the amir of the gate or by one of the amirs most in favour with the master.

Nearly all writing cases of the august chancellery and of the secret chancellery were in brass, plated and incrusted with gold and silver. The one we give here is quite curiousby its ornamentation formed of arabesques and birds.

Vessel Inlaid with Bronze, Decorated with Martichores (Pl. CLXXIII).—This small vase is now part of a private collection; it belonged in years gone by to the Chapter of Templars, and was then passed down to its present owner. The monsters known as *martichores* (which decorate everything) go back to a most distant period, although Herodotus makes no mention of them.

IVORY CASKET DECORATED WITH SILVER

Conserved in the Bayeux Cathedral (12th century)

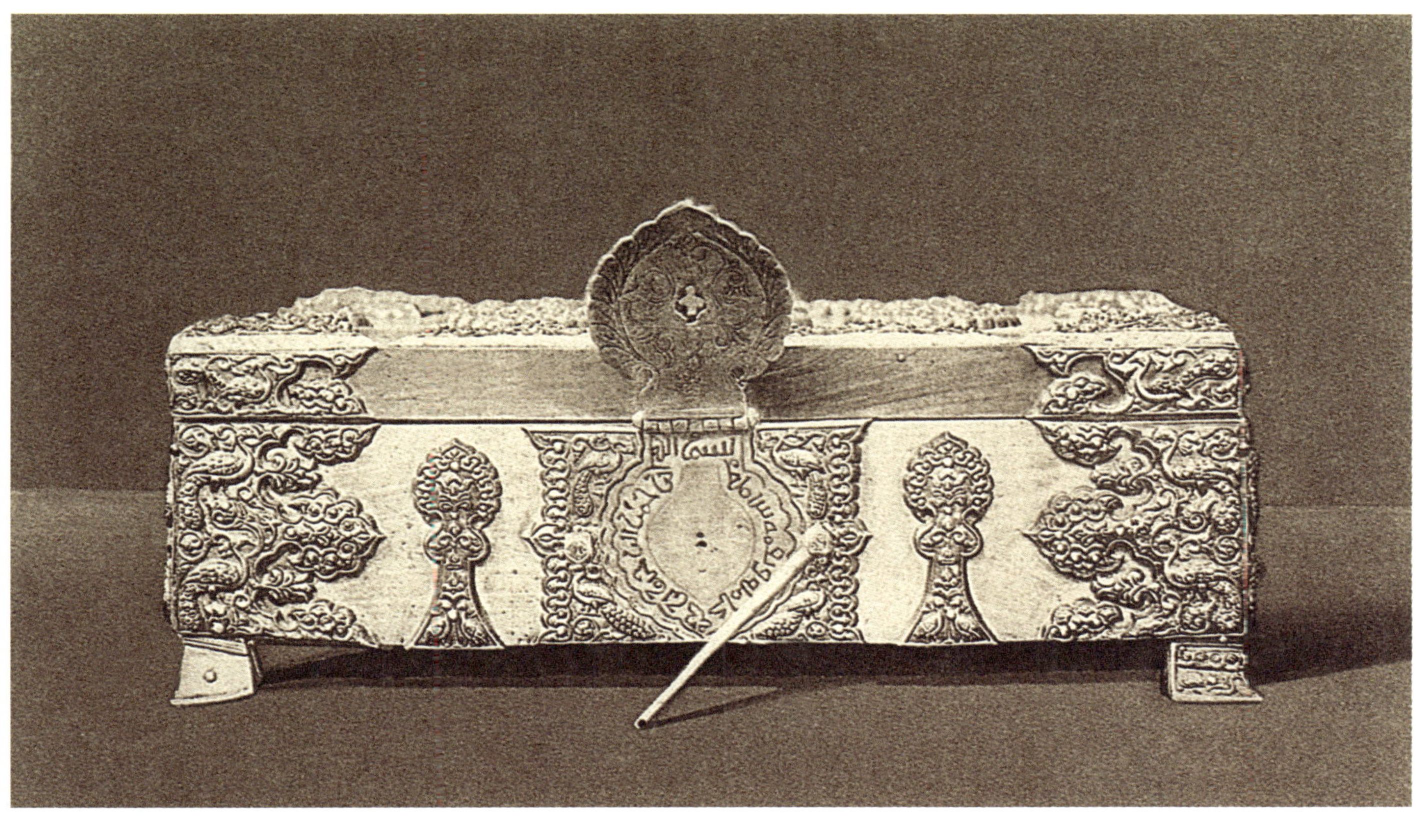

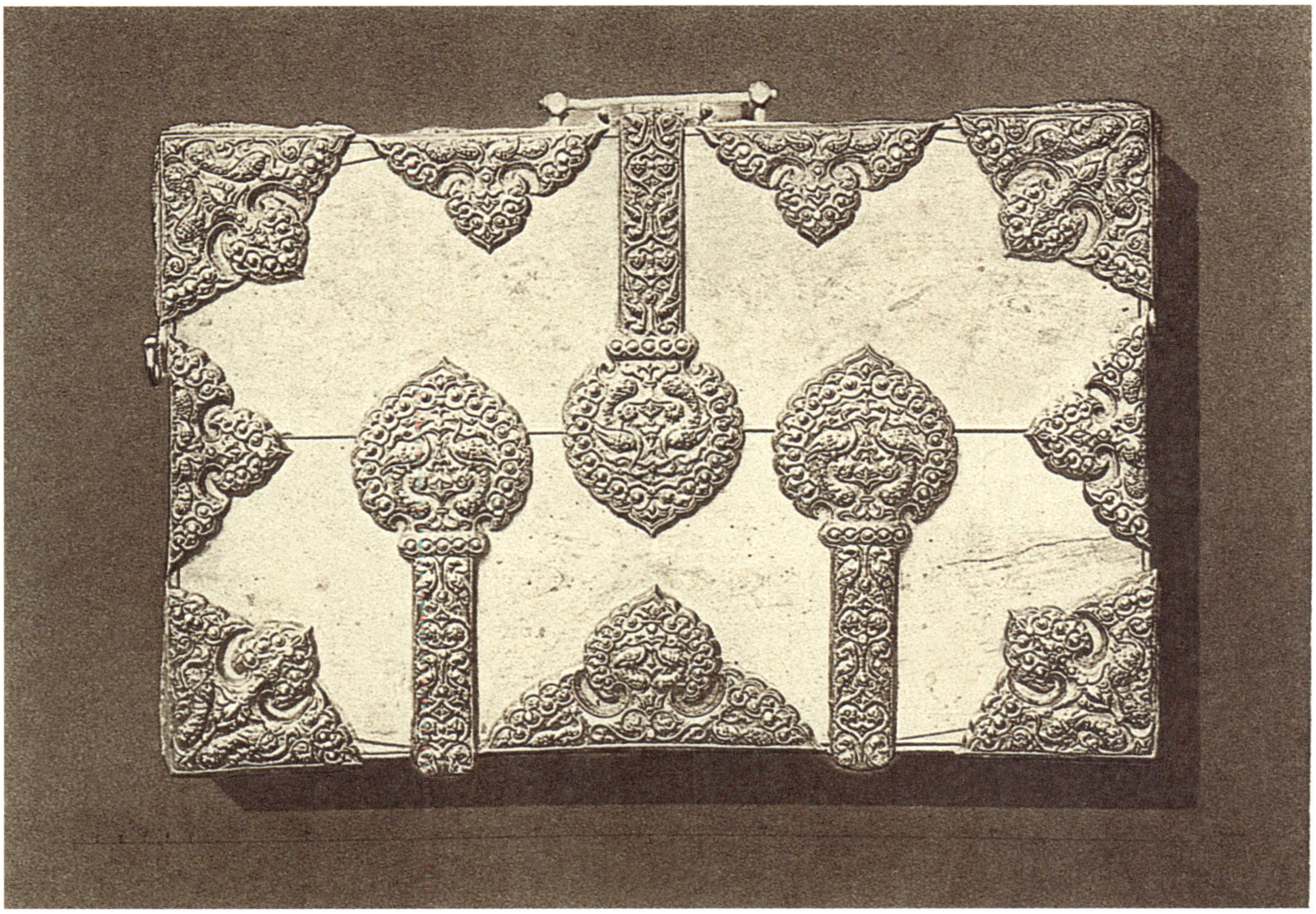

Plate CLVIII LAMP FROM THE TOMB OF SULTAN BAYBARS II
(14th century)

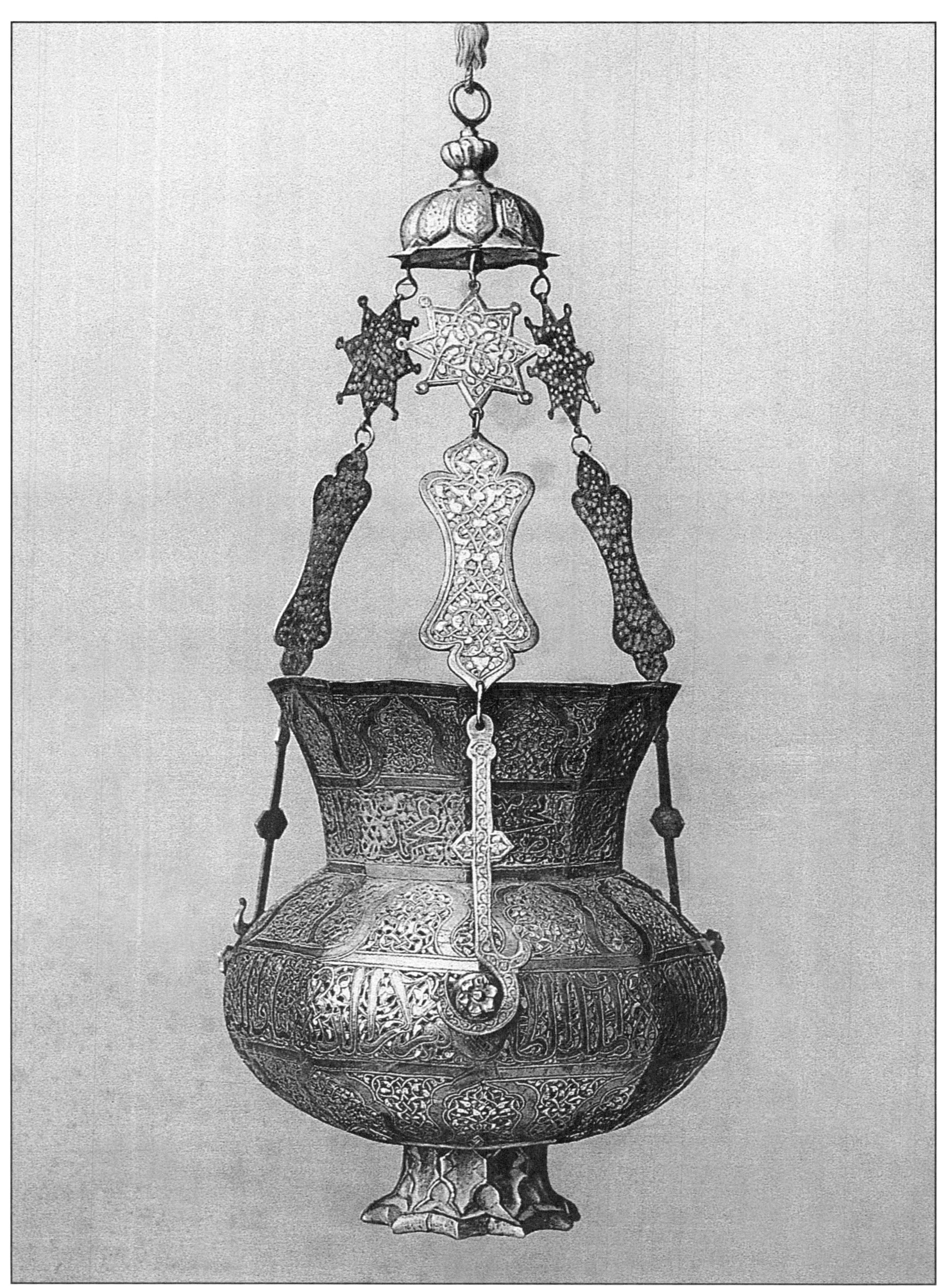

ORNAMENTAL DETAILS OF A SEDRIEH
(15th century)

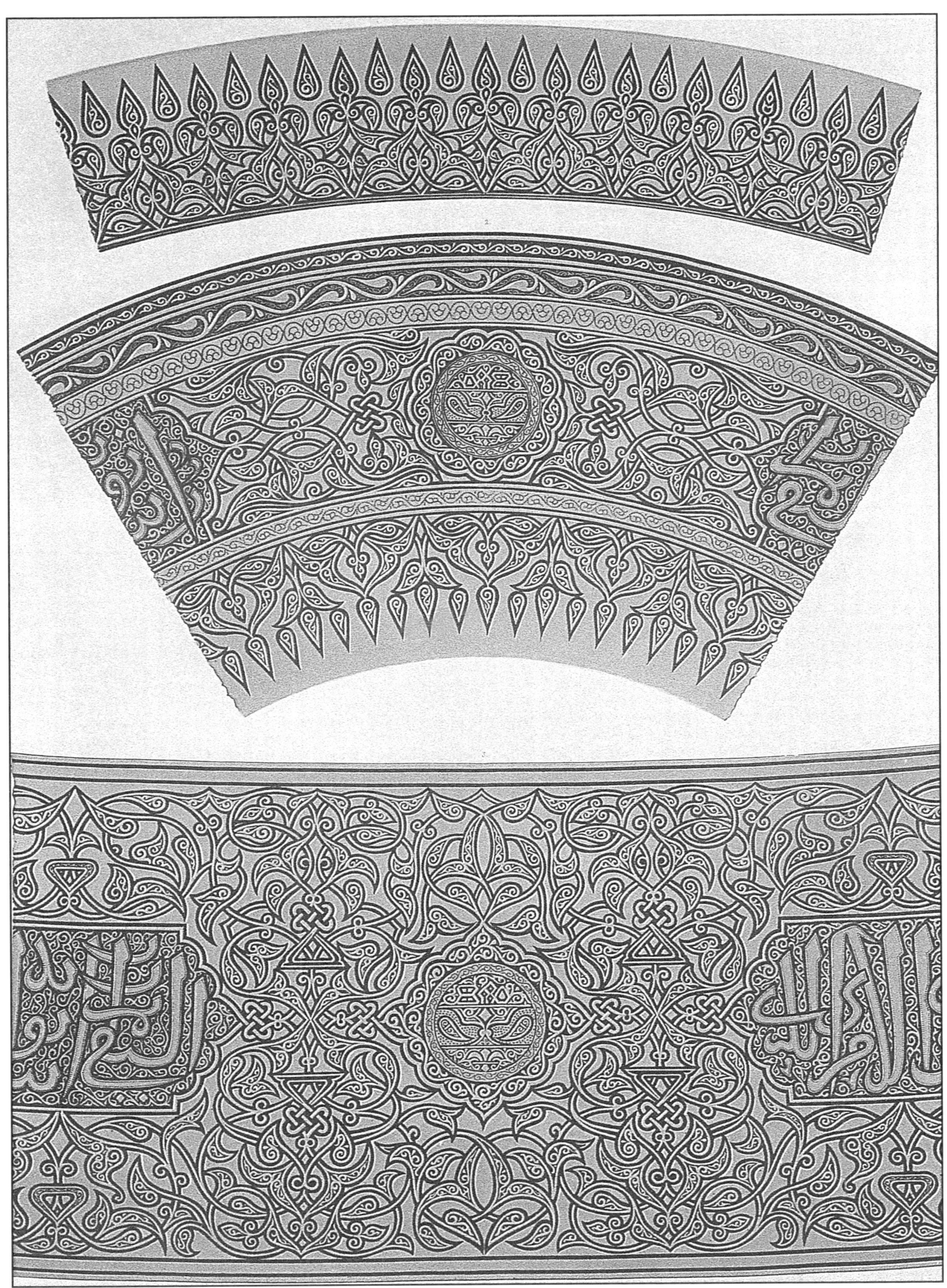

SMALL COPPER TRAY
(15th century)

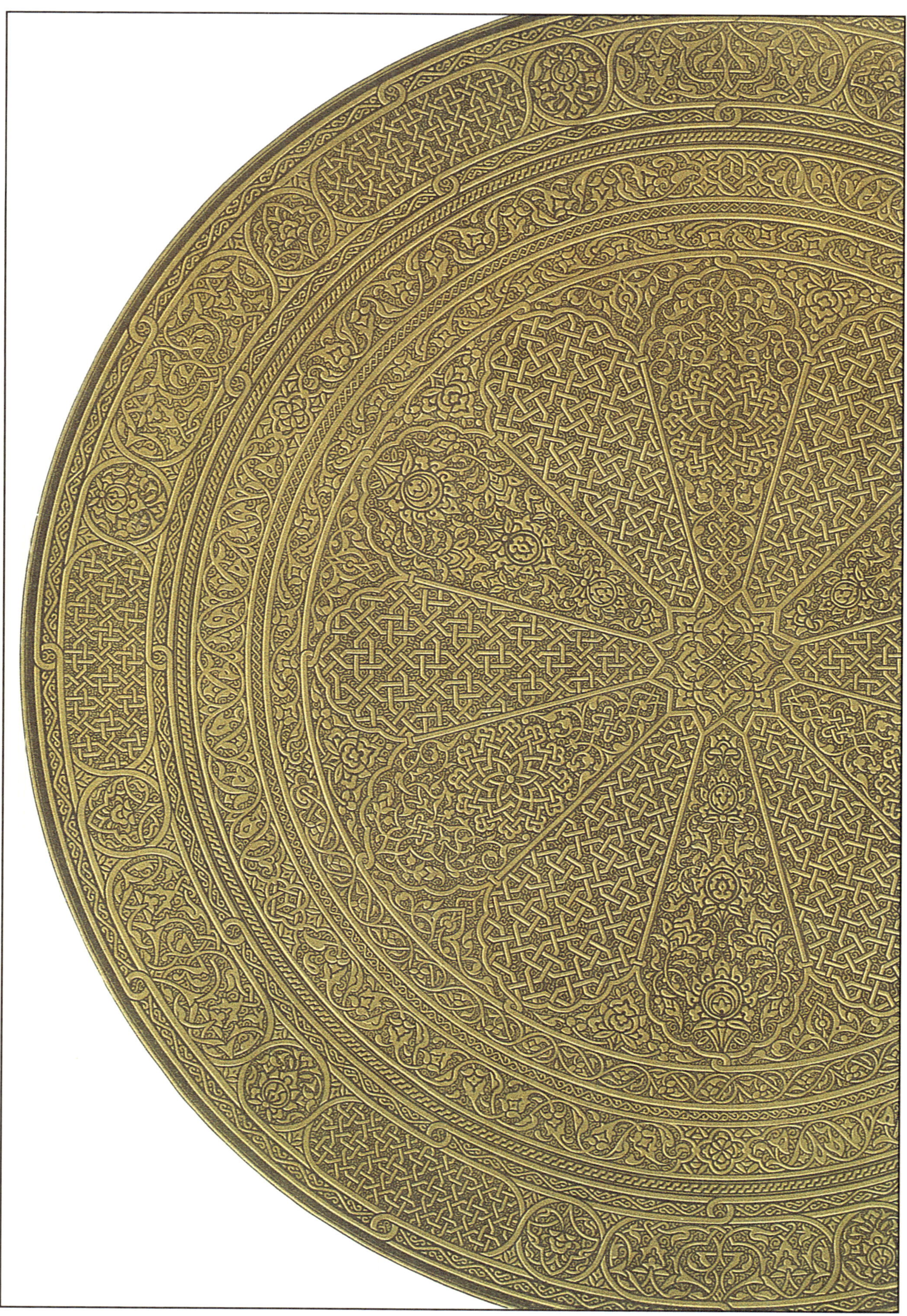

BRASS TRAY
(16th century)

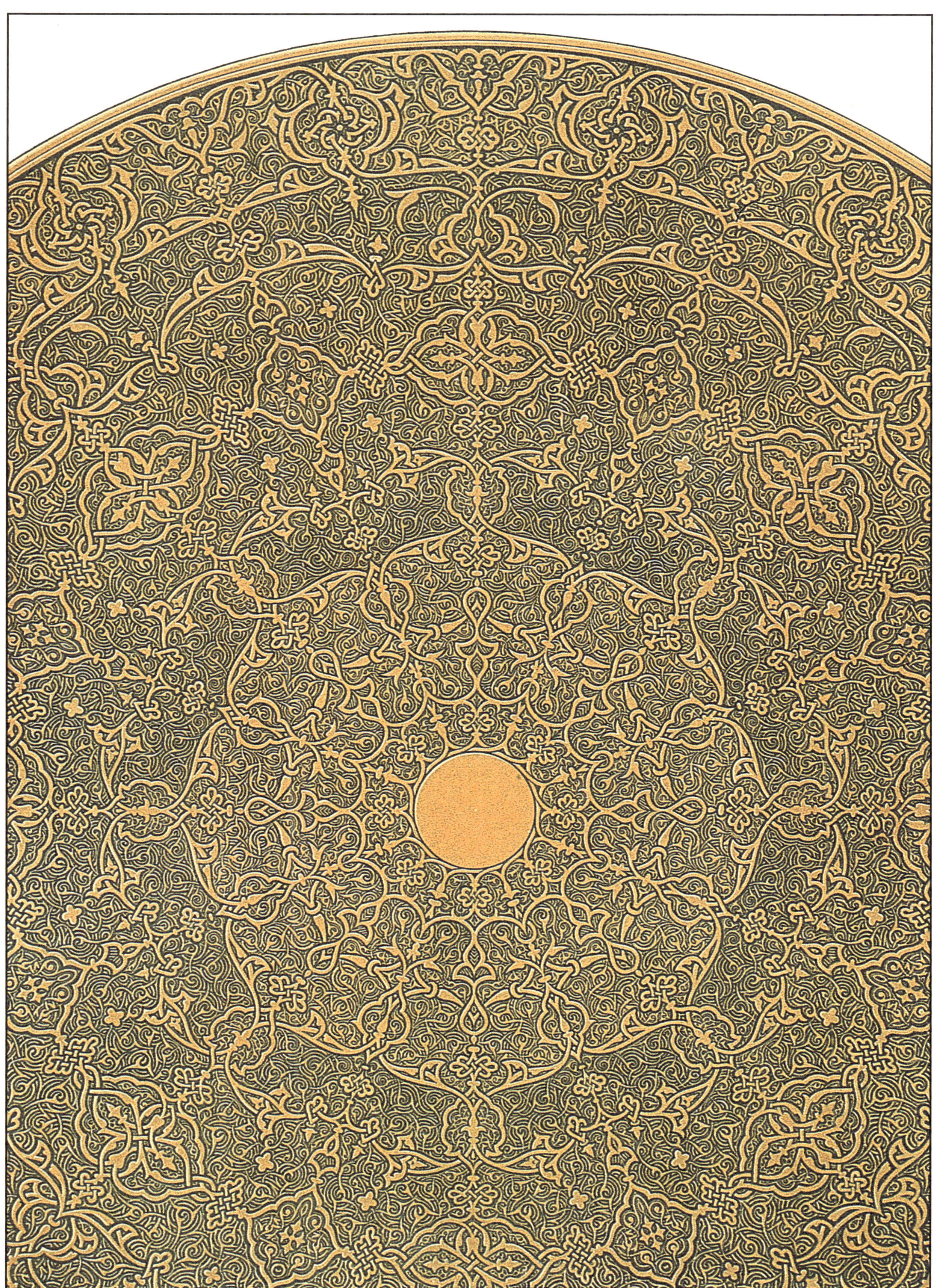

TINNED COPPER TRAY

Shelf of Sultan Barquq (16th century)

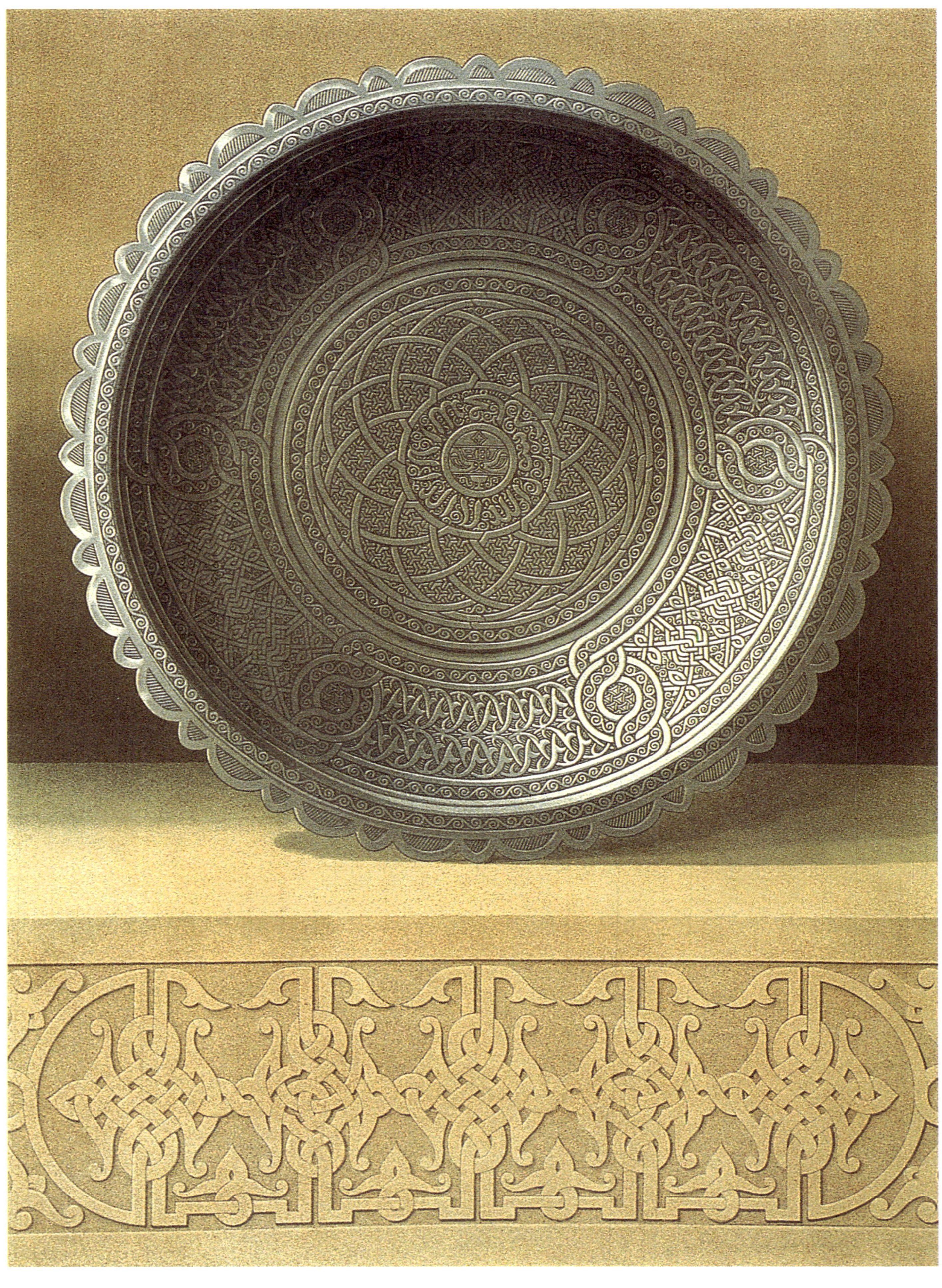

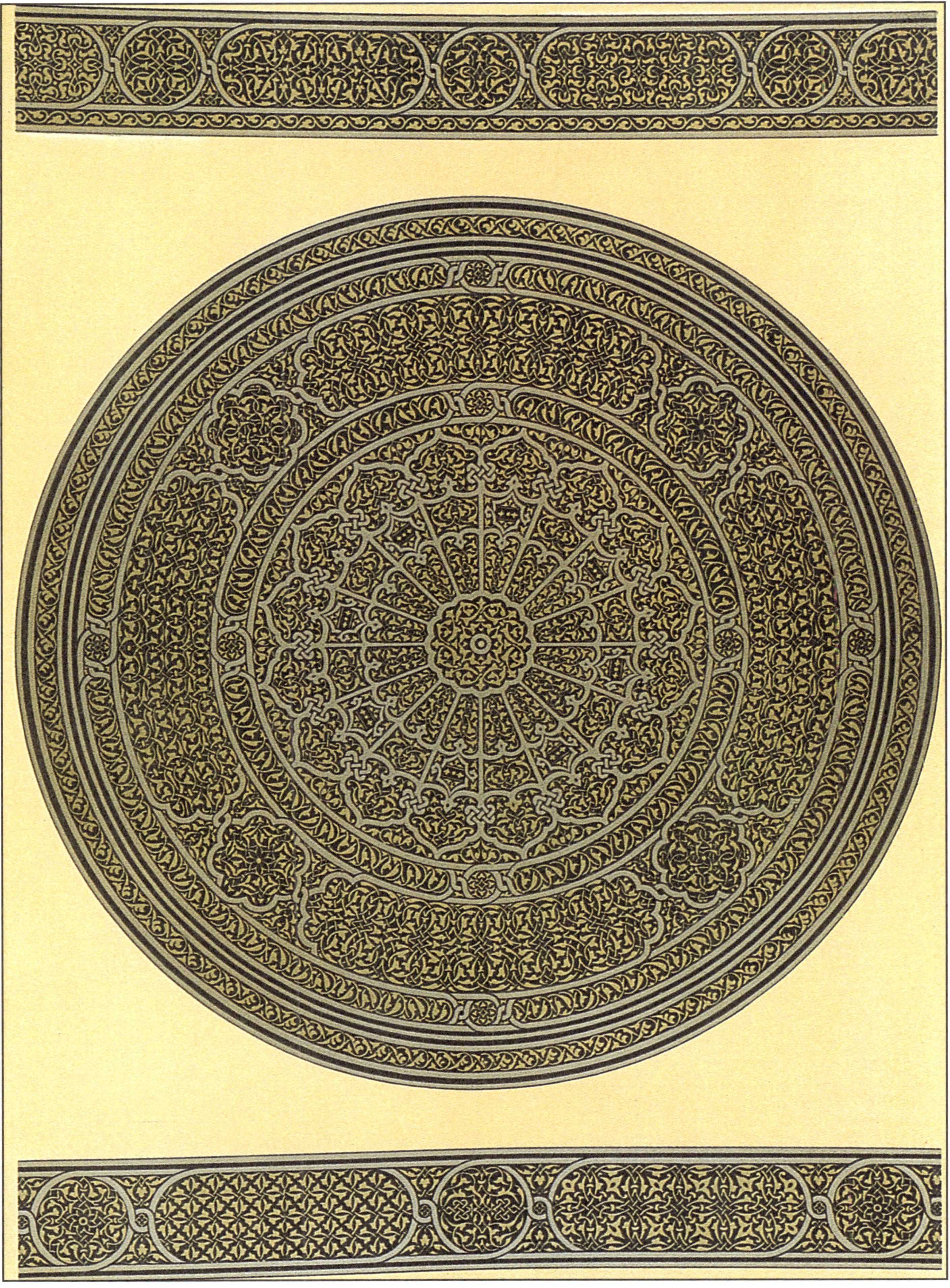

METAL HAND-MIRRORS

Backs

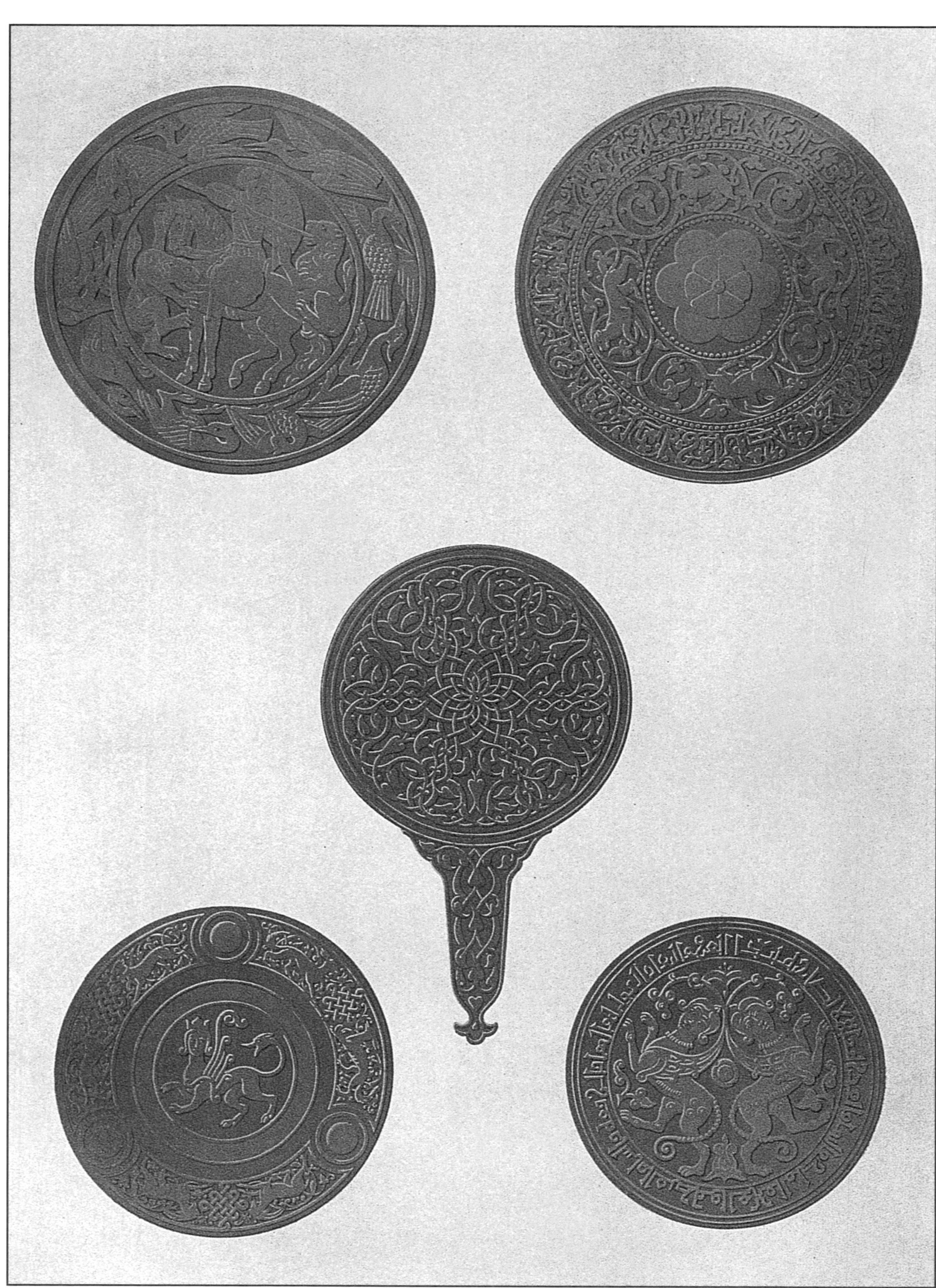

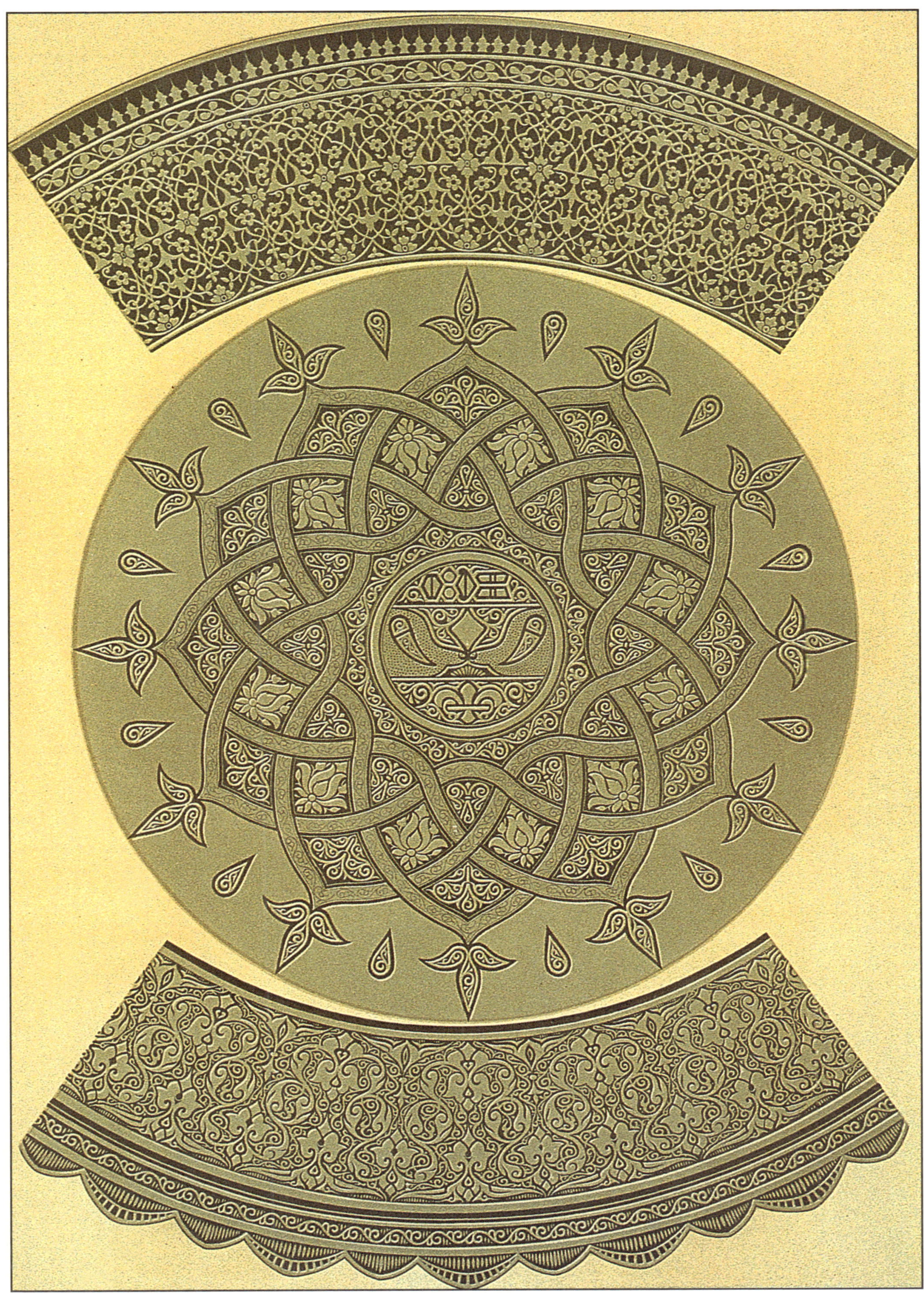

FURNISHINGS OF SULTAN MUHAMMAD IBN QALA'UN

Candlestick and Alcaraza Tray (14th century)

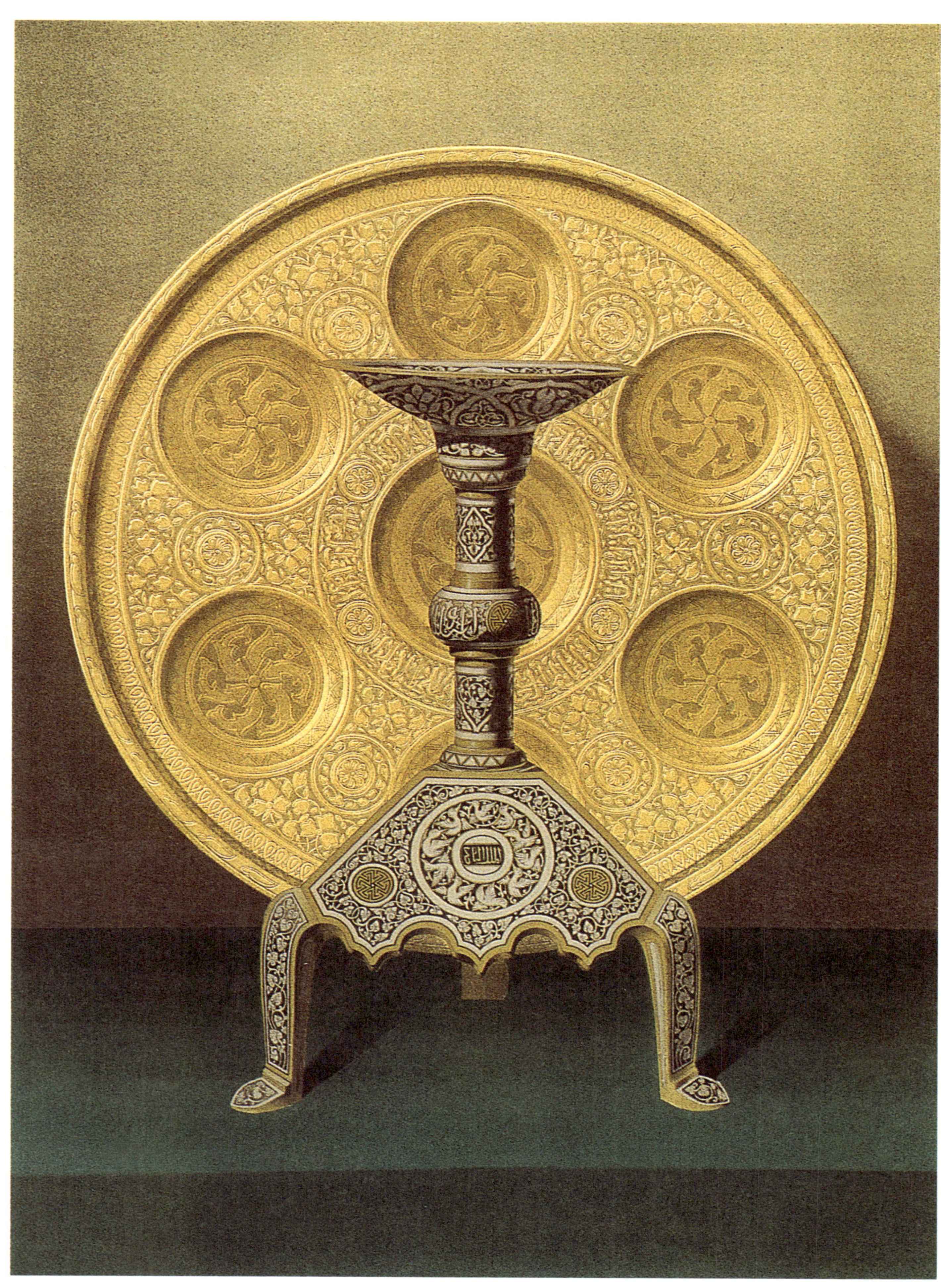

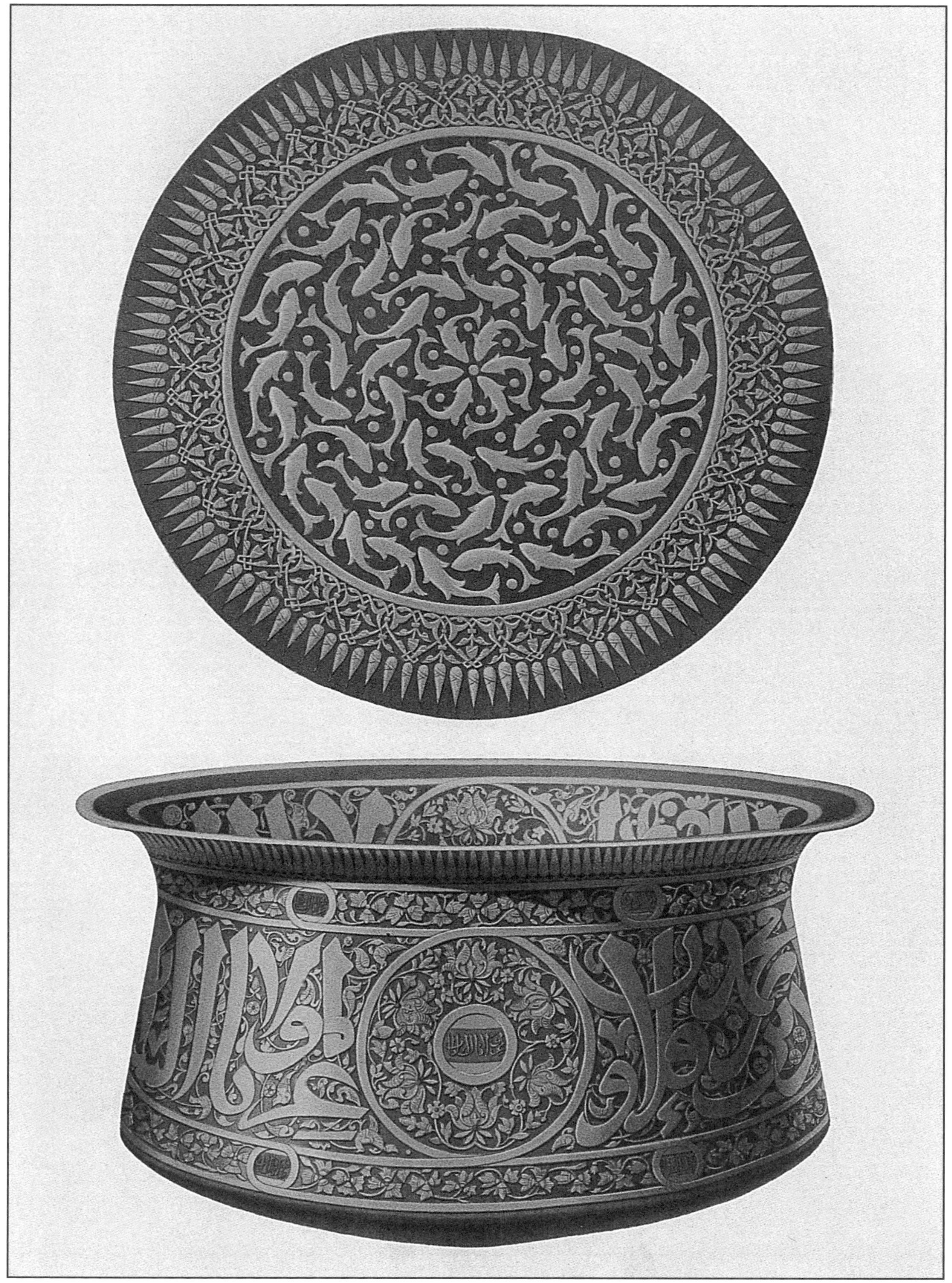

Inlaid Casket and Tray (16th century)

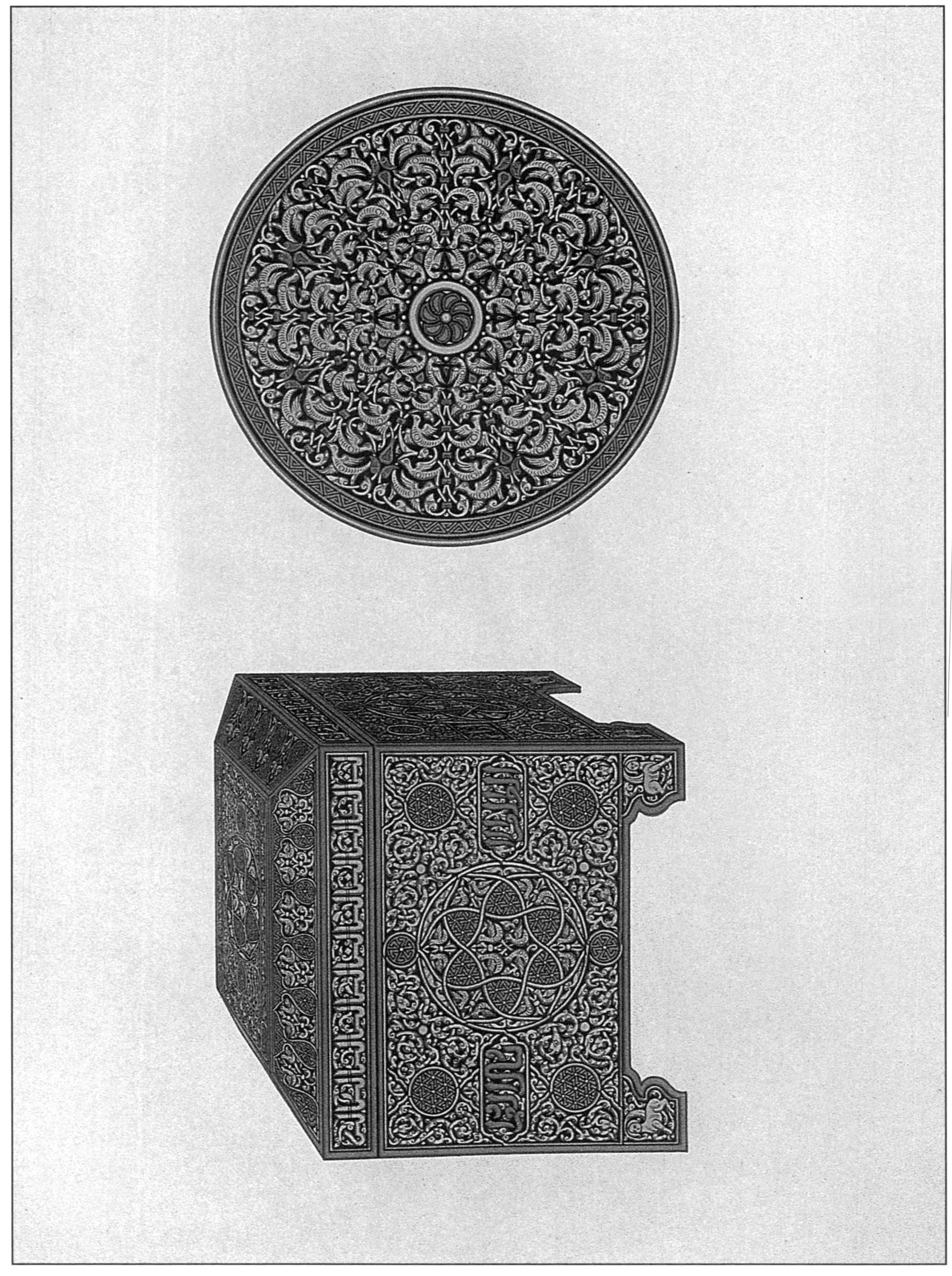

Candlesticks (14th century)

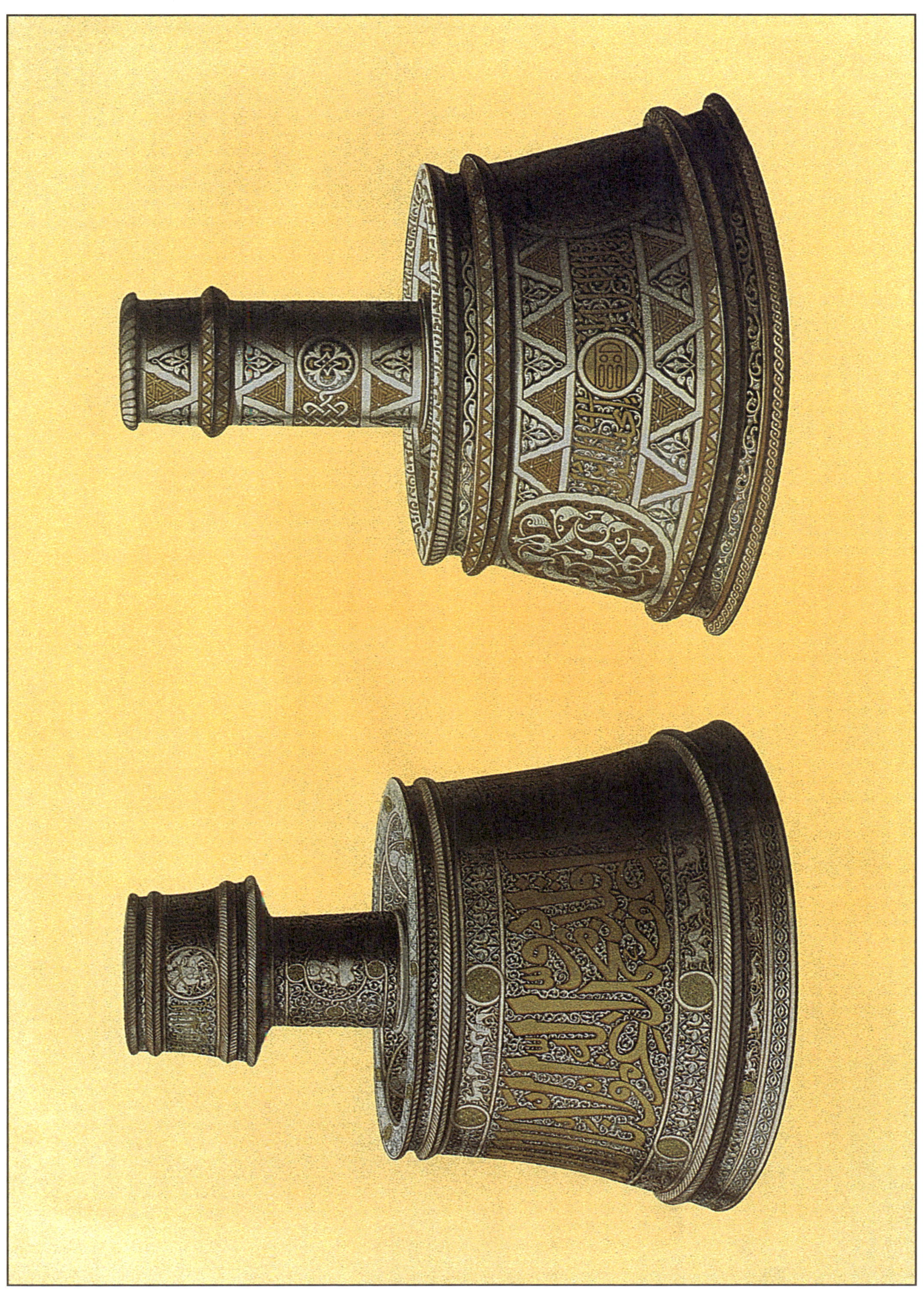

PENBOX OF SULTAN BAHRITE SHABAN

Details (14th century)

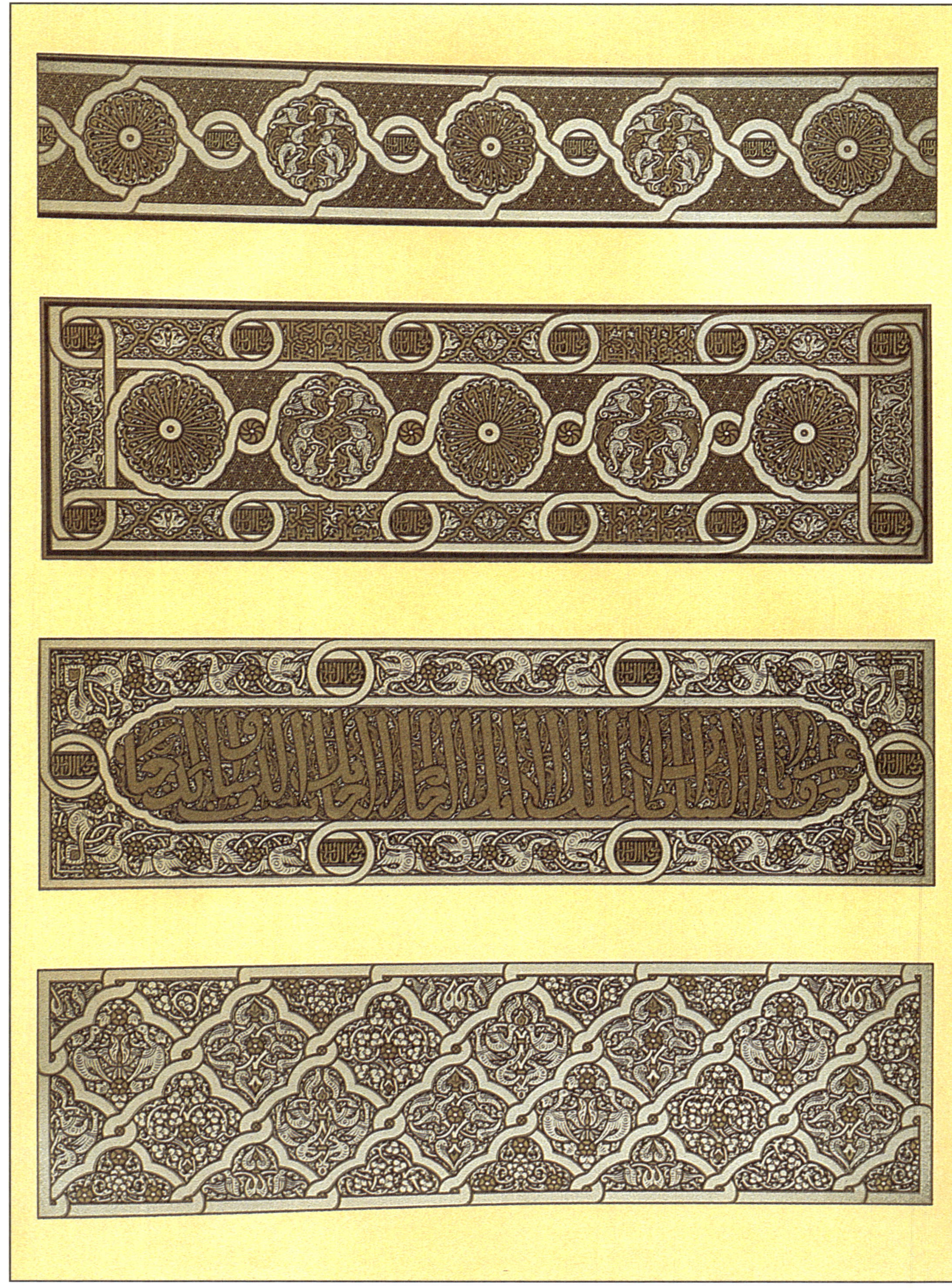

PENBOX OF SULTAN BAHRITE SHABAN
Whole and Details (14th century)

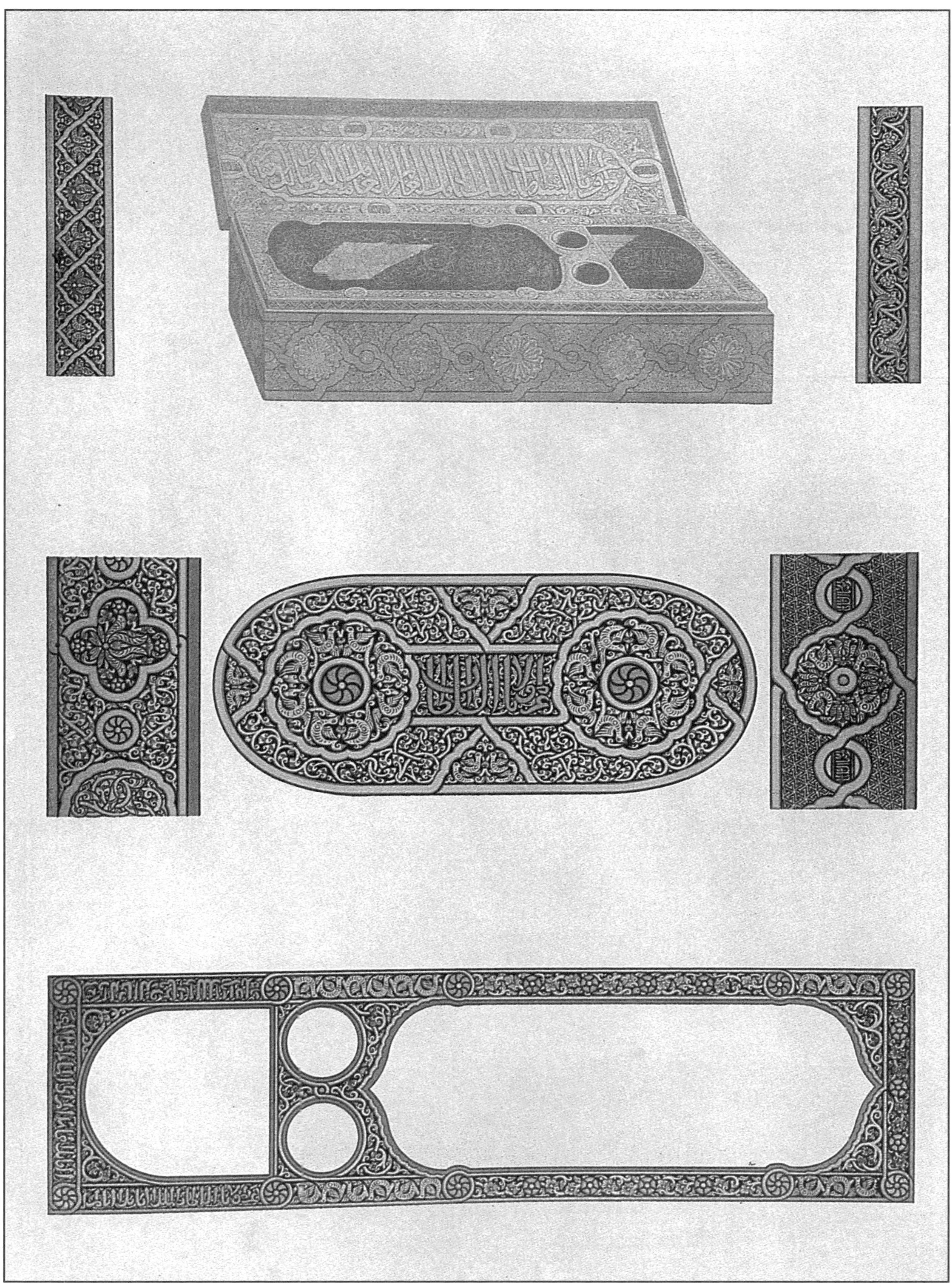

TWO COPPER SEDRIEHS

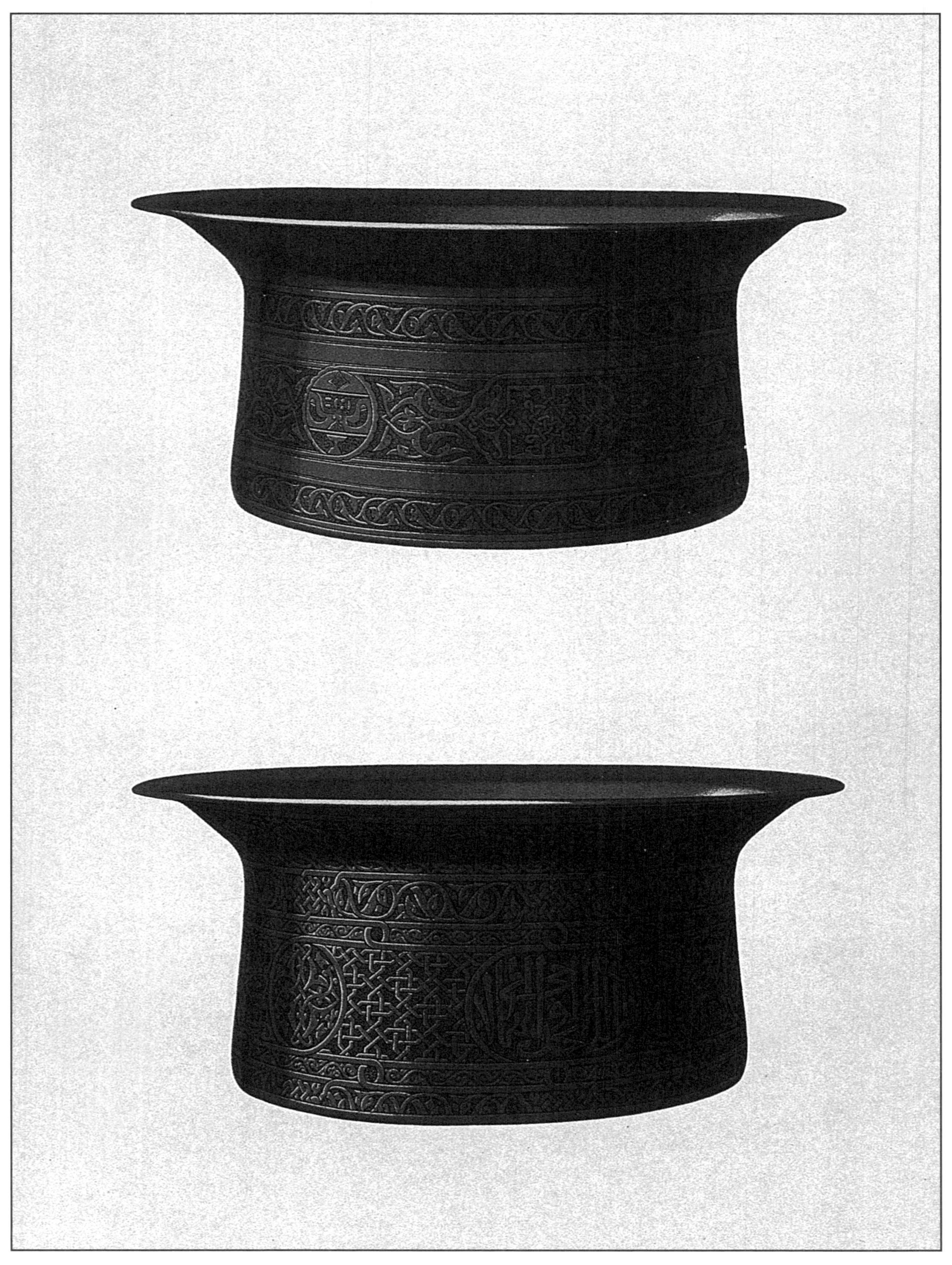

VESSEL INLAID WITH BRONZE

Decorated with martichores

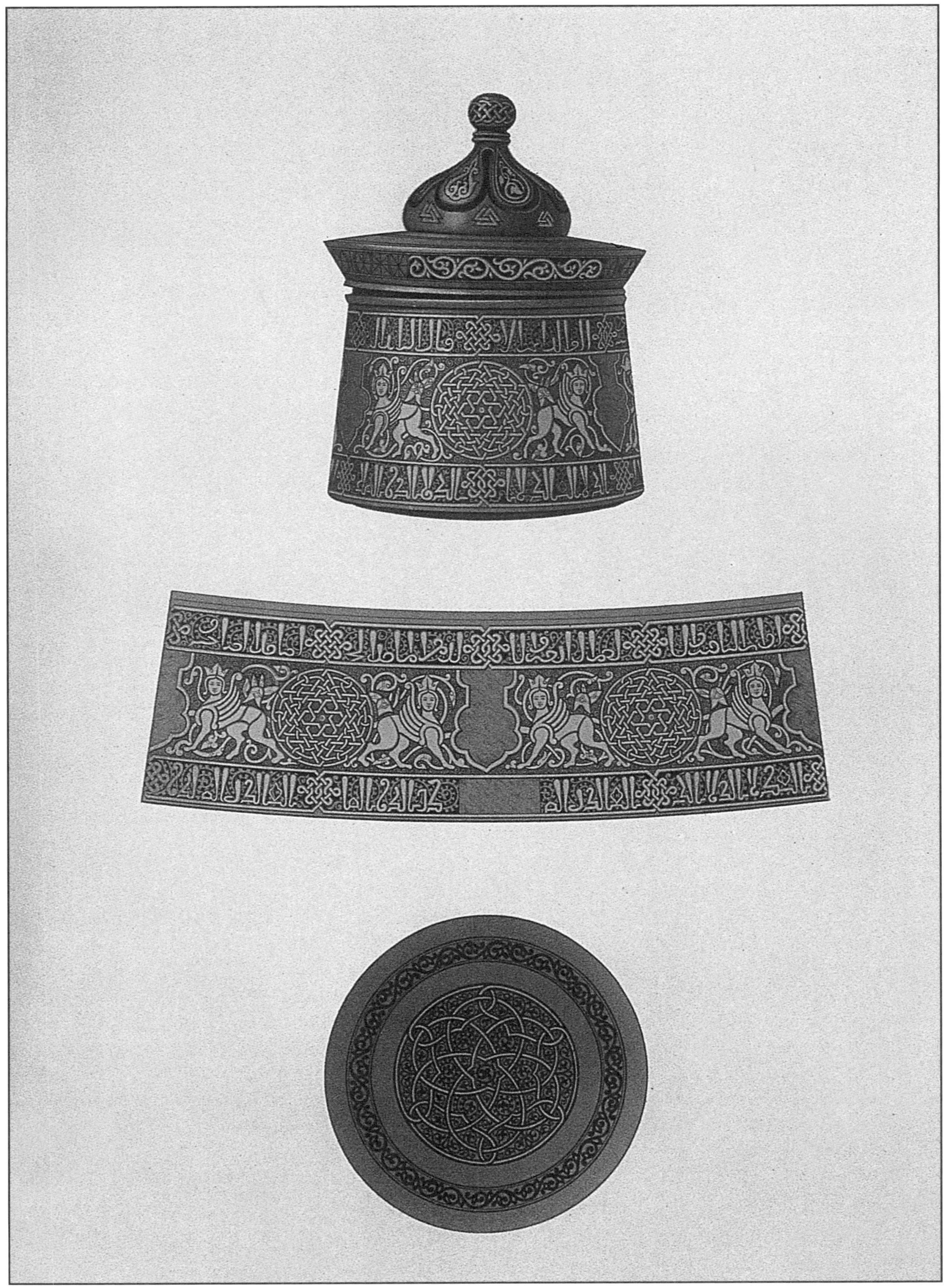

Plates CLXXIV to CLXXX
MANUSCRIPTS
Bindings and Applications of Paper Cutouts

Boook binding (Pl. CLXXIV).—Almost all Oriental bindings are lapjointed and of great beauty; we have only represented one or two since they all have ornaments printed on different grounds. We did not believe it necessary to add the cover, as this would only have complicated the design while adding nothing to the understanding of the plate.

Applications of paper cutouts (Pl. CLXXVI and CLXXVI).—These coloured papers, generally cut out with a penknife a half-dozen at a time, are glued upon different-coloured ground paper, and sometimes on silver or gold paper; they simulate in this inexpensive way painted panelling, and are suited to dwellings of people of little fortune. Those represented here were done by a Turkish artist, as seen in the rather heavy style of this decadent period.

Illustrations from Maqamat of al-Hariri (Pl. CLXXVII to CLXXX).—The manuscript from which were taken these interesting reproductions is a small folio rich in numerous and remarkable miniatures done by Yahia al-Wassetti, in the year 634 (1236 of the Christian era).

In Pl. CLXXVII, both natural and fantastic animals are found within the splendid foliated frame of the frontispiece.

These drawings seem to have been traced in haste, although a few are of more superior composition. Some parts are, in effect, boldy drawn, while others are timidly attempted. Heads and hands are poorly done and always reflect Persian sentiment and style. The folds of cloth are draped symmetrically and drawn like moiré. The animals are well treated and the plants, drawn in a fantastic fashion, are always charmingly ornamented.

Several heads are haloed, with no other purpose, in our view, than to better stand out from the surrounding confusion.

Clothing may provide precious information on the ornamentation of textiles during this period. It is apparent that manufacturers were already imitating these Kufic characters, and that there has been a stubborn refusal to recognise this in Oriental textiles. We believe that certain textiles considered until now to have been the work of Christian workmen or counterfeiters could well be authentic.

We have said that the frame, adorned with a succession of various animals, was taken from a copy belonging to a certain Yahia al-Wassetti, which is to say a native of Wassett, a small city in Mesopotamia. The small winged and haloed figures appear to be imitations of Byzantine paintings, or of certain other paintings of prior execution which we have sometimes found in Egyptian temples converted into churches.

The illustration of Plate CLXXIX, entitled *Mandarah*, shows a rather curious specimen of these small chalets, found in a wide variety of places, particularly in gardens and race courses.

BOOKBINDING, LAPJOINTED
Board, endpaper (16th century)

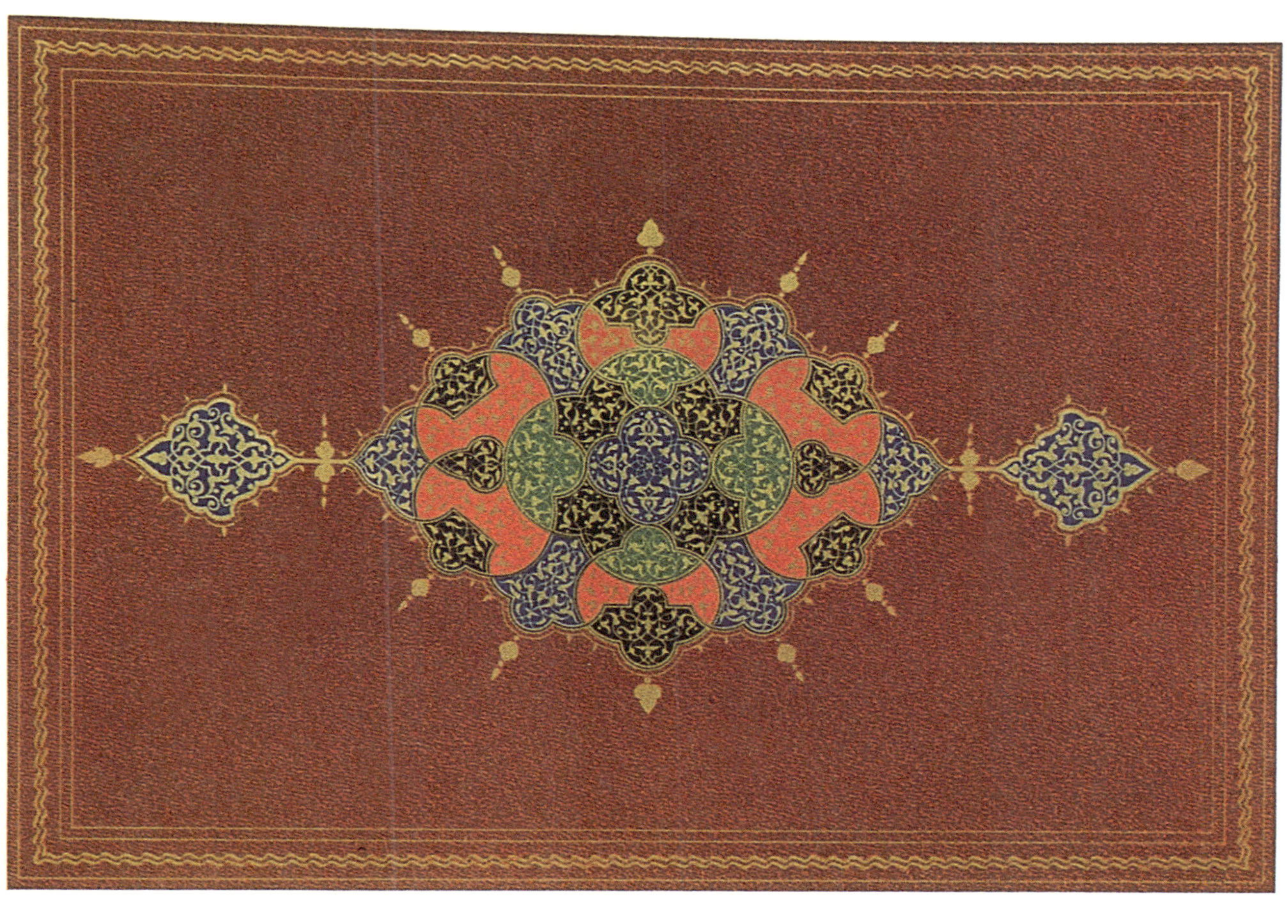

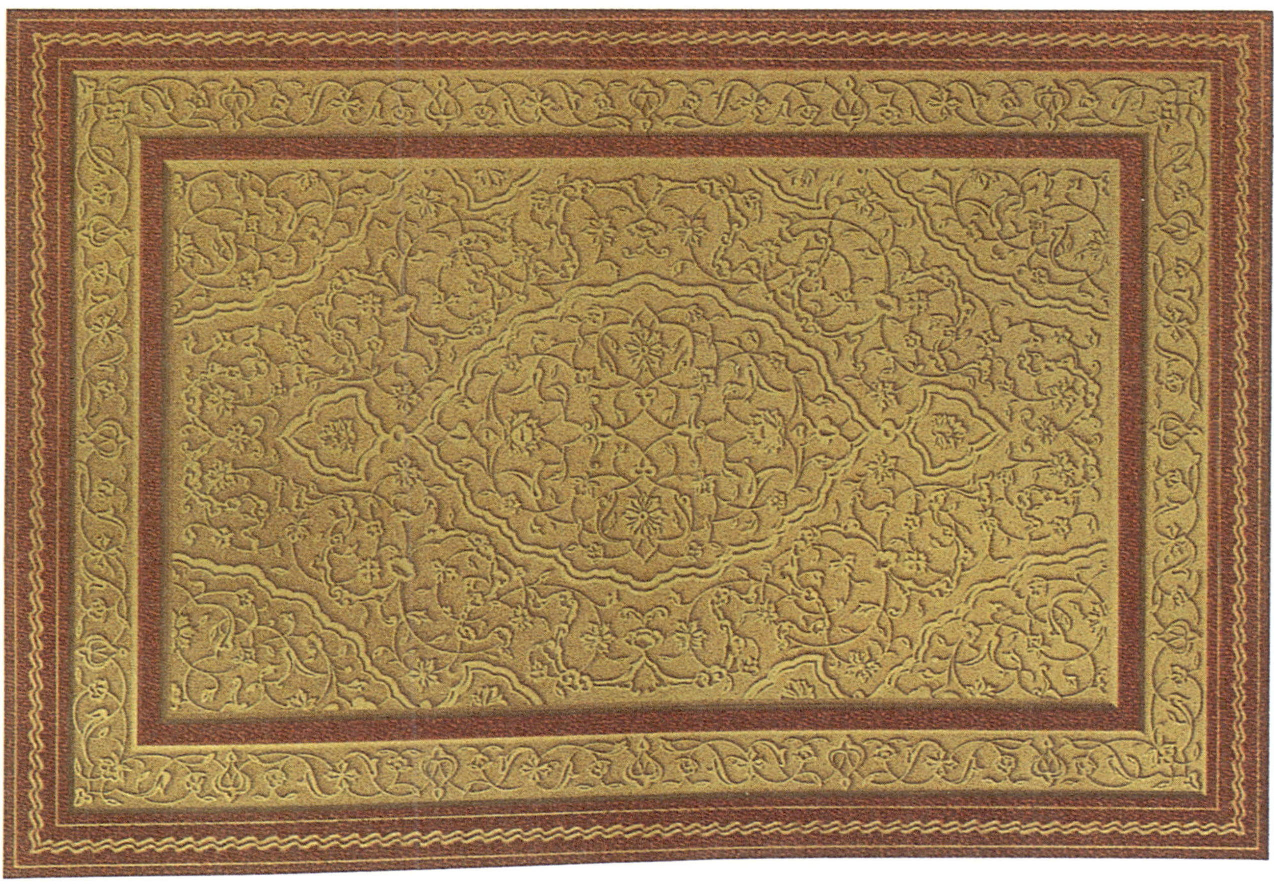

APPLICATIONS OF PAPER CUTOUTS
(End of 18th century)

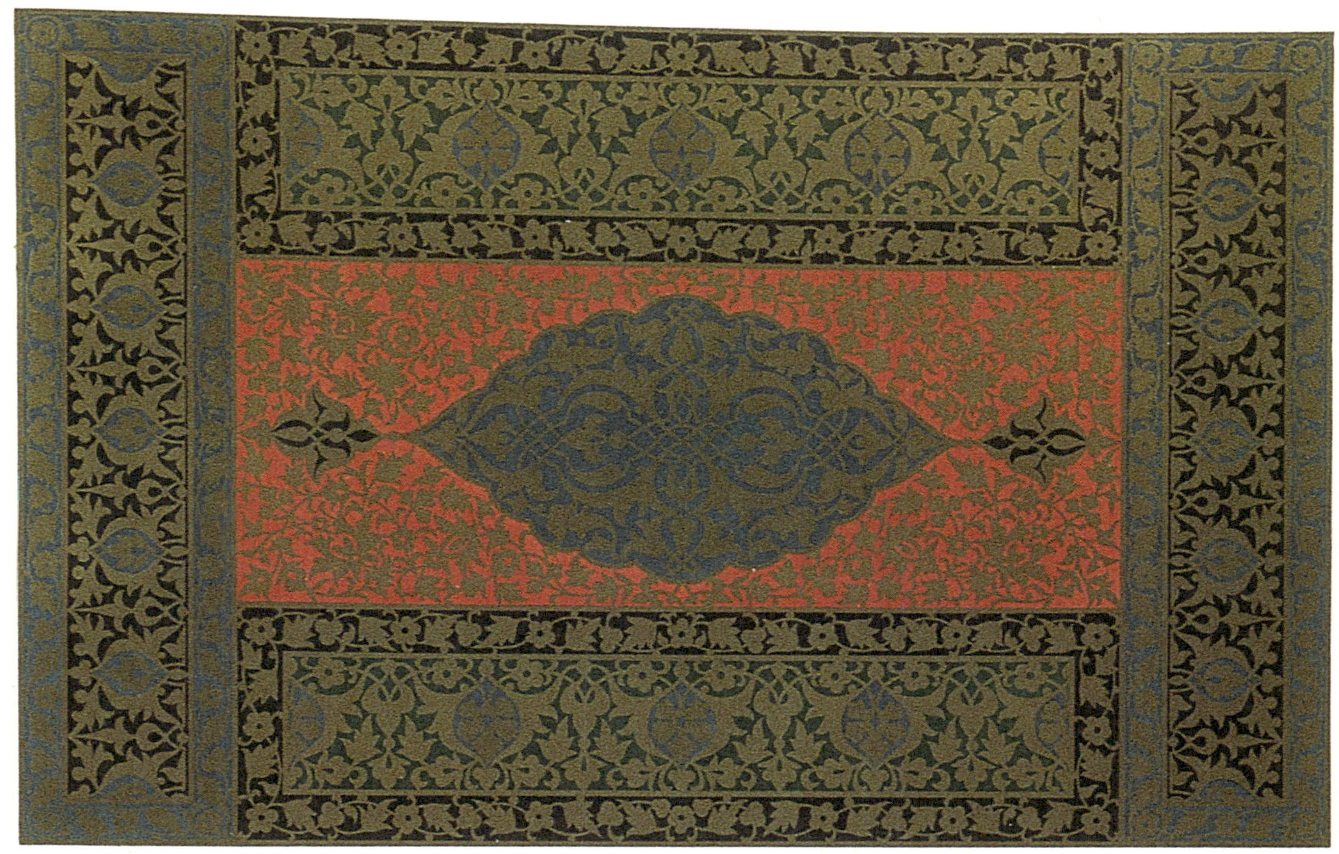

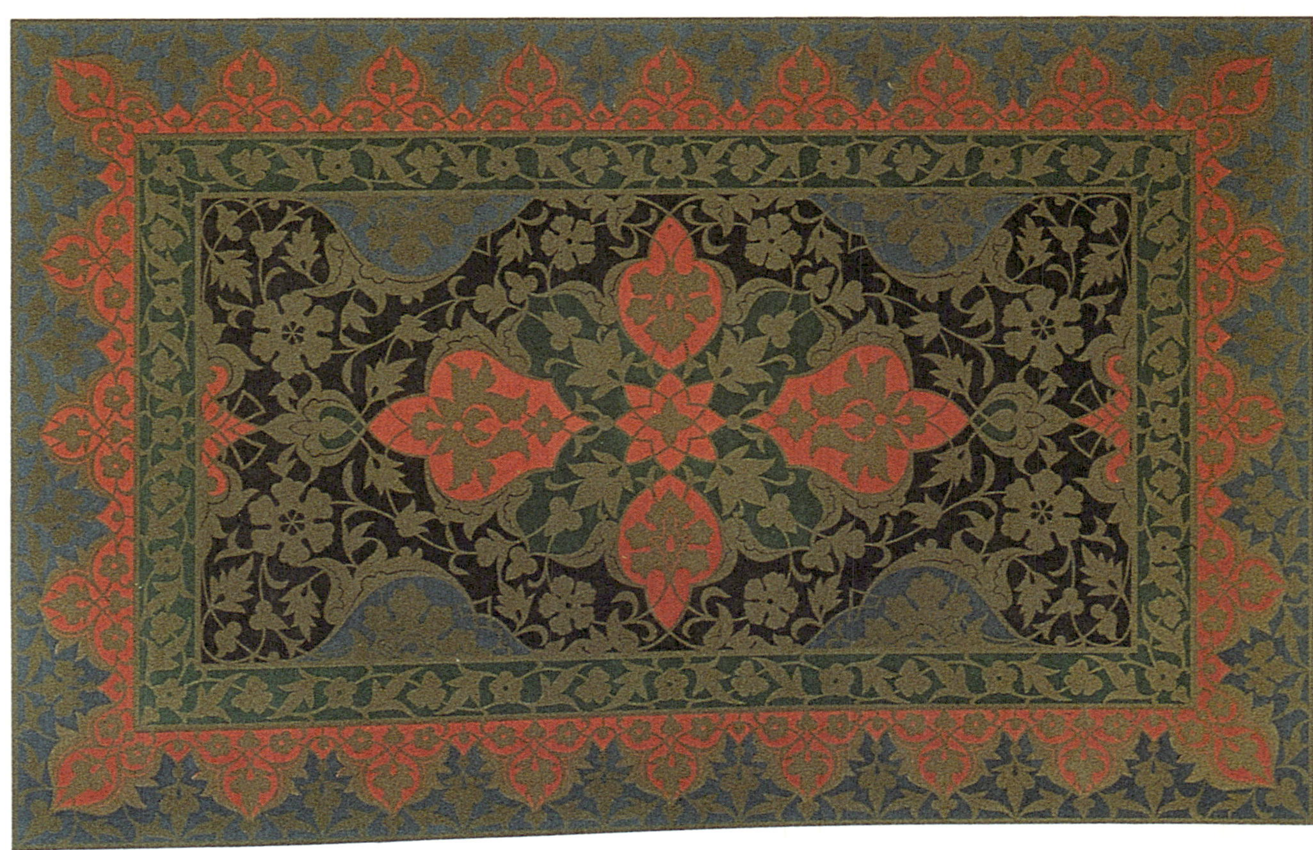

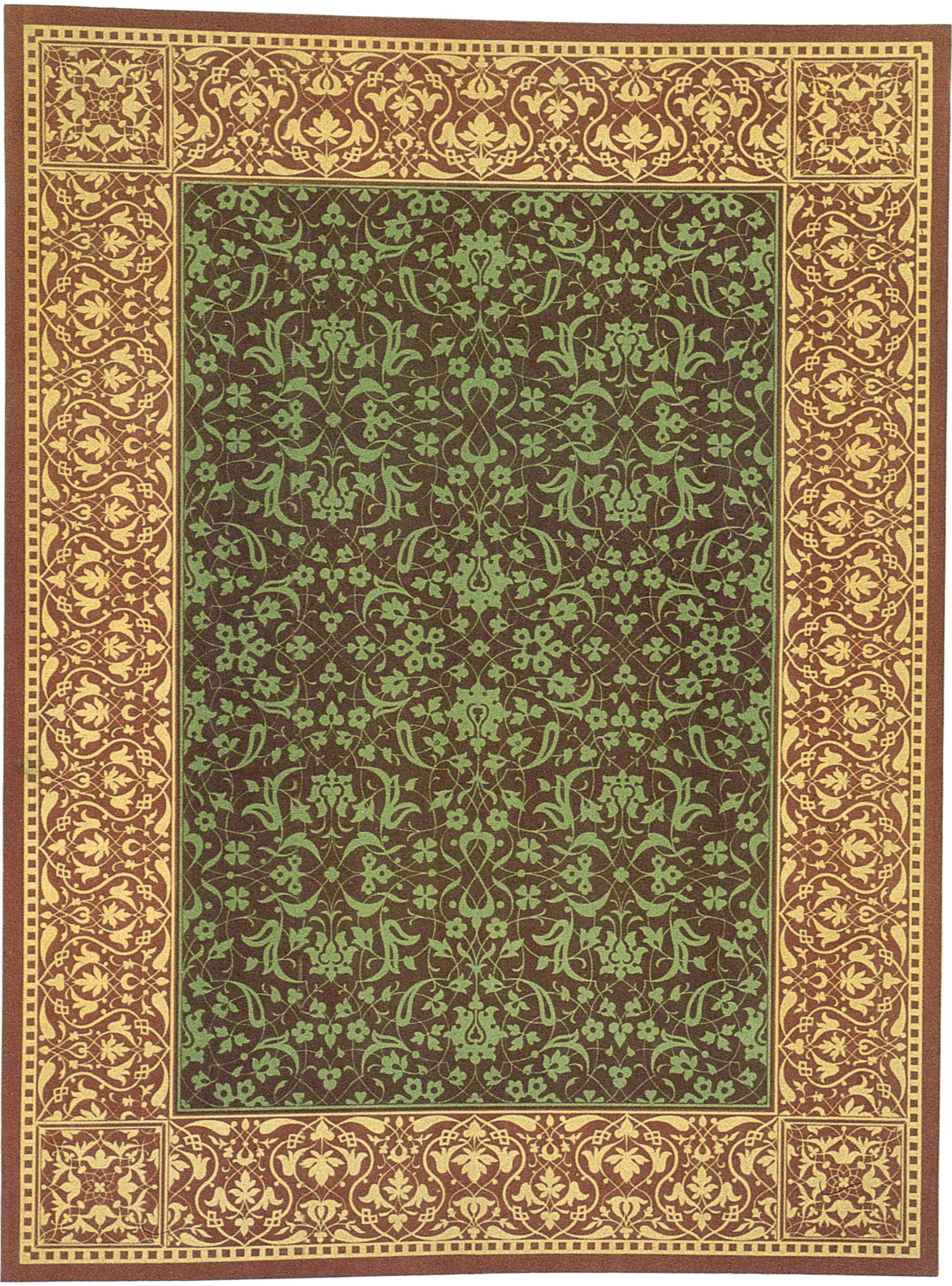

MAQAMAT OF HARIRI

Frontispiece (13th century)

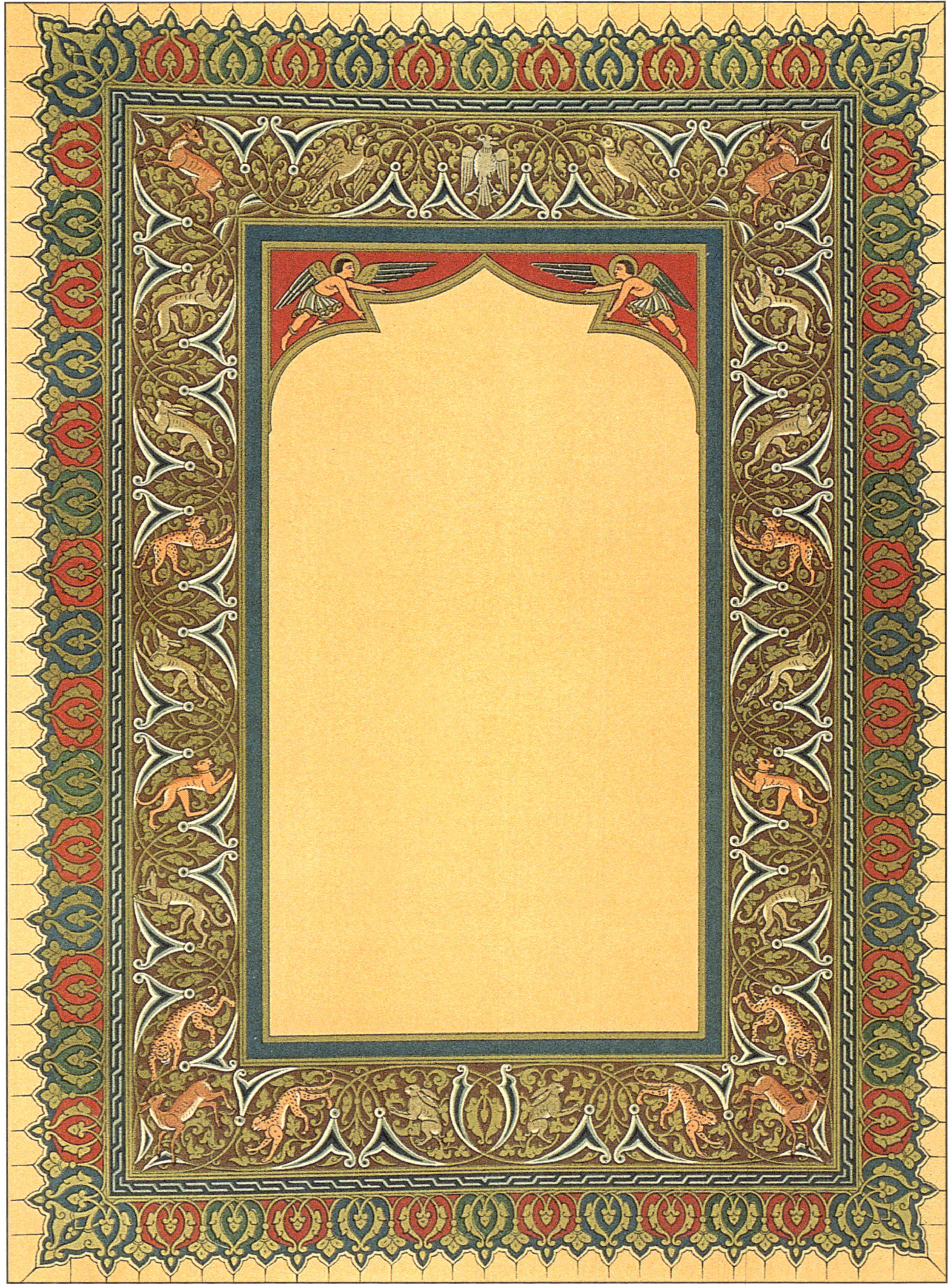

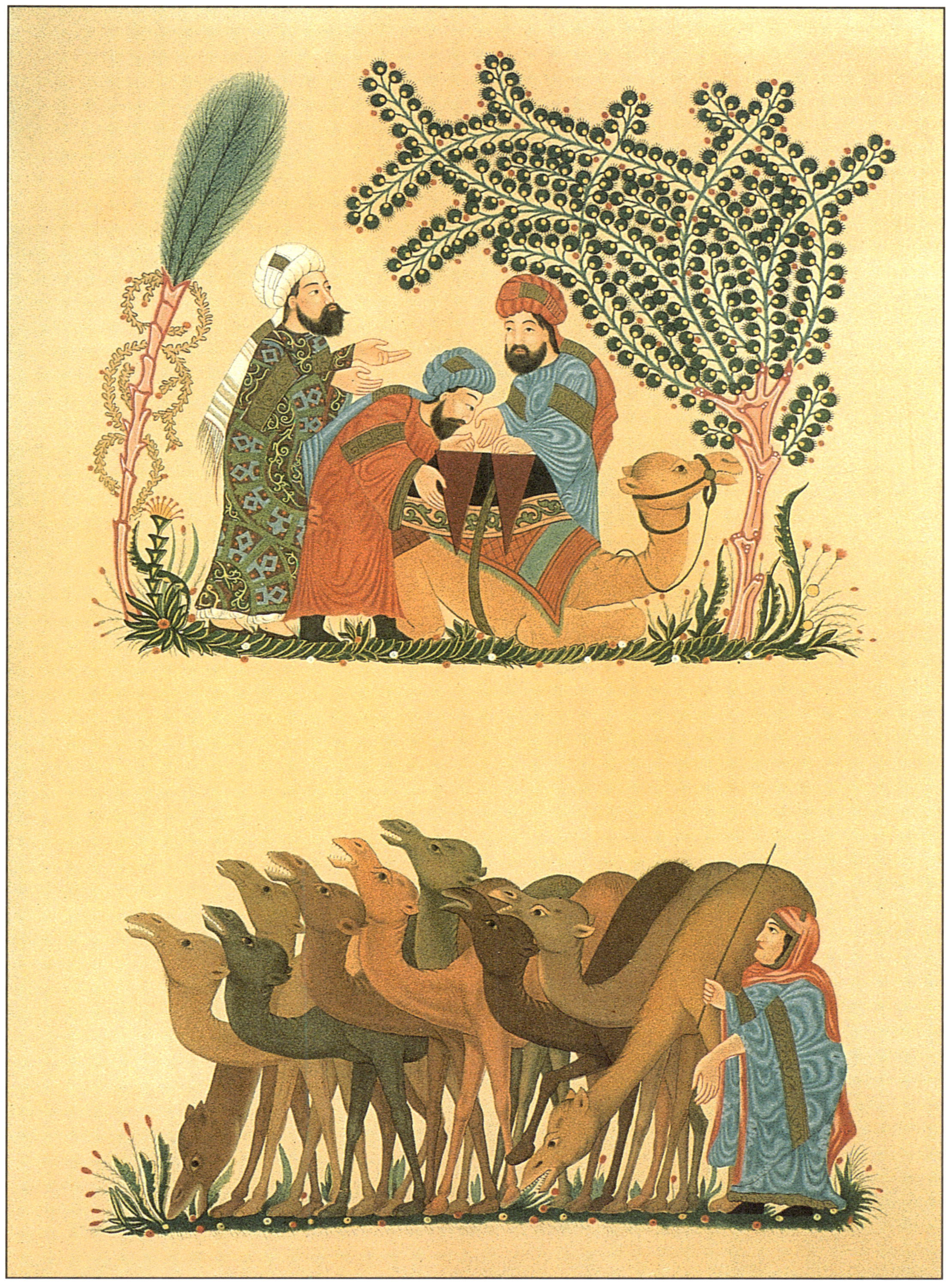

MAQAMAT OF HARIRI

Mandarah (13th century)

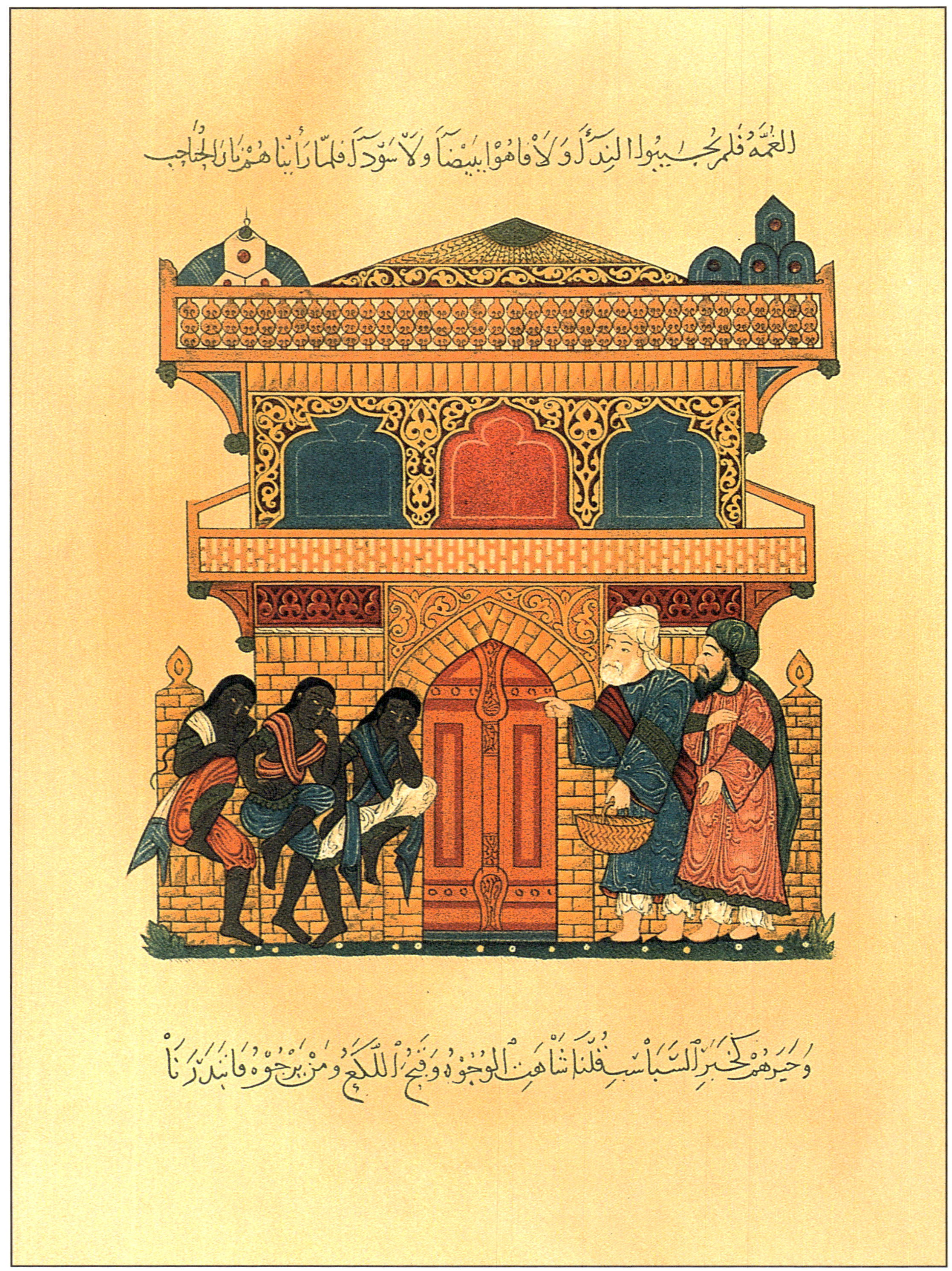

Caravan on the March (13th century)

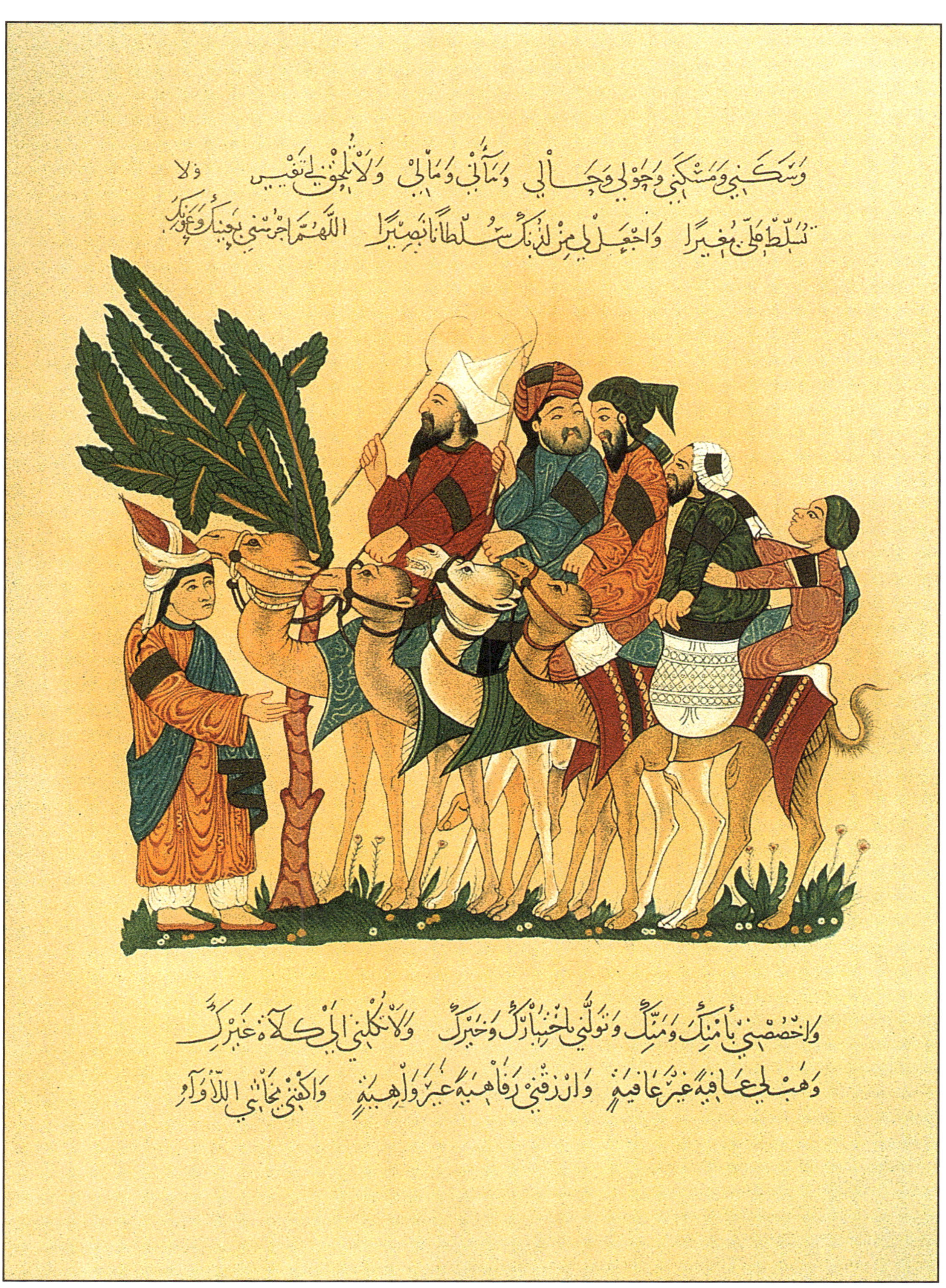

Plates CLXXXI to CC
KORANS

K*oran Ornamentation, Mosque of Qaysun* (Pl. CLXXXI).—The first page on the right reproduced here contains verses 76 and 77 of the 56th *sura* of the Koran; the 78th verse lies on the facing page with the same decoration. Written in kufic characters on these twin pages, the recommandation was often to be found at the beginning of this the book par excellence: "The sublime Koran, whose prototype is hidden in the volume, must only be touched by those in a state of purity".

The first page of the superb Koran of the Mosque of Qaysun, built, it is said, by a Tartar architect, contains only a few Kufic words. The middle features a polychromatic interlace which could be used for a ceiling; it is surrounded by a border imitating openwork ornaments, adorned with cabochons.

Last page of a Koran, Mosque of Sultan Barquq (Pl. CLXXXII).—The Koran of the Mosque of Sultan Barquq is one of the most elegant possessed by the city of Cairo. We could have been satisfied with giving a single specimen of the calligraphic and ornamental art of Arabic manuscripts in the 14th century, but we are able to offer for comparison another masterpiece from the same period. Plate CLXXII is an authentic reproduction of a magnificent Koran from the same century as the preceding motif. The veracity of our claim may be confirmed by referring to our text in Chapter VII.

Koran ornamentation, Tomb of Sultan al-Ghuri (Pl. CLXXXIII to CLXXXVII).—All those who visited the Egyptian Galleries at the 1867 Great Exhibition were able to admire in the showcases devoted to the Arts the superb pages of a Koran originally from one of the principal mosques of Cairo; these were displayed next to magnificent panelling, also originating from the pulpits of mosques.

We are convinced that this manuscript belonged to a *Waqf* of Sultan al-Ghuri written at the period of the founding of his mosque, sometime in the early 16th century.

Unfortunately, it was impossible to trace the double frontispieces which always adorn the beginning of this type of manuscript.

We were able to glean only the most attractive pieces which we have gathered and grouped together to compose five plates.

The variety of ornaments gives an exact idea of the decoration of manuscripts at this period in which Arabic art was already beginning to lose its primitive purity, although not yet weighted down by the Ottoman influence which was to dominate several years later after the conquest of Selim.

This Koran, from beginning to end, displays the same hand and the same style – the Arabic style; although constantly varying, it reluctantly conforms, here and there, to certain influences of Persia or Byzantium. It would have been of interest to the study of Arabic Art to compare its calligraphic ornamentations with those ornamentations covering the marble plaques and cupboard doors of the same mosque.

The tomb of Sultan al-Ghuri contained many relics and various splendidly decorated Korans. When the dome was repaired in 1858, one of the most handsome copies of this collection was removed from a transport cart and

1. See Prisse d'Avennes, *L'Art arabe d'après les monuments du Kaire,* volume of texts, same publisher.

sold to a Greek who brought it to Paris. The first page which contained the consecration of the book and the seal of the Sultan having been torn, an artist was put in charge of its restoration who then came to ask for our advice and entrusted us with the book. This was how we came to be allowed to copy at leisure ornaments we had only glimpsed, years before, in the hands of a caretaker of this tomb.

This Koran demonstrates that the ornamentation of manuscripts, even more so than the decoration of edifices, was a blend of all styles. The calligrapher who adorned it apparently wished to vary the chapter headings and, to do so, borrowed arabesques and characters from Islamic lands all over and from different periods.

In Plates CLXXXVIII to CXCI, we give several specimens of the ornamentation of Arabic manuscripts and Korans in the 16th and 17th centuries.

Moresque Koran (Pl. CXCII to CC).—Muhammad Abu Dahab endowed his mosque, built in the vicinity of al-Azhar, with this splendid Koran, said to have belonged to a Moroccan sultan, Sidi Muhammad. We have published the principal pages of this handsome manuscript, whose very pure and original Moresque style led all those who admired it at the 1867 Great Exhibition in Paris to believe it to be more ancient.

Apparently written and decorated in 1768 for Sultan Sidi Muhammad, Emperor of Morocco, the arabesques of this Koran are of very pure taste. A single glance at the manuscript reveals that it is written on Holland paper, bearing for watermark the motto *Pro Patria* above a crowned lion holding a two-edged sword in one paw and a bunch of arrows in the other, and followed by a knight armed from head to toe – all in a style indicative of the 18th century.

Moreover, the reading of the long inscriptions on the two last pages reveals to us that this splendid *Mashaf* was indeed executed in the year 1182 of the Hegira (1768 of the Christian era) for a Moroccan sultan of the Sherifian Dinasty. The inscriptions read as follows: "Glory to the unique God, may blessings and salvation be on he who has no prophet after him. He who commands the transcription of this noble Koran, which glorifies and honors God on high, is the master, the noble one, the glorious one, he who has high origins, in whom resides all honour and whose shining fame is appreciated by men, he whose virtues gladden the century, he whose odour of generosity gives flowers a perfume wafting all around, our master, the prince of Believers, the Caliph of God, Sultan Sidi Muhammad, son of Sultan our master Abd-Allah, son of Sultan our master Ismail. Year 1182 (1728 of the common era)". "Bequeathed by Mohammed-Bey Abou-Dahab, to his mosque, year 1188 (1774)". Above is found his seal.

The magnificent arabesques which decorate this volume always present two facing pages decorated in the same way, barring several minor details. Gilded lines and arabesques are the same, but other parts are coloured in a different manner, resulting in a symmetry and variety which give them much charm. As a general rule, the interlace which forms the frame or diagram is blue, outlined in gold in one, then chrome equally outlined in gold in the other, or emerald green in the one and kermes scarlet in the other. The arabesques which decorate the interiors vary in colour according to no fixed rule. Gold, which dominates everywhere and outlines nearly all the ornaments, transforms each page into a leaf of gold, covered in cloisonné enamels. Very different from the arabesques admired in other illuminated manuscripts, most of these pages are decorated in an entirely architectural manner, which renders them doubly precious.

Each subject is coloured in seven to eight acid colours: lemon yellow, orangey colour, pink, red, crimson, blue, green and black. Gold encircles or shapes all the ornaments. Yellow, orangey and green grounds are pointillé or decorated in black while blue and kermes scarlet grounds are pointillé or decorated in white.

Motifs 1, 3, 6, 9 and 13 offer complete fac-similes. Motif 3 reproduces the first chapter of the Koran and the beginning of the second *sura*. Motifs 4, 5, 7, 8, 10 and 14 contain half-pages only; the text has not been reproduced in order to focus on the ornamentation and colouring.

There are beautiful motifs of doors and panelling therein that would be hard to come upon today.

These Moresque ornaments, published to serve as points of comparison with ornaments of Cairo from the same period, bring their contingent of varieties to our collection of arabesques and in so doing, allow it to present specimens of ornamentation from nearly all the Islamic lands.

KORAN ORNAMENTATION

Mosque of Qaysun (14th century)

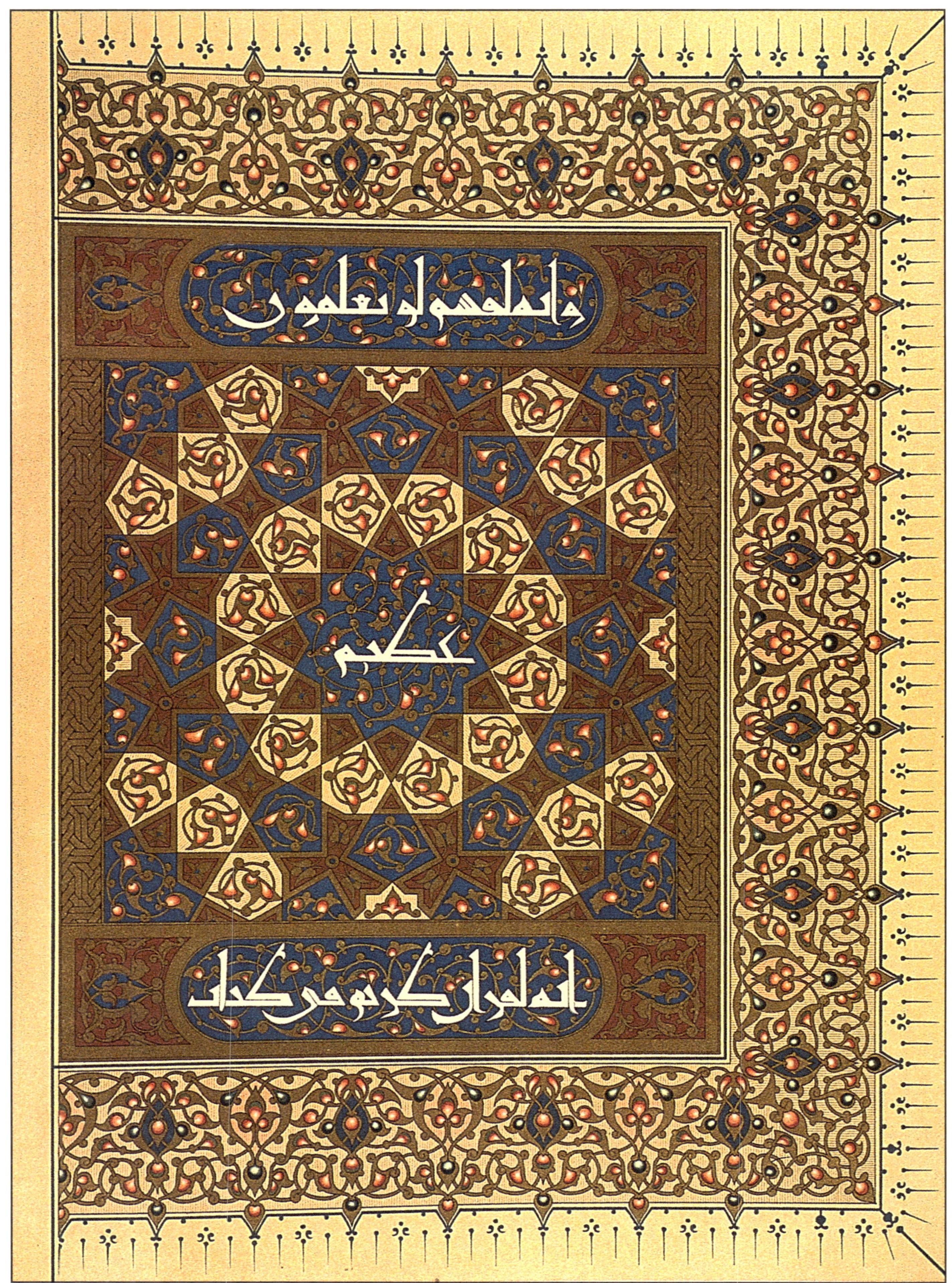

LAST PAGE OF A KORAN

Mosque of Sultan Barquq (End of 14th century)

Plate CLXXXII

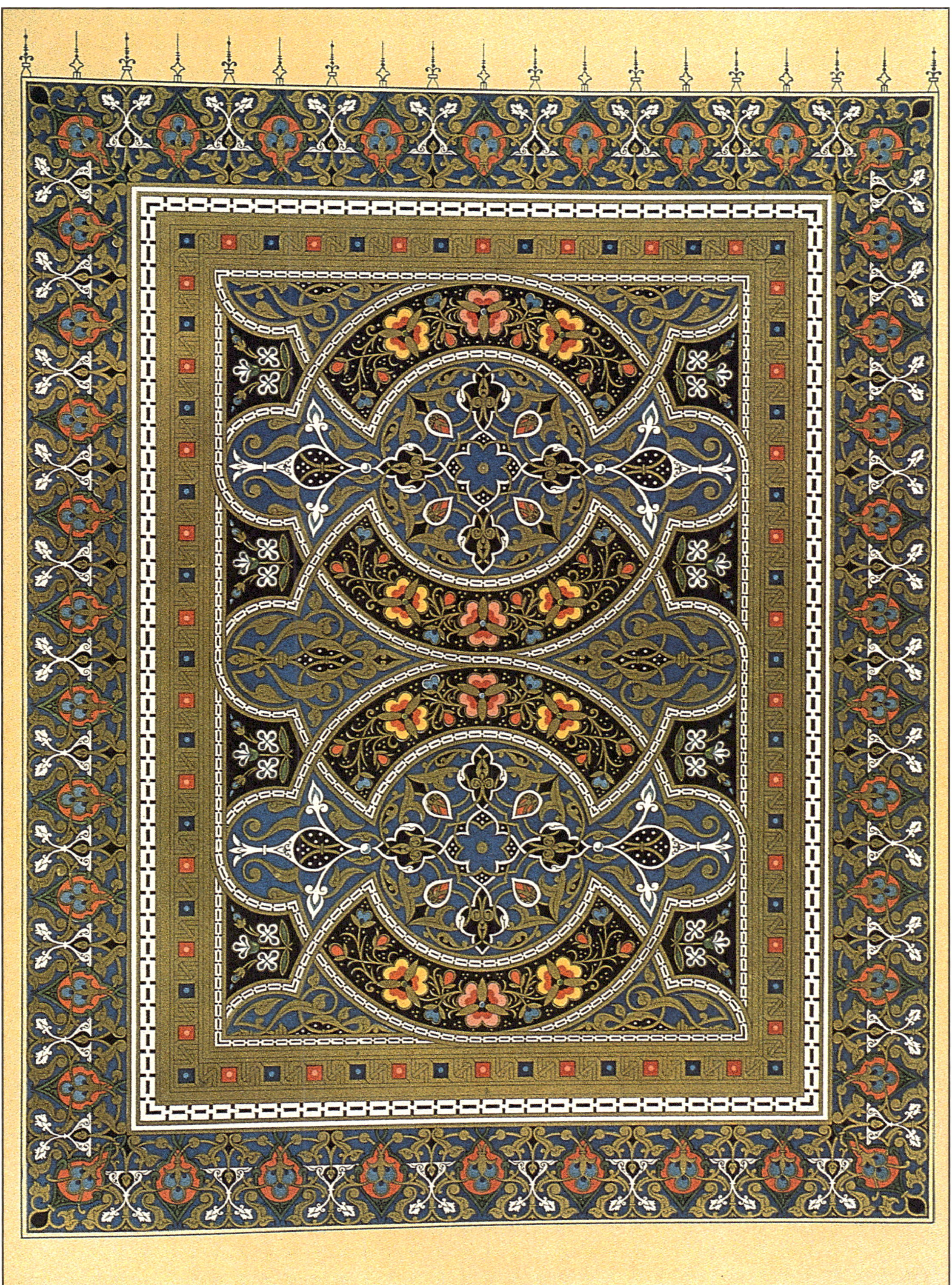

KORAN ORNAMENTATION

Tomb of Sultan al-Ghuri (16th century)

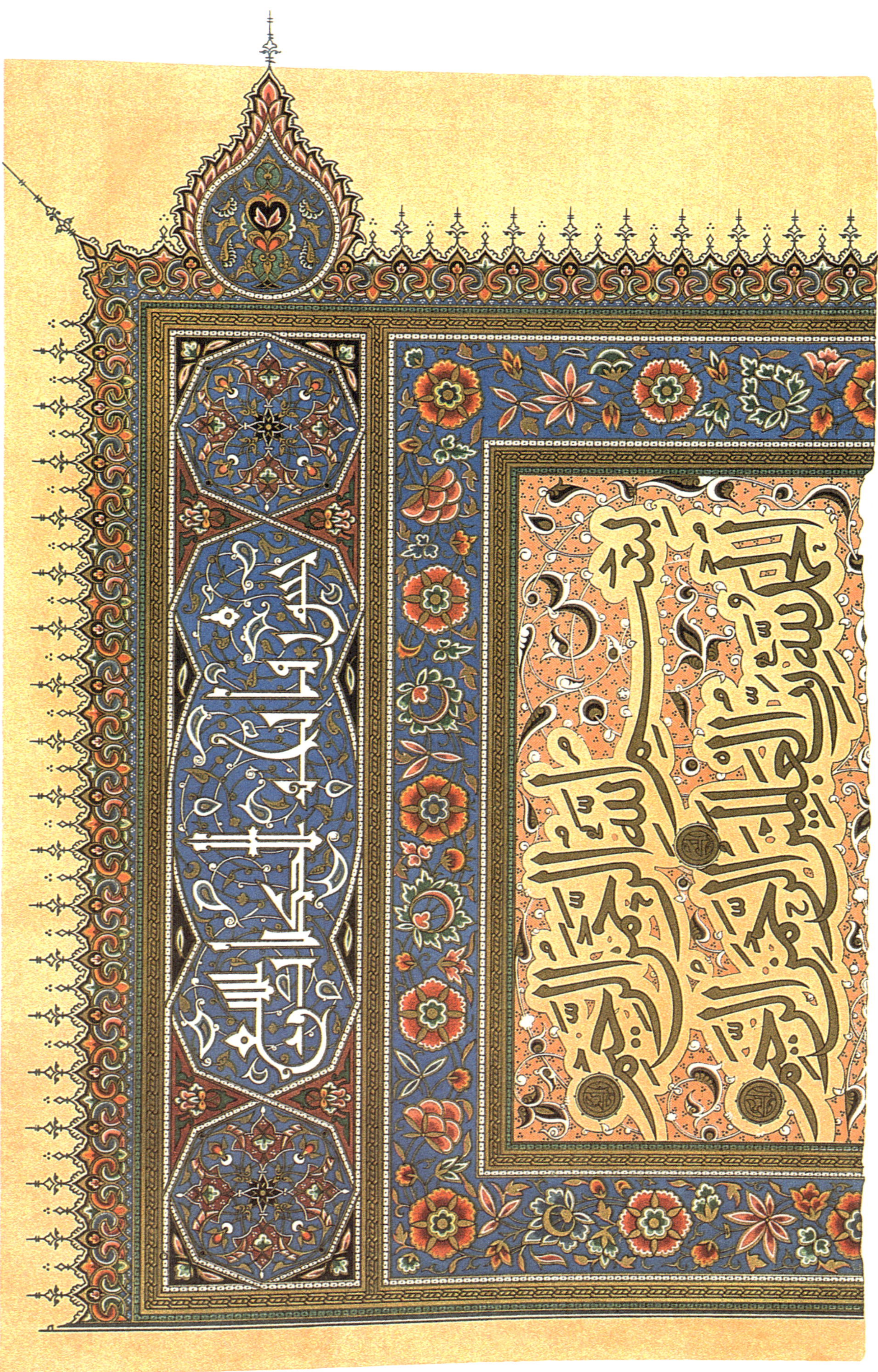

KORAN ORNAMENTATION

Tomb of Sultan al-Ghuri (16th century)

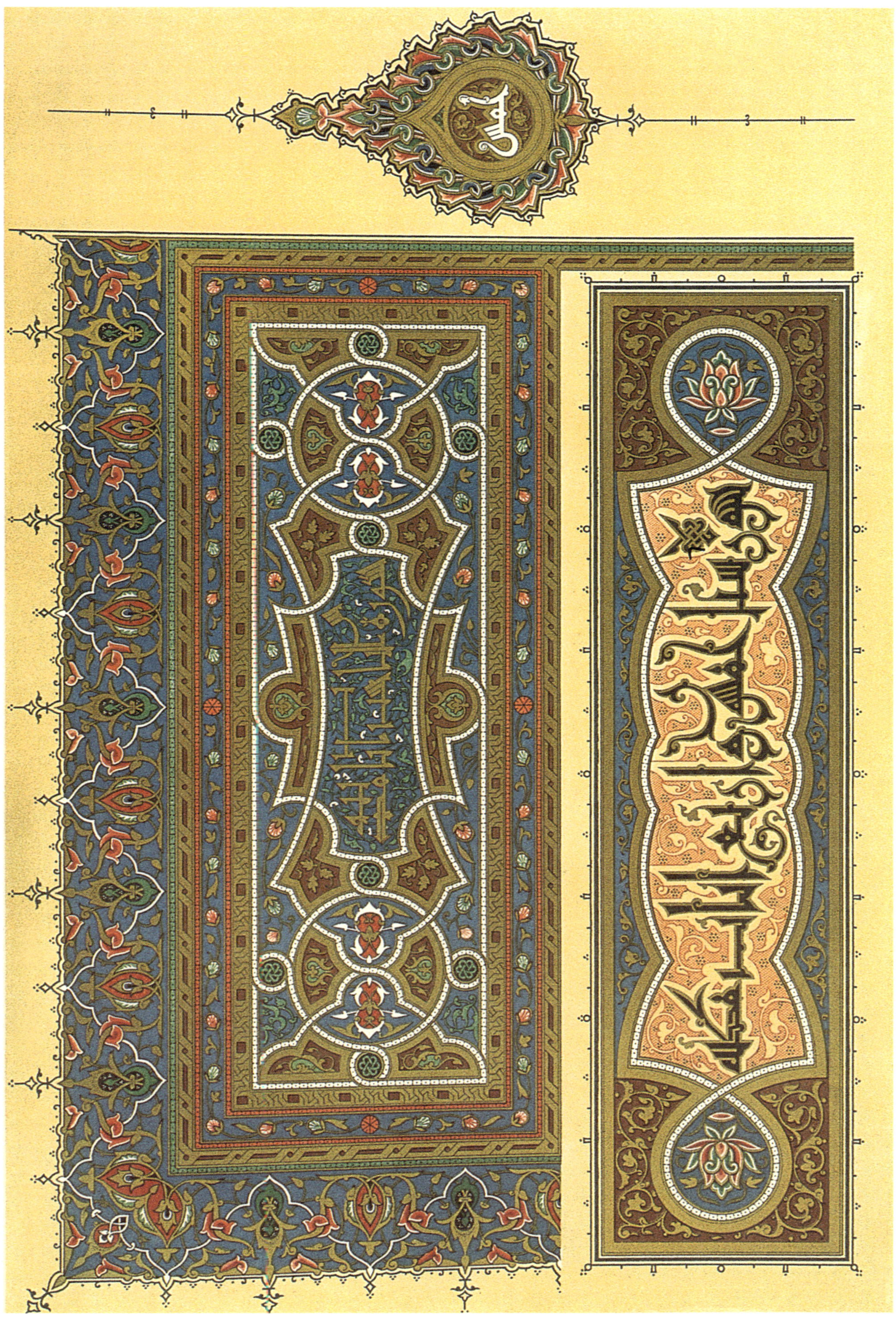

KORAN ORNAMENTATION

Tomb of Sultan al-Ghuri (16th century)

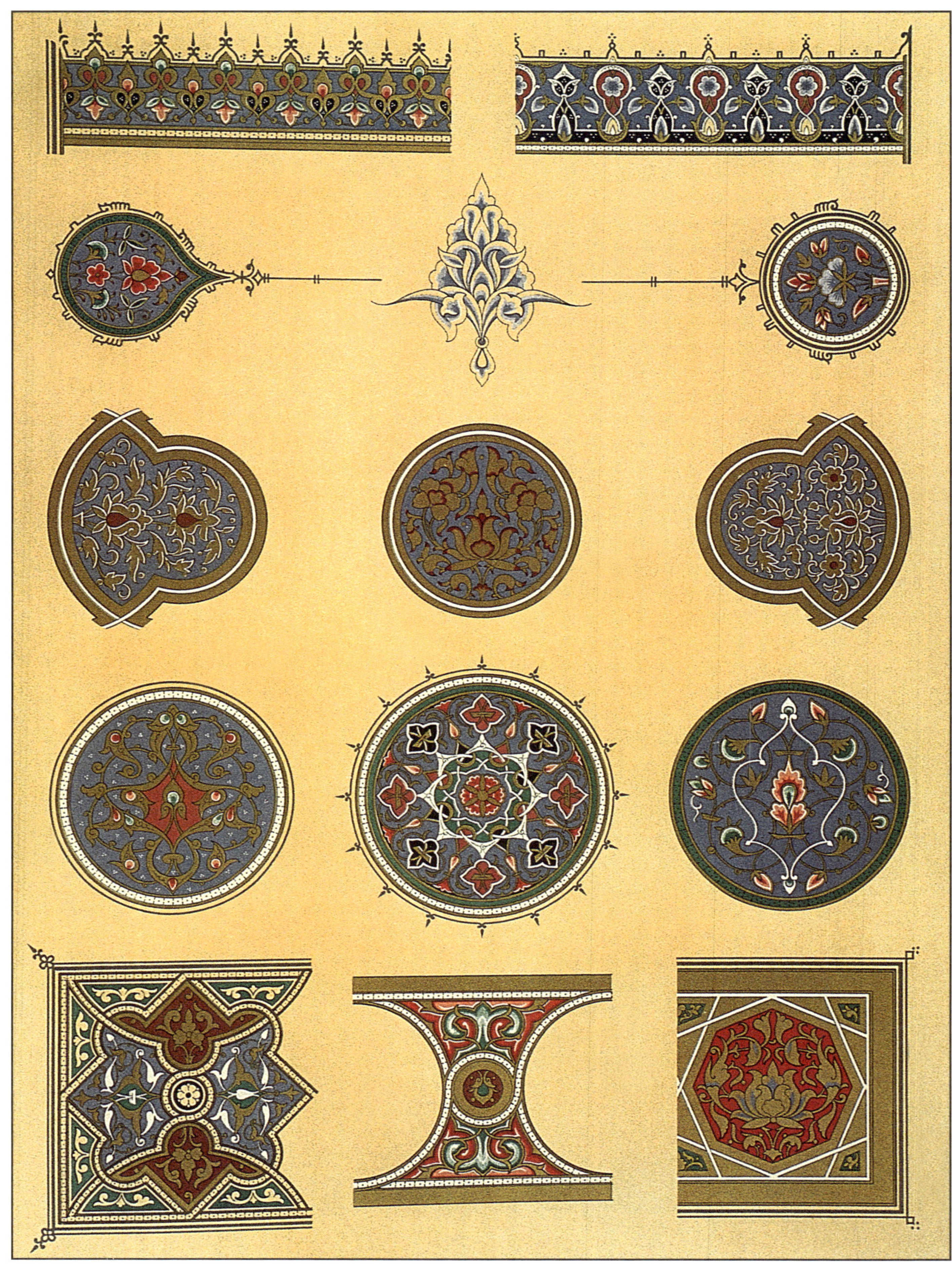

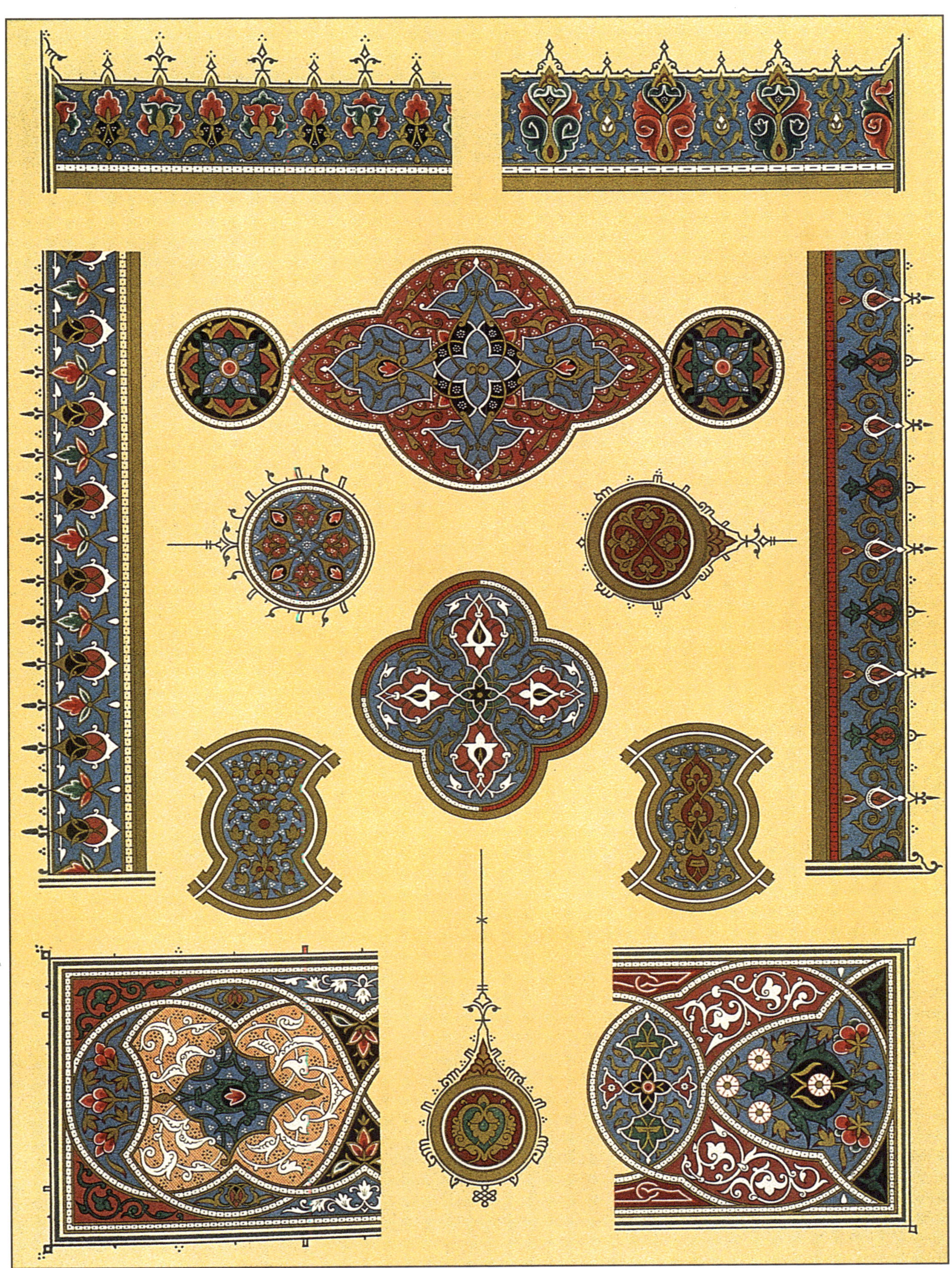

Plate CLXXXVII

FRONTISPIECE AND DETAILS FROM AN ARAB KORAN

(17th century)

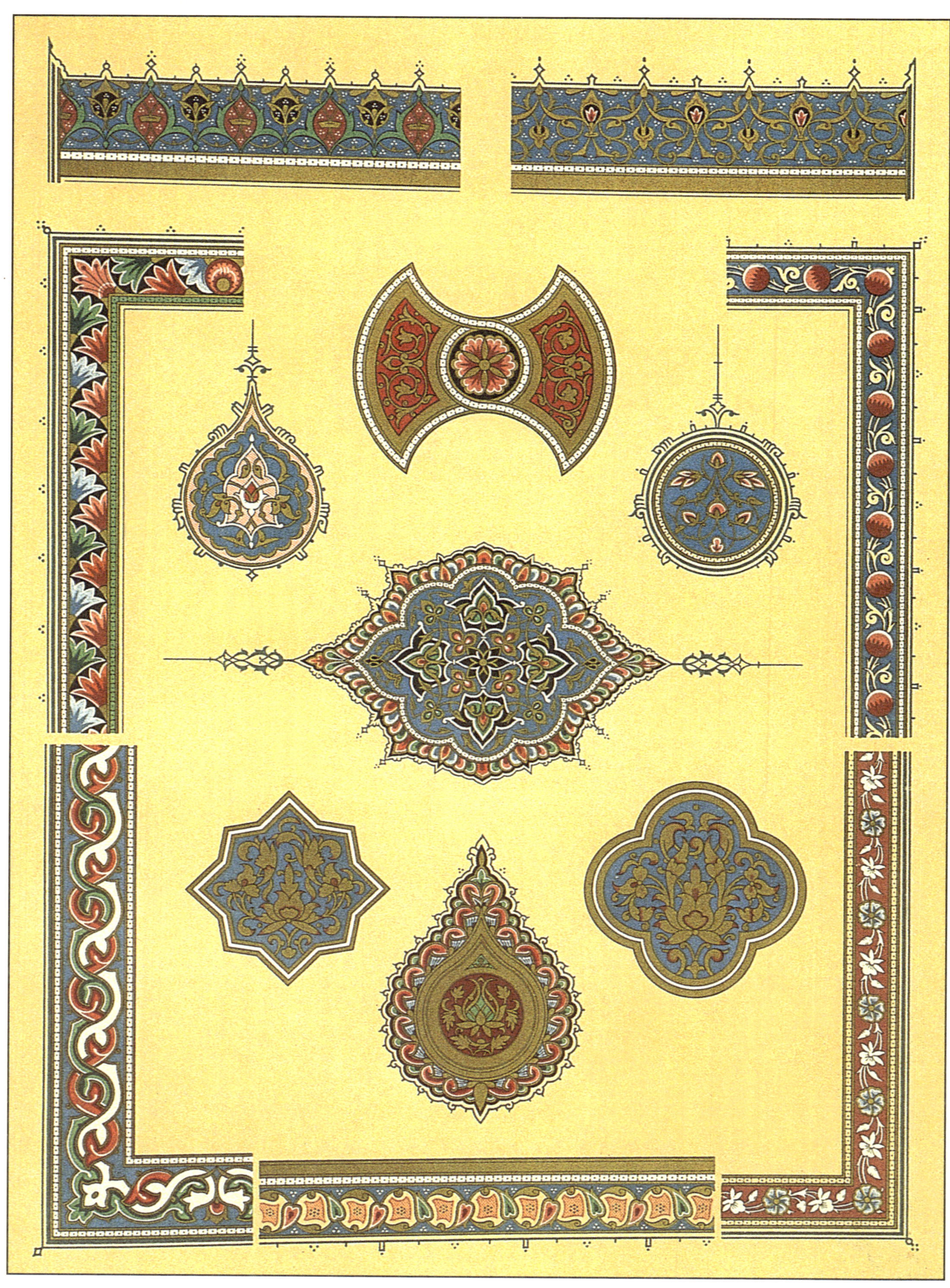

PAGE FROM AN ARAB MANUSCRIPT
(16th century)

Plate CLXXXVIII

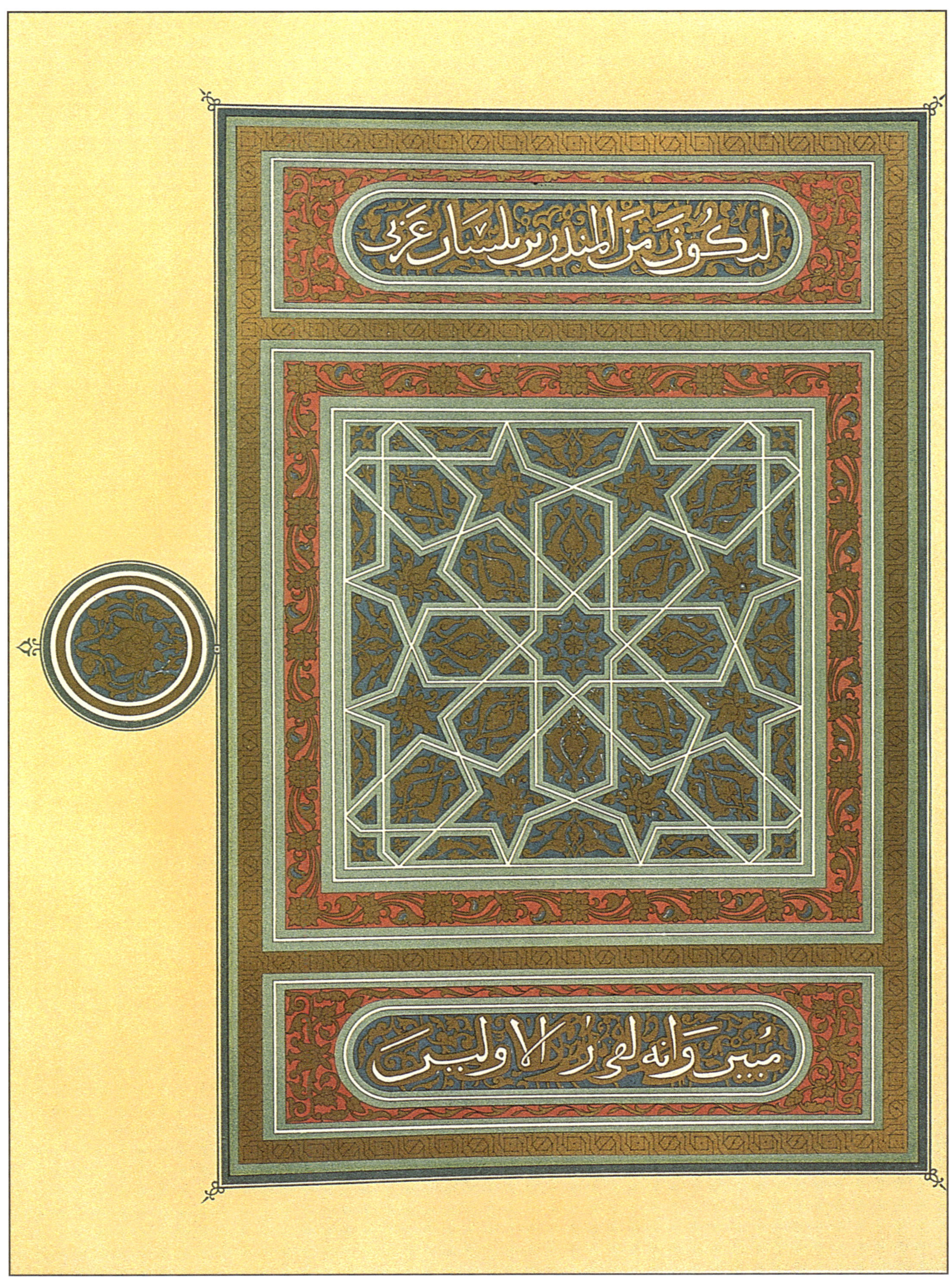

Plate CLXXXIX

FRONTISPIECE AND DETAILS FROM AN ARAB KORAN

(17th century)

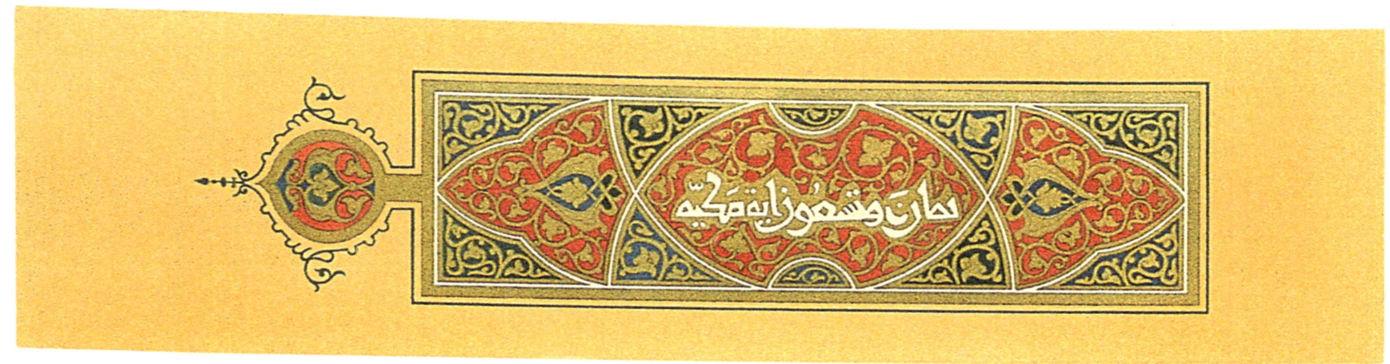

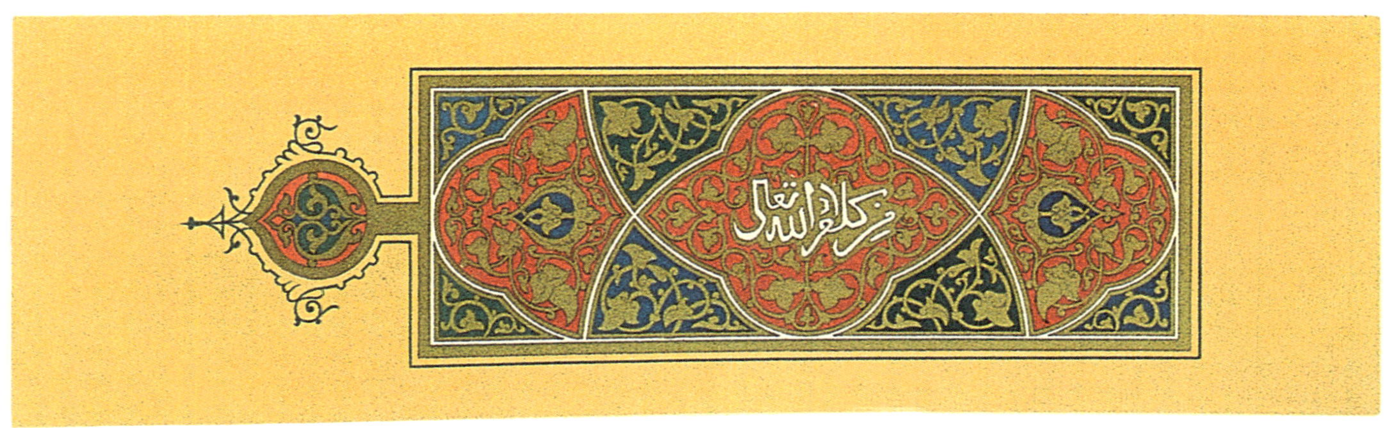

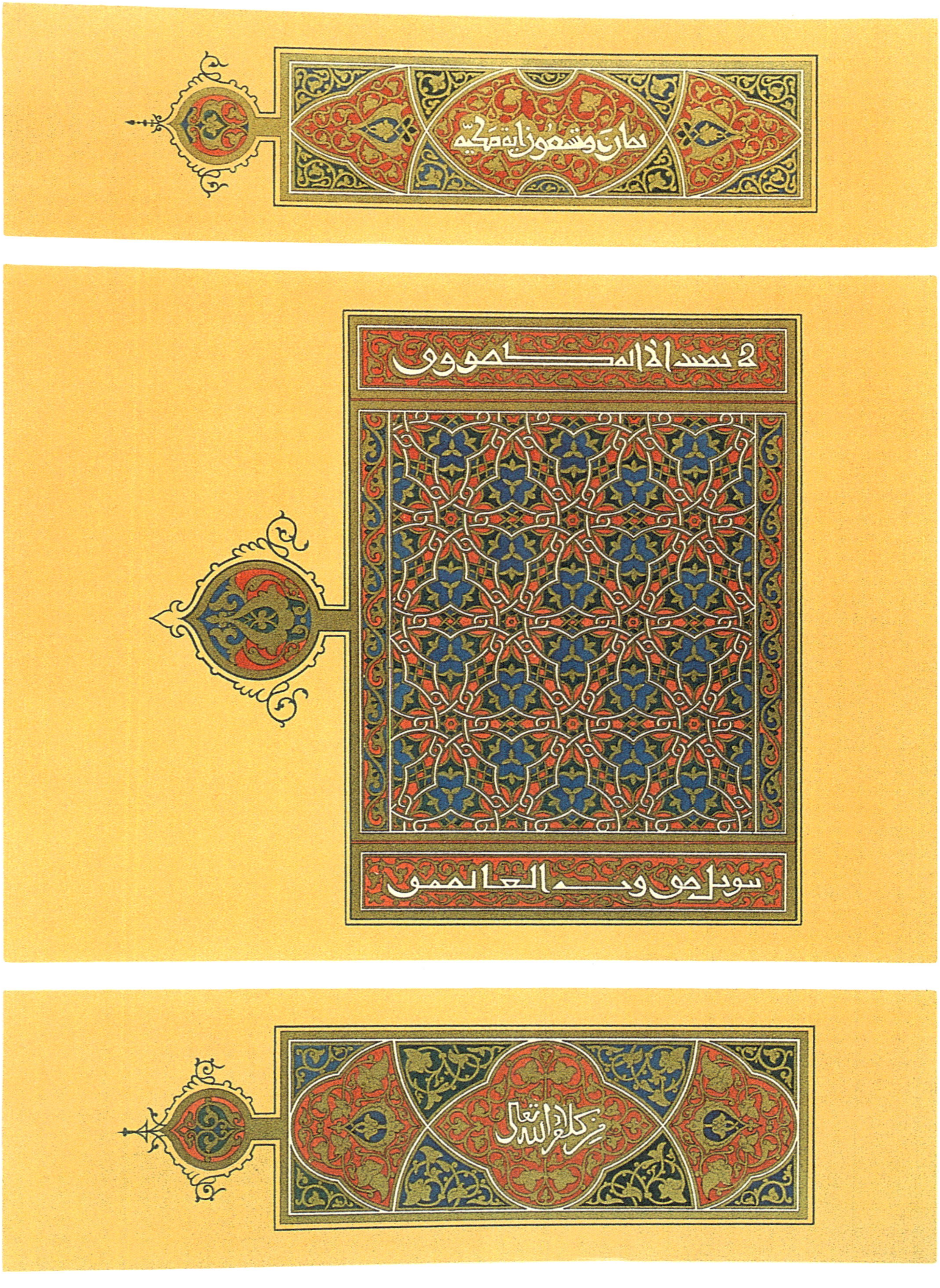

ORNAMENTATION DETAILS FROM AN ARAB KORAN

(17th century)

Plate CXC

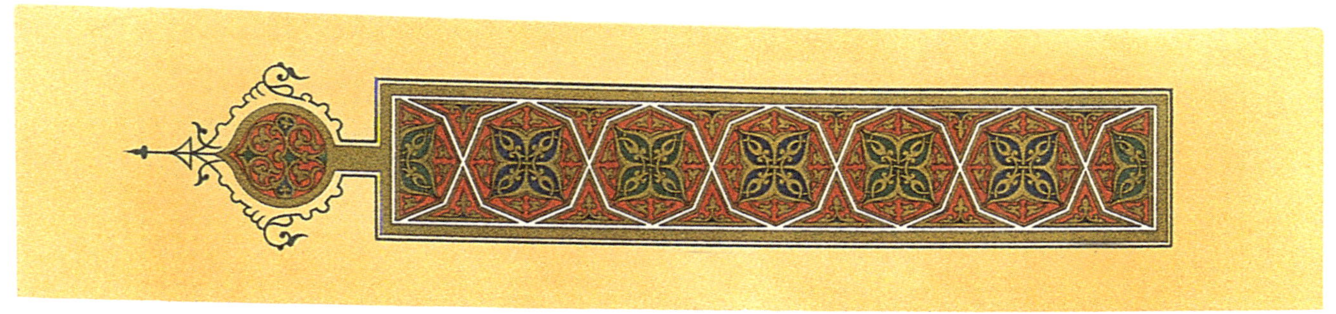

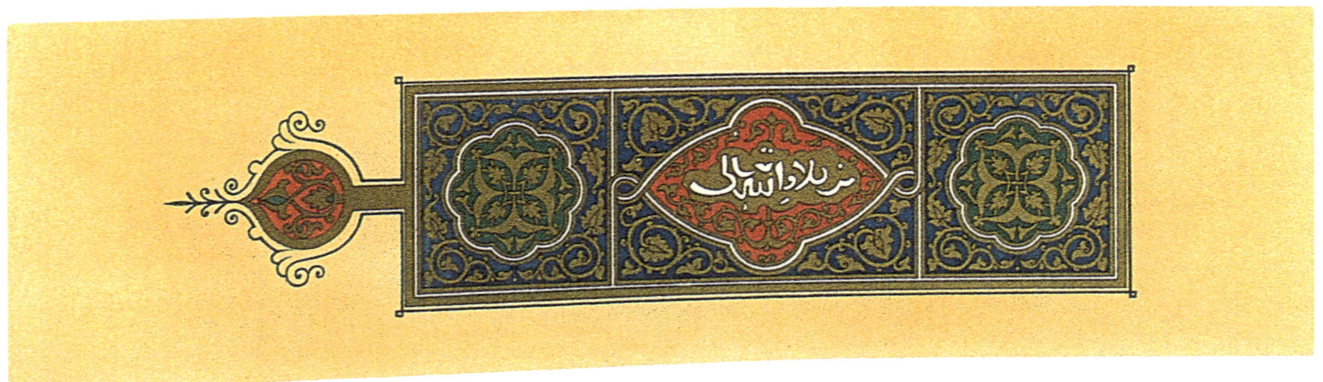

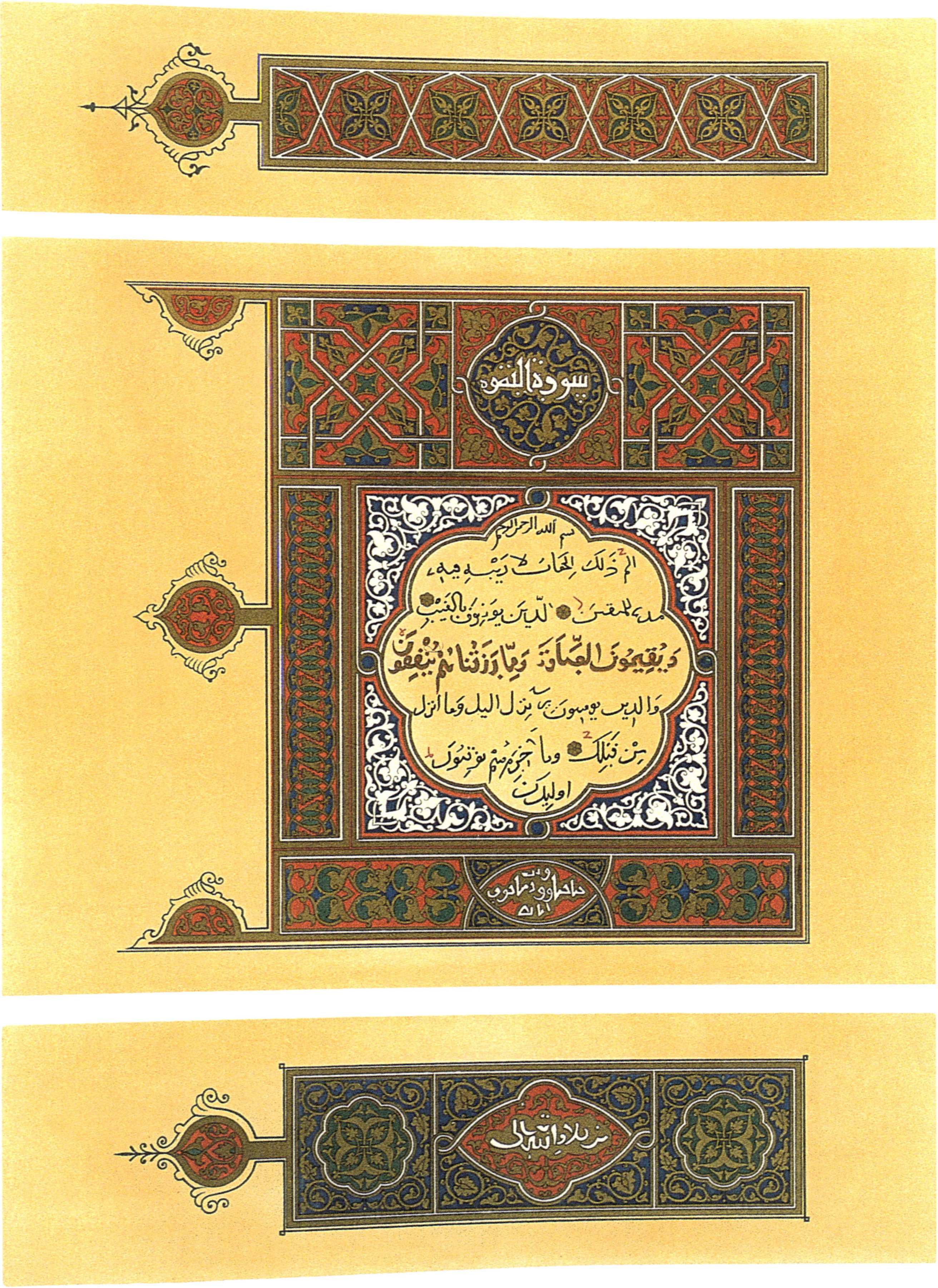

Plate CXCI ORNAMENTATION DETAILS FROM AN ARAB KORAN
(17th century)

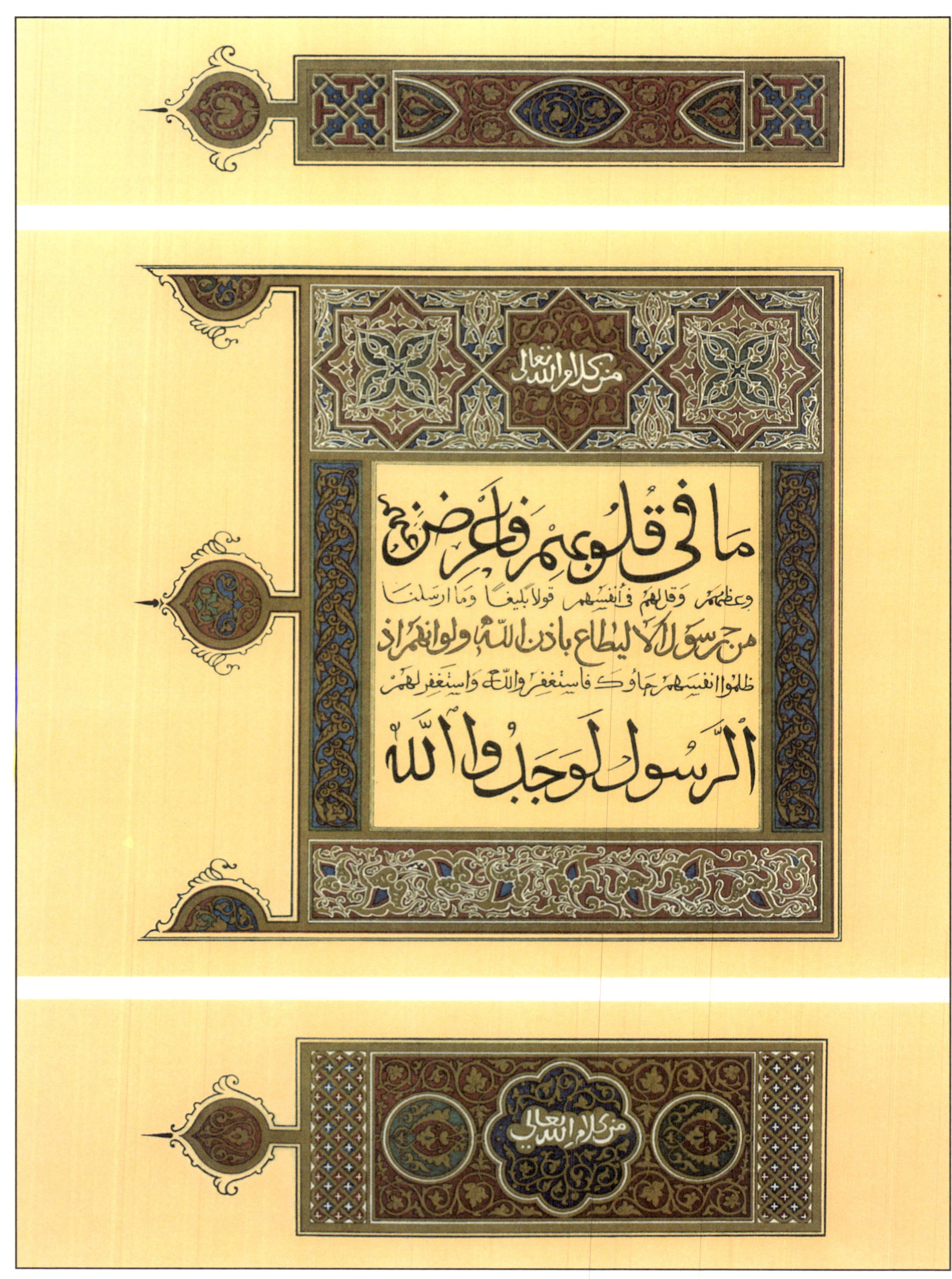

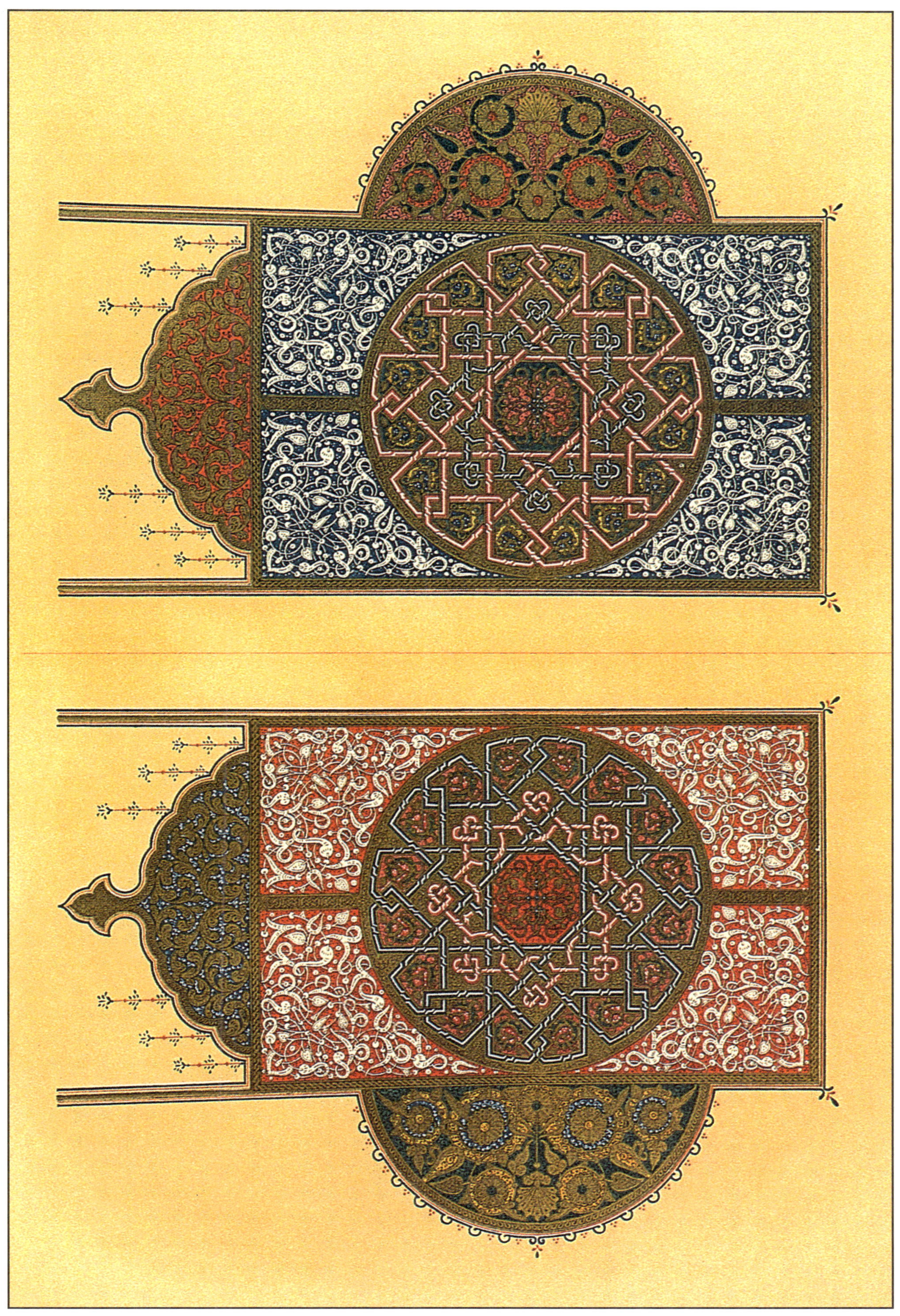

Plate CXCIII

FIRST PAGES FROM A MORESQUE KORAN

(18th century)

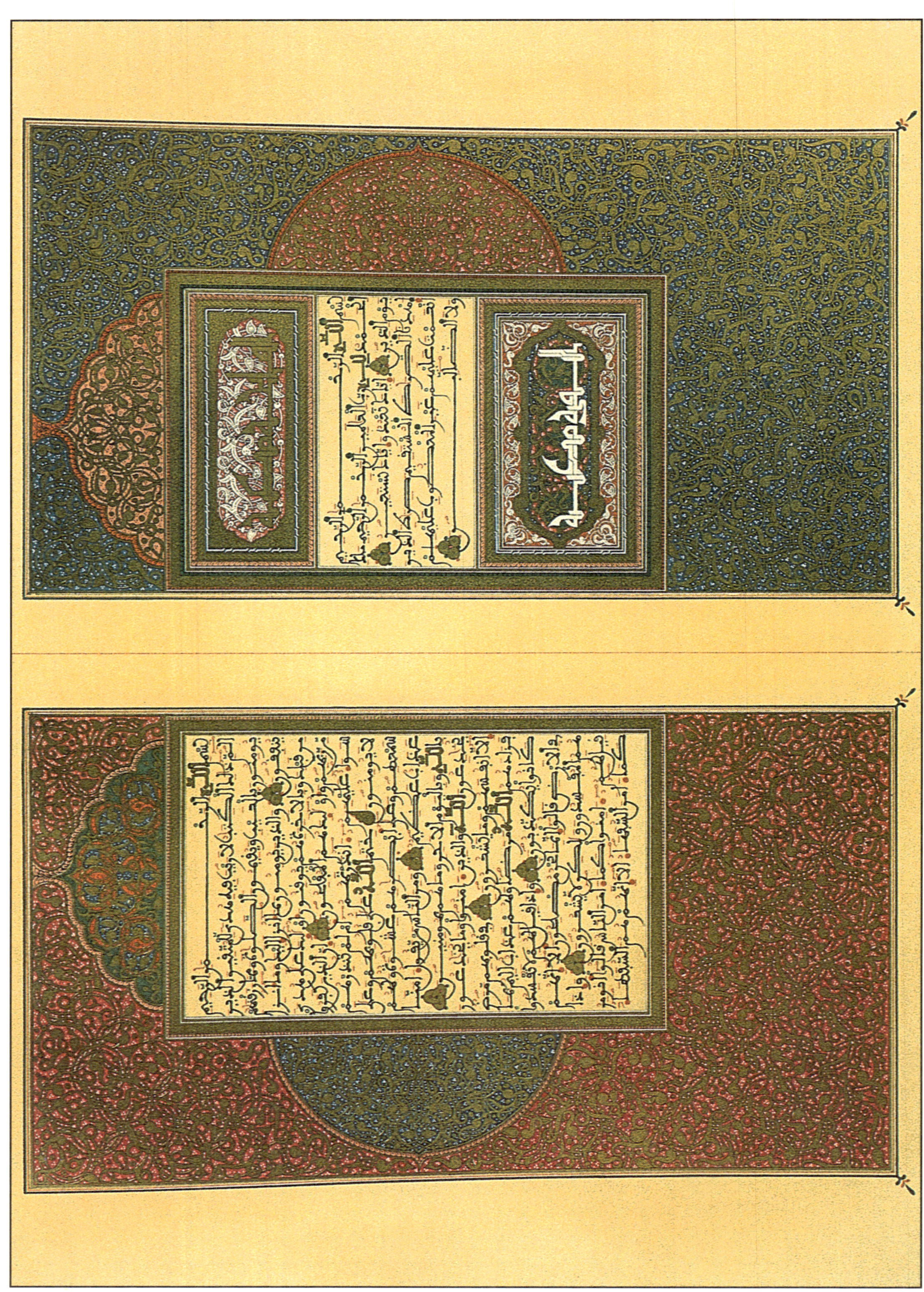

DOUBLE PAGES FROM A MORESQUE KORAN

(18th century)

Plate CXCIV

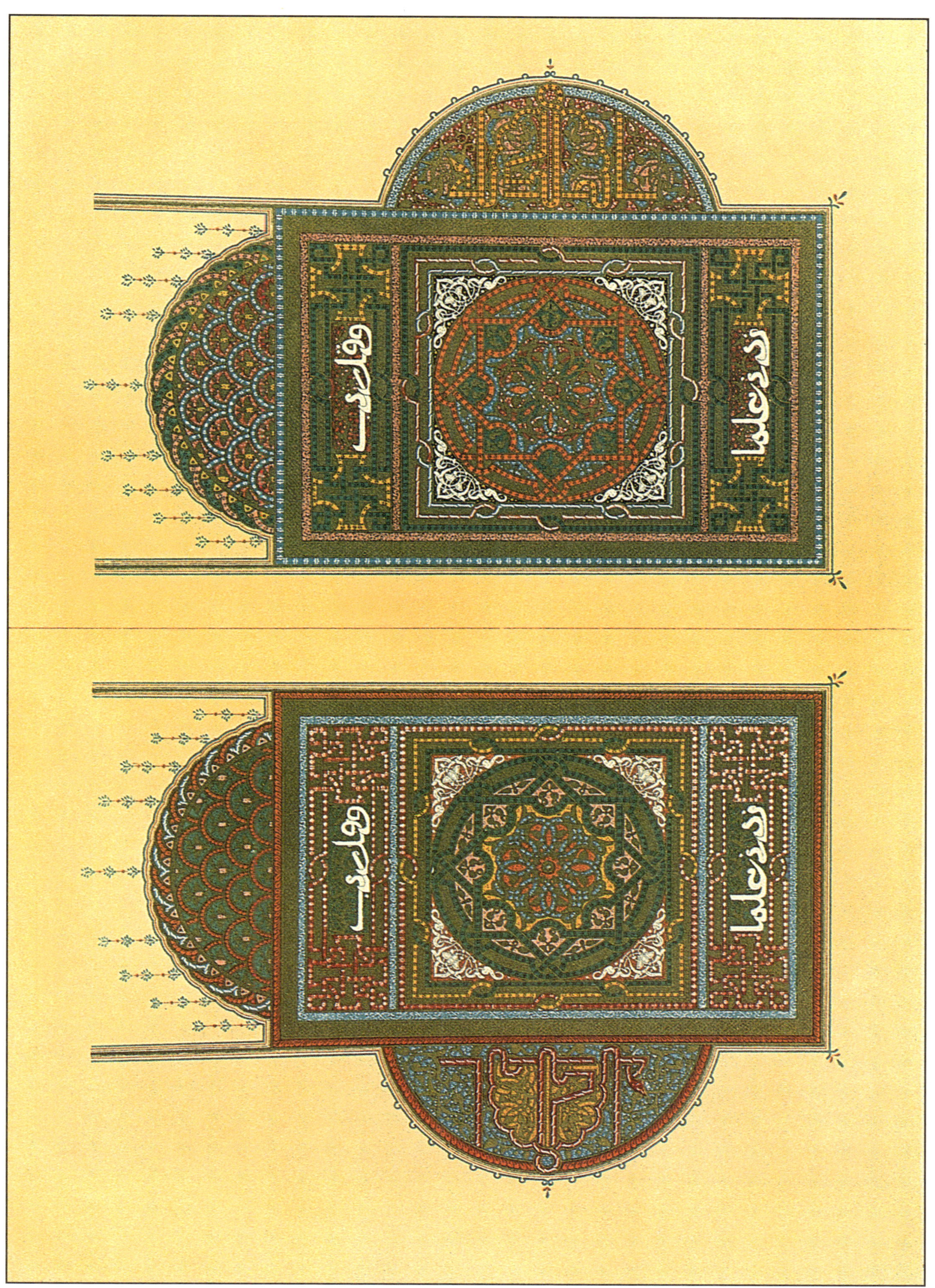

ORNAMENTATION FROM A MORESQUE KORAN

(18th century)

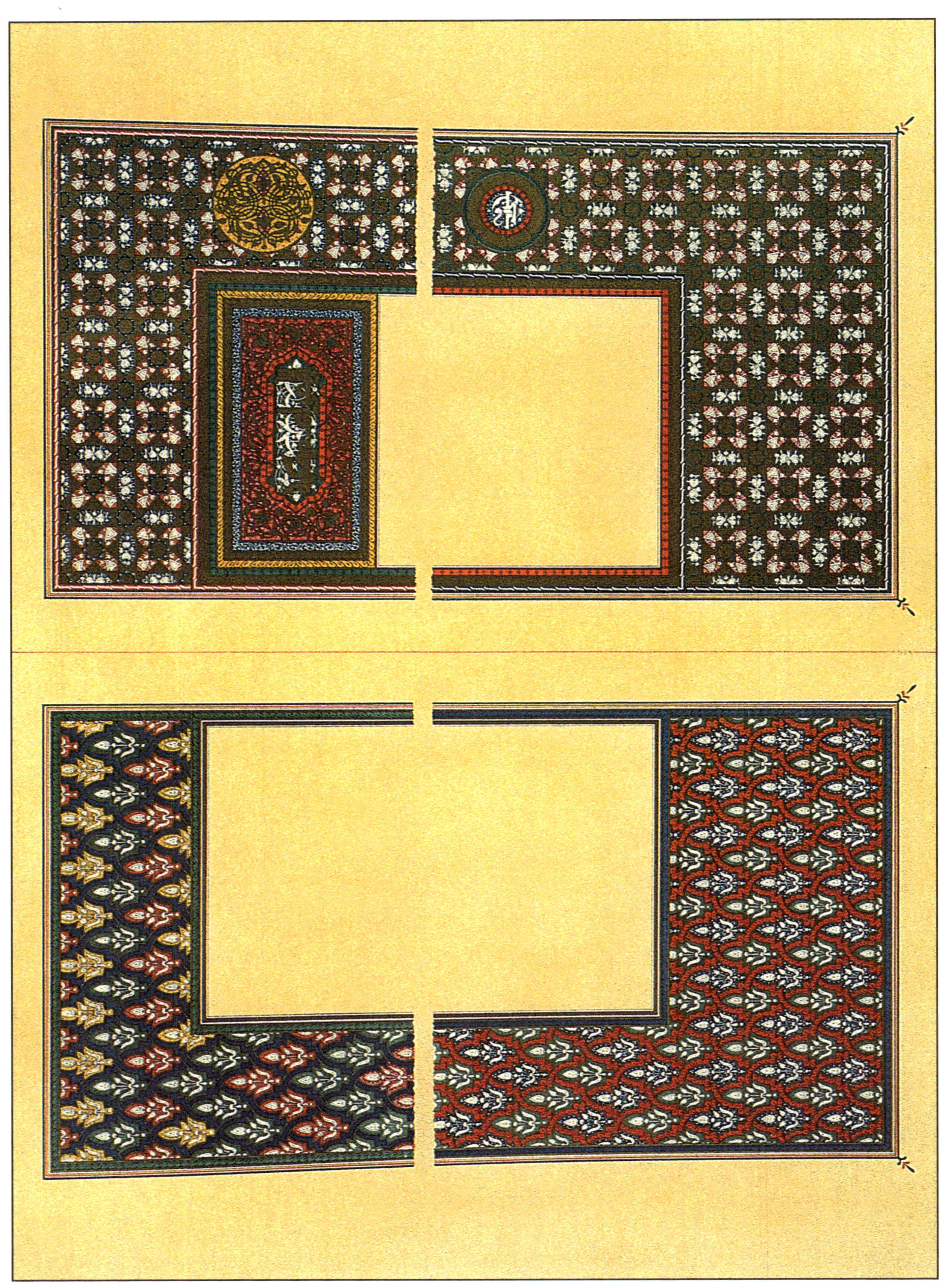

ORNAMENTATION FROM A MORESQUE KORAN (18th century) — Plate CXCVI

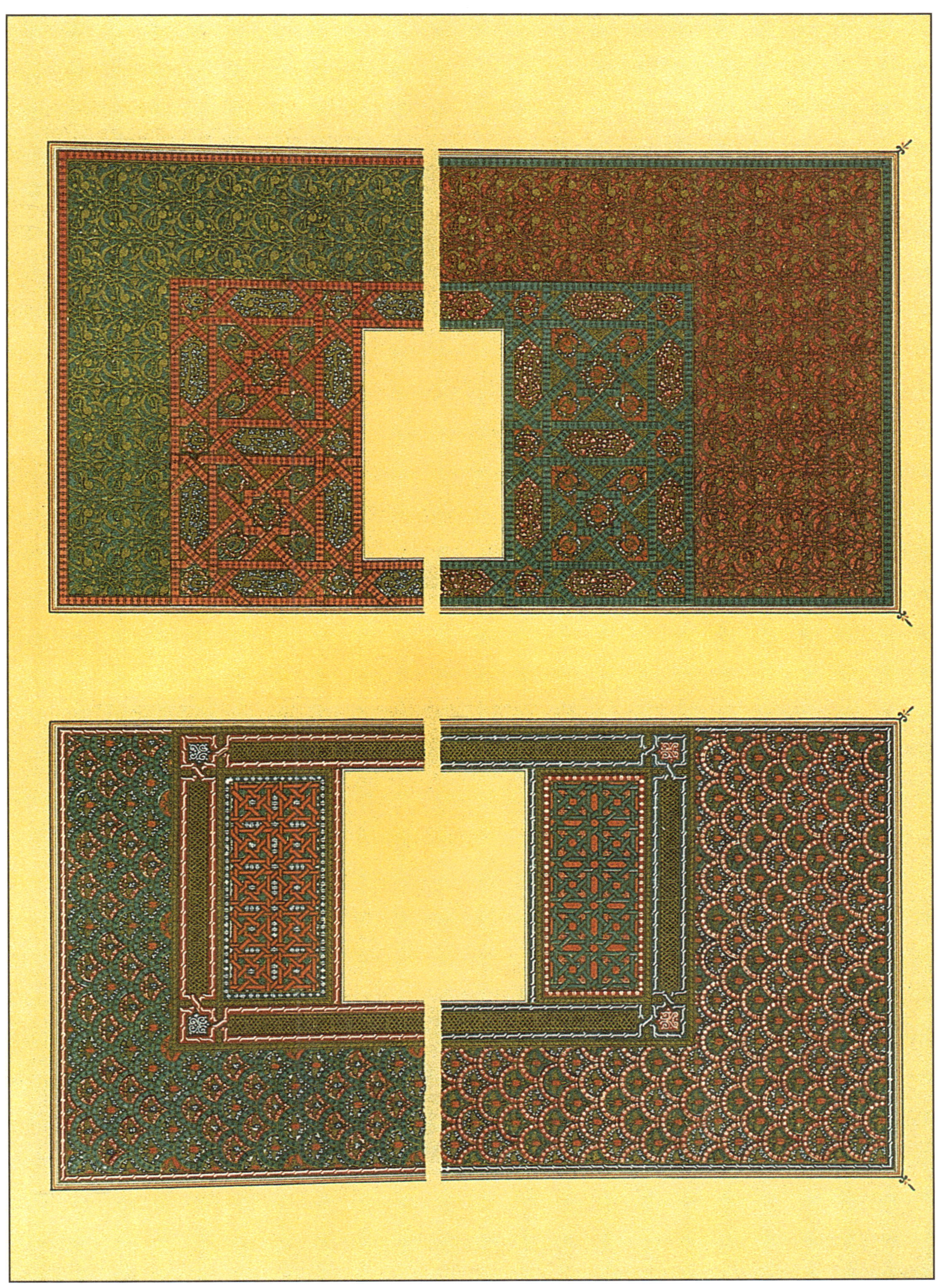

DOUBLE PAGES FROM A MORESQUE KORAN

(18th century)

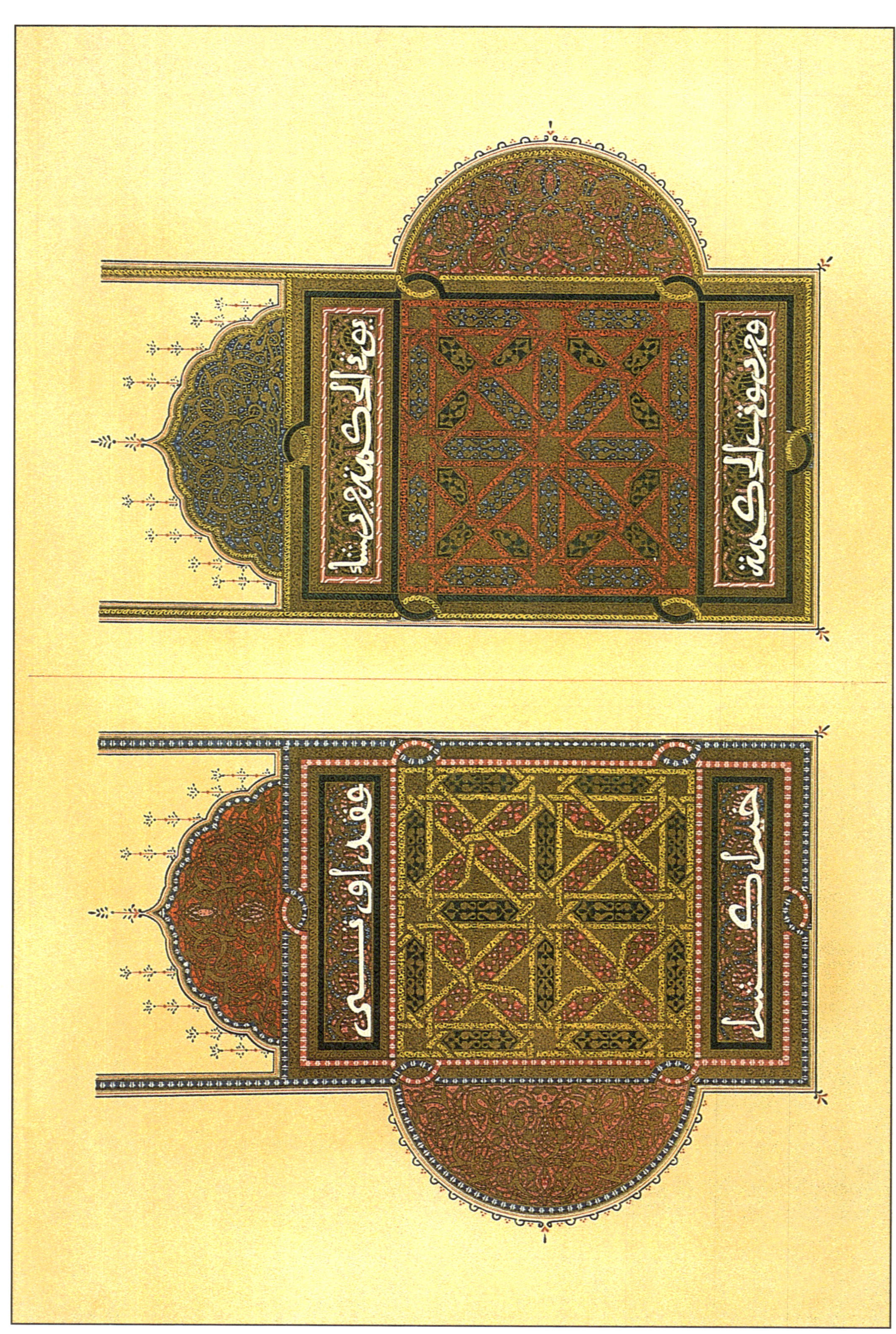

ORNAMENTATION FROM A MORESQUE KORAN
(18th century)

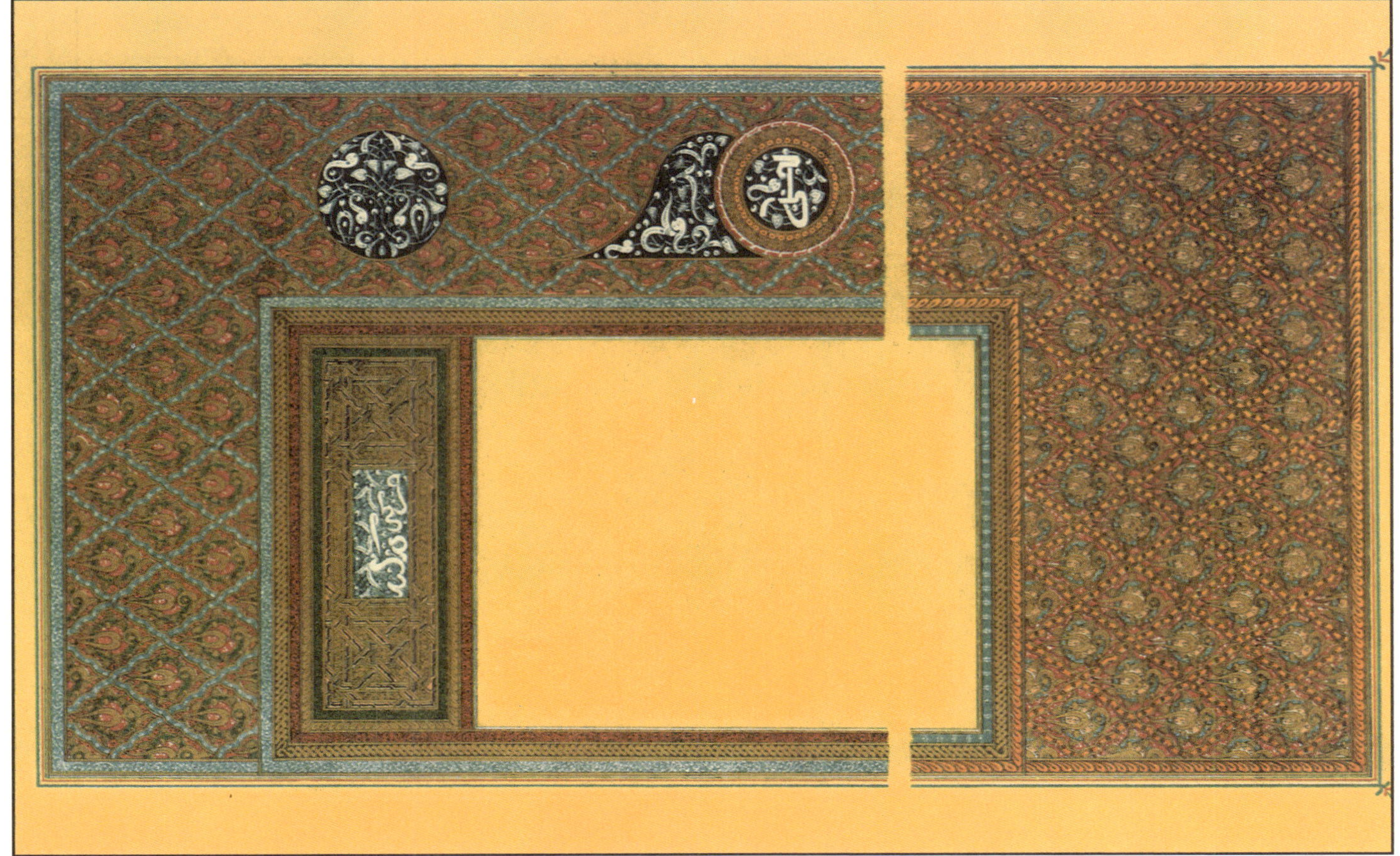

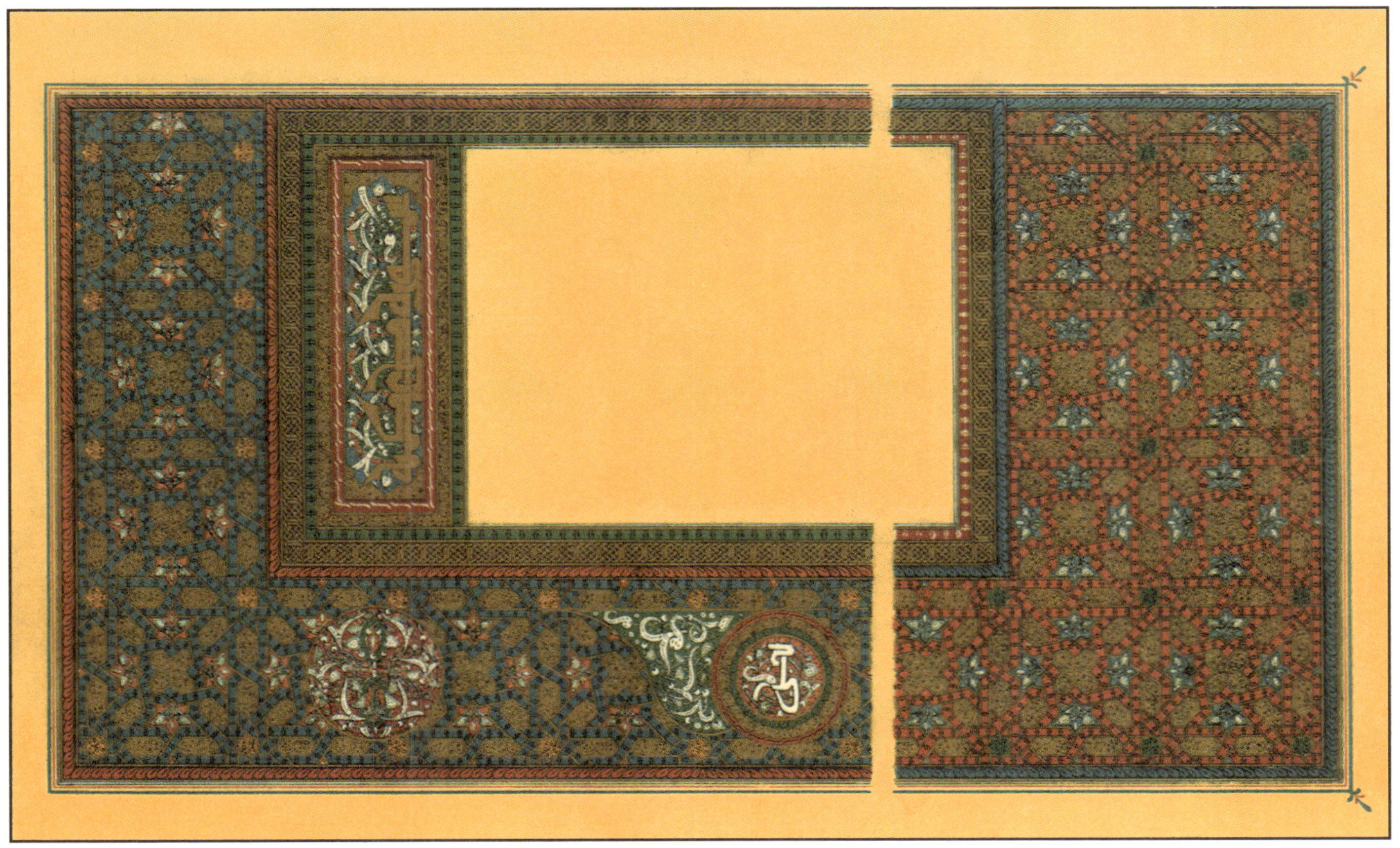

Plate CXCIX

DOUBLE PAGES FROM A MORESQUE KORAN

(18th century)

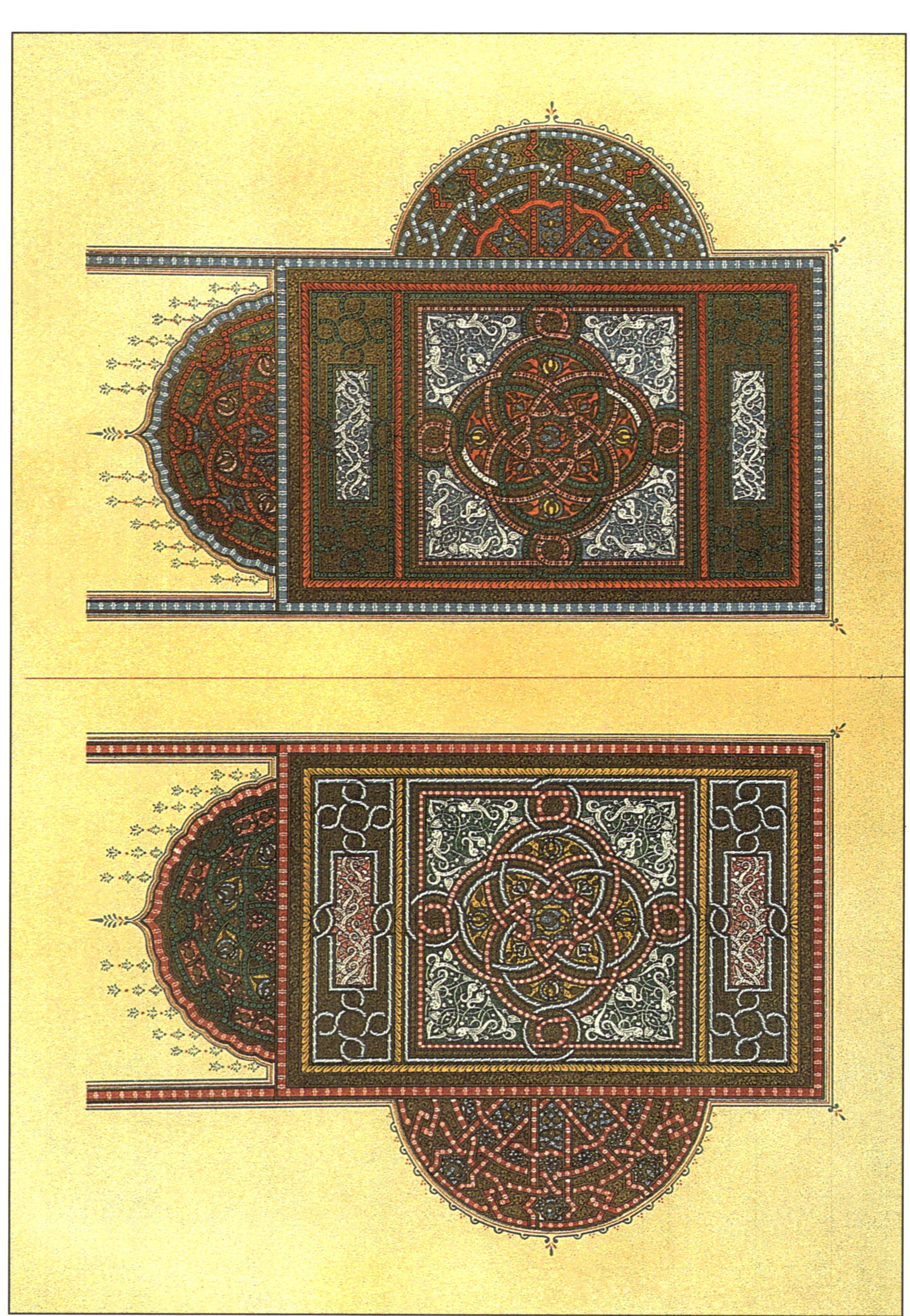

DOUBLE PAGES FROM A MORESQUE KORAN
(18th century)

Plate CC

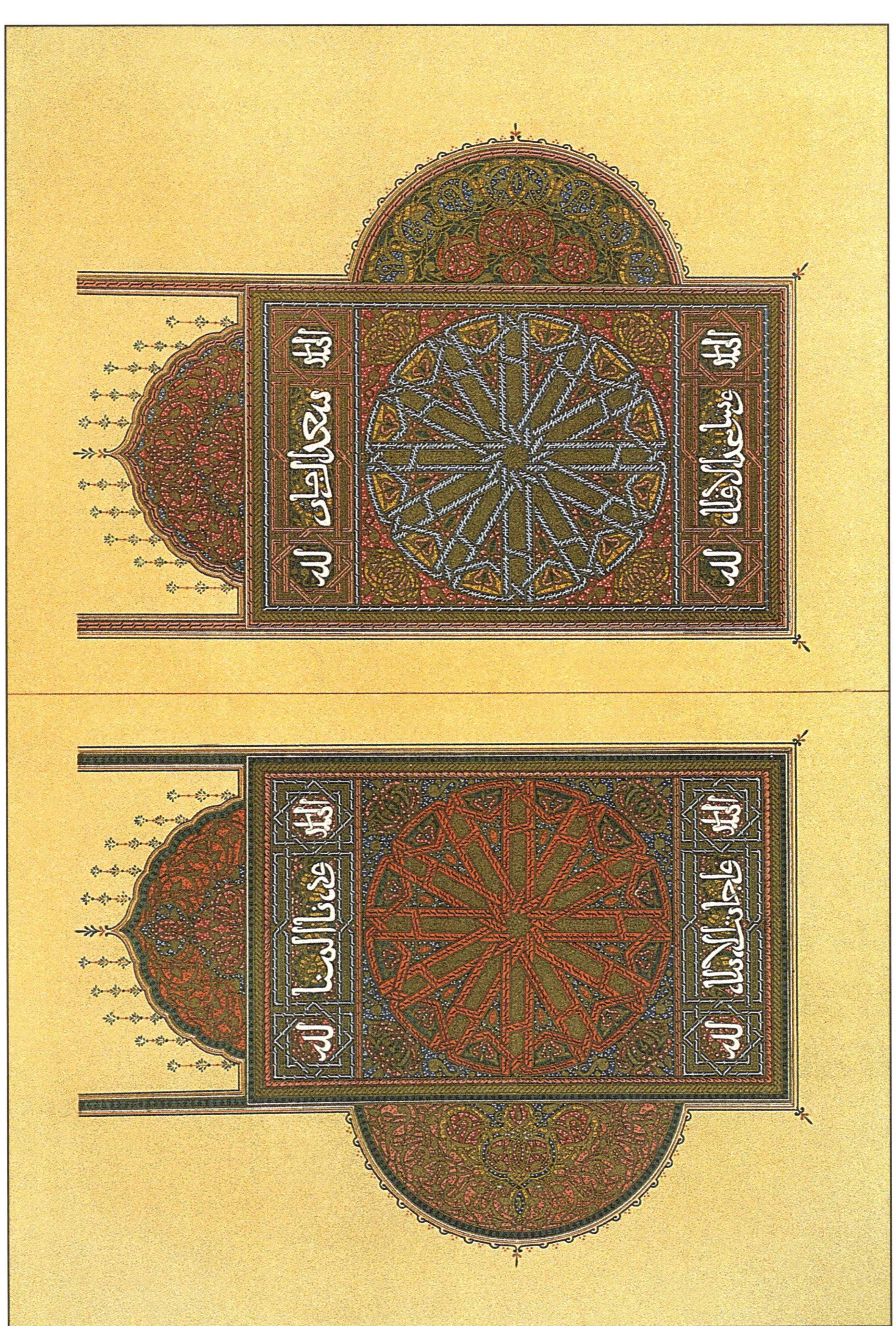

BIBLIOGRAPHY

CARRÉ (J.M.). *Voyageurs et écrivains français en Égypte,* Cairo, 1932.
COSTE (P.). *Architecture arabe et monuments du Kaire,* 1837-1839.
DAWSON (W.R.). *Who was who in Egyptology,* London, 1972.
Description de l'Égypte ou Recueil des observations et des recherches qui ont été faites en Égypte pendant l'expédition de l'armée Française, Imprimerie Impériale, Paris, 1809-1822.
DEWACHTER (M.). « Exploitation des manuscrits d'un égyptologue du XIXe siècle: Prisse d'Avennes », in *Bulletin de la société française d'égyptologie,* No. 101, Paris, 1984.
DEWACHTER (M.). Un Avesnois: l'égyptologue Prisse d'Avennes, in *Mémoires de la société archéologique et historique de l'arrondissement d'Avesnes,* 1988, pp. 143-167.
JONES (O.) et GOURY (J.). *Plans, Elevations, Sections and Details of the Alhambra,* London, 1836-1845.
JONES (O.). *The Grammar of Ornament,* London, 1865.
La Décoration arabe, décors muraux, plafonds, mosaïques, dallages, boiseries... extrait du grand ouvrage L'Art arabe de Prisse d'Avennes, A. Daly, n.d., Paris. (comprises 110 black and white plates).
PRISSE D'AVENNES. *Histoire de l'art égyptien d'après les monuments depuis les temps les plus reculés jusqu'à la domination romaine.* Text by P. Marchandon de la Faye, after the notes by Prisse d'Avennes. Paris, A. Bertrand, 1879.
VOLNEY. *Le Voyage en Syrie et en Égypte,* Paris, 1787.
ZANNIER (I.). *Le Grand Tour,* Venice, 1997.

TABLE OF CONTENTS

Photoengraving: Édilog, Paris

Printed in Italy
July 2001
Dépôt légal 3e trimestre 2001